The WTO and sustainable development

"One of the most pressing challenges with which the WTO is confronted today is how to reconcile free trade and sustainable development. The relationship between the two issues is complicated and they sometimes seem incompatible. Yet the maintenance of free trade helps economic development on a sustainable basis if these two issues are put into a proper relationship. Professor Gary Sampson's analysis of this challenge is sharp and his suggestions are full of wisdom. I regard this book to be a very important contribution to the study of the WTO."

– **Mitsuo Matsushita**, *founding member of the WTO Appellate Body, and Professor of Law at Seikei Law School, Tokyo, Japan*

"For trade to contribute to sustainable development, it is pertinent that WTO must shift the trade balance more in favour of developing countries and change its paradigm from promoting "free" to "fair" trade, especially if trade is also aimed to alleviate poverty.
It is in this context that I welcome Professor Gary Sampson's book and hope that it will stimulate intellectual discourse for changing our mindset by putting fair trade in the mainstream of sustainable development and poverty alleviation."

– **Emil Salim**, *former Minister of Population and Environment, Indonesia, and former Chairman of the Preparatory Committee for the World Summit on Sustainable Development, Johannesburg, 2002.*

It has long been established that improved market access for developing country exports and the economic growth that this can generate make the WTO a powerful potential ally of economic development. Sustainable development, however, embraces not only the alleviation of poverty but also the protection of the environment and the achievement of important social objectives. With the passage of time, the interface between the WTO and sustainable development has expanded considerably, the result being that its responsibilities embrace far more aspects of sustainable development than did its predecessor – the GATT.
The WTO now addresses the harmful effects of fisheries subsidies, access to essential medicines for impoverished people, liberalization of trade in goods and services beneficial to the environment, and numerous other high-priority issues on the sustainable development agenda.
That the multilateral trading system is an important tool to carry forward international efforts to achieve sustainable development is well recognized by governments. The World Summit on Sustainable Development in Johannesburg emphasized the significant potential contribution that trade can make to sustainable development, and WTO members identified sustainable development as both a core objective for the work of the WTO itself and a high priority for the

Doha Development Agenda. The challenge governments now face is to take the necessary action to ensure that trade does indeed promote sustainable development. However, to turn good intentions into results requires both a clear identification of those areas of policy where there is an overlap between trade and sustainable development, as well as constructive proposals as to how to ensure trade and sustainable development are mutually supportive.

In *The WTO and Sustainable Development*, Professor Gary Sampson addresses this need. He identifies an inventory of policy issues that fall within the overlap between trade and sustainable development, and analyses the implications of this overlap. He also presents policy options that are both ambitious and realistic, the pursuit of which could contribute to more coherent and mutually supportive action on the part of governments to both trade and sustainable development. This book is a useful contribution to the literature and should be of interest to a large part of the international community, including government officials, academics, the business community, and both intergovernmental and non-governmental organizations.

– *Dr Supachai Panitchpakdi, UNCTAD Secretary-General and former WTO Director General (2002–2005)*

The UNU-IAS was inaugurated in April 1996. Its mission statement is "Advancing knowledge and promoting learning for policymaking to meet the challenges of sustainable development".

UNU-IAS conducts research, postgraduate education, and capacity development, both in-house and in cooperation with an interactive network of academic institutions and international organizations. The Institute's research concentrates on exploring the key catalysts and drivers of sustainable development, which often depend on our capacity to harmonize, if not optimize, the interaction between societal and natural systems. This includes the development and use of new technologies and approaches; the study of major trends and pressures such as urbanization, regionalization, and globalization; as well as the exploration of integrated approaches to policy-making, decision-making, and sustainable development governance.

UNU-IAS website: http://www.ias.unu.edu

UNITED NATIONS
UNIVERSITY

UNU-IAS
Institute of Advanced Studies

The WTO and sustainable development

Gary P. Sampson

**United Nations
University Press**

TOKYO · NEW YORK · PARIS

9874390

© United Nations University, 2005

The views expressed in this publication are those of the author and do not necessarily reflect the views of the United Nations University.

United Nations University Press
United Nations University, 53-70, Jingumae 5-chome,
Shibuya-ku, Tokyo, 150-8925, Japan
Tel: +81-3-3499-2811   Fax: +81-3-3406-7345
E-mail: sales@hq.unu.edu   general enquiries: press@hq.unu.edu
http://www.unu.edu

United Nations University Office at the United Nations, New York
2 United Nations Plaza, Room DC2-2062, New York, NY 10017, USA
Tel: +1-212-963-6387   Fax: +1-212-371-9454
E-mail: unuona@ony.unu.edu

United Nations University Press is the publishing division of the United Nations University.

Cover design by Joyce C. Weston

Printed in Hong Kong

UNUP-1115
ISBN 92-808-1115-0

Library of Congress Cataloging-in-Publication Data

Sampson, Gary P.
 The world trade organization and sustainable development / Gary P. Sampson.
  p.   cm.
 Includes bibliographical references and index.
 ISBN 9280811150 (pbk. : alk. paper)
 1. World Trade Organization. 2. Sustainable development. 3. International trade—Environmental aspects. I. Title.
HF1385.S26   2005b
338.9'27—dc22   2005018004

Contents

Foreword

The world trading system and the role it plays in international economic and political relations have changed dramatically in the past half-century. Barriers to trade have been greatly reduced, trade itself has mushroomed, new and far-reaching rules governing trade have been written, and many more countries have now joined the World Trade Organization (WTO) and therefore play by those rules. This timely book investigates one important, sometimes controversial, aspect of this change – the relationship between trade and sustainable development. Given the evolution of the rules-based trading system, as well as the growing attention paid to policies designed to achieve sustainable development, there has been an increasing overlap between what have now become "trade" policies and policies relating to sustainable development.

It is not really in question whether or not this overlap ought to exist. In my view, the factual position is that it simply does exist. It is a natural outcome of the definition of sustainable development, as well as the objectives of the multilateral trading system. In common usage, the term "sustainable development" means securing a growth path that provides for the needs of the present generation without compromising the ability of future generations to meet their own needs. From a policy perspective, the pursuit of sustainable development requires a careful balancing between progress in each of its pillars: policies designed to advance economic development, for instance; to conserve the environment; and to ensure social progress. On the trade side, the WTO of course seeks to raise standards of living and to ensure full employment and a steadily growing volume of real income with the expansion of world production and trade. These days, however, the WTO simply cannot ignore the need to promote and preserve the environment, or indeed to enhance the means for doing so in a manner consistent with different levels of economic development. But an additional responsibility assigned to the WTO compared with its predecessor, the General Agreement on Tariffs and Trade (GATT), is to provide for the optimal use of the world's resources in accordance with the objective of sustainable development. In other words, the achievement of sustainable development is a formal goal of the WTO.

Yet, it is not only the formal business of objective-setting that has increased the relevance of sustainable development for the WTO. The manner in which the trading system has evolved over the past half-century has significantly changed the link between trade and sustainable development. First, there is more trade for the rules to apply to. Because world trade has grown more rapidly than world production in almost every year since the Second World War, it follows automatically that countries now trade a far greater share of their production than they did half a century ago. The rules apply to more countries too. Originally there were 23 members of the GATT; this number is now approaching 150 in the WTO, with another 27 countries in the process of accession. The result is that WTO rules that bear on "traditional" trade are now relevant for more than one-third of world production.

Impressive as this figure is, trade rules themselves have been expanded in consecutive trade Rounds. Minimum standards relate to intellectual property rights and can be enforced by the WTO even if no goods or services cross the border (for instance in relation to counterfeit goods). Similarly, the most important means of delivering services internationally are dealt with by the WTO. These include the commercial presence of foreign service suppliers with no cross-border movement of the service itself. The other "behind the border" agreements are important as well. The Subsidies Agreement is one example because it relates to domestic practices, as are disciplines relating to safeguard action against surges of imports, and measures to ensure that production standards, technical regulations and conformity assessment procedures are not unfair protection.

As a result, both the daily work of the WTO as well as the multilateral negotiations held under its auspices have come more and more to address key issues of public concern that far transcend those associated with the conventional political economy of trade policy. For example, agricultural negotiations naturally embrace sensitive questions relating to the "multi-functionality" of agriculture, and the Agreement on Trade-Related Intellectual Property Rights (TRIPS) addresses matters of access to essential medicines for poor countries without the means to produce them. The

Agreement on Sanitary and Phytosanitary Measures (SPS) already tackles the controversial question of the role of the precautionary principle in the absence of scientific evidence, and also bears on critical policies relating to public health. In addition, the issues dealt with in the normal course of WTO business have been expanded through the process of continuing negotiations. Addressing concerns relating to subsidies that lead to the depletion of fish stocks and negotiations on the relationship between the WTO rules and multilateral environment agreements provide current examples. All these matters are on centre stage in discussions relating to sustainable development.

Given the increased importance of trade and the rules that govern it, we have also seen the WTO's rules and practices evolving in response to the new challenges of the broader international agenda. These rules assume an even greater importance than did those under the GATT, reach deeper into the regulatory frameworks of all member countries and are, unlike in some other institutions, legally enforceable. This latter point is of particular relevance. When disagreements arise over WTO rights and obligations, poor and rich members alike can take these disagreements to the greatly strengthened dispute settlement mechanism of the WTO. Unlike the GATT, the WTO process is hard for the rich and powerful countries to thwart: Panel and Appellate Body reports are adopted unless there is a consensus against them. Moreover, the rule of negative consensus, backed up by a mechanism providing for compensation or sanctions in the case of non-compliance, has greatly increased public awareness of the WTO's existence. As a consequence, public interest has heightened, particularly in the light of recent high-profile disputes that extend into some of these new, sensitive areas. These disputes deal with the role of science in risk management (for example, in the *Hormones* case), the conservation of endangered species (for example, in the *Shrimp-Turtle* case), the cross-border movement of genetically modified organisms, and measures to protect public health (for example, in the *Asbestos* case). On occasion the rulings of the WTO dispute settlement process have even raised questions relating to the compatibility of trade rules with sustainable development. In other words, do trade and sustainable development find themselves on a natural collision course?

Overlap does seem inevitable, but I do not see any need for collision. I am firmly of the view that policies bearing on both trade and sustainable development can – and indeed must – be consistent and mutually supportive. From a trade perspective, the key elements in creating such a system come in the form of establishing fair and balanced rules for trade, enforcing them efficiently, and continuing trade opening in goods and services to promote economic development – particularly that of developing countries. I am not alone in holding this view. At the Ministerial meeting in Doha in 2001, trade ministers reaffirmed their commitment to sustainable development and once again expressed the common view that the aims of upholding and safeguarding an open and non-discriminatory multilateral trading system and acting for the protection of the environment and the promotion of sustainable development can and must be mutually supportive. Less than one year later, at the World Summit on Sustainable Development in Johannesburg, environment ministers called for urgent action to promote an open, equitable, rules-based, predictable and non-discriminatory multilateral trading system that benefits all countries in the pursuit of sustainable development. They also called for the successful completion of the work programme contained in the Doha Ministerial Declaration. There is clearly common ground in terms of objectives in the worlds of both trade and sustainable development, and this is as it should be.

At this point in history, however, the challenge is to put into practice what we preach. How will the work of the WTO evolve against the backdrop of the increasing importance of trade and trade rules? In addressing this question, my starting point is a simple one: trade opening and the reduction of trade barriers have been, remain and will remain essential to promote growth and development, to improve standards of living and to tackle poverty reduction, and also to provide the means to protect and preserve the environment. Nonetheless, trade opening is neither natural nor automatically beneficial, in and of itself. It needs a system based on rules coupled with adequate domestic policies. Since the creation of the GATT, some important steps have been taken towards the construction of this system and we can be proud of them. But there remains a lot to do; hence the launching of the new multilateral trade Round in Doha in 2001.

High on the "what to do" agenda is of course to ensure that trade opening and sustainable development can work together for the poorest countries. For them, there must be an assurance that their concerns will be listened to and acted upon. Absent this, there will be no successful conclusion to the Round. Many of these countries have undertaken new and demanding obligations, and rightfully look to improved market access in both goods and services to support their export-led growth strategies. Their legitimate expectation is that the WTO will provide a forum in which their views can be effectively expressed and their concerns adequately dealt with. Least developed countries in particular have not benefited as they should from the multilateral trading system, and creative and ambitious solutions must be found to ensure that they too benefit fully from trade-led growth. Only then can they be lifted out of their desperate economic situation through a multilateral trading system that is effective and equitable. Only then can they develop in a truly sustainable manner.

Indeed, to ensure that trade opening contributes more to development, the current WTO Round has been designated "the Doha Development

Agenda". I know from my former life as an EU Trade Commissioner, and therefore as one of the authors of this programme, that it represents a promise of fairer trade opening. To lead these negotiations in the right direction should therefore be our priority number one, our priority number two, our priority number three. This Round is in large measure a response to the recognition that, although exports from developing countries have tripled in just 20 years, the new possibilities unleashed by the world trade system remain unequally divided and unequally utilized by the different members of the club. Perhaps the rules themselves remain unequal, or perhaps making the necessary adjustments is too difficult a task for the weakest countries. Whatever the reason, it is the results and the perception of the results that count. There remains so much to do that the priority must be to re-balance the international trade system in favour of developing countries.

However, although the promotion of economic development and the contribution it can make to providing the resources necessary to improve environmental and social conditions have long been recognized, multilateralism is now confronted by new issues that the GATT never had to tackle. Many of these come from the trade and sustainable development overlap which I outlined above. Against this backdrop, the value of this book on *The WTO and Sustainable Development* is clear to me. It is a crucial first step in identifying and exploring the issues that fall under the umbrellas of sustainable development and the expanded agenda of trade policy. Only then can there be a full appreciation of the implications of the decisions taken.

In this respect, a crucial question that emerges throughout this book is whether a clearer mission for the WTO in support of sustainable development implies major institutional reforms. I do not think so. Yes, the WTO must reinforce its efficiency and legitimacy. It must be more interested in practical questions of organization and implementation, and in assuring better coherence with other international institutions. Having described this organization as "medieval" at the conclusion of two Ministerial conferences, as I have, I could hardly say otherwise. We learn more from our failures than from our successes, as ever. To surmount the difficulties confronting the WTO, it must adapt. To achieve this, the WTO must better integrate its work in the landscape of actors, states and international governance organizations. But the fundamental objective of the WTO has to remain the construction of fair trade rules to guarantee better, more long-lasting, more predictable and more transparent trade opening.

Pascal Lamy
WTO Director-General
Former European Union Commissioner for Trade (1999–2004)

Acknowledgements

In the period since joining the General Agreement on Tariffs and Trade (GATT) in 1987, I have had the opportunity to direct a number of divisions in both the GATT and the World Trade Organization (WTO), including the Development Division and the Trade and Environment Division. One thing that particularly struck me is the extent to which issues relating to sustainable development have increasingly appeared on the trade agenda. Against this backdrop, it seemed useful to explore the implications of this expanded agenda from a policy perspective. This book is the result of that enquiry.

The following chapters have greatly benefited from participation in many GATT and WTO meetings, a large number of conferences, and discussions with colleagues too numerous to acknowledge individually. Nevertheless, I would like specifically to mention Edwini Kessie, Serafino Marchese and Jorge Vigano of the WTO Secretariat, with whom I have discussed many aspects of the book. I would also like to thank Maria Pillinini of the WTO Secretariat for her input on matters relating to WTO rules and developing countries. In addition, I have benefited from exchanges with Bradnee Chambers of the Institute of Advanced Studies (IAS), particularly relating to international law and the environment. Sam Johnson, also of the IAS, provided helpful comments on a number of institutional and legal considerations relating to multilateral environment agreements. As far as basic research is concerned, I am very much indebted to both Mathieu and Gregory Sampson for their valuable and skilful contributions to many of the topics addressed in this book.

I would like also to thank Professor Hans van Ginkel, Rector of the United Nations University, and Professor Zakri, Director of the Institute of Advanced Studies, for their institutional support and general encouragement.

I would like particularly to thank the Ford Foundation for the financial assistance and other support it provided for this project. In many ways this study is a natural progression from an earlier volume entitled *The Role of the WTO in Global Governance*, also funded by the Ford Foundation and published by the United Nations University Press. Whereas in the earlier study a number of prominent policy makers addressed the question of the appropriate role for the WTO in global governance, this volume represents an enquiry into the relationship between the WTO, governance and the trade-related aspects of sustainable development.

1

Introduction and overview

Introduction

One of the potentially most important trade meetings in history took place in Doha, Qatar, from 9 to 14 November 2001, when a new round of multilateral trade negotiations – the Doha Development Agenda – was launched. At Doha, trade ministers told the world: "We strongly re-affirm our commitment to the objective of sustainable development ... We are convinced that the aims of upholding and safeguarding an open and non-discriminatory multilateral trading system, and acting for the protection of the environment and the promotion of sustainable development can and must be mutually supportive."[1]

Less than one year later, in September 2002, the World Summit on Sustainable Development (WSSD) – the largest intergovernmental meeting ever – took place in Johannesburg, South Africa. On this occasion, environment ministers called for urgent action to continue "to promote open, equitable, rules-based, predictable and non-discriminatory multilateral trading and financial systems that benefit all countries in the pursuit of sustainable development [and] support the successful completion of the work programme contained in the Doha Ministerial Declaration". They "welcomed the decision contained in the Doha Ministerial Declaration to place the needs and interests of developing countries at the heart of the work programme of the Declaration".[2]

My objective in this book is to review the relationship between trade policies as conducted in the World Trade Organization (WTO) and policies designed to promote sustainable development. Although many may understandably balk at the notion, I conclude that the WTO has unquestionably gravitated towards becoming a *World Trade and Sustainable Development Organization*. Some may or may not like this fact, but it is – by design or by default – a reality of the day.

In elaborating this proposition, we first need to address the questions of what trade policy is and which policies are designed to promote sustainable development. In broad terms, if trade policy is what the WTO deals with, then its objectives should offer some guidance as to the boundaries of trade policy. Its objectives are both ambitious and far-reaching: to raise standards of living and to ensure full employment and a steadily growing volume of real income with the expansion of world production and trade. Similarly, the WTO is to seek to protect and preserve the environment, and to enhance the means for doing so in a manner consistent with different levels of economic development. An additional responsibility assigned to the WTO compared with its predecessor, the General Agreement on Tariffs and Trade (GATT), is to provide for the optimal use of the world's resources in accordance with the objective of sustainable development.[3]

Convention has it that sustainable development means *securing a growth path where providing for the needs of the present generation does not mean compromising the ability of future generations to meet their own needs*. From a policy perspective, the pursuit of sustainable development requires a careful balancing between progress in each of its pillars: economic development; conservation of the environment; and improving social conditions.

The means available to the WTO to achieve its ambitious goals are the *liberalization* of trade and the conduct of trade according to multilaterally agreed *rules and procedures*. Both the liberalization of trade and the rules that govern trade have become inextricably linked with economic development, conservation of the environment and improving social conditions. In this respect, the working hypothesis of the WTO is that trade liberalization removes restrictions in the market, efficiently allocates resources and contributes to their optimal use. As a result, it increases production and income, promotes economic development, and makes more resources available for economic development, environmental management and improving social conditions. WTO rules ensure predictability and stability in a trading system based on, *inter alia*, non-discriminatory trading relations coupled with a powerful dispute settlement system. The conclusion is that both trade liberalization and trade rules are important contributors to sustainable development.

Despite the fact that there have been many contributions in both the theoretical and applied literature refining the definition of sustainable development, the concept remains somewhat vague – at least for providing a solid basis on which to identify policies to promote it. Setting the boundaries for the purposes of this book is therefore not a simple task. However, since the following chapters are about policy, one way to proceed is to consider the boundaries to be the policy issues addressed in the various forums devoted to sustainable development. Hundreds of government officials from diverse national administrations attended the World Summit on Sustainable Development in Johannesburg. The Declarations that emerged from the meeting identified and prioritized key issues. In addition, government officials regularly attend the meetings of the United Nations Commission on Sustainable Development and the United Nations Environment Programme and discuss the same or similar issues. Many specialized agencies of the United Nations – including multilateral environment agreements – deal directly or indirectly with many aspects of sustainable development, as does the International Labour Office. There is also a vast array of non-governmental organizations that focus on sustainable development[4] and chambers of commerce that have business and sustainable development as their focus.[5] Reviewing the issues that emerge in these deliberations in the light of the WTO work schedule provides useful insights into which policy issues deal with the interface between trade and sustainable development.

There is also guidance from academic circles. Although not necessarily addressed in the context of sustainable development, a great deal of intellectual activity has revolved around the extent to which there should be formal linkages between WTO rules and domestic policies relating to economic development, environmental management, labour standards and human rights. A key question that emerges in this debate is whether trade policy should be used as an instrument to promote sustainable development by obliging countries to adopt harmonized environment, labour and other standards in the conduct of international trade.[6]

Adopting this approach identifies a vast area of enquiry. The most important common area of policy concern for both trade and sustainable development is arguably the relationship between the trade liberalization successfully concluded under the GATT – and now the WTO – and economic development. Some remain unconvinced about the positive relationship, but the picture that increasingly emerges from empirical studies is that, although there are many influences bearing on economic growth, the adoption of liberal trade policies, through both expanded market access and domestic trade liberalization, generally promotes higher economic growth. The fact that trade is conducted according to enforceable rules on a non-discriminatory basis means that countries can pursue their own domestic policies to achieve their own national goals without sanctions applied by others.

However, the WTO has greatly expanded its reach compared with the GATT. Its obligations are more intrusive and many issues not normally considered to be in the domain of trade policy are being dealt with by the WTO. These are many and varied. There are *negotiations* in the WTO on the role of fisheries subsidies in fish stock depletion, and on the relationship between WTO rules and multilateral environment agreements. There are *disputes* over endangered species, public health and genetically modified organisms. There are *Agreement*s that deal with access to essential medicines and the patenting of life forms, and that have implications for the conservation of biodiversity. All of these matters find themselves squarely on the sustainable development agenda.

Yet sustainable development per se does not loom large on the agenda of the WTO. At most it is dealt with only obliquely.[7] There may be a number of reasons for this. One is that sustainable development, because of its very nature, is dealt with in different ways in different forums. Being interdisciplinary, it finds itself – albeit it in a fragmented way – as part of the work programme of international lawyers, economists and political scientists. The same is true for government officials, who come from a variety of ministries in their national administrations. Institutionally, there is no overarching body in the WTO that addresses sustainable development. Moreover, little attention is paid to it by governments that pride themselves on the enforceability of the legal rights and obligations they have created; they do not wish to invest too heavily in a concept that appears vague and of little use in legally binding agreements. The implication is that, at most, sustainable development should appear in Preambular language or be included in Ministerial Declarations – as indeed it is. In addition, developing countries approach sustainable development in the WTO with mistrust. Its emphasis on intergenerational equity – prioritizing growth between present and future generations – has the potential to downplay the urgency of improving the distribution of income between the rich and the poor of world today. Also, if sustainable development means focusing on environmental or labour standards, it could bring a new form of conditionality to world trade. Developing countries strongly resist its inclusion in the WTO on these grounds.

Many of the issues that now confront the WTO and are also firmly on the sustainable development agenda are the result of a conscious policy on the part of members to expand the reach of the WTO. Many other issues, however, have gravitated to the WTO on a de facto basis, and some people question whether the WTO is the appropriate body to be dealing with such matters. Even if it is, does it have the capacity to deal with them? It already has an overloaded agenda and other institutions have the skill and expertise to deal with such matters. My own experience is that those involved in various fields of policy-making have very different views as to what the WTO should be.[8] This lack of clarity about the role of the WTO has led to controversy.

The WTO is fiercely criticized by those who argue that its rules constitute an unwanted intrusion into the domestic affairs of sovereign states. For example, the rules impede the proper workings of democratically elected governments by denying them the possibility to discriminate in trade against goods produced in an environmentally unfriendly manner or without respect for core labour standards or universally accepted human rights. The reach and power of the WTO should therefore be *shrunk*. Others take the opposite view and even consider that new subject areas, such as the critical areas of competition policy, investment and government procurement, should be added to the existing WTO agenda (as was the case in the Uruguay Round with intellectual property and trade and services).

There are also those who think that the reach of the WTO should not only be extended horizontally but also be deepened. The trade community should accept that social norms are inextricably linked with the international economic system and provide the common moral and legal underpinnings for the formulation of policies relating to development, the environment and social objectives. Integrating social norms into all aspects of economic policy-making – including trade policy – would ensure that markets are not only open and efficient, but also fair and just.

Indeed, there are those who defend the organization on the basis of its past performance, and on these grounds wish to maintain the status quo. They argue that the multilateral trading system at the beginning of the twenty-first century is the most remarkable achievement ever in institutionalized global economic cooperation.[9] It does not intrude on national sovereignty as charged. On the contrary, it protects weaker countries by preventing more powerful countries from unilaterally imposing their preferred social and political standards via trade sanctions. WTO rules prevent powerful countries riding roughshod over less powerful ones, and ensure the policy space for other multilateral treaties to be negotiated to deal with environmental and social matters. Viewed through this prism, the concepts, principles and rules of the WTO should be consolidated through experience – and not shrunk or further stretched in any direction.

At the heart of these issues is the question of what role should be assigned to the WTO in relation to sustainable development. Could the WTO be rendered more useful in promoting sustainable development by enforcing – or even creating – standards that achieve social and environmental goals? This raises fundamental questions with respect to national sovereignty vis-à-vis international obligations. From a national sovereignty perspective, it is clearly important that WTO member governments retain the policy autonomy to implement whatever measures are necessary to achieve developmental, environmental and social goals. At the same time, from a trade policy perspective, market access rights obtained through bound liberalization commitments should not be undermined by what are paraded as legitimate measures in the pursuit of national policies. A key responsibility of the WTO as a *trade* organization is to police the use of disguised restrictions on trade to undermine negotiated commitments.

Although legitimizing discrimination on the basis of how goods and services are produced would profoundly change the nature of the WTO, it is precisely here that the greatest pressure is brought to bear on the WTO to create linkages with non-traditional trade areas. Trade measures to enforce environmental or labour standards where neither such standards *nor* trade measures have been agreed to by all affected parties are considered by many to be an infringement of national sovereignty and not to be the proper role of a trade organization. Yet the thought of importing goods that have degraded the environment, accelerated the extinction of endangered species, or been produced with child labour is clearly anathema to many. The question is not whether such matters should be dealt with at the international level; the controversy turns on whether the WTO is the appropriate body to deal with them.

Some argue that there currently exists a strong multilateral rules-based trade regime, attained through the WTO, which is essential to developing a system of governance of global markets. It is reasoned that the trading system cannot act in isolation when there exists a wide variety of issues that rightfully belong on the trade agenda. In my view, a strong argument can be made that a trade policy organization such as the WTO should not be responsible for many of the non-conventional trade issues that are gravitating towards it. The United Nations and its specialized agencies are charged with advancing the pillars of sustainable development, and a case can be made that these institutions should be strengthened and given the resources they need to carry out their tasks successfully, so that the WTO does not have to deal with the wider agenda that it now seems to be acquiring.

But this is most unlikely to happen. Putting it bluntly, there is not the same willingness as in the WTO to forgo national sovereignty and accept strong compliance mechanisms in treaties negotiated under the auspices of the United Nations and its specialized agencies. This fact has been lamented on a number of occasions by Kofi Annan, the Secretary-General of the United Nations, as well as by the heads of United Nations agencies.[10] It should also be lamented by the WTO, if for no other reason than self-interest. If the political will is lacking to strengthen the United Nations specialized agencies, the implications may be an even wider gap to be filled by the WTO.

A basic premise in what follows is that governments should be free to pursue their own policies without other countries imposing their preferences through trade sanctions. The WTO is a trade organization and was not conceived of as an environment or labour organization. Had it been, it would not have the 150 members it has at present. The WTO can best fulfil its role by maintaining clear and fixed legal rights relating to market access commitments, coupled with flexible procedures under which governments can negotiate for the modification of legal commitments when they wish to accommodate more important social policies. Nowhere is this clearer than in the interface between trade and sustainable development.

So where does all this take us in terms of policy? To my mind, there are two important questions. What is in reality the *current role* of the WTO in matters relating to sustainable development? And what is the *proper role* of the WTO in the pursuit of sustainable development? Addressing these two questions raises a number of important policy considerations. The objective of this book is to identify them, explore them, and make policy recommendations that are both ambitious and realistic.

In doing so, I do not advocate a greater role for sustainable development in the WTO in terms of the legal rights and obligations of members. What I contend is that, as a minimum, there should be a stocktaking of the issues that characterize the interface between trade and sustainable development. Thus, an important objective of this book is to present an inventory of issues that could represent an agenda for such a stocktaking. My intention is not only to draw attention to the fact that the WTO in reality deals with many issues relating to sustainable development, but also to make policy suggestions about how they could be dealt with. To my mind, viewing the activities of the WTO through the prism of sustainable development throws light on a number of policy options available to WTO members in some of the most challenging areas it deals with.

In the absence of such an approach, the criticisms that the WTO now faces will in large measure remain linked to the many different perceptions of what is the proper role of trade policy in the global economy. In the broadest perspective, in a perfect world, meeting the challenges facing the global economy requires a coherent approach and institutional structure at the global level. This means the existence of institutions that determine the substantive policies and public processes with a clear delineation of the responsibilities of the various actors involved, that are mutually consistent and supportive, and that operate in an effective, accountable and legitimate manner. The fact of the matter is that there is no world government to determine the appropriate division of labour among existing multilateral institutions, or to decide when new organizations need to be created or existing ones closed down. Thus, the goals of the institutions should be to facilitate the attainment of agreed policy objectives through cooperation, while providing for the avoidance and resolution of any disputes that may arise in the pursuance of these objectives.

Overview

The intention of this book is of course not to address all issues where trade and sustainable development policies intersect. This would be an impossible task. Not all readers will agree on the issues I have chosen, and many may have different views on those that are dealt with. Although some topics are obvious candidates, others are not. One obvious candidate, for example, is the work in the WTO Committee on Trade and Environment, which is specifically mandated in its terms of reference to take into account sustainable development. So too is the work of the Committee on Trade and Development. Other issues are of importance, but of a different nature. For example, I take up the arguments that the WTO is undemocratic, non-transparent and non-accountable to the public because these criticisms are frequently advanced by institutions dealing with sustainable development.

Another consideration is that, of the three pillars of sustainable development (economic development, the environment and considerations such as human rights and labour standards), I pay more attention in the following chapters to the environment and to development. Both have a tradition of being dealt with systematically in the GATT and WTO. Whereas Committees on Trade and Environment, as well as Trade and Development, have existed in the GATT or WTO for some years, there are no committees on trade and labour standards, human rights, public health or, for that matter, sustainable development. Nevertheless, even in the absence of WTO committees dedicated to particular issues, many issues of social concern emerge in other WTO forums. These too will be addressed. Examples include access to essential medicines and sharing the benefits of traditional knowledge in the Committee on Trade-Related Aspects of Intellectual Property Rights, fisheries subsidies in the Rules Committee, eco-labelling in the Technical Barriers to Trade Committee, protection of public health in the Sanitary and Phytosanitary Committee, and endangered species and public health in the dispute settlement process.

This book is directed to those in the trade community and those with a direct interest in sustainable development. It is interdisciplinary and deals with both economic and legal issues, and the implications of the conclusions are important for international relations. It also aims to be educative in approach, in the sense of raising questions, identifying issues and proposing solutions to them. For this reason, parts of the book may contain more detail than is necessary for those with a specialized knowledge of the particular topic. For example, environmentalists may be familiar with multilateral environment agreements (MEAs) and the workings of institutional considerations relating to environmental governance, and those more interested in trade may be familiar with multilateral trade institutions and specific accords such as the General Agreement on Trade in Services, all of which are discussed in detail.

The orientation of the book is towards making useful policy suggestions. Some come in the form of specific proposals; others assign a priority to questions to be addressed in present and future negotiations; some just raise issues. Where policy conclusions are drawn, the intention is to be both ambitious and realistic at the same time – in other words, to take into account the substance as well as the political and institutional realities that would bear on the acceptability of the proposals. This approach is built on the knowledge, for example, that proposals involving a change in the rights and obligations of WTO members are difficult to secure. WTO members have reached agreement on the basis of a balance of rights and obligations. Upsetting this balance might well require renegotiation of other Agreements, and even ostensibly minor changes in rules can result in unachievable outcomes. Negotiators rarely make concessions to negotiating partners without extracting some return payment, so a snowballing effect is often the pattern. The outline of the book is as follows.

In chapter 2, I review institutional efforts at the intergovernmental level over the past 50 years to address one of the key aspects of sustainable development – namely environmental management. I trace the policy orientation to the trade and environment debate in the GATT and then the WTO. I reason that at the time of its creation, and for the following decades, the GATT was concerned with environmental measures primarily as potential barriers to market access. Although, over time, the complexity of the trade and environment issues confronting the GATT increased greatly, the general approach adopted by the GATT was carried over to the WTO. The nature of the environment-related issues now under consideration at the WTO has certainly broadened well beyond the original concerns about the environment. The issues extend to discrimination among imports on the basis of environmental standards, seen as a precursor to discrimination based on standards including labour or human rights, and questions relating to extra-territoriality have moved onto centre stage through dispute settlement rulings. Most importantly, I conclude that the approach of the WTO towards the environment and other aspects of sustainable development still reflects a concern over the potential use of trade measures as barriers to trade, although clearly the emphasis is on the manner in which trade and the environment can be mutually supportive. Trade liberalization can improve resource allocation, increase growth and make more resources available to improve the environment. The challenge is how to operationalize these relationships.

Chapter 3 investigates in greater detail how the link between trade liberalization and sustainable development has been dealt with in the WTO from a substantive perspective. Although I acknowledge the role of trade liberalization in promoting growth, the focus of the chapter is on the relationship between trade liberalization and sustainability assessment scenarios, as well as on win–win scenarios – how to reap the benefits from removing trade restrictions and distortions that damage the environment, and how the removal of trade barriers could improve market access opportunities for developing countries in the same sectors. Examples include the environmental benefits that accrue from the removal of agricultural subsidies (which lead to an excessive use of fertilizers), or of fisheries subsidies (which lead to overcapacity of the fishing fleets and to fish stock depletion). In both cases the removal of subsidies could result in expanded export earnings for developing countries. I place particular emphasis on the fishery sector because it provides a useful case study. It shows, among other things, the constructive role that public interest groups can play in highlighting issues and information that are crucial to activate and support the negotiating process in the WTO. These efforts have surely contributed to this sector being a focus of attention and singled out for special treatment by governments in the Doha Development Agenda.

In chapter 4, I address a number of provisions in the WTO Agreements – most notably the GATT-1994 – that have a particular relevance for sustainable development. I focus on non-discrimination and how it has been interpreted in recent contentious dispute settlement rulings. A number of important questions arise as to the true purpose of certain trade measures and the grounds on which some measures that are important for sustainable development can be considered necessary to achieve a certain policy goal. Is the aim and effect of the measure to renege on legally binding market access commitments that the WTO is bound to protect, or does it pursue a legitimate policy goal without being unnecessarily trade restrictive? The importance of this chapter is underscored by the fact that it examines the extent to which WTO provisions circumscribe the policy options available to national governments in pursuing sustainable development. What becomes apparent in this exercise is the extent to which a number of the key terms in the WTO Agreements are open to interpretation, and the importance this has for policies relating to sustainable development. I review some selected dispute rulings and conclude that how sustainable development is dealt with in the future is in many ways in the hands of WTO Panels and the Appellate Body.

Chapter 5 addresses the implications for the WTO of the growing consumer demand for improved product and service standards that has come with higher income levels. The result is a growing number of increasingly sophisticated technical regulations and standards defining specific characteristics of a product: its size, shape, design, functions and performance, or the way it is labelled or packaged before it is put on sale. Governments are free under the WTO to limit the import of certain goods in order to protect public health, safety and the environment through the enforcement of mandatory standards to which imported goods must conform. However, for the WTO to fulfil its role as a trade body, such standards should be no more restrictive than necessary to achieve the legitimate purpose and should not undermine market access commitments. In other words, these regulations should not be designed to impede the free flow of trade. Distinguishing which measures are designed to implement legitimate policy choices and which are unnecessary obstacles to trade places the WTO in an increasingly difficult situation as the sophistication of regulations increases.

Because the WTO and the MEAs represent two different bodies of international law, it is important for the relationship between them to be coherent and fully understood by all concerned. This is not currently the case and chapter 6 discusses the potential problems of any clash between the two global regimes. To remove this possibility, and to avoid the WTO being the arbiter of environmental disputes, requires effective MEAs characterized by clearly specified trade measures that may be taken for environmental purposes, broad-based support in terms of country membership and a robust dispute settlement system.

Chapter 7 also deals with a controversial issue. Few topics generate as much public agitation as recent developments in biotechnology. Although gene modification has been with us since time immemorial, public sentiment has changed with the introduction of genetic engineering, which permits the transfer of genetic material between organisms that would never be able to breed in the natural environment. The regulation of living genetically modified organisms (GMOs) and products derived from them provides an excellent case study of how issues of central importance to sustainable development can find themselves on the WTO agenda. This has not been by design, but rather through the normal application of WTO rules and agreements crafted well before the concerns relating to biotechnology emerged. Issues relating to biotechnology enter the WTO stage due to market access considerations (restrictions on the cross-border movement of living GMOs and food products derived from them), ethical considerations (the patenting of life forms), equity considerations (access to essential medicines), and many others.

Chapter 8 deals with the WTO General Agreement on Trade in Services (GATS). This Agreement is the result of the Uruguay Round and therefore a relatively new addition to the body of international trade law. It is far from being a user-friendly agreement, and it has become the target of attack by those who see it as a vehicle for the privatization of government-owned activities, such as water supply and other public utilities, health services and education. They believe it will lead to the deregulation of services activities more generally. I argue that the GATS contains very few compulsory obligations, and additional obligations are undertaken at the discretion of the importing country. To provide a clearer understanding of how intrusive the GATS is – or is not – when it comes to domestic policy formulation, I offer a more analytical explanation of the Agreement than one would get from a simple reading of the text.

In chapter 9, I trace the manner in which developing countries' concerns about the multilateral trading system have been dealt with, from the early days of the GATT to the present. My starting point is that the WTO system should provide the legal flexibility for developing countries to implement the most appropriate development strategies, although this begs the question of what is an appropriate development strategy for a developing country. There are very different views in this respect. I conclude that development strategies and legal flexibilities should reflect the very diverse nature of developing countries' economies, resource endowments, institutions, and other national characteristics. I fully appreciate the desire of many developing countries to continue the current *generic* approach of special and differential treatment while maintaining self-selection in the absence of graduation. I document the WTO processes surrounding the negotiation of special and differential treatment with the intention of gaining insights into the complex, time-consuming and frustrating nature of WTO negotiations.

Chapter 10 looks at the changing importance of the WTO and how perceptions of its role in global affairs have evolved over time. I also address charges that the WTO is undemocratic, non-transparent and non-responsive to the needs of the citizens of its member countries. Too frequently, the WTO's critics fail to register that the WTO is in fact composed of 150 governments acting in accordance with multilateral rules that have been adopted on a consensus basis.

Chapter 11 turns to one of the important features of the World Summit on Sustainable Development – the search for a more coherent system of global governance in order to deal effectively with sustainable development at the global level. There have been many proposals over the years as to how this can be achieved, not the least important being the call for a World Environment Organization on a par with the World Trade Organization. In this chapter, I look at the functioning of the WTO and address the question of whether or not it is a useful model for a WEO. If it is not, can useful lessons be learned from a close examination of the key characteristics of the WTO?

In the final chapter of the book I look at the need for greater coherence in global policy-making and at developments in this respect within the WTO in the past. I draw attention to the fact that, whereas governments have seen a need for greater coherence in policies between the WTO, the World Bank and the International Monetary Fund, similar attention has not been given to coherence in the relationship between the WTO and the specialized agencies of the United Nations. I advance a number of policy proposals, starting from the basic proposition that, by identifying issues in a "bottom–up" manner, solid foundations can be built for a more coherent system of global governance in relation to sustainable development. In the bigger picture, however, the chapter returns to the question of the role of the WTO in global governance.

Notes

1. See WTO, *Doha Declarations: The Doha Development Agenda*, Geneva: WTO Secretariat, 2001, para. 6.
2. WTO, *Report of the World Summit on Sustainable Development*, Geneva: WTO Secretariat, WT/CTE/W/220/Rev.1, 20 December 2002, para. 47 (a).
3. The objectives of the WTO are spelled out in the Preamble to the Agreement Establishing the World Trade Organization. This and the texts of the Agreements and other legal instruments for which the WTO is responsible can be found in World Trade Organization, *The Results of the Uruguay Round of Multilateral Trade Negotiations: The Legal Texts*, Geneva: WTO Secretariat, 1994. The contents of this volume will be referred to as the WTO Agreements in what follows. Another important point for the following is that the GATT no longer exists as an institution; its functions have been taken over by the WTO, which entered into force in January 1995. The original GATT (referred to as the GATT-1947) lives on as part of the Uruguay Round Agreements in an updated form as the GATT-1994. In what follows, the governments that constitute the membership of the WTO will be referred to as the WTO members. For convenience and consistency, the GATT contracting parties (the usual terminology) will be referred to as GATT members.
4. The Canadian International Institute for Sustainable Development is one example. Others, for example the International Centre for Trade and Sustainable Development in Geneva, focus even more finely on *trade* and sustainable development and consequently have the WTO as their primary focus.

5. Examples include the World Business Council on Sustainable Development and the International Chamber of Commerce.
6. See, in particular, Jagdish Bhagwati and Robert H. Hudec, *Fair Trade and Harmonisation*, vols I and II, Cambridge, MA: MIT Press, 1997.
7. As noted, sustainable development is an objective identified in the Preamble to the Agreement Establishing the WTO. It is referred to in the terms of reference of the Committee on Trade and Environment and in the Appellate Body ruling in the *Shrimp-Turtle* case. It appears from time to time in WTO Ministerial Declarations, including the Doha Development Agenda.
8. In the course of research carried out under a project funded by the Ford Foundation, a number of prominent personalities responded positively to a request to offer their views on the role of the WTO in global governance. These views were on occasion very different. They are published in Gary P. Sampson (ed.), *The Role of the WTO in Global Governance*, Tokyo: United Nations University Press, 2000.
9. See Martin Wolf, "What the World Needs from the Multilateral Trading System", in Sampson (ed.), *The Role of the WTO in Global Governance*, chapter 9.
10. Kofi Annan, "Foundations for a Fair and Free World Trade System", in Sampson (ed.), *The Role of the WTO in Global Governance*, chapter 1.

2

Institutional considerations

Introduction

Fulfilling the mandates that emerged from the Doha Ministerial Meeting in Qatar and the World Summit on Sustainable Development (WSSD) in Johannesburg requires a coherent approach at the national, regional and multilateral levels to the three pillars of sustainable development: economic development, protection of the environment and the effective implementation of social policies. It requires a set of institutions that are coherent, mutually consistent and supportive, and operate in an effective, accountable and legitimate manner. A practical question that can usefully be addressed is how close the international institutional structure today is to this ideal, and what we can learn from past experience.

Many question the value of large ministerial meetings such as these, particularly as Declarations are frequently statements of good intentions and best endeavours. Nevertheless, they do offer guidance to more operational policy-making on a number of fronts by identifying areas for future negotiation, listing priorities for future work and providing political support and direction for the substantive work of various national, regional and global institutions. However, although ministers can declare good intentions, the task of assigning national resources to give the Declarations operational content, or of concluding the negotiations launched by them, invariably proves more difficult.

In terms of the orientation of the Declarations, however, it would appear that governments agree on how the trading system should contribute to sustainable development: the common theme of both Declarations is that trade liberalization can lead to growth, which can contribute to sustainable development providing it is coupled with effective environmental management and social policies. The presumption is that environmental protection preserves the natural resource base on which economic growth is premised, and trade liberalization leads to the economic growth needed to generate the resources for adequate environmental protection. In this respect, a coherent approach by institutions at the national and international level is critical to ensure that environmental policies do not intentionally act as obstacles to trade liberalization and that trade rules do not stand in the way of adequate domestic environmental protection.

Since the World Trade Organization (WTO) certainly has a positive contribution to make in this respect, it is instructive to review the past experience of the General Agreement on Tariffs and Trade (GATT) and the WTO to see how they have dealt institutionally with the link between trade, the environment, and now sustainable development. However, this requires an appreciation of the manner in which the link between trade and environment has been viewed in the GATT and the WTO in the past, and whether this approach has been carried over to those issues that link trade and sustainable development today. The intention is not to record institutional developments as such; this has been done comprehensively elsewhere.[1] The intention is to gain insights into how the approach has, or has not, evolved, resulting in the institutional arrangements that we see today. Also, the focus is very much on trade and the environment rather than other aspects of the trade and sustainable development interface. Chapter 9 deals principally with economic development, for example, and the environmental and social aspects of sustainable development are addressed at various stages throughout the book.

My own view is that what lies at the heart of much of the debate that surrounds the *appropriate* contribution of the WTO to sustainable development is, not surprisingly, disagreement in relation to the perceived link between trade and the environment – and other aspects of sustainable development. I will explore in later chapters how the link is open to interpretation and the role of the WTO legal processes in this respect.

The outline of this chapter is as follows. First, I look at the institutional background in the GATT and the WTO to trade and environment. I then address developments in the early 1990s when hostilities vis-à-vis the GATT increased considerably. I describe the GATT and WTO response, but the main focus is the evolving approach in institutional thinking about the relationship between trade and the environment. I examine the outcome of the Uruguay Round and, in particular, the functioning of the Committee on Trade and Environment. Although this Committee has been extensively criticized, I advance a defence of its contribution. I follow this with a discussion of trade and environment after the Uruguay Round, at the time of the launching of the Doha Development Agenda, and the relationship between the Doha Agenda and the World Summit on Sustainable Development (WSSD). I conclude that even a casual review of the outcome of the WSSD indicates that the subject matter dealt with by the WTO overlaps to a very large extent with that on the sustainable development agenda.

Institutional background

There was a leap in international concern regarding the implications of future global growth for the environment and social development following the publishing of the Club of Rome's report *The Limits to Growth* in 1972.[2] The main conclusion was that, if current trends continued, the global system would "overshoot" and collapse by the year 2000. To avoid that disastrous route, both population growth and economic growth would have to cease. Although the report was severely criticized, it was certainly successful in popularizing the notion that there were "outer limits" to the world's resources and that development was circumscribed by the finite size of these resources. The report became a milestone.

Concerns relating to the physical limits of the world's resources led to the convening of the United Nations Conference on the Human Environment in Stockholm in 1972. The Stockholm Conference, the first attempt by the international community to address the relationships between the environment and development at the global level, certainly placed concerns about global resources squarely on the global agenda. It provided a policy framework within which to develop an international approach to development and the environment. It led to the creation in 1972 of a Secretariat in the United Nations – the United Nations Environment Programme (UNEP) – as a focal point for coordination within the UN system and to act its environmental conscience.[3]

Prior to the Stockholm Conference, however, a much narrower concern had emerged in the GATT with respect to the potentially restrictive impact of environmental policies on international trade. There was a fear that anti-pollution measures could become major obstacles to trade, with the possible emergence of what was later to be identified as "green protectionism". The Director-General of the GATT Secretariat submitted to the Stockholm Conference a document warning of the "real danger that in attempting to combat pollution, governments may unwittingly introduce new barriers to trade".[4] What is of particular interest for present purposes is that this report does much more than express a concern about market access being restricted by measures to protect the environment. With considerable insight, the report, prepared under the direction of Jan Tumlir, drew attention to what has since emerged as a major issue in the trade and sustainable development debate: namely, how should the GATT deal with regulations that restrict trade but relate to the production processes in the foreign country that produced the product rather than to the imported product itself? Could an environmentally unfriendly production process in another country be the basis for trade restriction in the importing country when applying GATT rules?

In specific terms, the report was concerned that production costs would differ across countries owing to divergent regulations dealing with pollution standards. Taxes or subsidies that were based on the method of production – to tax polluting activities or to subsidize environmentally friendly ones – should not, in the view of the report, be a basis for discrimination in trade. In fact, in generalizing the proposition, it is remarked that a difference in costs resulting from government regulations "does not make them unique: national standards concerning labour, social security, taxation and safety already have a varying impact on costs from one country to another which GATT does not recognise as grounds for protection".[5] The report made clear some three decades ago that legitimizing or penalizing different national choices relating to the protection of the environment, labour, health and other social considerations was not in the domain of the GATT and the multilateral trading system.

There was an institutional response. The Director-General called on GATT members to prepare for pollution measures that could have a negative impact on market access. Thus, in November 1971, the GATT General Council established a Group on Environmental Measures and International Trade (the EMIT Group) with a mandate "to examine upon request any specific matters relevant to the trade policy aspects of measures to control pollution and protect the human environment especially with regard to the application of the provisions of the General Agreement taking into account the particular problems of developing countries".[6] The Group was to report on its activities to the General Council.

The creation of the Group was controversial at the time. A number of countries did not see the need for it. Developing countries, in particular, voiced their early concerns about dealing with environmental matters in the GATT, and the potential for an encroachment on national sovereignty. The counter-argument was that the Group was simply a defensive measure against possible future developments. Agreement was eventually reached to establish the Group, but the Director-General did not see any particular urgency for it to meet. This view was shared by governments and, notwithstanding the nomination of a chairman, the rather extraordinary outcome was that the newly established Group did not meet at any time during the next two decades.

Nevertheless, the ensuing years saw institutional developments in the GATT of importance for the environment. Broadly speaking, they were driven not by a concern for the environment per se, but rather by a concern that such measures to protect the environment could be protectionist in intent (or effect) and create unnecessary barriers to trade. During the Tokyo Round of trade negotiations (1973–1979), the Agreement on Technical Barriers to Trade (or Standards Code) was adopted by a number of GATT members; it was a plurilateral agreement, and eventually 30 governments joined. It called for non-discrimination in the preparation, adoption and application of technical regulations and standards, advocated the use of international standards, and recognized that no country should be prevented from taking measures for the protection of the environment or human, animal and plant life and health. The crucial balancing obligation was that such measures could be taken as long as they were not applied in a manner that would constitute a disguised restriction on trade. The Code also stipulated that international standards could be deviated from for an open-ended variety of reasons – including the protection of the environment and health. Given the broad definition of standards, the Agreement had potentially important implications for environmental management. Indeed, the seeds were sown for the intense debate that was to come later about what were legitimate grounds for the protection of the environment or human, animal and plant life and health (see chapter 5).

A more specific environmental concern emerged at the November 1982 GATT Ministerial Meeting in Geneva relating to products that were prohibited in developed countries and exported to developing countries. Importing developing countries suffered the consequences in terms of harm to human, animal or plant life or health or the environment. In 1989, a Working Group on the Export of Domestically Prohibited Goods was established in the GATT. The Group met 15 times but, when its mandate expired in 1991, no agreement had been reached on how to resolve the issue. It was, however, incorporated into the terms of reference of the Committee on Trade and Environment in 1994 (see below), and provides an early example of how trans-boundary environmental problems are better dealt with by multilateral and regional agreements outside the WTO. Discussions revealed that the control of exports of hazardous wastes is a national responsibility requiring a high degree of specific expertise, and as a result is better dealt with at the multilateral level through a multilateral environment agreement (MEA), not through a trade agreement. This indeed proved to be the case with the entry into force of the Basel Convention on the Transboundary Movements of Hazardous Wastes dealing with chemicals, pharmaceuticals and hazardous wastes. What is important, however, is that the rules of such MEAs are consistent with those of the GATT, and that the parties to the MEA fully appreciate the implications of the provisions in terms of GATT commitments (see chapter 6).

At the global level, the focus of the environment community at the time was primarily on the biophysical environment, including wildlife management, soil conservation, water pollution, land degradation, desertification, the depletion of the ozone layer, climate change, and deforestation. As a result of these concerns, it is not surprising that the 1980s saw a proliferation of MEAs targeting specific environmental problems.[7] Some of these agreements contained trade measures heralding a new concern in the GATT: could such agreements be hijacked for protectionist purposes, and were environmental problems being addressed by unnecessary barriers to trade?

The growth of global environment agreements led to a search for a long-term strategy that would facilitate integrated action on the part of a number of governments and international institutions. Because environment and development were now clearly both on the global agenda, a search had already begun for a concept of development that related to the limits of the natural resource base. In 1983, the General Assembly established the World Commission on Environment and Development to address the relationship between environment and development, and to propose long-term environmental strategies. The report that emanated from the Commission, entitled *Our Common Future* (the Brundtland Report), was issued in 1987. It adopted the term "sustainable development" and drew attention to the link between the environment and development by identifying poverty as a principal cause of environmental degradation.[8] It reasoned that greater economic growth, fuelled in part by increased international trade, could generate the necessary resources to combat what had become known as the "pollution of poverty". The conclusion was that existing decision-making structures and institutional arrangements, both national and international, simply could not cope with the demands of sustainable development. An increasing number of actors would need to grapple with the environmental dimensions of activities previously not recognized as having environmental implications.

The introduction of the notion of sustainable development onto the global agenda was met with a great deal of scepticism by a number of developing countries. The thought of sacrificing development today to preserve the environment for future generations raised the suspicion that the immediacy of development needs would be traded off against a much longer-term goal of environmental protection. Laudable as this goal might be, developing countries were not prepared to contribute to rectifying global environmental problems that they considered not to be of their making, while conforming to new environmental standards that were never faced by developed countries during their own economic development. A trade-off was required somewhere in the negotiating process to convince them that negotiating on the basis of sustainable development was in their interests.

Of importance for present purposes is that a new round of multilateral trade negotiations – the Uruguay Round (1986–1994) – had been launched. In fact, throughout the 1980s there had been continuing and difficult negotiations to establish the agenda for what was to become the most comprehensive round of trade negotiations in history. The goal of the negotiations (launched in Punta del Este in Uruguay) was the "liberalization and expansion of world trade to the benefit of all countries, especially less-developed contracting parties, including the improvement of access to markets".[9] The negotiations held a great deal of promise for developing countries.

It is interesting from an institutional perspective that there was acknowledgement that the GATT should respond to the "evolving international economic environment, through ... enhancing the relationship of the GATT with the relevant international organizations ... coupled with a need to foster concurrent co-operative action at the national and international levels to strengthen the inter-relationship between trade policies and other economic policies affecting growth and development".[10] What was to become apparent in later negotiations, if it was not clear at the time, was that governments were looking to improve coherence in global policy-making, but only between the WTO, the World Bank and the International Monetary Fund. Organizations with responsibilities in the area of environment, labour standards or other social norms were certainly not to be part of the package (see chapter 12).

However, the lack of attention to sustainable development in the Punta del Este Declaration was not surprising, if for no other reason than that the concept had yet to be adopted by the international community. Somewhat more surprising perhaps is that, given the attention focused on the global environment at the time, there was no reference at all to environment in the final Declaration. As the negotiations progressed, however, the late 1980s and early 1990s were, as noted, characterized by a significant growth in the number of MEAs. It was against this backdrop that the Director-General was requested at the Ministerial Meeting in Brussels in December 1990 to convene the EMIT Group for the first time. Austria, Finland, Iceland, Norway, Sweden and Switzerland (the countries of the European Free Trade Area) reasoned that the acceptance of "sustainable development" had established a link between environmental protection and development, and that the EMIT Group should address the trade-related environmental implications. The Brussels Ministerial Meeting ended in failure and no effect was given to the EFTA request.

Outside of the GATT, however, sentiments were running high that the GATT was acting in an irresponsible manner by disregarding the increasing importance attached to sustainable development, and, in particular, to the link between trade and the environment.[11] The EFTA group pursued the initiative, and in February 1991 again requested the Director-General to convene the EMIT Group. Although this attempt was also unsuccessful, a debate was launched in the GATT to identify measures taken on environmental grounds that could affect the existing provisions in the GATT and Tokyo Round instruments.[12] A recurring theme was the important distinction between legitimate environment-related measures, protectionist measures and the implications for GATT rules. Although developing countries continued to make clear their reservations about bringing environmental considerations into the GATT, the EMIT Group was finally convened later in 1991.[13] It had a three-point agenda: an examination of trade provisions contained in existing multilateral environment agreements; the multilateral transparency of national environmental regulations likely to have trade effects; and the trade effects of new packaging and labelling requirements aimed at protecting the environment. Thus, the subject matter under discussion had broadened beyond the implications of environment measures as impediments to trade.

The Group met from November 1991 to January 1994, and determined the parameters of what was to be the future approach of the GATT to trade and environment. The broad thrust was that the GATT was not equipped to review national environment priorities, to set environmental standards or to develop global policies on the environment. Further, there need not be any policy contradiction between the values of the multilateral trading system and countries acting individually or collectively to promote sustainable development. If problems of policy coordination did occur, however, it was considered important to resolve them in a way that did not undermine the multilateral trading system. On the other hand, trade rules should not present an unjustified obstacle to the implementation of legitimate environmental measures. With respect to existing GATT rules, they were considered already to be sufficient to accommodate trade measures to protect the environment, and exceptions to GATT rules were available specifically for this purpose. An open, secure and non-discriminatory trading system, underwritten by the GATT rules and disciplines, would facilitate environmental conservation and protection by ensuring a more efficient resource allocation and generating real income growth.[14]

The meetings of the EMIT Group coincided with both the final stages of the Uruguay Round and the convening of the United Nations Conference on Environment and Development (UNCED) – the "Earth Summit" – in Rio de Janeiro in 1992. The link between developments in the GATT, the ongoing negotiations in the Uruguay Round and the timing of UNCED is important. As noted above, some trade-off was required to convince developing countries to accept the objective of sustainable development within the context of international negotiations. This task was facilitated by the link that they envisaged between trade liberalization, improved market access and growth in the Uruguay Round. Operationalizing this link would contribute to poverty alleviation and therefore sustainable development. The logic was that a successful conclusion of the Uruguay Round would in itself contribute significantly to sustainable development, as long as the successful conclusion was measured in terms of improved access to the markets of developed countries.[15]

The UNCED summit was a major event, with over 100 heads of state and government, representatives from 178 countries, and some 17,000 participants meeting in Rio de Janeiro. One of its principal outputs was the *Rio Declaration on Environment and Development*, which contained a 40-chapter Programme of Action (*Agenda 21*).[16] This called for, *inter alia*, the creation of a Commission on Sustainable Development (CSD) to: ensure effective follow-up to UNCED; enhance international cooperation and rationalize intergovernmental decision-making; and examine progress in the implementation of *Agenda 21* at all levels. In 1992, the UN General Assembly set out the terms of reference for the CSD, its composition, guidelines for the participation of non-governmental organizations (NGOs), the organization of work, its relationship with other UN bodies, and the Secretariat arrangements. The CSD held its first meeting in June 1993 and has met annually since. It has institutionalized, within the United Nations, a continuing dialogue on sustainable development.[17]

With respect to the textual outcome of UNCED, what is quite striking for present purposes is the similarity between the guiding principles on trade-related sustainable development and the GATT approach described above. A potted summary of the relevant parts of *Agenda 21* runs along the lines that an open, multilateral trading system makes possible a more efficient allocation and use of resources, and contributes to an increase in production and incomes, and therefore to lessening demands on the environment. Importantly, to better address the problems of environmental degradation, governments should cooperate to promote a supportive and open international economic system that would lead to economic growth and sustainable development. UNCED recognized the relationship between open economies, improved market access, growth and sustainable development. Additionally, it was recognized that domestic measures targeted to achieve certain environmental objectives might need trade measures to render them effective but, if trade policy measures were necessary, they should be based on the principle of non-discrimination and be the least trade-restrictive necessary to achieve the objectives. Furthermore, there should be an obligation to ensure transparency in the use of trade measures related to the environment and to give consideration to the special conditions and developmental requirements of developing countries. Environment-related regulations or standards, including those related to health and safety standards, should not constitute a means of arbitrary or unjustifiable discrimination or a disguised restriction on trade. According to UNCED, the most important contribution the GATT could make to sustainable development was to conclude the Uruguay Round successfully, implying – much to the displeasure of many – that the only obligation for GATT members in meeting their sustainable development obligations was to complete their ongoing negotiations successfully.[18] All of the above could just as easily have come from trade ministers.

Despite commitments to improved market access, developing countries remained deeply suspicious of sustainable development, particularly as a number of environmental groups were working hard to convince their governments to integrate environment more comprehensively into the trade agenda in Geneva, precisely at the time when the Rio Conference had been successfully concluded. Were developed countries – pushed by their own environmental groups – thinking of backtracking on their UNCED and Uruguay Round commitments to improve market access, transfer technology and provide additional resources for developing countries? One conclusion was that there was a retreat from the holistic approach to sustainable development agreed at Rio. Were developed countries backtracking from the *Agenda 21* reassurance to avoid unilateral action to deal with environmental challenges outside the jurisdiction of an importing country?[19] The experience in Geneva pointed to backtracking taking place.[20]

In 1991, a high-profile – and well-documented – dispute between Mexico and the United States served to confirm developing countries' suspicions. In this instance, US trade restrictions on Mexican tuna caught using purse-seine nets, which resulted in the incidental kill of dolphins, drew attention to the potential for unilateral trade measures to be taken for environmental purposes. Mexico appealed to the GATT dispute settlement process on the grounds that the US embargo was inconsistent with the rules of international trade. The Panel ruled in favour of Mexico, thereby serving to focus attention on what was to be a source of considerable grievance – and remains so – for a number of environmentalists. The ruling created the perception that, for the GATT and later for the WTO, there was a clear hierarchy of trade policy vis-à-vis environment policy, with trade policy coming out on top. Trade priorities were seen as destined to ride roughshod over environmental concerns.

The significance of this case was considerable, not least because it served to shift the focus from environmental measures that could be impediments to trade to the enforcement of preferred environmental standards extra territorially through trade sanctions. The ruling mobilized environmental groups to push for an integrated approach at the global level that would harmonize international trade law with international law generally and take seriously the goal in the WTO Preamble to use the world's resources in accordance with the objective of sustainable development.[21]

Important as this ruling was from an environmental perspective, it was equally of concern to developing countries for systemic reasons – much of which is relevant for the broader range of sustainable development issues that were to emerge in the coming years. The ruling had confirmed that imported products could not be discriminated against under GATT rules because of the manner in which they were produced abroad. The same argument had been articulated two decades earlier in the report by Jan Tumlir mentioned above.[22] What this translated into was that the United States was obliged to provide Mexican tuna (as a product) with treatment no less favourable than that accorded to US tuna (also as a product), regardless of how the tuna itself was harvested. That products that were physically the same could not be discriminated against in this manner had far-reaching implications for the broader debate on sustainable development (see chapter 4). Traded products made by workers whose core labour or human rights were not respected could not be discriminated against, and trade restrictions could not be used as a tool to enforce standards. Although the report was never adopted, it rang alarm bells for developing countries, reinforced their opposition to unilateral measures, and raised their suspicions that trade restrictions would be legitimized through multilateral environment agreements.

Institutional developments in the WTO

Although discussion in the GATT was at a preliminary stage in the early 1990s, the trade and environment debate nevertheless figured prominently on the trade agenda elsewhere; the "Greening of the GATT" became a catch cry for environmentalists.[23] A proliferation of scholarly and popular contributions debated whether conflict between trade and environment policies was unavoidable.[24] Life was also injected into the debate from the GATT side via a timely and influential report – at least from a trade perspective – that elaborated and consolidated the approach to trade and environment in the GATT. Its relevance is also underscored by the fact that the GATT Secretariat had been specifically requested to contribute to the proceedings of UNCED, and this was one of two reports sent by the Director-General in response.[25] Its main thrust was a consolidation of the view that, when adverse production and consumption externalities are adequately integrated into decision-making processes, trade liberalization and the attainment of environmental objectives can be mutually supportive. For trade-induced growth to be sustainable, appropriate environmental policies determined at the national level need to be put in place. This was not seen to be a GATT responsibility. The report recognized that taxes and regulations applied to products and processes are frequently the most effective means to internalize externalities, but such regulations may well differ significantly across countries as a result of differences in, *inter alia*, comparative advantage.

There are two issues here, the first relating to comparative advantage and the second to extra territoriality. With respect to comparative advantage, the GATT report stipulates that "differences in environmental policies are properly regarded as domestic choices reflecting among other factors the domestic trade offs between income and environment and that such differences can well be an additional source of gainful trade among nations".[26] Thus, different environmental standards should not in themselves be considered an argument for restricting imports. Thus, GATT rules must be flexible enough to accommodate different policy choices, but still fulfil the GATT's role as a trade organization by policing measures that are protectionist in intent or that constitute unnecessary obstacles to trade. In terms of extraterritoriality, the closely related issue is whether the manner in which a product is produced can be a basis for discrimination in trade. Here the conclusion was that, whereas a domestic production process can be regulated in any manner thought fit by the national government to safeguard the life of humans, animals and plants within the jurisdiction of the importing country, it should not be possible under GATT rules to make access to domestic markets dependent on the environmental policies or practices of the exporting countries.

As this approach was gaining acceptance in the GATT, members instructed the EMIT Group to review the relevant sections of *Agenda 21* and report to the GATT General Council. However, it was agreed at this stage that any UNCED follow-up should await the outcome of the Ministerial Meeting in Marrakesh in April 1994 that concluded the Uruguay Round.

There were in fact a number of developments in the Uruguay Round of importance for sustainable development. The Standards Code was to become the Technical Barriers to Trade (TBT) Agreement, with all WTO members being parties. The Agreement on Sanitary and Phytosanitary Measures (SPS) was also a product of the Uruguay Round, and future events were to confirm that it had important implications for public health and environment-related matters. The Agreement on Agriculture, the General Agreement on Trade in Services, the Agreement on Subsidies and Countervailing Measures, and the Agreement on Trade-Related Aspects of Intellectual Property Rights (TRIPS) all formally recognized their potential impact on the environment. The strengthened dispute settlement system and the newly created Appellate Body were to prove important in the interpretation of provisions relating to trade, environment and sustainable development in the WTO, and the goal of sustainable development was recognized in the Preamble of the Agreement Establishing the WTO (see chapter 4).

Further, the reference to sustainable development in the Preamble now proved acceptable to developing countries. The *Tuna-Dolphin* case had allayed some fears, and the Preamble reflected a negotiated balance of interests: the pursuit of sustainable development must be consistent with the needs and concerns of countries at different levels of economic development. The Preamble was a clear reaffirmation of Rio Principle 7, with common but differentiated responsibilities for governments in promoting sustainable development. It was understood on the part of developing country negotiators that developed countries were accepting a greater responsibility to meet the costs of sustainable development owing to their larger role in environmental degradation as well as their economic capacity to do so. On their side, developing countries needed to develop to meet their needs; developed countries would provide adequate financial resources and technology transfer to facilitate their transition to sustainable development.

As a result of the work in the EMIT Group and the UNCED, another outcome of the Marrakesh Ministerial Meeting came in the form of a Decision on Trade and Environment. The Decision restated that there should be no policy contradiction between the multilateral trading system and protecting the environment while promoting sustainable development. It also called for the establishment of a Committee on Trade and Environment (CTE) to take over from the EMIT Group.[27]

The work programme of the CTE was to be broader than the agenda of the EMIT Group. The Committee was given a two-fold mandate that draws a clear link between trade, environment and sustainable development. It is first to identify the relationship between trade measures and environmental measures in order to promote sustainable development, and second to make appropriate recommendations on whether any modifications of the provisions of the multilateral trading system are required in this respect. In line with their concerns in bringing sustainable development to the WTO, developing countries were certainly not *demandeurs* when it came to creating the Committee on Trade and Environment. However, there was some reassurance in the terms of reference of the Committee that there would be no new WTO obligations, because future work was confined to trade-related aspects of the environment and, in this context, only those environmental measures with trade effects. Additionally, the CTE could make only *recommendations* for modifications of rules.

The Committee met for the first time in February 1995. It reported to the WTO General Council and is still operational. It has a standing agenda of 10 items that has not changed since its inception. It meets formally at least twice a year, and in an informal mode whenever considered necessary. It includes all WTO members and a number of observers from intergovernmental organizations. The Committee has discussed relations with non-governmental organizations but, despite a number of requests, there are no NGO observers. The early work of the CTE is comprehensively described in its Report to Ministers at the first WTO Ministerial Meeting in 1996 in Singapore. More recent meetings are described in the various reports of the CTE as well as the Annual Reports of the WTO. In addition, there are detailed summaries, commentaries and evaluations of the work of the CTE by academics and NGOs.[28] In the rest of this section, I selectively describe some aspects of the work of the Committee. These gave rise to tensions between developed and developing countries that served to shape much of the agenda in the CTE and elsewhere in the WTO for matters that are important for sustainable development.

The standing agenda of 10 items has been taken up in two "clusters of work". Broadly speaking, the first relates to *market access* and the second to *linkages* between the WTO and multilateral environment agreements. The clustering has been, and remains, an important feature of the work of the Committee for reasons that far transcend concerns over efficiency and effectiveness. Developing countries originally insisted on this grouping to ensure that improved market access – their only real interest in the trade and environment debate – was not lost as developed countries pursued their own agendas relating to trade measures taken for environmental purposes. Developing countries were not prepared to contemplate trade-offs between rule change with systemic implications (such as creating automatic acceptance of MEA-endorsed measures as exceptions from GATT obligations) and improved market access. For them, improving market access would be one way to straighten what they perceived to be a lop-sided trade and environment agenda and render it useful for development purposes. Against this backdrop, it was unlikely from the outset that the CTE would reach agreement "to make appropriate recommendations" for changes in rules.

The principal item in the first cluster (market access) relates to so-called win–win scenarios. These will be addressed in some detail in chapter 3; suffice it at this stage to note that this item addresses the environmental benefits that flow from removing trade restrictions and distortions that result in damage to the environment (win number one). If the right sectors and measures are chosen, this could improve market access opportunities for developing countries (win number two). Clearly, the win–win approach is in line with the overall GATT objective of removing trade restrictions and distortions. Nevertheless, even this mandate was viewed with suspicion by developing countries, which saw it as a potential new form of conditionality. Improved market access could be conditioned on their own governments' removing trade restrictions and adopting certain environmental standards dictated by the developed countries. Given their refusal to review their own environmentally unfriendly trade restrictions, the discussion has been rather one-sided, with the only environment-related trade restrictions under discussion being those in developed countries.

Another important market access agenda item has been the relationship between WTO rules and environmental taxes, standards and other regulations. This will be taken up in chapter 5. However, one particularly contentious issue in terms of regulations has been the use of labelling schemes based on life-cycle analysis; namely, the labelling of products according to the environmental effects of their production, consumption and eventual disposal. The relevant issue here turns on the fact that production methods vary across countries because of resource endowment and other factors and so does their effect on the environment. If an eco-label is required, this raises the issue of the comparability and acceptability of different criteria for receiving the label, and whether they are based on non-product-related process and production methods. The suspicion on the part of developing countries has been that eco-labelling schemes could be used as a barrier to their exports by necessitating labelling according to production standards in the importing countries. The same would apply to the packaging material used and requirements prescribing its recovery, re-use, recycling or disposal. These requirements can increase costs for exporters and result in discriminatory treatment owing to different environmental resource endowments and constraints in different countries.[29]

With respect to the second cluster, dealing with *linkages* between the WTO and MEAs, the task that has confronted the CTE since its inception has been how to deal with trade provisions in MEAs that may be at variance with WTO obligations. This topic is addressed in chapter 6. The concern for developing countries is the imposition of trade measures – sanctioned by MEAs reflecting the preferred standards of developed countries – that restrict their own market access possibilities. It was also thought that the discussion of this topic could be used tactically by developed countries to squeeze out discussion of what was of real interest to developing countries; namely, improved market access through win–win liberalization. Other matters on the MEA agenda related to whether the TRIPS Agreement promoted the transfer of technology to enable developing countries to fulfil their obligations under various MEAs. Discussion has also focused on the protection of traditional rights and knowledge and how to proceed if there were to be a conflict between the TRIPS Agreement and the Convention on Biological Diversity. These issues are elaborated in chapters 6 and 7.

Criticisms and future of the CTE

Ever since its first Report to Ministers in Singapore in 1996, the CTE has been heavily criticized for a "failure" to fulfil what many considered to be its principal task, namely, recommending modifications of the provisions of the multilateral trading system.[30] A number of developments, in particular the *Tuna-Dolphin* ruling, led many in the environment community to conclude that WTO rules did indeed need to be modified to take into account trade-related environmental considerations. But changing rules in the WTO is not a simple task and, in my view, the contribution of the CTE has been particularly constructive in the absence of rule change. In other words, many of the criticisms of the CTE are misplaced.

First of all, by not recommending rule change at the Singapore Ministerial Meeting and since, a policy choice has indeed been made by the trade negotiators – namely, that rule change is not appropriate. There are many reasons for this recommendation. First, discussions in the CTE have revealed the complexities associated with formulating environmental policies, coupled with an awareness on the part of trade officials that they have neither the expertise nor the mandate to deal with many of the problems they are expected to address by those outside the process. WTO members have constantly stressed that the WTO is neither an environmental standard-setting organization nor an enforcement agency for environmental standards. Various reports of the Committee and rulings of the Appellate Body have stressed that the solution to trans-boundary environmental problems lies in the negotiation of multilateral and regional environment agreements. In this respect, four considerations are important. First, because no environment dispute has ever come to the WTO where an MEA was the justification for a WTO-inconsistent measure, it has been hard to convince officials that there is a sufficiently serious problem to be addressed through rule change. As a general rule in the WTO, members tend to favour the adage "if it's not broken, don't fix it". Second, with respect to changing rules, because of their binding nature, members will agree to a rule change only if the outcome is clear and without risk. Unlike many environmental agreements, the WTO's dispute settlement process, with its threat of retaliation and compensation, is the Damocles sword hanging over those who have to live with the interpretation of the new rules – in both the trade and the environment communities. Third, of the hundreds of disputes dealt with by the GATT and WTO, only eight environment-related disputes have been brought to either institution, and all have ultimately had a satisfactory conclusion. However, they could all have been better handled outside the WTO (see chapter 4). Finally, there has been a greatly increased understanding of the complexity of the issues at hand. In large measure, this is due to CTE meetings at which secretariats of various MEAs have been invited to present relevant information with respect to the rules and objectives of their agreements.[31] These sessions have clearly facilitated a mutual understanding of the linkages between the multilateral environment and trade agendas and of environmental problems in general, and have thereby built awareness of how trade and environment can be mutually supportive without changing rules.

Another consideration in evaluating the contribution of the CTE and criticisms of it is that there have in some cases been false expectations about what the CTE can and cannot do. Although its mandate is broad, it does not extend to many of the concerns environmentalists have had with the WTO, and certainly not to the broader agenda of sustainable development. Dispute settlement cases provide an example. Even discussing – much less acting on – the outcomes of environment disputes such as *Tuna-Dolphin* or *Shrimp-Turtle* was simply not possible given the distribution of responsibilities in the WTO (see chapter 4). This mandate rests with the Dispute Settlement Body. The same is true for much of the discussion relating to rules and eco-labelling, which takes place in the TBT Committee. The controversial topic of NGO access to WTO processes has been discussed in the General Council, health measures in the SPS Committee, and development issues in the Committee on Trade and Development. There are many other examples. For some, the CTE was wrongly perceived as a Committee on Sustainable Development.

After a decade of meetings addressing a standing agenda, it seems to me that change is required. Has the CTE outlived its usefulness? The relevance of this question is underscored by the fact that some of the key issues that have been under consideration in the Committee are no longer of importance or have been relocated elsewhere in the WTO. Negotiations to deal with fisheries subsidies have been referred to the Negotiating Group on Rules, and the Special Session of the CTE has agreed that the Market Access for Non-Agricultural Products Group should conduct the negotiations on environmental goods and services. The Committee on Agriculture is dealing with trade-distorting agricultural subsidies, and a Special Session of the CTE deals with negotiations relating to MEAs. Furthermore, a number of the agenda items (such as trade in domestically prohibited goods) are simply no longer relevant or even discussed.

The Committee will not, however, be wound up, for a variety of reasons. Doing so would require the approval of all WTO members, and this will not be forthcoming. It serves at least one useful purpose in political terms and for a number of governments. Even in the extreme case that the CTE did not have a substantive agenda to address, it constitutes a process whereby governments can reassure domestic interest groups that questions of concern to them are on the WTO agenda and under review, or at least that a forum exists for them to be discussed. Most importantly, even as it functions today, the CTE provides a channel of communication to outside interest groups via public symposiums, provides a forum for representatives of different MEA secretariats to keep trade officials abreast of recent developments in their own treaties, and serves as a focal point for discussions of technical cooperation in the field of trade and environment. Nevertheless, changes in the functioning of the CTE are required. In particular, its terms of reference are out of date and a number of the standing agenda items are completely irrelevant. Agenda items that are important are being dealt with elsewhere, and items could be discussed that are of greater relevance today than those identified over a decade ago. The question is how to proceed.

In my view, there should be a meeting of the CTE dedicated to assessing whether or not the existing agenda items still require further discussion, and as a consequence whether some (or all) items should be dropped from the agenda. There should also be a discussion of what positive lessons can be drawn from past experience, and how the CTE should function in the future. A new agenda needs to be decided upon, which would look very different from the existing one. The directive for the CTE to review the existing situation in this manner would have to come from ministers. Therefore, I would suggest that this proposal be under consideration at the next WTO Ministerial Meeting.

I have argued that the CTE has been extremely useful for obtaining a better understanding on the part of both trade and environment officials with respect to the linkages between trade and environment policies, and it should continue to be so. However, the time has now come to reconsider its agenda and future usefulness. It is with that perspective in view that other parts of this book propose ways in which some of the matters of relevance to sustainable development can be more effectively dealt with by alternative means (win–win scenarios in chapter 3, standards in chapter 5, MEAs in chapter 6, etc.).

Given the language on sustainable development in the Preamble of the WTO Agreement, various Ministerial Declarations referring to sustainable development, and the fact that the environment and development are inextricably linked under the heading of sustainable development, a logical institutional arrangement would be for the WTO Committee on Trade and Development and the WTO Committee on Trade and Environment to combine to create a Committee on Sustainable Development. That this would appear to be a logical step is perhaps all the more so as both the Doha Development Agenda[32] and the WSSD encourage the Committee on Trade and Environment and Committee on Trade and Development to identify aspects of the Doha Development Agenda negotiations to achieve an outcome that benefits sustainable development.[33] The possibility of creating a Committee on Sustainable Development in the WTO has been raised informally in the past, but it has never been close to acceptance by WTO members. Moreover, although many parts of the Doha Development Agenda have been neglected, paragraph 51 must surely take the prize. Governments have no desire formally to discuss development and environment under a sustainable development agenda at the WTO. Nevertheless, a joint meeting of the committees with an input from public interest groups would potentially be of considerable value. This will be returned to in chapter 12.

Doha and Johannesburg

At the meeting in Doha, ministers also launched negotiations on trade and the environment – in particular, on the relationship between existing WTO rules and specific trade obligations set out in multilateral environment agreements. The negotiations are to be limited to the applicability of existing WTO rules among parties to the MEA in question. There are also to be negotiations on the procedures for regular information exchange between MEA secretariats and the relevant WTO committees and on the criteria for the granting of observer status. The reduction or elimination of tariff and non-tariff barriers to environmental goods and services is also to be negotiated. In principle, the fact that governments agreed to negotiate on such matters elevates the trade and environment deliberations beyond mere discussions to the status of negotiations. This, however, has not led to any higher degree of importance being assigned to the issue to date, and has served only to add complications as WTO members struggle with how to interpret the mandate and agree on the key terms (for example, what is an MEA for the purposes of negotiations, and indeed what is it that is being negotiated?). These complications apart, it is difficult to see why it should be trade officials who negotiate something that is so critical to the environment community.

As elsewhere in the Doha Development Agenda, these negotiations are being conducted under the Trade Negotiations Committee (TNC), with specific areas being addressed in special groups; the chairperson of each group reports on a regular basis to the TNC. Since the Doha Ministerial Session, in the case of trade and the environment work has been split into two separate tracks: (i) the negotiating track (paragraph 31), conducted in the CTE Special Session (CTESS), and (ii) the regular work of the CTE (paragraphs 32 and 33), conducted under the CTE Regular Session. The discussions of the CTESS have been largely information sessions, held with the participation of representatives of multilateral environment agreements. A long-standing issue in the CTE prior to the Doha Ministerial Conference was whether fisheries subsidies contribute to fish stock depletion and, if so, how the WTO should respond. These negotiations have been referred to the Negotiating Group on Rules in the context of negotiations on the Agreement on Subsidies and Countervailing Measures. Negotiations on the reduction and elimination of tariff and non-tariff barriers on environmental goods were also launched and this item is being taken in by the Market Access for Non-Agricultural Products Group.

As far as its regular work is concerned, ministers instructed the CTE to give particular attention to three areas: first, the effect of environmental measures on market access, particularly those situations in which the elimination or reduction of trade restrictions and distortions would benefit trade, the environment and development; second, the relevant provisions of the TRIPS Agreement; and, finally, labelling requirements for environmental purposes. Work on these issues should include the identification of any need to clarify relevant WTO rules. Ministers also recognized the importance of technical assistance and capacity-building in the field of trade and environment to developing countries, in particular the least developed among them, and encouraged the sharing of expertise and experience on national environmental reviews. The CTE was to report on this work to the Fifth Ministerial Conference in Cancún, Mexico (paragraph 33).

As noted, one potentially important development was that, at Doha, ministers mandated the Committee on Trade and Environment and the Committee on Trade and Development to monitor how sustainable development was dealt with in all ongoing negotiations. To this end, the CTE has commenced a process that involves sector-by-sector secretariat briefings on the environmental aspects of the negotiations (paragraph 51).

What is remarkable is the degree of overlap, and coherence, in the ministerial statements emerging from Doha and the World Summit in Johannesburg. The references to the role of the multilateral trading system in promoting sustainable development and the breadth of coverage of issues that the WSSD considers to be of relevance to its own agenda, yet which find themselves on the trade agenda, are quite staggering.

In the broadest perspective, in Doha, ministers strongly reaffirmed the traditional GATT/WTO approach to trade and environment, the evolution and characteristics of which are described in the earlier parts of this chapter. Ministers restated their conviction that "the aims of upholding and safeguarding an open and non-discriminatory multilateral trading system, and acting for the protection of the environment and the promotion of sustainable development can and must be mutually supportive".[34] From Johannesburg we learn that "[s]tates should cooperate to promote a supportive and open international economic system that would lead to economic growth and sustainable development in all countries to better address the problems of environmental degradation",[35] and that a "universal, rule-based, open, non-discriminatory and equitable multilateral trading system, as well as meaningful trade liberalization, can substantially stimulate development worldwide, benefiting countries at all stages of development".[36] This exact wording could also have come from the meeting in Doha.

This commonality of approach is of course commendable, and indeed it is in principle what governments are actively seeking in attempting to bring greater coherence to global policy-making. But what is striking is that the Johannesburg Declaration addressees such a large part of the vast expanse of issues that are squarely on the Doha Development Agenda of negotiations – or vice versa. This is apparent from the appendix to this chapter, which juxtaposes the relevant texts of the WSSD Declaration and the Doha Development Agenda to make the point.

As a potted summary, however, it can be noted that both Declarations announce a common commitment to uphold and safeguard the open and non-discriminatory multilateral trading system and to act for the protection of the environment and the promotion of sustainable development. These objectives are seen as being mutually supportive. Cooperation is considered necessary to promote a supportive and open international economic system that would lead to economic growth to better address the problems of environmental degradation. There is a recognized need in both Declarations for an improved effort to ensure that developing countries, and especially the least developed among them, secure a share in the growth of world trade commensurate with the needs of their economic development. Provisions for special and differential treatment are seen in both Declarations to be an integral part of the WTO Agreements, and the integration of developing countries into the multilateral trading system requires meaningful market access, support for the diversification of their production and export base, and trade-related technical assistance and capacity-building. Both Declarations support the successful completion of the work programme contained in the Doha Ministerial Declaration as a means to achieve these objectives.

Institutionally, the WTO Committee on Trade and Environment and the WTO Committee on Trade and Development are singled out in both Declarations to act as a forum to identify and debate developmental and environmental aspects of the negotiations in order to benefit sustainable development. In fact, there is specific mention in both statements of the need within the CTE to prioritize the elimination or reduction of trade restrictions and distortions, which would benefit trade, the environment and development. Both outcomes identify the need to promote sustainable development by removing market distortions, including restructuring taxation and phasing out harmful subsidies, where they exist. In the context, there is a need to clarify and improve WTO disciplines on fisheries subsidies, taking into account the importance of this sector to developing countries.

In more specific terms, both Declarations encourage the voluntary use of environmental impact assessments as an important national-level tool to better identify trade, environment and development interlinkages and support the reduction or elimination of tariff and non-tariff barriers to environmental goods and services. They both also seek to promote mutual supportiveness between the multilateral trading system and the multilateral environment agreements, while recognizing the importance of maintaining the integrity of both sets of instruments.

Both Declarations are on common ground that, under WTO rules, no country should be prevented from taking measures for the protection of human, animal or plant life or health, or of the environment, and that trade measures for environmental purposes should not constitute a means of arbitrary or unjustifiable discrimination or a disguised restriction on international trade. Unilateral actions to deal with environmental challenges outside the jurisdiction of the importing country should be avoided. Environmental measures addressing trans-boundary or global environmental problems should, as far as possible, be based on an international consensus.

The detailed contents of the Declarations with respect to improved market access in the areas of non-agricultural and agricultural products are striking. Both take note of the non-trade concerns reflected in the negotiating proposals submitted by WTO members and confirm that non-trade concerns will be taken into account in the negotiations as provided for in the Agreement on Agriculture, in accordance with the Doha Ministerial Declaration.

Attention is drawn to the importance of the Doha Declaration on the TRIPS Agreement and Public Health, in which it has been agreed that the TRIPS Agreement does not and should not prevent WTO members from taking measures to protect public health. There is a reaffirmation that the Agreement can – and should – be interpreted and implemented in a manner supportive of WTO members' right to protect public health and in particular to promote access to medicines for all. There is also a reaffirmation regarding the importance of internationally recognized core labour standards and the work under way in the International Labour Organization (ILO) on the social dimension of globalization.

What is striking in all of this is the extent to which the WSSD Declaration addresses issues that one way or another find themselves squarely on the agenda of the WTO. Many of these issues are addressed in the Declaration with specific reference to the ongoing work of the WTO, and others are important by inference. If there was any doubt about the proposition that the WTO is a world trade and sustainable development organization, it should be dispelled through a review of the WSSD Declaration along with the Doha Development Agenda.

Conclusion

What is needed as a minimum is a stocktaking of the relationship between the multilateral trading system and policies undertaken in the pursuit of sustainable development. In the absence of a coherent system addressing the relationship between the WTO and sustainable development, the criticism that the WTO now faces will in large measure remain linked to the many different perceptions of what is the proper role of trade policy in the global economy. Clarifying the role of the WTO in matters relating to sustainable development is an absolute priority for the international community if the enormous contribution that the multilateral trading system has made to world economic growth and stability over the past 50 years is to continue for the next half-century and beyond.

In chapter 12, I propose that there is a need to bring greater coherence to global economic policy-making. In the Uruguay Round, a FOGS (Functioning of the GATT System) Group was created, which produced a Ministerial Declaration on the Contribution of the World Trade Organization to Achieving Greater Coherence in Global Economic Policy-making.[37] This Declaration served as the basis for the comprehensive and formal agreements that were struck between the WTO, the World Bank and the International Monetary Fund to guide them in their future collaboration. In this Declaration, the ministers recognized that "difficulties, the origins of which lie outside the trade field, can not be redressed through measures taken in the trade field alone. This underscores the importance of efforts to improve other elements of global economic policy-making to complement the effective implementation of the results achieved in the Uruguay Round." They acknowledged that the "inter- linkages between the different aspects of economic policy require that the international institutions with responsibilities in each of these areas follow consistent and mutually supportive policies". The Declaration stated that the "World Trade Organization should therefore pursue and develop cooperation with the international organizations". The basic thrust of this Declaration would appear to be equally applicable to bringing greater coherence to global trade and environment policy-making. This could well be the objective of a FOWTOG (Functioning of the World Trade Organization Group).

Chapter 12 also identifies an institutional peg on which to hang such an initiative. As noted earlier, in the Doha Declaration, ministers agreed that the Committee on Trade and Development and the Committee on Trade and Environment should each act as a forum to identify and debate developmental and environmental aspects of the negotiations in order to help achieve the objective of having sustainable development properly reflected.

Appendix

This appendix compares the text of the Doha Development Agenda and the report of the World Summit on Sustainable Development.[38]

Sustainable development

DDA: "We strongly reaffirm our commitment to the objective of sustainable development, as stated in the Preamble to the Marrakesh Agreement. We are convinced that the aims of upholding and safeguarding an open and non-discriminatory multilateral trading system, and acting for the protection of the environment and the promotion of sustainable development can and must be mutually supportive" (para. 6).
WSSD: "States should cooperate to promote a supportive and open international economic system that would lead to economic growth and sustainable development in all countries to better address the problems of environmental degradation" (para. 101).

WSSD: "A universal, rule-based, open, non-discriminatory and equitable multilateral trading system, as well as meaningful trade liberalization, can substantially stimulate development worldwide, benefiting countries at all stages of development" (para. 141).

Commitment to development

DDA: "we shall continue to make positive efforts designed to ensure that developing countries, and especially the least-developed among them, secure a share in the growth of world trade commensurate with the needs of their economic development. In this context, enhanced market access, balanced rules, and well targeted, sustainably financed technical assistance and capacity-building programmes have important roles to play" (para. 2).

WSSD: "Welcome the decision contained in the Doha Ministerial Declaration to place the needs and interests of developing countries at the heart of the work programme of the Declaration, including through enhanced market access for products of interest to developing countries" (para. 47a).

WSSD: "Continue to promote open, equitable, rules-based, predictable and non-discriminatory multilateral trading and financial systems that benefit all countries in the pursuit of sustainable development. Support the successful completion of the work programme contained in the Doha Ministerial Declaration and the implementation of the Monterrey Consensus" (para. 47a).

WSSD: "Review all special and differential treatment provisions with a view to strengthening them and making them more precise, effective and operational, in accordance with paragraph 44 of the Doha Ministerial Declaration" (para. 92a).

Special and differential treatment

DDA: "We reaffirm that provisions for special and differential treatment are an integral part of the WTO Agreements. We note the concerns expressed regarding their operation in addressing specific constraints faced by developing countries, particularly least-developed countries. In that connection, we also note that some Members have proposed a Framework Agreement on Special and Differential Treatment (WT/GC/W/442). We therefore agree that all special and differential treatment provisions shall be reviewed with a view to strengthening them and making them more precise, effective and operational. In this connection, we endorse the work programme on special and differential treatment set out in the Decision on Implementation-Related Issues and Concerns" (para. 44).

DDA: "We recognize that the integration of the LDCs into the multilateral trading system requires meaningful market access, support for the diversification of their production and export base, and trade-related technical assistance and capacity building. We agree that the meaningful integration of LDCs into the trading system and the global economy will involve efforts by all WTO Members. We commit ourselves to the objective of duty-free, quota-free market access for products originating from LDCs" (para. 42).

WSSD: *"Call on developed countries that have not already done so to work towards the objective of duty-free and quota-free access for all least developed countries' exports, as envisaged in the Programme of Action for the Least-Developed Countries for the Decade 2001–2010" (para. 93).*

Integration of least developed countries (LDCs)

DDA: "... to help least-developed countries secure beneficial and meaningful integration into the multilateral trading system and the global economy. We are determined that the WTO will play its part in building effectively on these commitments under the Work Programme we are establishing" (para. 3).

DDA: "We endorse the Integrated Framework for Trade-Related Technical Assistance to Least Developed Countries (IF) as a viable model for LDCs' trade development. We urge development partners to significantly increase contributions to the IF Trust Fund and WTO extra-budgetary trust funds in favour of LDCs. We urge the core agencies, in coordination with development partners, to explore the enhancement of the IF with a view to addressing the supply-side constraints of LDCs and the extension of the model to all LDCs, following the review of the IF and the appraisal of the ongoing Pilot Scheme in selected LDCs. We request the Director-General, following coordination with heads of the other agencies, to provide an interim report to the General Council in December 2002 and a full report to the Fifth Session of the Ministerial Conference on all issues affecting LDCs" (para. 43).

WSSD: *[Small island developing countries] "Work to ensure that, in the ongoing negotiations and elaboration of the WTO work programme on trade in small economies, due account is taken of small island developing States, which have severe structural handicaps in integrating into the global economy, within the context of the Doha development agenda" (para. 58f).*

WSSD: *[Africa] "Improve market access for goods, including goods originating from African countries, in particular least developed countries, within the framework of the Doha Ministerial Declaration, without prejudging the outcome of the WTO negotiations and also within the framework of preferential agreements" (para. 67c).*

WSSD: "Recognizing the major role that trade can play in achieving sustainable development and in eradicating poverty, we encourage WTO members to pursue the work programme agreed at the Fourth WTO Ministerial Conference" (para. 90).

WSSD: "Support the Doha work programme as an important commitment on the part of developed and developing countries to mainstream appropriate trade policies in their respective development policies and programmes" (para. 90b).

WSSD: "Commit to actively pursue the WTO work programme to address the trade-related issues and concerns affecting the fuller integration of small, vulnerable economies into the multilateral trading system in a manner commensurate with their special circumstances and in support of their efforts towards sustainable development, in accordance with paragraph 35 of the Doha Declaration" (para. 94).

Role of the CTD and CTE

DDA: "The Committee on Trade and Development and the Committee on Trade and Environment shall, within their respective mandates, each act as a forum to identify and debate developmental and environmental aspects of the negotiations, in order to help achieve the objective of having sustainable development appropriately reflected" (para. 51).

WSSD: "Encourage the WTO Committee on Trade and Environment and WTO Committee on Trade and Development, within their respective mandates, to each act as a forum to identify and debate developmental and environmental aspects of the negotiations, in order to help achieve an outcome which benefits sustainable development in accordance with the commitments made under the Doha Ministerial Declaration" (para. 97a).

Trade restrictions and distortions

DDA: "We instruct the Committee on Trade and Environment, in pursuing work on all items on its agenda within its current terms of reference, to give particular attention to:

(i) the effect of environmental measures on market access, especially in relation to developing countries, in particular the least-developed among them, and those situations in which the elimination or reduction of trade restrictions and distortions would benefit trade, the environment and development" (para. 32).

WSSD: "Provide incentives for investment in cleaner production and eco-efficiency in all countries, such as state-financed loans, venture capital, technical assistance and training programmes for small and medium-sized companies while avoiding trade-distorting measures inconsistent with the rules of the World Trade Organization" (para. 16b).

WSSD: "Continue to promote the internalization of environmental costs and the use of economic instruments, taking into account the approach that the polluter should, in principle, bear the costs of pollution, with due regard to the public interest and without distorting international trade and investment" (para. 19b).
WSSD: "Promote ... sustainable development through the use of improved market signals and by removing market distortions, including restructuring taxation and phasing out harmful subsidies, where they exist, to reflect their environmental impacts with such policies taking fully into account the specific needs and conditions of developing countries with the aim of minimizing the possible adverse impacts on their development" (para. 20p).

Environmental impact assessment

DDA: "We take note of the efforts by Members to conduct national environmental assessments of trade policies on a voluntary basis" (para. 6).
WSSD: "Encourage the voluntary use of environmental impact assessments as an important national-level tool to better identify trade, environment and development inter-linkages. Further encourage countries and international organizations with experience in this field to provide technical assistance to developing countries for these purposes" (para. 97d).

TRIPS and the Convention on Biological Diversity

DDA: "We instruct the Council for TRIPS, in pursuing its work programme including under the review of Article 27.3(b), the review of the implementation of the TRIPS Agreement under Article 71.1 and the work foreseen pursuant to paragraph 12 of this Declaration, to examine, *inter alia*, the relationship between the TRIPS Agreement and the Convention on Biological Diversity, the protection of traditional knowledge and folklore, and other relevant new developments raised by Members pursuant to Article 71.1. In undertaking this work, the TRIPS Council shall be guided by the objectives and principles set out in Articles 7 and 8 of the TRIPS Agreement and shall take fully into account the development dimension" (para. 19).
WSSD: "With a view to enhancing synergy and mutual supportiveness, taking into account the decisions under the relevant agreements, promote the discussions, without prejudging their outcome, with regard to the relationships between the Convention and agreements related to international trade and intellectual property rights, as outlined in the Doha Ministerial Declaration" (para. 44r).

Subsidies – Fisheries

DDA: "In the light of experience and of the increasing application of these instruments by Members, we agree to negotiations aimed at clarifying and improving disciplines under the Agreements on Implementation of Article VI of the GATT 1994 and on Subsidies and Countervailing Measures, while preserving the basic concepts, principles and effectiveness of these Agreements and their instruments and objectives, and taking into account the needs of developing and least-developed participants. In the initial phase of the negotiations, participants will indicate the provisions, including disciplines on trade distorting practices, that they seek to clarify and improve in the subsequent phase. In the context of these negotiations, participants shall also aim to clarify and improve WTO disciplines on fisheries subsidies, taking into account the importance of this sector to developing countries. We note that fisheries subsidies are also referred to in paragraph 31 [i.e. "note that fisheries subsidies form part of the negotiations provided for in paragraph 28"]" (para. 28).

WSSD: *"Take action, where appropriate, to phase out subsidies in this area that inhibit sustainable development, taking fully into account the specific conditions and different levels of development of individual countries and considering their adverse effect, particularly on developing countries"* (para. 20q).

WSSD: *"Eliminate subsidies that contribute to illegal, unreported and unregulated fishing and to over-capacity, while completing the efforts undertaken at WTO to clarify and improve its disciplines on fisheries subsidies, taking into account the importance of this sector to developing countries"* (para. 31f).

WSSD: *"Support completion of the work programme of the Doha Declaration on subsidies so as to promote sustainable development and enhance the environment, and encourage reform of subsidies that have considerable negative effects on the environment and are incompatible with sustainable development"* (para. 97b).

The WTO and MEAs

DDA: "With a view to enhancing the mutual supportiveness of trade and environment, we agree to negotiations, without prejudging their outcome, on:

the relationship between existing WTO rules and specific trade obligations set out in multilateral environmental agreements (MEAs). The negotiations shall be limited in scope to the applicability of such existing WTO rules as among parties to the MEA in question. The negotiations shall not prejudice the WTO rights of any Member that is not a party to the MEA in question; and

procedures for regular information exchange between MEA Secretariats and the relevant WTO committees, and the criteria for the granting of observer status" (para. 31).

WSSD: "With a view to enhancing synergy and mutual supportiveness, taking into account the decisions under the relevant agreements, promote the discussions, without prejudging their outcome, with regard to the relationships between the Convention and agreements related to international trade and intellectual property rights, as outlined in the Doha Ministerial Declaration" (para. 44r).

WSSD: "Promote mutual supportiveness between the multilateral trading system and the multilateral environmental agreements, consistent with sustainable development goals, in support of the work programme agreed through WTO, while recognizing the importance of maintaining the integrity of both sets of instruments" (para. 98).

Environmental goods and services

DDA: "With a view to enhancing the mutual supportiveness of trade and environment, we agree to negotiations, without prejudging their outcome, on:

the reduction or, as appropriate, elimination of tariff and non-tariff barriers to environmental goods and services" (para. 31).

WSSD: "Support voluntary WTO compatible market-based initiatives for the creation and expansion of domestic and international markets for environmentally friendly goods and services, including organic products, which maximize environmental and developmental benefits, through, inter alia, capacity-building and technical assistance to developing countries" (para. 99b).

Eco-labelling

DDA: "We instruct the CTE, in pursuing all items on agenda with its current terms of reference to give particular importance to ... labelling requirements for environmental purposes" (para. 31(iii)).

WSSD: "Develop and adopt, where appropriate, on a voluntary basis, effective, transparent, verifiable, non-misleading and non-discriminatory consumer information tools to provide information relating to sustainable consumption and production, including human health and safety aspects. These tools should not be used as disguised trade barriers" (para. 15e).

Sanitary and Phytosanitary Measures

DDA: "The outcome of this work as well as the negotiations carried out under paragraph 31(i) and (ii) shall be compatible with the open and non-discriminatory nature of the multilateral trading system, shall not add to or diminish the rights and obligations of Members under existing WTO agreements, in particular the Agreement on the Application of Sanitary and Phytosanitary Measures, nor alter the balance of these rights and obligations, and will take into account the needs of developing and least-developed countries" (para. 32).

WSSD: *"Develop production and consumption policies to improve the products and services provided, while reducing environmental and health impacts, using, where appropriate, science-based approaches, such as life-cycle analysis" (para. 15c).*

WSSD: *"Improve policy and decision-making at all levels through, inter alia, improved collaboration between natural and social scientists, and between scientists and policy-makers" (para. 109).*

WSSD: *"Promote and improve science-based decision-making and re-affirm the precautionary approach as set out in principle 15 of the Rio Declaration on Environment and Development" (para. 109f).*

Market access – Agriculture

DDA: "We commit ourselves to comprehensive negotiations aimed at: substantial improvements in market access; reductions of, with a view to phasing out, all forms of export subsidies; and substantial reductions in trade-distorting domestic support. We agree that special and differential treatment for developing countries shall be an integral part of all elements of the negotiations and shall be embodied in the Schedules of concessions and commitments and as appropriate in the rules and disciplines to be negotiated, so as to be operationally effective and to enable developing countries to effectively take account of their development needs, including food security and rural development" (para. 13).

WSSD: *"Call upon WTO members to fulfil the commitments made in the Doha Ministerial Declaration, notably in terms of market access, in particular for products of export interest to developing countries, especially least developed countries" (para. 92).*

WSSD: *"Fulfil, without prejudging the outcome of the negotiations, the commitment for comprehensive negotiations initiated under article 20 of the Agreement on Agriculture as referred to in paragraphs 13 and 14 of the Doha Ministerial Declaration, aiming at substantial improvements in market access, reductions of with a view to phasing out all forms of export subsidies, and substantial reductions in trade-distorting domestic support, while agreeing that the provisions for special and differential treatment for developing countries shall be an integral part of all elements of the negotiations and shall be embodied in the schedules of concession and commitments and, as appropriate, in the rules and disciplines to be negotiated, so as to be operationally effective and to enable developing countries to effectively take account of their development needs, including food security and rural development. Take note of the non-trade concerns reflected in the negotiating proposals submitted by WTO members and confirm that non-trade concerns will be taken into account in the negotiations as provided for in the Agreement on Agriculture, in accordance with the Doha Ministerial Declaration" (para. 92c).*

Market access – Non-agriculture

DDA: "We agree to negotiations which shall aim, by modalities to be agreed, to reduce or as appropriate eliminate tariffs, including the reduction or elimination of tariff peaks, high tariffs, and tariff escalation, as well as non-tariff barriers, in particular on products of export interest to developing countries. Product coverage shall be comprehensive and without *a priori* exclusions. The negotiations shall take fully into account the special needs and interests of developing and least-developed country participants, including through less than full reciprocity in reduction commitments, in accordance with the relevant provisions of Article XXVIII *bis* of GATT 1994 and the provisions cited in paragraph 50 below. To this end, the modalities to be agreed will include appropriate studies and capacity-building measures to assist least-developed countries to participate effectively in the negotiations" (para. 16).

WSSD: "Call upon WTO members to fulfil the commitments made in the Doha Ministerial Declaration, notably in terms of market access, in particular for products of export interest to developing countries, especially least developed countries, by implementing the following actions, taking into account paragraph 45 of the Doha Ministerial Declaration: Aim to reduce or, as appropriate, eliminate tariffs on non-agricultural products, including the reduction or elimination of tariff peaks, high tariffs and tariff escalation, as well as non-tariff barriers, in particular on products of export interest to developing countries. Product coverage should be comprehensive and without a priori exclusions. The negotiations shall take fully into account the special needs and interests of developing and least developed countries, including through less than full reciprocity in reduction commitments, in accordance with the Doha Ministerial Declaration" (para. 92b).

Health

DDA: "We recognize that under WTO rules no country should be prevented from taking measures for the protection of human, animal or plant life or health, or of the environment at the levels it considers appropriate, subject to the requirement that they are not applied in a manner which would constitute a means of arbitrary or unjustifiable discrimination between countries where the same conditions prevail, or a disguised restriction on international trade, and are otherwise in accordance with the provisions of the WTO Agreements" (para. 6).

WSSD: "Trade policy measures for environmental purposes should not constitute a means of arbitrary or unjustifiable discrimination or a disguised restriction on international trade. Unilateral actions to deal with environmental challenges outside the jurisdiction of the importing country should be avoided. Environmental measures addressing trans-boundary or global environmental problems should, as far as possible, be based on an international consensus" (para. 101).

Access to medicines

DDA: "We stress the importance we attach to implementation and interpretation of the Agreement on Trade-Related Aspects of Intellectual Property Rights (TRIPS Agreement) in a manner supportive of public health, by promoting both access to existing medicines and research and development into new medicines and, in this connection, are adopting a separate Declaration" (para. 17).

WSSD: "Address the public health problems affecting many developing and least developed countries, especially those resulting from HIV/AIDS, tuberculosis, malaria and other epidemics, while noting the importance of the Doha Declaration on the TRIPS Agreement and Public Health, in which it has been agreed that the TRIPS Agreement does not and should not prevent WTO members from taking measures to protect public health. Accordingly, while reiterating our commitment to the TRIPS Agreement, we reaffirm that the Agreement can and should be interpreted and implemented in a manner supportive of WTO members' right to protect public health and in particular to promote access to medicines for all" (para. 100).

Labour standards

DDA: "We reaffirm our declaration made at the Singapore Ministerial Conference regarding internationally recognized core labour standards.

We take note of work under way in the International Labour Organization (ILO) on the social dimension of globalization" (para. 8).

WSSD: "Promote international cooperation to assist developing countries, upon request, in addressing child labour and its root causes, inter alia, through social and economic policies aimed at poverty conditions, while stressing that labour standards should not be used for protectionist trade purposes" (para. 13).

Technical assistance

DDA: "We recognize the needs of developing and least-developed countries for enhanced support for technical assistance and capacity building in this area, including policy analysis and development so that they may better evaluate the implications of closer multilateral cooperation for their development policies and objectives, and human and institutional development. To this end, we shall work in cooperation with other relevant intergovernmental organisations, including UNCTAD, and through appropriate regional and bilateral channels, to provide strengthened and adequately resourced assistance to respond to these needs" (para. 21).

DDA: "We recognize the importance of technical assistance and capacity building in the field of trade and environment to developing countries, in particular the least-developed among them. We also encourage that expertise and experience be shared with Members wishing to perform environmental reviews at the national level. A report shall be prepared on these activities for the Fifth Session" (para. 33).

DDA: "We confirm that technical cooperation and capacity building are core elements of the development dimension of the multilateral trading system, and we welcome and endorse the New Strategy for WTO Technical Cooperation for Capacity Building, Growth and Integration. We instruct the Secretariat, in coordination with other relevant agencies, to support domestic efforts for mainstreaming trade into national plans for economic development and strategies for poverty reduction. The delivery of WTO technical assistance shall be designed to assist developing and least-developed countries and low-income countries in transition to adjust to WTO rules and disciplines, implement obligations and exercise the rights of membership, including drawing on the benefits of an open, rules-based multilateral trading system. Priority shall also be accorded to small, vulnerable, and transition economies, as well as to Members and Observers without representation in Geneva. We reaffirm our support for the valuable work of the International Trade Centre, which should be enhanced" (para. 38).

WSSD: "Enhance the delivery of coordinated, effective, targeted trade-related technical assistance and capacity-building programmes, including to take advantage of existing and future market access opportunities, and to examine the relationship between trade, environment and development" (para. 47e).

WSSD: "Implement the outcomes of the Doha Ministerial Conference by WTO members, further strengthen trade-related technical assistance and capacity-building, and ensure the meaningful, effective and full participation of developing countries in multilateral trade negotiations by placing their needs and interests at the heart of the work programme of the World Trade Organization" (para. 48).

WSSD: "Implement substantial trade-related technical assistance and capacity-building measures and support the Doha Development Agenda Global Trust Fund established after the Fourth WTO Ministerial Conference as an important step forward in ensuring a sound and predictable basis for WTO-related technical assistance and capacity-building" (para. 90c).

WSSD: "Implement the New Strategy for WTO Technical Cooperation for Capacity-Building, Growth and Integration endorsed in the Doha Declaration" (para. 90d).

WSSD: "Fully support the implementation of the Integrated Framework for Trade-Related Technical Assistance to Least Developed Countries, and urge development partners to significantly increase contributions to the Trust Fund of the Framework, in accordance with the Doha Ministerial Declaration" (para. 90e).

WSSD: "In accordance with the Doha Declaration as well as with relevant decisions taken at Doha, we are determined to take concrete action to address issues and concerns raised by developing countries regarding the implementation of some WTO agreements and decisions, including the difficulties and resource constraints faced by them in fulfilling those agreements" (para. 91).

WSSD: "Build the capacity of commodity-dependent countries to diversify exports through, inter alia, financial and technical assistance, international assistance for economic diversification and sustainable resource management, and address the instability of commodity prices and declining terms of trade, as well as strengthen the activities covered by the Second Account of the Common Fund for Commodities to support sustainable development" (para. 95).

WSSD: "Encourage efforts to promote cooperation on trade, environment and development, including in the field of providing technical assistance to developing countries, between the secretariats of WTO, UNCTAD, UNDP, UNEP and other relevant international environmental and development and regional organizations" (para. 97c).

Small economies

DDA: "We agree to a work programme, under the auspices of the General Council, to examine issues relating to the trade of small economies. The objective of this work is to frame responses to the trade-related issues identified for the fuller integration of small, vulnerable economies into the multilateral trading system, and not to create a sub-category of WTO Members. The General Council shall review the work programme and make recommendations for action to the Fifth Session of the Ministerial Conference" (para. 35).

WSSD: *"Enhance the capacities of developing countries, including the least-developed countries, landlocked developing countries and small island developing States, to benefit from liberalized trade opportunities, through international cooperation and measures aimed at improving productivity, commodity diversification and competitiveness, community-based entrepreneurial capacity, and transportation and communication infrastructure development" (para. 47c).*

Institutional cooperation

DDA: "We welcome the WTO's continued cooperation with UNEP and other inter-governmental environmental organizations. We encourage efforts to promote cooperation between the WTO and relevant international environmental and developmental organizations, especially in the lead-up to the World Summit on Sustainable Development to be held in Johannesburg, South Africa, in September 2002" (para. 6).

WSSD: *"Recognizing the major role that trade can play in achieving sustainable development and in eradicating poverty, we encourage WTO members to pursue the work programme agreed at the Fourth WTO Ministerial Conference" (para. 90).*

WSSD: *"Strengthen collaboration within and between the United Nations system, international financial institutions, the Global Environment Facility and WTO" (para. 140b).*

Accession

DDA: "We therefore attach great importance to concluding accession proceedings as quickly as possible. In particular, we are committed to accelerating the accession of least-developed countries" (para. 9).

WSSD: *"Facilitate the accession of all developing countries, particularly the least-developed countries, as well as countries with economies in transition, that apply for membership of WTO" (para. 90a).*

Greater coherence in policy-making

DDA: "We are aware that the challenges Members face in a rapidly changing international environment cannot be addressed through measures taken in the trade field alone. We shall continue to work with the Bretton Woods institutions for greater coherence in global economic policy-making" (para. 5).

WSSD: "Strengthen collaboration within and between the United Nations system, international financial institutions, the Global Environment Facility and WTO" (para. 140b).

WSSD: "Ensure that there is a close link between the role of the Council in the follow-up to the Summit and its role in the follow-up to the Monterrey Consensus, in a sustained and coordinated manner. To that end, the Council should explore ways to develop arrangements relating to its meetings with the Bretton Woods institutions and WTO, as set out in the Monterrey Consensus" (para. 144f).

WSSD: "Stress the need for international institutions both within and outside the United Nations system, including international financial institutions, WTO and GEF" (para. 151).

WSSD: "Enhance the effectiveness and coordination of international institutions to implement Agenda 21, the outcomes of the World Summit on Sustainable Development, relevant sustainable development aspects of the Millennium Declaration, the Monterrey Consensus and the outcomes of the fourth WTO ministerial meeting, held in Doha in November 2001" (para. 151b).

WSSD: "Strengthen cooperation among UNEP and other United Nations bodies and specialized agencies, the Bretton Woods institutions and WTO, within their mandates" (para. 154).

Notes

1. See, in particular, GATT, *Trade and Environment: Factual Note by the Secretariat*, Geneva: GATT Secretariat, L/6896, 18 September 1991, as well as Håkan Nordström and Scott Vaughan, *Trade and the Environment*, Geneva: WTO Secretariat Special Studies, 1999.
2. See D. H. Meadows, D. L. Meadows, J. Randers and W. H. Behrens, *The Limits to Growth*, New York: Universe Books, 1972.
3. For a review of the Stockholm Conference and the ensuing evolution of environment institutions, see UNEP, *Global Environment Outlook 3*, Nairobi: UNEP, 2002, in particular, Part One entitled "Integrating Environment and Development: 1972–2002".
4. GATT, *Industrial Pollution Control and International Trade*, GATT Studies in International Trade, Geneva: GATT Secretariat, 1971, p. 4.
5. Ibid., p. 16.
6. See GATT, *Trade and Environment*, L/6896, p. 5.

7. Some of the major MEAs of the 1980s were: the 1982 United Nations Convention on the Law of the Sea (UNCLOS); the 1987 Montreal Protocol on Substances that Deplete the Ozone Layer (implementing the 1985 Vienna Convention for the Protection of the Ozone Layer); and the 1989 Basel Convention on the Control of Transboundary Movements of Hazardous Wastes and Their Disposal. In 1989, the Intergovernmental Panel on Climate Change (IPCC) was established by UNEP.

8. See WCED, *Our Common Future*, Oxford: Oxford University Press, 1987.

9. GATT, *Ministerial Declaration on the Uruguay Round*, Geneva: GATT Secretariat, MIN.DEC, 20 September 1986, p. 3.

10. Ibid., p. 3.

11. Steve Charnovitz, for example, later expressed the exasperation of the environmental community at the time by linking the origins of the ensuing intensified trade and environment debate (see below) to the opposition to the creation of the EMIT Group at the Brussels Ministerial Meeting. According to Charnovitz, it was "yet another sign of the GATT's antipathy for the environment". See Steve Charnovitz, "The World Trade Organization and the Environment", *Yearbook of International Environmental Law*, Vol. 8, 1997, p. 104.

12. GATT, *Outline of Points for Structured Debate on Environmental Measures and Trade*, Geneva: GATT Secretariat, Spec(91)21, 29 April 1991.

13. See GATT, *Trade and Environment*, L/6896.

14. This is a very brief synopsis of the contents of the report. For the full report, see GATT, *Report by Ambassador H. Ukawa (Japan), Chairman of the Group on Environmental Measures and International Trade, to the 49th Session of the Contracting Parties*, Geneva: GATT, L/7402, 2 February 1994.

15. This has been elaborated by one of the key negotiators of the time, Magda Shahin, "Trade and the Environment: How Real Is the Debate?", in Gary P. Sampson and W. Bradnee Chambers (eds), *Trade, Environment, and the Millennium*, 2nd edn, Tokyo: United Nations University Press, 2002, pp. 45–80.

16. Other significant outputs included the UN Framework Convention on Climate Change, the Convention on Biological Diversity, and the Statement of Forest Principles.

17. For a useful summary, see UNEP, *Global Environment Outlook 3*.

18. United Nations, *Report of the United Nations Conference on Environment and Development*, Rio de Janeiro, 3–14 June 1992, Chapter 1, Objectives 2.9(a), p. 3.

19. UNCED strongly endorsed the negotiation of MEAs to address global environmental problems. *Agenda 21* of the Conference states that measures should be taken to "avoid unilateral action to deal with environmental challenges outside the jurisdiction of the importing country. Environmental measures addressing trans-border or global environmental problems should, as far as possible, be based on international consensus." See United Nations, *Agenda 21: The United Nations Programme of Action from Rio*, New York: United Nations, 1993, Chapter 2.

20. See Shahin, "Trade and the Environment: How Real Is the Debate?".

21. Charnovitz, "The World Trade Organization and the Environment", p. 106.

22. GATT, *Industrial Pollution Control and International Trade*.

23. See, in particular, Dan Esty, *Greening the GATT*, Washington D.C.: International Institute for Economics, 1994.

24. See Jagdish Bhagwati, "Trade and Environment: The False Conflict?", in Durwood Zaelke, *Trade and the Environment: Law, Economics and Policy*, Washington D.C.: Island Press, 1993; also Kym Anderson and Richard Blackhurst (eds), *The Greening of World Trade Issues*, London: Harvester Wheatsheaf, 1992, and GATT, *International Trade 1990–1: Volume 1*, Geneva: GATT Secretariat, 1992, chapter 3 ("Trade and the Environment"), pp. 19–47. See also Duncan Brack (ed.), *Trade and Environment: Con-*

flict or Compatibility?, London: Royal Institute of International Affairs and Earthscan, 1997, and Richard Eglin, "Trade and Environment in the World Trade Organisation", *The World Economy*, Vol. 18, No. 6, 1995.

25. See GATT, *International Trade 1990–1: Volume 1*, Chapter 3. The Director-General also submitted GATT, *Trade and Environment*, L/6896.

26. See GATT, *International Trade 1990–1: Volume 1*, Chapter 3.

27. The Ministerial Decision on Trade and Environment, containing the mandate of the WTO Committee on Trade and Environment, is in Annex A of WTO, *Legal Texts: The Results of the Uruguay Round of Multilateral Trade Negotiations*, Cambridge: Cambridge University Press, 2002. A Decision on Trade in Services and the Environment was also adopted by ministers. The Decision instructs the CTE to examine and report on the relationship between services trade and the environment.

28. See WTO, *Report of the Committee on Trade and Environment*, Geneva: WTO, WT/CTE/1, 12 November 1996. See also WTO, *Trade and Environment: Special Studies 4, Trade and the Environment in the GATT/WTO*, Geneva: WTO Secretariat, 1999, Annex 1; Gregory C. Shaffer, "The World Trade Organization under Challenge: Democracy and the Law and Politics of the WTO's Treatment of Trade and Environment Matters", *Harvard Environmental Law Review*, Vol. 25, No. 1, 2001.

29. Wood, for example, is used for packaging in many Asian countries, but is not regarded as recyclable in Europe and therefore pays a penalty in the marketplace.

30. For a critique of the work of the Committee at the time of the Singapore Ministerial Meeting, see Steve Charnovitz, "A Critical Guide to the WTO's Report on Trade and the Environment", *Arizona Journal of International and Comparative Law*, Vol. 14, No. 2, 1997.

31. The most recent of these information sessions involved representatives from the Convention on International Trade in Endangered Species of Wild Fauna and Flora; the Basel Convention on the Control of Transboundary Movements of Hazardous Wastes and Their Disposal; the Rotterdam Convention on Prior Informed Consent; and the draft Persistent Organic Pollutants Convention. The Intergovernmental Forum on Forests, the UN Framework Convention on Climate Change and the Executive Secretary of the Convention on Biological Diversity were also represented at this session.

32. WTO, *Doha Declarations: The Doha Development Agenda*, Geneva: WTO Secretariat, 2001, para. 51.

33. WTO, *Report of the World Summit on Sustainable Development, Note by the Secretariat*, Geneva: WTO Secretariat, WT/CTE/W/220/Rev.1, 20 December 2002, para. 7a.

34. WTO, *Doha Declarations: The Doha Development Agenda*, para. 6.

35. WTO, *Report of the World Summit on Sustainable Development: Note by the Secretariat*, para. 95.

36. Ibid., para. 47(a).

37. See WTO, *The Results of the Uruguay Round of Multilateral Trade Negotiations: The Legal Texts*, Geneva: WTO Secretariat, 1994.

38. The sources referred to are WTO, *Doha Declarations: The Doha Development Agenda*, and WTO, *Report of the World Summit on Sustainable Development*. Both texts are available at ⟨http://www.wto.org⟩.

3

Trade liberalization, market access and sustainable development

Introduction

There may be differing views on the nature of the relationship between trade liberalization and sustainable development, but the existence of the relationship is not denied. The working premise of the World Trade Organization (WTO) is that trade liberalization and sustainable development are mutually supportive, and that putting into effect the link between them is in many ways the *raison d'être* of the Doha Development Agenda that emerged from the Doha Ministerial Meeting in Qatar in 2001. The World Bank has estimated that liberalization of merchandise trade with a supportive domestic policy environment would result in gains of around 5 per cent of income in developing countries and lift 300 million people out of poverty by 2015. If greater opening of services trade were to occur as well, including increased movement of natural persons (see chapter 8), the benefits would be substantially greater. It is argued that no other area of international economic cooperation – for example, debt relief or official development assistance – holds out such a promise. According to the World Bank: "In addition to bolstering investor confidence in the short term, a Doha Round agreement that slashed trade barriers, particularly in agriculture, would stimulate trade and raise incomes around the world, leading to a substantial reduction in global poverty."[1] Poverty alleviation is one pillar of sustainable development.

Although this may be the working hypothesis of the WTO and the Bretton Woods institutions, there is certainly no consensus that trade liberalization automatically promotes sustainable development. In fact, from an environmental or social perspective, the contribution of trade liberalization to sustainable development is seen by some to be rather sinister. Trade expansion is perceived as an anti-environmental/anti-social force driven by the desire for increased profits, jobs, consumption and production. This in turn is believed to lead to an accelerated attrition of the world's non-renewable resources, such as fossil fuels and minerals, and an overexploitation of water, air, forests and other renewable resources. Although it is agreed that removal of poverty is the number one obstacle to achieving sustainable development, trade liberalization is carried out on the basis of rigged trade rules that in no way ensure the elimination of poverty.[2] When viewing the link between trade liberalization and sustainable development, some consider it lamentable that these features of trade liberalization have not been the subject of Ministerial Declarations.

Those promoting the virtues of trade liberalization would not deny that trade liberalization and growth can be harmful to the environment, or that liberalization per se will not necessarily achieve sustainable development. In fact, it may indeed be harmful. For market-based economists, the welfare of society can be undermined when market prices fail to capture the effects of environmentally damaging activities and therefore send misleading signals relating to the optimal use of environmental resources. Distorted prices can obscure the abundance of underutilized environmental resources, contribute to the excessive depletion of exhaustible resources, generate new environmental problems, and contribute to the excessive use of environmentally damaging inputs. In these circumstances, more trade is not good for the environment. Nor does trade-induced growth in any way ensure an equitable distribution of the gains from trade. Indeed, the failure to redistribute the gains from trade can exacerbate inequality.

The important question that emerges from this is what the role of the WTO should be in dealing with these trade-related concerns. The WTO response is that, for benefits to be realized and for trade-induced growth to be sustainable, national environmental, income distribution and social policies should be put in place. The view is that trade liberalization is not the cause of environmental degradation, poverty or unacceptable social conditions, nor are trade instruments the first-best policy for addressing such matters. Quite the contrary. The most significant part of the relationship passes indirectly through effects on levels and patterns of production, consumption and income distribution. The argument runs that, if such problems accompany trade-induced growth, this is the result not of bad trade policy but of bad environment policy, income distribution policy or social policies.

Although the WTO by definition takes responsibility for negotiated trade liberalization, its members have repeated on numerous occasions that they do not consider the WTO to be responsible for setting environmental and social standards and enforcing them. Nor is it the responsibility of the WTO to redistribute the gains from trade in countries that have benefited from trade expansion or to protect those that are adversely affected. In the WTO tradition, it would be considered an encroachment on national sovereignty to meddle in the national economic, environmental and social programmes of member states. This argument is buttressed by the fact that, at the multilateral level, agreements outside the WTO are already in place to deal with concerns of this nature.

Against this backdrop, an important question confronting the WTO is how to facilitate the positive links between trade liberalization and sustainable development. I address this question in this chapter, as follows. First I provide an overview of approaches to identifying the relationship between trade liberalization and sustainable development. I then describe a methodology adopted in the WTO to exploit a positive link: the so-called win–win scenarios. I examine agriculture, fisheries and environmental goods and services in this context. I place particular emphasis on the fisheries sector, not least because of the importance assigned to it in the Doha Development Agenda. It constitutes an interesting case study for a variety of reasons. The chapter closes with a conclusion.

Liberalization and resource allocation

Given the complexities of the links between trade liberalization, economic growth, the environment and social considerations, it is not surprising that there have been calls for a multilateral framework to facilitate the assessment of the impact of trade liberalization on sustainable development. After making such a proposal in 1994, the United Nations Commission on Sustainable Development was mandated by governments to provide the institutional coordination necessary to undertake an assessment of the environmental and social development aspects of trade policies. The nature and current status of review in the case of WTO members have been usefully summarized.[3] The Worldwide Fund for Nature (WWF) and the United Nations Environment Programme (UNEP) have also developed comprehensive methodologies for assessing the environmental impact of trade measures, and the Organisation for Economic Co-operation and Development (OECD) has developed Guidelines on the Development of Sustainable Development Strategies.[4]

The specifics in terms of coverage and techniques used in these models of assessment differ but, broadly speaking, they all develop tools to evaluate the impact of changes in various regulations (including tariffs and other trade barriers) on one or more aspects of sustainable development. The objective is to improve the efficiency, effectiveness and transparency of governmental decisions that have an impact on sustainable development. Although the techniques differ, two major categories of effects are common to the assessment methodologies: first, the legal effects of obligations undertaken via a trade agreement that necessitates changes to domestic regulations; and, second, changes in trade flows and general economic activity as a consequence of trade liberalization. These are relevant for trade and sustainable development issues. A scoping or screening exercise is required to ascertain which trade measures deserve attention.

There have been a number of suggestions that WTO members should commit themselves to conducting sustainability/environmental impact assessment studies to precede, accompany or evaluate the implications of trade liberalization. The idea has not gained formal support for action in the WTO. There are a number of reasons for this, some practical and others political.

One practical consideration is the uncertainty surrounding the proper timing of assessments. Should they be carried out prior to negotiations to liberalize trade or at various stages during the negotiations themselves? Alternatively, should they take place after the finalization of the agreement? In addition, the task of evaluating the environmental effects of trade liberalization is complicated by the fact that changes in resource usage and consumption patterns are difficult to measure. Even establishing links between changes in the pattern of trade and its effects on the environment and social conditions reflects different priorities and values. In fact, the very nature of externalities is that the costs and benefits occur outside the market framework and are not valued by it. Finally, but very importantly, only a minority of countries have adequate environmental data to carry out such an assessment.

Nevertheless, the resistance on the part of most WTO members to carving out a role for the WTO in this area is driven principally by political considerations. Reviewing the local impact of trade liberalization is considered to be a national choice; it should not be a precondition for trade liberalization within the context of WTO deliberations. As frequently noted, particularly by developing countries, the WTO is in the business of promoting growth through expanded trade, and is not, according to its current terms of reference, responsible for implementing or evaluating the effectiveness of environmental management and sustainable development policies. For developing countries, if conditions are imposed with respect to predetermined environmental standards before liberalization can take place, this is a clear breach of national sovereignty, probably a form of disguised protectionism, and creates a precedent for labour and other standards that would have to be met. Not surprisingly, the Doha Development Agenda assigns a low priority to environmental assessments. Ministers decided merely to "take note of the efforts by Members to conduct national environmental assessments of trade policies on a voluntary basis".[5] The key word is *voluntary*; there is no obligation to link trade liberalization and sustainable development formally through sustainable development impact assessment studies.[6]

Yet trade liberalization can lead to adverse environmental results and an evaluation of its impact on sustainable development is of primary importance. It is an area of joint concern of the WTO – though not as a monitoring or enforcement agency – and other organizations, such as UNEP, the OECD, the United Nations Conference on Trade and Development (UNCTAD) and the United Nations Development Programme (UNDP). The policy prescription that emerges is for a coordinated and comprehensive approach, including the creation of a number of formal and informal linkages between the relevant institutions. The WTO Secretariat could contribute in an informal manner. This would be consistent with the Agreement Establishing the WTO: namely, the need to establish working relations with other international organizations (Article V:1) and for the General Council to make appropriate arrangements for effective cooperation with other intergovernmental organizations that have responsibilities related to those of the WTO.

Win–win ...

The terms of reference of the Committee on Trade and Environment (CTE) require WTO members to examine the effects of environmental measures on market access, as well as the environmental benefits of removing trade restrictions and distortions. In the jargon of the CTE, trade liberalization in industrial countries that results in the removal of environmentally unfriendly measures has the potential to result in what could be described as "win–win" outcomes. Countries "win" when they remove environmentally harmful trade restrictions in their own countries; other countries "win" when their exports grow owing to the improved market access that follows.

The positive relationship between trade liberalization and the environment manifests itself through, first, improved production and consumption patterns with the removal of environmentally harmful trade restrictions; second, a reduction in poverty through trade expansion, growth and the encouragement of a sustainable rate of natural resource exploitation in the exporting country; third, an increase in the availability of environment-related goods and services through market liberalization; and, fourth, more resources available through trade-led growth for environment management programmes. In reality, a "win–win–win–win" scenario presents itself.

There are many good reasons for promoting a win–win approach. It gives force to the commitment of WTO members in the Preamble to the Agreement Establishing the WTO to use the world's resources optimally and in accordance with the objective of sustainable development. It provides evidence of the willingness of WTO members to protect and preserve the environment, and to enhance the means for doing so, precisely when they are being criticized for not doing enough. Adopting this approach assists in creating a more positive image for public interest groups that have been hostile to the WTO for not doing enough to promote sustainable development. Importantly, with improved market access being the light at the end of the tunnel, the agenda item of trade liberalization holds attraction for developing countries, where few other advantages are seen in the trade and environment debate (see chapter 2). Finally, by adopting a win–win approach, public support can be garnered for undertaking reform in sectors where some interest groups might be adversely affected by policy reform (e.g. agriculture) but where reform is in the interests of the community at large (e.g. an environmentally improved countryside).

In carrying out this work, there is a real opportunity for WTO members – and the CTE in particular – to work constructively with public interest groups. It seems fair to say that the local knowledge of environmentalists in terms of assessing the environmental impact of trade restrictions far exceeds that of trade officials. The potential for useful work in this area has become apparent in the success that international organizations (e.g. UNEP) and public interest groups (e.g. WWF) have had in drawing attention to the fact that the WTO may be able to take action regarding environmentally harmful fisheries subsidies.[7] This advocacy has spawned a series of publications, proposals and meetings to address the damaging consequences of fisheries subsidies.

However, there are several important relevant considerations when reviewing the work in the WTO. First, as noted in chapter 2, the CTE has been confined exclusively to examining the positive effects on the environment in *industrial* countries of the removal of trade restrictions and distortions. The possibility of developing countries removing their own environmentally harmful trade restrictions and distortions has never been under discussion. In a sense this is unfortunate. However, the reason is political. It is based on developing countries' fear that improved market access in the developed countries would be offered in exchange for the removal in developing countries of trade restrictions considered environmentally harmful by the importing countries. If the justification for environmental trade restrictions in developing countries were under examination, their view is that this would bring added pressure to adopt norms and standards devised by the developed countries and probably inappropriate for their own countries. In most general terms, developing countries have consistently resisted creating a link whereby their improved market access is contingent upon meeting predetermined standards or adopting certain policies domestically, be they related to the environment, labour conditions, or anything else.

A second consideration relates to the fact that not all trade-related measures adversely affect the environment. Quite the contrary. Subsidies used to encourage the use of environmentally friendly technology or subsidies to promote the adaptation of existing facilities to new environmental requirements imposed by law and/or regulations are both examples. Other examples include measures that correct for excessive resource use as part of a well-constructed environmental management policy. However, the intention of the win–win approach is clearly not to question measures to improve the environment that do not unnecessarily restrict trade. Another consideration is that removing trade restrictions and distortions is rarely synonymous with an unambiguous improvement in environmental quality per se. As noted earlier, the impact of regulation on the environment is complex, even when examined within the context of well-constructed sustainability impact assessment exercises. Although removing a trade restriction or distortion may be an important component in an environmental management strategy, its removal is not in itself a guarantee of improved environmental quality.

The important question from a practical perspective is whether or not win–win situations really exist. Work on several fronts has revealed that they do, and that there is plenty of scope for action. Research by the OECD has revealed that OECD countries provide approximately US$400 billion in subsidies every year, with about three-quarters going to agriculture, one-tenth to transport, and the rest to fisheries and forestry, energy production and manufacturing. There has been a shift towards less environmentally harmful support in agriculture since the mid-1980s, but progress has been slow. The OECD believes much more can be done. In fact, harmful support for the agricultural sector amounts to about US$235 billion per year. Some of the US$6 billion in fisheries subsidies in developed countries goes to general services that support fisheries infrastructure and enhancement programmes that contribute to over-fishing. Estimates of energy subsidies range between US$20 billion and US$80 billion per year. Subsidies to coal and peat production are among the most harmful to the environment, and support to the coal industry is estimated at about US$5 billion per year for developed countries.[8]

Agriculture

Agriculture is estimated to be responsible for 40 per cent of nitrogen emissions and 30 per cent of phosphorous emissions into surface water in developed countries. It is the main source of groundwater pollution. Methane and nitrous oxide emissions from livestock operations and rice production also contribute to global warming. The use of pesticides and their build-up in groundwater and surface water pose risks to the health of people and to wildlife. Groundwater systems are increasingly under threat from contamination and withdrawals that exceed the capacity of aquifers to recharge.[9]

It has long been recognized that reducing domestic supports and export subsidies in the agricultural sector can in many instances lead to more sustainable production. Research has shown that agricultural subsidies have led to harmful land use, increased applications of agrochemicals, the adoption of intensive animal production practices and overgrazing, the degradation of natural resources, the loss of natural wildlife habitats and biodiversity, reduced agricultural diversity, and the expansion of agricultural production into marginal and ecologically sensitive areas. Agricultural assistance through output-related policies in many industrial countries has imposed high costs in terms of lost market access opportunities for more competitive suppliers. Benefits in the form of a *first win* – improved environment – could come from the removal of some of the agricultural trade distortions. The WTO Agreement on Agriculture provides for the long-term reform of trade in agricultural products and domestic policies. One significant aspect is the commitment to reduce domestic support for production, particularly in the form of production-linked agricultural subsidies.

There is also the potential for further wins. There is a clear development dimension to agricultural trade liberalization. First, there are direct links. Many developing countries have an export capacity in agricultural products. If market access restrictions are removed, their exports will increase. In fact, developed country support to agriculture coupled with restrictions on imports is estimated to cause annual welfare losses of US$19.8 billion for developing countries. This is equivalent to approximately 25 per cent of their annual development assistance.[10] As such, it significantly reduces developing countries' ability to provide the necessary resources for environmental and social sustainability.

Second, quantitative studies reveal that government intervention through trade-related measures depresses world agricultural prices, with the result that poor farmers stay poor. And low prices and rural poverty induce farmers to cultivate marginal lands that are subject to erosion and runoff. More forests are cleared for the extension of agricultural land for cultivation. Attempts by developing country governments to offset low prices by providing input subsidies for fertilizers and pesticides lead to the same soil erosion and intensive chemical use as in highly protected agricultural markets, but they also involve greater threats to the health of local farmers and consumers from the incorrect application of agro-chemicals. In short, the removal of trade restrictions in the agricultural sector in developed countries could well touch on some of the most impoverished developing countries, many of which benefited little from the tariff reductions and preferences accorded to manufactured goods.

Although discussions on win–win situations in agriculture have proceeded in the CTE, they have now been overtaken by the more broad-based negotiations in the Special Sessions of the Committee on Agriculture, dealing with the ongoing Doha Development Agenda: removal of export subsidies, reduction of domestic support and improved market access. Knowing the environmental damage that can arise from trade restrictions in this area should increase popular support and stiffen the backbone of politicians and administrators involved in agricultural reform.

There has been a resistance to removing some aspects of government intervention in the agricultural sector in the search for "sustainable" production through the response to what have been referred to as *non-trade concerns*. These have been reflected in the negotiating proposals submitted by members in the Doha Development Agenda, which itself confirms that non-trade concerns will be taken into account in the negotiations. The friends of non-trade concerns (the European Union and its candidate member states, Japan, Korea, Norway, Switzerland and some developing countries) consider a number of policy areas such as rural development, environment protection, food safety, food security, animal welfare, consumer information and labelling to be outside the negotiations. Others consider them to be nothing more than a pretext for continuing trade-distorting domestic support measures. The United States and the Cairns Group of 17 agricultural exporting countries, for example, are of the view that any such concerns should be addressed through measures that target specific policy objectives and that are WTO consistent and transparent and do not distort trade.

One further interesting development relating to agriculture that links the Doha negotiations on agriculture to sustainable development is the Conference of the Parties to the Convention on Biological Diversity

(CBD). At its Seventh Meeting in Kuala Lumpur in February 2004,[11] trade concerns were most overtly raised in the context of a draft decision on providing "positive incentives" for the conservation and sustainable use of biodiversity, as well as removing/mitigating "perverse incentives" that encourage practices leading to degradation and loss of biodiversity. Some countries (Australia and Brazil) expressed concern that initiatives to legitimize positive incentives/subsidies were in effect an attempt to promulgate disguised trade restrictions. In the view of the CBD Secretariat, the process of reducing trade-distorting domestic support policies has the potential to generate synergies with the objectives of the Convention on Biological Diversity to conserve and sustainably use biological diversity.[12]

One final consideration is that the treatment of forest products goes hand in hand with the agricultural sector. The removal of support to agriculture can reduce the pressure for agricultural extension into ecologically marginal land, including forest areas. Many types of measures are known to affect trade in this sector, including tariffs and tariff escalation, subsidies, export taxes and restrictions, certification of sustainable forest management and labelling of forest products, market transparency for forest products, the promotion of less-used forest species, and financing and technology to improve sustainable forest management and increase value-added processing of wood and wood products.

Of these measures, tariff escalation is believed to be the main source of trade restriction and distortion in this sector. It can distort production patterns and have a second-round negative effect on developing countries. Export taxes and other restrictions on unprocessed timber exports are used by some timber-exporting countries to encourage forest-based industrialization. They are reinforced by other measures giving preferential treatment to domestic processing industries, such as supplying raw materials to local producers at below world market prices with an inefficient use of raw materials as a result. In certain cases they are used to compensate domestic processors for tariff escalation and other market access barriers faced in major export markets. Again, there is considerable scope for a win–win approach.

Environmental goods and services

There is no general agreement on what constitutes an environmental good or service. Should the definition include only goods and services that are directly used to minimize or correct environmental damage, or should it extend to goods and services that are produced, used or disposed of in a way that has a minimal impact on the environment? Defining the scope of the industry, however, is difficult even if goods and services produced in an environmentally friendly manner are excluded. There are multiple possible end uses of many environmental goods and services, and they are not specifically identified as such in standard industry nomenclatures.

Nevertheless, a common description of environmental goods and services (in the absence of environmentally friendly goods) includes those that measure, prevent, limit, minimize or correct environmental damage to water, air and soil, as well as problems related to waste, noise and eco-systems. These include cleaner technologies and products and services that reduce environmental risk and minimize pollution and resource use, such as energy-efficient machinery, wastewater treatment equipment, air pollution scrubbers and processes to reduce or eliminate chrome in leather tanning. Adopting this narrower definition, it has been estimated that the production of environmental goods and services already exceeds US$250 billion per annum.[13]

In this sector, as in others, it is in the interest of all WTO members that environmentally sound goods and services be made available on the international market at the cheapest prevailing world prices. Cheaper environmental goods and services mean that limited environmental protection budgets can be stretched further, expanded market opportunities can encourage technological progress, and economies of scale can increase efficiency.

There seems little reason not to advance rapidly in the negotiated liberalization of environmental goods and services. In practice, though, governments seek "concessions" in negotiations even when acting in their own interests. In recent years, however, traditional cross-sectoral trade-offs have not always been necessary to encourage governments to enter into sectoral trade-liberalizing negotiations: examples include information technology, pharmaceutical products, basic telecommunications and financial services.[14] In this respect, ministers agreed in the Doha Development Agenda to negotiations on "the reduction or, as appropriate, elimination of tariff and non-tariff barriers to environmental goods and services". This, they say, will enhance "the mutual supportiveness of trade and environment".[15] Following the logic of other sectoral agreements, there seems little justification in not rapidly agreeing to a sectoral agreement for liberalizing environmental goods and services.

The negotiations, however, appear to be stalled precisely over devising a classification for environmental goods and services for the purposes of liberalization. A great deal has been written about how to classify environmental goods and services. That the negotiations are stalled on this matter is unfortunate. There is, however, a parallel, which emerged in the Uruguay Round negotiations on trade in services with respect to the classification of sectors and subsectors to be used as a basis for the negotiation of country schedules containing the bound degree of openness. There too was a need to break an impasse. In the absence of a natural scientific definition of services, delegations requested the Secretariat to propose a list of what could be considered services for the purposes of negotiations. The Secretariat reviewed the existing nomenclatures and drew up a suggested list of sectors and subsectors. This remains the basic working document for the negotiated liberalization of services today. There seems little reason why this should not be the course of action to take in order to advance the negotiated liberalization of environmental goods and services.

Fisheries subsidies: A useful case study

Background

Scientific evidence has consistently shown a downward trend in the world's fish stocks. The result is that there are now few underexploited resources and an increasing number of overexploited ones. The factors that explain fish stock decline are many and varied. Apart from an overcapacity of fishing fleets, specialists single out open access to fish resources as a result of the absence of property rights. Not all oceans – and certainly not the high seas – are subject to property rights, and the migratory nature of fish populations makes it impossible to assign such rights.[16] Other factors leading to fish stock decline include inappropriate fisheries management practices, marine pollution, increased mortality of non-commercial fish by-catch, and various other practices that adversely affect marine biodiversity and their habitats. Another candidate is subsidies, which are widespread in the fisheries sector. Although their precise identification and quantification are unknown, a common view is that they are a major contributor to the current state of fleet overcapacity and to the mismanagement of fisheries resources. The conclusion is that their reduction or removal would result in less capital flowing into the sector, lower fish-harvesting levels, and the facilitation of sustainable fisheries management systems.

Concern about the effects of fisheries subsidies on fish stocks is not new. Many international initiatives over the past decade have emphasized the adverse effects of subsidies on fish stocks. The UN Commission on Sustainable Development (CSD) listed among the actions required for the implementation of Chapter 17 of *Agenda 21* the urging of governments "to reduce subsidies to fishing industry and abolish incentives leading to over-fishing".[17] One year later, the CSD noted the urgent need for "governments to consider the positive and negative impact of subsidies on the conservation and management of fisheries through national, regional and appropriate international organizations and, based on these analyses, to consider appropriate action".[18] The Committee on Fisheries of the Food and Agriculture Organization (FAO) reported that "frequent use of direct and indirect subsidies in fisheries often aggravated excess capacity".[19] At the regional level, Asia-Pacific Economic Cooperation (APEC) has investigated fisheries subsidies, as has the Fisheries Committee of the OECD. UNEP has also sponsored a series of useful workshops on fisheries subsidies and sustainable fisheries management and reported on the outcomes to the CTE.[20]

The WTO on centre stage

The WTO finds itself on centre stage in dealing with the issue of subsidies, and the reasons are clear. The WTO is already the custodian of multilateral rules to discipline subsidies. The WTO Agreement on Subsidies and Countervailing Measures (SCM) is the only multilateral agreement that not only monitors the use of subsidies but also provides for countervailing measures. In addition, the WTO is an organization concerned with trade distortions, and fisheries subsidies clearly have the potential to distort trade. The FAO has estimated that 37 per cent of all fish products enter international trade and 20 per cent of fishery revenues come from government support.[21] The effect of the subsidies is to limit access to common fisheries resources for non-subsidized fleets, which, it is argued, is unquestionably a barrier to trade for all non-subsidizing countries.[22]

In addition, the WTO is mandated to promote development, and one-half of world exports of fish and fish products come from developing countries. Subsidies distort production – and therefore trade patterns – and limit the exports from developing countries. Also, as emphasized throughout this book, the WTO has among its objectives the optimal use of the world's resources in accordance with the objective of *sustainable development*. In the area of fisheries subsidies, the WTO has the opportunity to show its seriousness in addressing a mandate of considerable importance to many. Moreover, it has a powerful dispute settlement system to enforce any agreements reached on disciplining fisheries subsidies.

In short, it would be hard to deny that the WTO has an important potential responsibility in this area. This view is reflected in national submissions to the CTE. In particular, a number of countries have formed a group to highlight the beneficial contribution that the elimination of environmentally damaging and trade-distorting subsidization of the fisheries sector would make to the conservation and sustainable use of fish stocks and the promotion of sustainable development. They have been declared the "Friends of the Fish".[23]

Reaching agreement?

Moving ahead on this front is not without its complications. One involves unravelling the complex causal factors leading to fish stock depletion and assessing their relative importance, including the relative importance of fisheries subsidies in terms of the total needs of fisheries management. There is also a question of institutional jurisdiction. It has been argued that 95 per cent of fish are caught in national waters and only 5 per cent on the high seas. The conclusion that is drawn is that problems should be tackled by the UN Convention on the Law of the Sea (UNCLOS) and not by the WTO.[24] It is also argued that most of the major subsidizing members are also major consumers, and have relatively limited exports. Another consideration is the variety of purposes served by fisheries subsidies, and therefore their very diverse nature. They are used to reduce operating costs, harvesting costs, fishing vessel construction or maintenance costs, or are provided indirectly by way of income support and as part of fisheries management schemes. Subsidies to reduce vessel fuel costs can encourage long-range harvesting, and subsidies to vessel construction will increase total fleet capacity. There are direct subsidies based on total output and measured in terms of days at sea or as a percentage of total catch, and subsidies on a fleet's idle capacity. Not all subsidies are necessarily damaging to the environment. Subsidies have the potential to contribute to sustainable fisheries management schemes by reducing fleet capacity, retraining those in the fisheries sector, enhancing fish stocks, promoting vessel and fishing buy-backs to take vessels out of use, and encouraging technological improvements.

Further, there are significant practical problems that arise in applying the existing provisions of the Subsidies Agreement to the fisheries sector. In particular, the heterogeneous nature of fisheries products and the economic structure of the industry make it more difficult to identify the sort of market distortions at which subsidy disciplines are directed.[25]

Information on fisheries subsidies holds the key to many of the questions relating to their nature, purpose and relative importance. Here there is a serious information gap. Because subsidies at the national level should be notified to the WTO in accordance with the Subsidies Agreement, they should constitute an important source of valuable information. However, the poor quality of fisheries notifications, coupled with the inaccessibility of information on government programmes in the fisheries sector, has made it difficult to develop authoritative assessments of the value and nature of subsidies. In fact, not even 10 per cent of the subsidies in the fisheries sector of WTO members have been notified to the WTO Secretariat.[26]

Another consideration is the difference in views on the appropriateness of the WTO Subsidies Agreement to deal with fisheries subsidies. Although the WTO prohibits certain types of subsidies and provides remedies in situations where a subsidy has adverse effects on another member, its rules primarily address trade distortions arising from subsidization, not their environmental effects.[27] For example, subsidies in an importing country can reduce market access for the exports of non-subsidizing countries or unfairly promote exports to other countries. Subsidized exports can also squeeze out non-subsidized exports in third-country markets. Although these situations are addressed in the Subsidies Agreement and remedial action is provided for, the Agreement does not – as it stands – adequately address the trade, environment and development impacts of fisheries subsidies. It was not crafted to respond to the distinctive production distortions that subsidies can cause in the fisheries sector, because fisheries subsidies have consequences well beyond the distortion of competitive relationships provided for in the Subsidies Agreement. They distort access to shared fish stocks and limit access for other countries through depleting an exhaustible resource. Material injury may be incurred (a requirement for action in the Subsidies Agreement), but the concept of injury as it has been developed in the context of the Subsidies Agreement is not geared to deal with this sort of situation. As a result, countervailing duties, as provided for in the Agreement, may be of little relevance in such instances, because they can be applied only to imports into the complaining member's market.

Commitment to an outcome

Given these various concerns, WTO members have reached agreement on two important fronts: first, that there should be *negotiations* in this sector; and second, because of the peculiarities of fisheries subsidies, that the negotiations should be aimed at clarifying and improving disciplines under the Subsidies Agreement while taking into account the needs of developing and least developed countries. In the initial phase of the negotiations, governments are to identify the provisions that they seek to clarify and improve on.[28] In operational terms, the negotiation of fisheries subsidies has been transferred from the CTE to the Group on Rules, one of seven negotiating bodies established to deal with the Doha Development Agenda.[29] However, national positions on how to proceed remain far apart. I describe the broad contours of the country positions below, but it should be noted that there are important nuances.

Although the "Friends of the Fish" propose the elimination of harmful fisheries subsidies, they acknowledge that their removal will not in itself ensure the sustainable use of fish resources. Appropriate domestic and international environmental and conservation policies are needed, but the elimination of trade restrictions and distortions is nevertheless an important prerequisite for building sustainable fisheries management.[30] "Friends of the Fish" further acknowledge that, although some fisheries subsidies might have beneficial effects, there is a clear role for the WTO in removing harmful ones.[31]

At the other end of the spectrum, Japan and Korea challenge the notion that subsidies are responsible for the depletion of fish stocks, and cite various sources to support the notion that no reasoned determination has been made on the causality between fisheries subsidies and the depletion of stocks.[32] Their view is that the available quantitative information diverges widely depending upon sources and, until more is known in this respect, negotiations would be premature. They advocate a broader approach that looks at the various factors influencing overexploitation, such as illegal fishing, and favour taking into account socioeconomic aspects.

The European Union has reasoned that only some fisheries subsidies lead to overcapacity. It sees a need for increased research and analysis to determine the most effective way for the industry to downsize. Although not opposed to discussions on this issue at the WTO, the European Union stresses the need for negotiations to take into account the importance of the sector to developing countries, the role of international fishery conventions and work under way in other relevant international forums. Within the European Union, the self-declared "Friends of Fishing" – France, Greece, Ireland, Italy, Portugal and Spain – have been most reluctant to address fisheries subsidies.

Classifying subsidies

A first question to be addressed is how to classify fisheries subsidies. Only then can the extent to which the Subsidies Agreement applies, and whether the provisions of the Subsidies Agreement are directly relevant, be established.[33] As a result, there have been various attempts to define subsidies in familiar WTO terms. For example, all fisheries subsidies of a commercial nature, directly geared towards lowering costs, increasing revenues, raising production (by enhancing capacity), or directly promoting overcapacity and over-fishing, have been referred to as "red light" subsidies, which should be expressly prohibited.[34] Under this classification, the remaining subsidies would be permitted to the extent that they are sufficiently accredited and notified in the WTO. Since subsidies always affect trade, no member should be permitted adversely to affect the trade interests of other members.

The European Union has proposed the prohibition of capacity-enhancing subsidies – subsidies for marine fishing fleet renewal (e.g. construction of vessels, increases in fishing capacity); and subsidies for the permanent transfer of fishing vessels to third countries, including through the creation of joint enterprises with third-country partners. Certain types of subsidies, however, would be permitted to reduce fishing capacity and to mitigate the negative social and economic consequences of restructuring the fisheries sector. These subsidies should be clearly defined in order to ensure they are not used to circumvent the prohibition of capacity-enhancing subsidies and non-actionable subsidies.[35]

Another approach would supplement the "red light" approach, and create a "dark amber" category of subsidies. These subsidies would be *presumed* to be harmful unless the subsidizing government could affirmatively demonstrate that no overcapacity/over-fishing or other adverse trade effects have resulted from the subsidy. If the presumption was not rebutted, such subsidies would be actionable.[36] For example, subsidies that exceed a certain value of production could be presumed to cause "serious prejudice", but the presumption could be rebutted if certain criteria were met, such as showing that the subsidy was not being used to fish in a fishery that is over-fished, or that effective restrictions were placed on the operation of the programme so that it does not result in over-fishing.[37]

Expectations

One response to the difficulties encountered in the present process could be that the WTO should never have engaged in dealing with what is clearly an environmental matter of great importance, the reasoning being that it has neither the experience nor the expertise to deal with such matters, whereas other institutions do. This would be disingenuous to say the least, and cast justified doubts on the credibility of the concern in the WTO with respect to the environment. The process that has led to this result was agreed to over a decade ago and appears clearly within the terms of reference of the CTE: namely, to identify the relationship between trade measures and the environment in order to promote sustainable development, and to make appropriate recommendations on whether any modifications of the provisions of the multilateral trading system are required. A decade of discussion has led to agreement that there are to be negotiations in this area.

Not to have a meaningful outcome would give substance to the criticism that the CTE has been nothing but a "talk fest" that has reneged on the commitment to modify the provisions of the multilateral trading system to promote sustainable development. The possibility is now there to deliver in an area of vital importance to environmentalists – or to explain to the outside world why inaction is appropriate. In this context, the President of WWF International has remarked that the issue of fisheries subsidies "presents the first instance of a WTO negotiation centred explicitly at the nexus of trade policy, natural resource economics, and environmental conservation ... the issue poses a fundamental test of the WTO's ability to regulate trade in the broadest public interest, and in cooperation with other relevant intergovernmental bodies."[38] But the task of meeting public expectations will not be an easy one. The most fundamental one is what sort of outcome could be reasonably expected.

If fisheries subsidies are leading to fish stock depletion and the Subsidies Agreement as it stands cannot discipline them, what is the way forward? Should the Subsidies Agreement be renegotiated to take account of the special case of fisheries subsidies? Should there be a stand-alone WTO Agreement on Fisheries Subsidies? If so, should it be a trade agreement to remove trade distortions in line with other WTO Agreements or a fully fledged environment agreement enforced by the WTO? Why is it that trade officials are dealing with such a technically difficult task as identifying the link between fisheries subsidies, fish stock management, the legally binding provisions to discipline subsidies and the compliance mechanism to enforce them? Why would WTO trade officials be any more likely to succeed in this area when so many specialists in a host of institutions have managed only to establish best endeavour commitments? Would the creation of such a stand-alone agreement be well received by the environment community, and would it create a precedent for more sectoral agreements of a similar character in the WTO?

It is important to recall that, although a number of WTO Agreements refer to the environment – and certainly have an impact on it – none of them establishes rights and obligations that deal directly with the environment. The terms of reference of the CTE, for example, stress the market access aspects of the link between trade measures and the environment. They are not directed to conservation of the environment as such. Also, the objectives of the Subsidies Agreement are to deal with governmental measures that distort trade, not to preserve the environment per se. Thus, for the WTO to be responsible for an agreement that has the environment as its focus would be to enter into a whole new area of intergovernmental agreements.

Options for the legal form of the new rules have been proposed and include, as a minimum: (i) modifications to the Subsidies Agreement, (ii) incorporation of fisheries subsidies into an expanded Agreement on Agriculture, or (iii) negotiation of a new WTO sectoral agreement. Against this backdrop, it has been argued that, "given the nature of the issues, the negotiation of a new WTO sectoral agreement appears the most attractive. A simple effort to amend the Subsidies Agreement would likely remain too focussed on correcting only traditional and provable trade distortions."[39] This, however, comes with a word of caution. The guiding principle should be for the WTO not to step over the thin green line. According to Schorr, this line separates the WTO's legitimate scope of competence from an inappropriate entanglement with environmental matters. It is called "thin" to convey a sense that it is not always easy to see, and may at times be easy to cross inadvertently.

But at the end of the day, the notion of an actual line is a misnomer. By its essence, a win–win–win issue is hybrid in character. The realms of economics and environmental management cannot be neatly separated; nor can the economics of fisheries be isolated from trade. When the question is close – and where spheres of policy necessarily overlap – the difference between an "environmental" issue and a "trade" issue can be little more than a matter of semantics, or of subjective perspective.[40]

Conclusion

What conclusions can be drawn from the above and what is the way forward? At a most general level, and from an economic perspective, different environmental resource endowments (such as the physical capacity to absorb pollution) are themselves a basis for differences in comparative advantage. Furthermore, different societies and individuals within them have different levels of tolerance for environmental degradation, apart from physical capacities. As long as national sovereignty prevails with respect to environmental priorities, the extent to which externalities are internalized will be determined by awareness of the environmental problem, the government's capacity to adopt the necessary policy measure to deal with it, the nation's physical capacity to absorb the environmental damage, and societal preferences relating to environmental conditions and the quality of life. This in turn will influence the impact on relative prices nationally and internationally. Trade restrictions can distort the good functioning of markets, and thus the exploitation of comparative advantage, just as they can frustrate the implementation of sound environmental management policies.

More specifically, with respect to fisheries subsidies, a number of observations may be useful. First, there is a learning exercise. An examination of how fisheries subsidies have been dealt with in the WTO shows how constructive pressure by public interest groups can bring important issues to the attention of negotiators. Although many intergovernmental organizations have been involved in discussing fisheries subsidies, there is little doubt that non-governmental organizations such as WWF have played a most useful role in raising the profile of the issue – certainly within the WTO.

A second observation is that, as far as the WTO is concerned, the discussion has been undertaken primarily in the CTE – and now the Rules Group – in a transparent manner. Summary records and background documents have been made freely available, and advocates of the removal of fisheries subsidies have been invited to WTO seminars to tell their story to government negotiators and others. A further advantage of this open process where summary records and national submissions are available to all is that, if "insufficient" progress is being made in the view of any particular interest group, the problem is seen to be not a recalcitrant WTO as such, but a failure of individual governments to agree (see chapter 10). Given that full information is at hand about which countries are responsible for the various positions adopted in the negotiations, it is clear where pressure needs to be applied in order to change country positions and move the debate forward in the direction sought by the interested parties.

Third, if disagreement over fisheries subsidies had been brought to the WTO as a dispute, this same openness would not have existed – even if public interest groups could view the proceedings, which they cannot do now. Only the views of the countries involved in the dispute would have been known, and without doubt, irrespective of the decision by the Panel and/or the Appellate Body, there would have been dissatisfaction on the part of some interest group, be it those supporting the "Friends of the Fish" or the "Friends of Fishing". The WTO, and in particular the dispute settlement system, would have been the object of attack. The Appellate Body has consistently made the point that environmental problems, such as the preservation of endangered species in the *Shrimp-Turtle* case, should be dealt with through negotiated agreement, not WTO litigation.

Another observation is that the work of the WTO can progress only by adopting a coherent approach that involves the many intergovernmental organizations already active in the area. It also needs to address the concerns and integrate the information coming from various non-governmental groups. However, as with other areas of sustainable development, the WTO should not be drawn into the role of a fisheries management or conservation body, or infringe the powers or autonomy of existing authorities, such as regional fisheries conventions. Intergovernmental organizations such as the FAO, UNEP, APEC and the

OECD provide research and policy analysis on fisheries resources, management and production. UNCLOS and the Straddling and Highly Migratory Stocks Agreement provide legal frameworks for the development and implementation of sound management regimes.

For those who are looking for a change in the Subsidies Agreement as a means to address the issue, it is unlikely that there will be the required consensus to reach this end. There are at least three reasons for this. First, the countries that are unwilling partners even in discussing the issue are not likely to change their stance so radically that they would agree to modifying a key WTO Agreement when consensus is required to do so. Second, even those who are prepared to accept a "sectoral" approach to fisheries subsidies fear that it would fragment the Subsidies Agreement and create a precedent for other sectors. In any event, and third, governments are unwilling to change rules in general, as witnessed on numerous occasions. Finally there are probably other means to deal with the situation, and it should be useful to look for precedents. There are indeed numerous precedents that fall far short of modifying the Subsidies Agreement. We have seen in the past an Understanding on Financial Services within the context of the General Agreement on Trade in Services, a Declaration to deal with access to essential medicines to accompany the TRIPS Agreement, a Decision on bringing greater coherence to global economic policy-making, an Understanding on how to deal with regional trade agreements to accompany the GATT-1947, and many other instruments to accommodate specific concerns effectively without modifying agreed texts. It should not be outside the capabilities of governments to find a similar instrument to deal with the adverse effects of fisheries subsidies.

The bottom line is, however, that, if the WTO cannot make a credible contribution to resolving the problems that are seen to exist between fish stocks and subsidies, the credibility of the institution itself will be severely undermined. To be successful, a means needs to be found within the WTO negotiations to ensure that governments phase out and avoid subsidies that contribute to excess fishing capacity, over-fishing and unsustainable fishing practices. With this in mind, a schedule for phasing out harmful fisheries subsidy programmes should be established and the introduction of new ones should be outlawed. There should be no restrictions on constructive government conservation programmes and special attention should be addressed to the needs of developing countries. In moving the process forward, one thing is certainly clear: information on fisheries subsidies is seriously lacking. There should be complete notification on the part of WTO members with respect to their obligations and, if these obligations are not fulfilled, a monitoring body should be created in order to ensure that the right sort of information is to hand.

Notes

1. World Bank, *Global Economic Prospects 2004*, Washington, D.C.: World Bank, 2004.
2. See OXFAM, *Rigged Rules and Double Standards: Trade, Globalization and the Fight against Poverty*, Oxford: OXFAM, 2002.
3. See WTO, *Environmental (Sustainability) Assessments of Trade Liberalisation Agreements at the National Level*, Geneva: WTO Secretariat, WT/CTE/W/171, 20 October 2000. See also C. George and C. Kirkpatrick, *Sustainability Impact Assessment of Proposed WTO Negotiations: Preliminary Overview of Potential Impacts of the Doha Agenda, Final Report*, Institute for Development Policy and Management, University of Manchester, 2003.
4. See UNEP, *Reference Manual for the Integrated Assessment of Trade-Related Policies*, Nairobi: UNEP, 2001. The OECD studies are described in OECD, *Working Together towards Sustainable Development*, Paris: OECD Secretariat, 2002, Annex 1. See also OECD, Workshop on "Methodologies for Environmental Assessment of Trade Liberalisation Agreements" held in Paris, 26–27 October 1999, and Commission for Economic Cooperation, *Free Trade and the Environment: The Picture Becomes Clearer*, Montreal: Secretariat of the Commission for Environment Cooperation in North America, 2002.
5. See WTO, *Doha Declarations: The Doha Development Agenda*, Geneva: WTO Secretariat, 2001, para. 6.
6. As far as the WSSD is concerned, ministers agreed to "[e]ncourage the voluntary use of environmental impact assessments as an important national-level tool to better identify trade, environment and development inter-linkages" and to "[f]urther encourage countries and international organizations with experience in this field to provide technical assistance to developing countries for these purposes". See WTO, *Report of the World Summit on Sustainable Development, Note by the Secretariat*, Geneva: WTO Secretariat, WT/CTE/W/220/Rev.1, 20 December 2002, para. 92.
7. In this respect see David K. Schorr, "Fishery Subsidies and the WTO", in Gary P. Sampson and W. Bradnee Chambers (eds), *Trade, Environment, and the Millennium*, 2nd edn, Tokyo: United Nations University Press, 2002, pp. 175–206.
8. These figures are drawn from OECD, *Working Together towards Sustainable Development*. The developed countries referred to are the OECD countries.
9. Ibid., pp. 38–39.
10. See World Bank, *World Development Report 2000/1*, Washington, D.C.: World Bank, 2001.
11. The Conference of the Parties requested "the Executive Secretary to further study the impact of trade liberalization on agricultural biodiversity, in collaboration with the United Nations Environment Programme, the Food and Agriculture Organization of the United Nations, the World Trade Organization and other relevant organizations". See Convention on Biological Diversity, *The Impact of Trade Liberalization on Agricultural Biological Diversity: Domestic Support Measures and Their Effects on Agricultural Biological Diversity, Note by the Executive Secretary*, Montreal: Secretariat of the Convention on Biological Diversity, UNEP/CBD/COP/INF/14, 18 December 2003.
12. They concluded that "more analytical and conceptual work is necessary on the appropriate design and implementation of such agri-environmental policies and programmes and their interplay with the reduction of trade-distorting domestic support measures." Ibid., p. 33.
13. WTO, *Environmental Benefits of Removing Trade Restrictions and Distortions: Addendum on Environmental Services*, Geneva: WTO Secretariat, WT/CTE/W/67, add. 1, March 1998.

14. Descriptions of all these agreements are available on the WTO website at ⟨http://www.wto.org/⟩.
15. See WTO, *Doha Declarations: The Doha Development Agenda*, para. 31(iii).
16. See WTO, *Approaches to Improved Disciplines on Fisheries Subsidies: Communication from Chile*, Geneva: WTO, TN/RL/W/115, 10 June 2003.
17. Commission on Sustainable Development, *Fourth Session, Protection of the Oceans, All Kinds of Seas, Including Enclosed and Semi-Enclosed Seas, and Coastal Areas and the Protection, Rational Use and Development of Their Living Resources, Report of the Secretary General*, New York: United Nations, E/CN.17/1996/3, 1996, Section IV, para. 18.
18. UNGASS, *Report of the Commission on Sustainable Development on Preparations for the Special Session of the General Assembly for the Purpose of an Overall Review and Appraisal of the Implementation of Agenda 21*, New York: United Nations, E/1997/60, 1997, para. 30.
19. FAO, *Report of the Twenty-Second Session of the Committee on Fisheries*, Rome: FAO, Fisheries Report No. 562, 17–20 March 1997, para. 11.
20. WTO, *Fisheries Subsidies and Sustainable Fisheries Management: Contribution by UNEP*, Geneva: WTO, WT/CTE/W/236, 17 June 2004.
21. See FAO, *State of World Fisheries and Aquaculture*, Rome: FAO, 2002.
22. This argument is developed in WTO, *Approaches to Improved Disciplines on Fisheries Subsidies: Communication from Chile*.
23. See WTO, *The Doha Mandate to Address Fisheries Subsidies: The Issues, Submission from Australia, Chile, Ecuador, Iceland, New Zealand, Peru, Philippines, and the United States*, Geneva: WTO, TN/RL/W/3, 24 April 2002. Other countries have now joined this group: Argentina, Bangladesh, Colombia, India, Indonesia, Malaysia, Mexico, Singapore, Thailand and Venezuela.
24. The WTO Secretariat has drawn up a list of regional fishing bodies regulating the catch of straddling and migratory species caught in the high seas throughout the world. See WTO, *Environmental Benefits of Removing Trade Restrictions and Distortions: The Fisheries Sector*, Geneva: WTO Secretariat Report, WT/CTE/W/167, 19 June 2001, Annex II.
25. WTO, *The Doha Mandate to Address Fisheries Subsidies: The Issues, Submission from Australia, Chile, Ecuador, Iceland, New Zealand, Peru, Philippines, and the United States*.
26. The environment-related fisheries subsidies that have been notified by members include regional structural adjustment programmes for fisheries in which conservation objectives are identified; various fisheries support schemes in which environmental conservation is cited; and support schemes to promote environmentally sound fish-harvesting methods.
27. For example, in relation to actionable subsidies, the serious prejudice provision (Article 6.3 of the WTO Subsidies Agreement) is concerned with subsidies altering competitive conditions in markets, either by undercutting prices or by displacing or impeding imports. Similarly, the injury provision in Article 15 is concerned with the effects on prices of subsidized imports into the domestic market of a complainant country.
28. See WTO, *Doha Declarations: The Doha Development Agenda*, para. 28. The reference to negotiations on fisheries subsidies is also included in the Trade and Environment section of the Doha Declaration (para. 31).
29. At the World Summit on Sustainable Development, governments agreed to "[e]liminate subsidies that contribute to illegal, unreported and unregulated fishing and to overcapacity, while completing the efforts undertaken at WTO to clarify and improve its disciplines on fisheries subsidies, taking into account the importance of this sector to

developing countries". See WTO, *Report of the World Summit on Sustainable Development*, para. 97b.

30. See the submissions to the WTO Committee on Trade and Environment: WTO, *Environmental and Trade Benefits of Removing Subsidies in the Fisheries Sector, Submission by the United States*, Geneva: WTO, WT/CTE/W/51, 19 May 1997; and WTO, *Item 6: The Fisheries Sector: Submission by New Zealand*, Geneva: WTO, WT/CTE/W/52, 21 May 1997.

31. WTO, *The Doha Mandate to Address Fisheries Subsidies: The Issues, Submission from Australia, Chile, Ecuador, Iceland, New Zealand, Peru, Philippines, and the United States*.

32. See WTO, *Japan's Basic Position on the Fishery Subsidy Issue: Item 6, Submission by Japan*, Geneva: WTO, WT/CTE/W/173, 23 October 2000; and WTO, *Japan's Contribution to Discussion on Fisheries Subsidies Issue*, Geneva: WTO, TN/RL/W/52, 6 February 2003. See also WTO, *Utilization of Subsidies and Their Positive Role in the Fisheries Sector: Communication from Korea*, Geneva: WTO, WT/CTE/W/175, 24 October 2000. Japan and Korea cite OECD, *Government Financial Transfers and Resource Sustainability*, Paris: OECD, 2002, which stated "most transfers (77%) are general services that are devoted to fisheries infrastructure and expenditure on activities, such as research and enforcement, that are essential for ensuring the sustainable use of fish stocks and the aquatic eco-system".

33. See WTO, *GATT/WTO Rules on Subsidies and Aids Granted in the Fishing Industry*, Geneva: WTO, WT/CTE/W/80, 9 March 1998. See also Schorr, "Fishery Subsidies and the WTO", as well as Seung Whe Chang, "WTO Disciplines on Fisheries Subsidies: A Historic Step towards Sustainability?", *Journal of International Economic Law*, Vol. 6, No. 4, 2003, pp. 879–921.

34. WTO, *Approaches to Improved Disciplines on Fisheries Subsidies: Communication from Chile*.

35. WTO, *Submission of the European Communities to the Negotiating Group on Rules – Fisheries Subsidies*, Geneva: WTO, TN/Rl/W/82, 23 April 2003.

36. A "dark amber" category could be modelled on the now expired Article 6.1 of the Subsidies Agreement.

37. WTO, *Possible Approaches to Improved Disciplines on Fisheries Subsidies: Communication from the United States*, Geneva: WTO, TN/RL/W/77, 19 March 2003.

38. See Preface to David Schorr, *Crafting New Rules on Fishing Subsidies in the World Trade Organisation: A WWF Position Paper and Technical Resource*, Gland, Switzerland: WWF, June 2004, p. 27.

39. See Schorr, "Fishery Subsidies and the WTO", p. 197.

40. Ibid., pp. 27–28.

4

Discrimination, WTO rules and sustainable development

Introduction

The WTO Agreements aim to improve the conditions of access to markets of members of the World Trade Organization, bind the results of negotiated liberalization of trade, and underpin the commitments with a predictable and stable set of legally enforceable rules. A trading system with these characteristics by its nature restricts the possibility for members to employ certain trade measures. Having committed themselves to a degree of market openness, if governments were free to afford protection to domestic producers arbitrarily, market access commitments would be undermined, as would predictability and stability in the trading system. One of the outcomes of accepting WTO rules is indeed to circumscribe national sovereignty by limiting the use of trade measures in certain situations.

However, no responsible government would forgo its right to pursue policies that it considers to be in its national interest. As a consequence, WTO rules, while limiting the freedom of governments, also ensure they retain the flexibility to implement policies to avoid damage to the environment, protect public health, enforce labour standards, or deal with any other areas of economic or social concern. Indeed, the WTO Agreements – and therefore the dispute settlement system – do not call into question the legitimacy of policies pursued by WTO members within their own borders.

Nevertheless, although governments are free to pursue their policy choices, they cannot adopt measures that have as their intention the restriction of trade or that are unnecessarily trade restrictive. This begs a number of closely related questions. Is the *aim* of the measure to meet a *bona fide* objective, or is it to protect domestic producers? Is the *effect* of the measure to create less favourable conditions for the imported good? Is the measure really *necessary* to achieve the legitimate policy goal or are there less trade-restrictive alternatives available? If the *aim and effect* of a trade measure is to renege on legally binding market access commitments, surely the WTO – as a trade organization – has the responsibility to protect the agreed commitments? Are there any conditions under which there is a role for the WTO in legitimizing trade sanctions that have as their objective the enforcement of the preferred standards of one country on another? The answers to these questions largely determine the constraints that the WTO places on many of the measures employed by governments when formulating policies relating to sustainable development. Finding answers to these questions is not easy.

Many of the WTO provisions that are most relevant in answering these questions are not clearly defined; their interpretation has been – and will be – the subject of discretion through the WTO dispute settlement process. WTO legal interpretations are far from definitive, and they vary according to circumstances. The questions then are how this discretion has been exercised to date and, more importantly, how it will be exercised in the future. The answers are all the more intriguing with respect to sustainable development, because the concept is found only in Preambular language and in Ministerial Declarations, whose legal status is not immediately apparent.

My objective in this chapter is to examine how a number of key WTO provisions have been interpreted in the past, speculate on their future interpretation and evaluate the implications for sustainable development. I shall place particular emphasis on the cornerstone of the multilateral trading system: non-discrimination. The focus will be the 1994 General Agreement on Tariffs and Trade (the GATT-1994): national treatment and most favoured nation treatment, as well as measures qualifying as exceptions in terms of legally justified discrimination. A great deal has been written on the interpretation of these provisions. However, my intention here is not to discuss the legal outcomes of the cases per se; rather it is to explore the implications of the interpretations for the relationship between the WTO and sustainable development.

The outline of the chapter is as follows. First, there is a background section, in which I address three topics. The first is non-discrimination and the closely related concept of "like" products. Exceptional circumstances can permit the use of measures that do not conform to WTO rules, so my second topic is the conditions under which exceptions can be taken. And third, since the dispute settlement system enforces the obligations in each of these areas, I outline it in some detail, not only because of its relevance for this chapter but because of its importance for other parts of this book. In the following sections I review some of the areas where the interpretation of the GATT-1994 is important for sustainable development. I address questions about how environmental taxes and other fiscal measures can – or cannot – be adjusted according to WTO rules in order to maintain domestic competitiveness, as well as questions relating to how the WTO has dealt with taxes and regulations that are discriminatory in their application but neutral with respect to origin. I explore the extent to which trade measures can or cannot be used to influence policy choices in other countries, which involves a first look at the importance of the existence of multilateral environment agreements (MEAs) for dispute settlement cases relating to sustainable development. I return to this topic in chapter 6. The focus throughout is on the policy implications.

Background

Non-discrimination and like products

The principle of non-discrimination underpins the rules-based multilateral trading system. It has two key components: the most favoured nation (MFN) clause contained in Article I of the GATT-1994 and the national treatment obligation found in Article III. MFN treatment means that, with respect to customs duties, charges and formalities, the most favourable treatment granted by any member to any product originating in, or destined for, any other country must be accorded to the *like product* for all other members. MFN applies equally for imports and exports; the overarching principle is that rules or measures must not discriminate between like products on the basis of their origin or destination.

National treatment requires that internal taxes, charges, laws and regulations should not be applied to imported or domestic products so as to afford protection to domestic production. The intention is to ensure that, after imported goods have entered a country, they are no longer subject to taxes and regulations that are designed only to protect domestic producers. As far as taxes are concerned, imports are not to be subject to taxes in excess of those applied to like domestic products.[1] In the case of regulations, imports should be accorded treatment no less favourable than that accorded to like products of national origin in respect of all laws and regulations.[2]

There is an important distinction between two types of discrimination when interpreting national treatment. First, there are measures that provide explicitly different treatment for imports and domestic goods, and whose effects (i.e. the taxes and regulations) are more burdensome for imports. This is referred to as de jure discrimination and is a clear violation of national treatment. Second, there are regulatory measures that make no distinction as to the origin of goods (i.e. are origin neutral), but nevertheless have a disproportionate impact on the imported good. This is referred to as de facto discrimination. An example of the former case would be the imposition of a new tax on imported goods but not on domestic goods. The tariff concession is undermined, and the *aim and effect* is to afford protection to a domestic producer. However, what if, in accordance with domestic priorities, there is a new fuel tax on large cars with low fuel efficiency, both domestic and imported? And what if only large cars are imported? The tax is origin neutral – applying both domestically and to imports – but it is more burdensome for the imported good. In such a case, a challenge may be lodged as to the true purpose of the measure employed and the criteria according to which the measure should be considered legitimate or otherwise. Another example could be mandatory marketing requirements for imported tropical timber harvested in an environmentally unfriendly manner. There may be no domestic production of this type of wood, but tropical timber may compete with domestically produced wood. The imported product is disadvantaged by an origin-neutral tax or regulation. Should the role of the WTO be to determine the true *aim* of the measure and whether its "effect" on trade is restrictive? If the answer to this question is yes, then, in practical terms, there is no alternative to the WTO delving into the domestic policies of WTO members.

In dealing with de facto discrimination, the first step is to establish that the imported good is indeed a like product, but is being discriminated against; tropical timber is *like* domestic timber but is discriminated against in terms of domestic regulations. In such cases, GATT jurisprudence supports the interpretation that the only kind of product distinction that can be recognized under the national treatment provisions is a distinction based on the nature of the product itself. Product distinctions based on characteristics of the production process that are not present in the product itself are not relevant in determining likeness. Thus, the challenges to an "origin-neutral" tax or regulation that imposes a greater burden on imports than on competing domestic products will normally be couched in terms of the imported good being *like* the domestic product but receiving less favourable treatment.

The concept of "like product" is central to the application of both MFN and national treatment. Products have generally been considered in GATT and WTO jurisprudence to be "like" based on their physical characteristics, end-use, consumers' preferences and tariff classification, keeping in mind that a government may create as many categories of products as it wishes, as long as they are based on product specificities rather than origin. Notwithstanding its importance, the interpretation of like product has never been definitively established in GATT and WTO jurisprudence. The colloquial usage of "like" means having the same physical characteristics or qualities as something else (such as an identical shape, size and colour). However, it also means "similar". This common understanding leaves many interpretive questions open in determining whether governments can legitimately discriminate between products for policy purposes. In particular, which characteristics or qualities are important in assessing the likeness of products? A diesel bus and an electric tram are *like* in that they both provide transport for the public, but they may be very different when it comes to protecting the environment. Second, there is no guidance in determining the degree or extent to which products must share qualities or characteristics in order to be like products. Adding one gene to many thousands of others can turn a non-offensive food product into an allergy nightmare for others. Third, the normal usage definition of "like" does not indicate from whose perspective likeness should be judged.[3] A slug and a snail are like products to a vegetable gardener but not to a French gourmet.

In more general terms, the manner in which MFN and national treatment are interpreted has important implications for the flexibility of governments in formulating domestic policies in areas that are critical for sustainable development.[4] As will become clear in the following, the interpretation of "like product" is crucial in this respect.

Exceptions

Flexibility exists for taking measures that would in normal circumstances be considered violations of WTO rules. If, in pursuing a preferred domestic policy option, a WTO obligation is breached, recourse can be sought to the General Exceptions Article XX of the GATT-1994. This provides that, in exceptional circumstances, governments may find it necessary to apply and enforce measures – such as quantitative restrictions – to protect public morals or human, animal or plant life or health (Article XX (b), or relating to the conservation of exhaustible natural resources (Article XX (g)). The measure for which the exception is sought is (according to Article XX) subject to the requirements that it does not constitute a means of arbitrary or unjustifiable discrimination, and that it does not represent a disguised restriction on international trade. Read together, Articles XX (b) and XX (g) mean that measures to promote sustainable development are available to WTO members, even if they are inconsistent with the normal obligations of the WTO Agreements.

Measures taken as exceptions have often been challenged through the dispute settlement process.[5] Under the GATT, six Panel proceedings involving an examination of environmental measures or human health-related measures under Article XX were completed. Of the six reports, three remain unadopted. Under the WTO, three disputes have so far led to the adoption of Panel and Appellate Body reports. In only one case did the ruling accept the legitimacy of the measure in question as an exception. As a result, a great deal of animosity has been directed towards the WTO by public interest groups that firmly believe that a variety of WTO-illegal measures should be available for sustainable development purposes. The denial of the use of these measures has led to the criticism that the trading system rides roughshod over concerns relating to sustainable development.

It is important to note in this context that none of the Panel or Appellate Body rulings has in any way questioned the legitimacy of the policy choice that is the object of the measures at issue. What has been questioned is whether the measures used to implement the policy chosen by the governments conform to WTO rules. If exceptions have to be sought, this is to address the justification for certain measures, not the legitimization of national policies. Indeed, GATT and WTO members would never have agreed to the job of WTO Panels and Appellate Body being to approve the policy choice of a government (protection of public health) rather than the measure to implement that policy (a ban on imported cigarettes with no corresponding domestic measures).

Settling disputes

The dispute settlement process of the WTO emerged from the Uruguay Round and is built on 50 years of experience with the GATT.[6] The current practices are inscribed in the Dispute Settlement Understanding (DSU). Any member of the WTO that believes benefits accruing to it under the WTO Agreements are being impaired by measures taken by another member can invoke the dispute settlement system. In most cases, a WTO member will claim that a measure enacted by another member violates one or more of the substantive provisions contained in a WTO Agreement. The Dispute Settlement Understanding is applicable in a uniform manner to all disputes under any WTO Agreement. To the chagrin of many, participation in the WTO dispute settlement system is not open to WTO observers, other international organizations, non-governmental organizations (NGOs), local governments or private persons. The mechanism is essentially intergovernmental, with private parties being represented by their respective governments. A Panel, however, may consult with any entity or person it wishes.

The DSU contains rules and procedures on both consultations and adjudication. It favours solutions mutually acceptable to the parties to the dispute, provided they are consistent with WTO Agreements. In the absence of a mutually agreed solution, the ultimate objective of the dispute settlement mechanism is to secure the withdrawal of the measure concerned if it is found to be inconsistent with WTO Agreements. If this cannot be achieved, the dispute will be adjudicated by Panels composed of experts convened on an ad hoc basis. The members of Panels are normally trade officials from Missions of WTO members located in Geneva. They act as panellists on a voluntary basis. Panel reports may be subject to appeal to the Appellate Body, a permanent group of seven experts in trade law who review the legal aspects of reports issued by Panels.

All WTO members are entitled to participate in the Dispute Settlement Body (DSB), which oversees the functioning of the DSU. Its primary task is to establish dispute settlement Panels, to adopt reports from Panels or the Appellate Body, and to authorize suspension of concessions and retaliation by one party if another party fails to implement the conclusions of a report.

When a Panel or the Appellate Body concludes that a measure is inconsistent with a covered Agreement, it must recommend that the member concerned bring the measure into conformity with that Agreement. The Panel or Appellate Body may suggest ways in which the member concerned could implement the recommendations.

Despite what many consider an admirable track record to date, the dispute settlement process is one of the most criticized aspects of the work of the WTO, particularly with respect to disputes that are important for sustainable development. The principal criticisms fall under two headings. The first relates to process and lack of openness; a common demand is that all hearings should be open to the public and that all briefs by the parties be made publicly available at the time of submission. The second criticism is substantive, and relates to the unpopular nature of the rulings.

Although the GATT's dispute settlement process was also attacked by environmentalists and others, one reason the chorus of criticism has risen in the case of the WTO is that the process moves forward more automatically than under the GATT. This makes the lack of outside involvement even more aggravating for some. The president of Worldwide Fund for Nature (WWF) International has remarked: "The speed, power, and efficiency of the system are both frightening and fascinating to environmental groups. It is the very power and authority of the system that has led to calls for reforms."[7] This automaticity is evident in, for example, the decision-making process. In general, the DSB takes decisions by consensus, as is the case throughout the WTO. In other parts of the organization, consensus means that no WTO member present at a meeting formally objects to the proposed decision. However, a radically different procedure is followed at four key stages in settling disputes: with the establishment of the Panel, the adoption of Panel reports, the adoption of Appellate Body reports, and the authorization for retaliation. At each stage, adoption follows unless there is a consensus *against* what is to be agreed. This rule of negative consensus makes decision-making quasi-automatic, in sharp contrast to the situation that prevailed under the GATT-1947, when reports of Panels could be adopted only on the basis of consensus. The DSU provides no opportunity for blockage in decision-making by the losing party, as frequently occurred in the GATT. Under the WTO, if one member votes for the report, it is adopted.

The Dispute Settlement Understanding provides for the payment of compensation and the application of sanctions in the case of non-compliance. The losing party in a dispute is expected to implement the Panel or Appellate Body recommendations, and there are incentives for doing so. If the government concerned fails within a reasonable period to follow the recommended course of action, the parties may agree to compensation. Without such an agreement, the winning member may retaliate under any WTO Agreement after obtaining DSB authorization.

There have been a number of proposals to make the dispute settlement process more open to public scrutiny. Currently, meetings between the panellists and the parties are closed, except for the parties to the dispute. They are open to neither WTO members who are third parties nor other WTO members. Third parties can make submissions to the Panels, along with the parties to the dispute, but other WTO members cannot. There are hearings of the Panel where third parties, but not other WTO members, can present their views. Since governments that are not direct parties to the dispute not third parties have no access to the process, it is hard to imagine their approving more access to the process for non-governmental organizations than they have themselves.[8]

In the view of some, the arguments in favour of greater participation by NGOs in the dispute settlement process are "overwhelming".[9] This is not, however, the view of the majority of WTO members. At the most fundamental level, many governments argue that the WTO is an intergovernmental organization and governments should represent the collectivity of their constituents. They also argue that to have a public discussion of national submissions at the same time as they are under discussion in the Panel – and the possibility of that discussion influencing the panellists – could jeopardize the case of parties to the dispute. This formula also conjures up visions of what has been described as "scorched earth" tactics, where defendants would employ every technical objection available to create serious obstacles to the Panel adjudicating the dispute. The simple reality is that under the pressure of domestic pressure groups, particularly in developed countries, there will most probably be an opening up of the dispute settlement process to the public. It may well take time (see below), because most WTO members (particularly developing countries) are of the view that this will not "enrich" the process when submissions are presented.

In determining a time horizon for change in dispute processes, it is important to consider the different groups that are interested in the outcome of a dispute and their access to the process under current procedures. At least five groups are involved: the parties to the dispute; the third parties that have a formal role to play in the dispute (i.e. in accordance with the DSU); the WTO members that are interested in the outcome of the dispute (perhaps from a systemic perspective); public interest groups; and a group comprising producers in both countries, producers in other competing countries and consumers in all countries. This last group has a very direct interest and is certainly the largest in terms of numbers. It is clear from the discussions in the review of the DSU that governments will not permit more rights to be given to non-governmental organizations and other groups than they themselves have. A practical reality is that, before the dispute process is made more publicly accessible, governments will have to decide on how they themselves are to be treated in this process.

Fiscal measures and non-discrimination

One area in which governments are understandably keen to maintain their autonomy is in the imposition of taxes to meet national goals. In well-functioning market-based economies, prices can register the relative scarcity of resources and consumer preferences, and thereby allocate resources efficiently. The welfare of society can be undermined, however, when market prices fail to capture the effects of certain activities and therefore send misleading signals relating to "the optimal use of resources" and other objectives of the WTO as stated in its Preamble to the Agreement Establishing the WTO. Resource misallocation undermines effective environmental management. Distorted prices can obscure the abundance of underutilized resources, accelerate the depletion of exhaustible resources, generate new environmental problems, and contribute to the excessive use of environmentally damaging inputs. The reasoning follows that, when adverse production and consumption externalities are adequately integrated into decision-making processes through the use of fiscal measures, trade and environment objectives can be mutually supportive. In such instances, a hierarchy of instruments is available to deal with environmental problems, and trade instruments are rarely the first-best among them.

Not surprisingly, taxes and charges are increasingly used in the pursuit of national policy objectives involving the correction of market failures of importance to sustainable development. Importantly, taxes, subsidies and other charges will vary across countries and affect the international competitiveness of tradable products, for example. There are good reasons for this. There may be different physical conditions leading to different pollution absorption capacities, with costs being internalized differently in various countries. An important question for present purposes is whether WTO rules inhibit countries from taxing as they wish and adjusting domestic taxes and other charges in order to maintain international competitiveness.

Taxes

The purpose of national treatment is to avoid the application and rebate of internal taxes and regulatory measures to afford protection to domestic production. Toward this end, members of the WTO are obliged to provide equality of competitive conditions for imported and domestic products. The intention of national treatment is to ensure that internal charges and regulations are not employed so as to frustrate the effect of tariff and other trade-liberalizing concessions.

In the absence of a harmonized taxation system between trading partners, and according to WTO rules, taxes can be adjusted at the border to preserve the competitive equality between domestic and imported products. Although this appears to be a straightforward exercise, there remains a considerable degree of controversy about which taxes can be imposed or rebated, and in what circumstances.[10]

For WTO purposes, there is an important distinction between taxes in this respect. *Indirect taxes* are those imposed directly or indirectly on products (such as sales, excise, turnover, value added, franchise, stamp, transfer, inventory and equipment taxes). There are also *direct taxes* imposed on the factors of production or inputs to the production process (such as taxes on wages, profits, interests, rents, royalties and other forms of income, and taxes on the ownership of real property). According to WTO practice, indirect taxes are eligible for tax adjustment on imports and exports, but direct taxes are not. The rationale for different treatment for indirect taxes is based on the premise that indirect taxes are shifted completely "forward" by the taxpayer, are eventually reflected in the final price of the product, and directly affect the international competitiveness of the product. In contrast, it is assumed that direct taxes are shifted "backward", in the sense that they are borne by the manufacturer, may not be reflected in the final price, and may not affect international competitiveness.

From a commercial perspective, the rebate of taxes in one country and not another can have the same effect as a subsidy. As far as border adjustment for subsidies is concerned, the WTO Agreement on Subsidies and Countervailing Measures endorses the distinction between direct and indirect taxes. The remission of indirect taxes in respect of the production of exported products is not considered to be an export subsidy, provided the amount of taxes remitted does not exceed the amount of taxes levied in relation to the production of like products sold for domestic consumption. On the other hand, adjustment with respect to the remission of direct taxes related to exports is considered to be an export subsidy.

Although this provides considerable scope for corrections of market failure, an additional point is that there are no limitations in this process regarding the policy objective of the tax or subsidy. For example, in accordance with the polluter pays principle, a tax on chemicals produced in a particular country may be designed to tax polluting production activities in that country. This tax may finance environmental programmes benefiting only those in the country concerned. It could be argued that this tax should not be eligible for border tax adjustment (in terms of an equivalent tax imposed on imported like chemical products) – the logic being that the importing country should tax only products of domestic origin that give rise to environmental problems. GATT/WTO jurisprudence is such that the tax adjustment rules do not distinguish between taxes with different policy purposes. Whether a sales tax is levied on a product for general revenue purposes or to encourage the rational use of environmental resources is not considered relevant for the determination of the eligibility of a tax for border tax adjustment.[11]

The above rules apply to taxes on tradable products. As countries develop their national response strategies to environmental problems, environmental taxes that apply directly to production processes are likely to play an increasingly important role. In fact, recent studies have addressed national measures such as energy efficiency standards or carbon and energy taxes applied to products exhausted in the production process. If taxes such as these are not applied to imports, they provide foreign competitors with an economic advantage. Carbon and energy taxes have been introduced in several European countries, and all include some form of compensatory measures for domestic industries, such as total exemptions for certain sectors, reduced rates for the most energy-intensive processes, ceilings for total tax payments, or subsidies for energy audits. Exemptions and other such features have been introduced

to accommodate the competitiveness concerns of energy-intensive industries. The important question from a WTO perspective is whether taxes
on products exhausted in the production process, as well as taxes on the
process that produced them, can be adjusted at the border.

Under existing WTO rules and jurisprudence, it is clear that border
tax adjustment is possible for indirect taxes levied on products. However,
the extent to which indirect taxes on inputs incorporated or exhausted in
the production process of the final product can be adjusted at the border
is open to interpretation.[12] Since environmental taxes and charges are at
least as much process oriented as product oriented, the interpretation of
WTO rules will have significant implications for the competitiveness of a
variety of industries.[13] What this translates into is that equivalent domestic taxes can be imposed on imported like products – domestic taxes, for
example, on the same imported coal and petroleum. As far as exports are
concerned, taxes could be rebated if they were levied on the product at
the domestic level – for example, domestic taxes on exported coal and
petroleum. This same understanding does not, however, extend to taxes
paid in the process of producing the good; for example, rebating domestic taxes levied on the energy consumed or the carbon emitted in the
production process.[14] A domestic tax can be applied legitimately to
imported fuel, but a tax cannot be applied on the energy consumed in
producing a ton of steel.

Subsidies

Subsidies have the potential to contribute positively to the environment
when they capture positive environmental externalities. On the other
hand, they may contribute negatively if they cause environmental stress
by encouraging the overuse of natural resources. Environmentalists have
suggested that multilateral trade rules should incorporate greater flexibility for providing subsidies to encourage activities that have a beneficial
impact on the environment. On the other hand, special agreements have
been sought to restrict the use of subsidies when they are seen to be
harmful for the environment. The initiative to deal with fisheries subsidies is a useful case study in this respect, and it is discussed in chapter 3.

The Uruguay Round Agreement on Subsidies and Countervailing
Measures defines certain kinds of subsidy as prohibited because they are
clearly harmful. Other subsidies are actionable and open to challenge
only if they are believed to cause adverse effects. The logic behind the
WTO treatment of subsidies is that domestic industries should not be
put at an unfair disadvantage by competition from goods that benefit
from government subsidies, and that countervailing measures to offset
those subsidies should not themselves be obstacles to fair trade. Because

subsidies result from the decisions of governments, the rules not only regulate the unilateral action (countervailing duties) that may be taken against subsidized imports, but also establish multilateral disciplines to control the use of subsidies themselves.

Only subsidies that are "specific", in the sense of being given to particular enterprises or industries, are subject to the disciplines of the WTO Agreement. The argument for this distinction is that multilateral rules are needed to regulate only subsidies that distort trade flows and the allocation of resources within an economy. All specific subsidies are classified into one of two categories. *Prohibited subsidies* are most clearly designed to affect trade, and are most likely to have adverse effects on the interests of WTO members. They fall into two groups: export subsidies, which are contingent on export performance; and import substitution subsidies, which are granted on the condition of the use of domestic rather than imported goods. The second category comprises *actionable subsidies*, which are not prohibited but can be challenged owing to adverse effects on the interests of other members (in the classic GATT manner of causing "serious prejudice", "injury" or "nullification and impairment" of benefits). First, a WTO member may impose a countervailing duty if it determines that subsidized imports are causing material injury to a domestic industry. Alternatively, a member may challenge an injurious subsidy before a WTO dispute settlement Panel. Second, nullification or impairment of benefits may arise when improved market access as a result of another member's tariff concession is undercut by a subsidy. Finally, serious prejudice (a wider concept) focuses on situations where a member's export interests are affected by subsidization.

During the Uruguay Round, both the positive and the negative contributions that subsidies may make to the environment were considered. The Subsidies Agreement (Article 8) singles out non-actionable subsidies or "green" subsidies, which could be either non-specific subsidies or specific subsidies involving assistance to industrial research and pre-competitive development activity, assistance to disadvantaged regions, or certain types of assistance for adapting existing facilities to new environmental requirements imposed by law and/or regulations. According to the Agreement, the Subsidies Committee was obliged to review the operation of this category of subsidies before the end of 1999. However, members were not able to reach consensus on this matter in the review process, so the provisions lapsed. At present, all subsidies (subject to the specific rules on export subsidies and domestic support to agricultural products) are either prohibited ("red") or actionable ("yellow").

The Subsidies Agreement does not apply to agricultural subsidies. These are covered by the Agreement on Agriculture. Making such subsidies non-actionable enabled members to capture positive environmental externalities when they arise. A number of authors have argued that there should be a reintroduction of such subsidies designed to meet social and environmental objectives. The Agreement on Agriculture seeks to reform trade in agricultural products and provides the basis for market-oriented policies. In its Preamble, the Agreement reiterates the commitment of members to reform agriculture in a manner that protects the environment. Under the Agreement, domestic support measures with minimal impact on trade (so-called "green box" policies) are excluded from reduction commitments. These include expenditures under environmental programmes, provided that they meet certain conditions.

Regulatory intentions

An important question for regulators is how their flexibility to regulate imported and domestic like products is restricted by WTO rules. If there is a traditional or conventional means of establishing "likeness" in the WTO, it is with reference to the Report of the Working Party on Border Tax Adjustments.[15] Four general criteria were developed in determining likeness. According to the Appellate Body, these four criteria translate into four characteristics that products should share to be "like": their physical properties; the extent to which they serve the same end-uses; the extent to which consumers perceive them as alternative means of satisfying a particular want or demand; and the international classification of the products for tariff purposes.

From an economic perspective, it would seem reasonable that like products should share essentially the same physical characteristics and a commonality of end-uses, as well as compete in the marketplace. If products did not compete, there would be thin grounds on which to claim that a product was discriminated against. However, the important question is whether competing in the marketplace is both a necessary and sufficient condition for establishing likeness. According to the Appellate Body, a great degree of discretion is involved in the interpretation of "like product" – the concept of "likeness" is a relative one that evokes the image of an accordion: "The accordion of *likeness* stretches and squeezes in different places as different provisions of the WTO Agreement are applied. The width of the accordion in any one of those places must be determined by the particular provision in which the term *like* is encountered, as well as by the context and the circumstances that prevail in any given case to which that provision may apply."[16]

Donald Regan has provided a useful example of the likeness between milk contained in biodegradable cardboard cartons and milk contained in non-returnable plastic containers.[17] The milk has the same physical characteristics and commonality of end-uses and competes in the market-place. Thus, the product meets the conventional criteria of likeness. But these products may well be regulated for sale in very different ways. If environmental legislation favours all milk sold in biodegradable car-tons, the regulation is origin neutral. But what if it is only milk in plastic containers that is imported? Are burdensome regulations relating to imported milk in plastic containers considered to be illegal within the context of national treatment?

Bob Hudec draws on past case history in the GATT and WTO to de-velop the elements of an *aims and effects* test.[18] His starting point is that, in accordance with national treatment, internal tax and non-tax regula-tions "should not be applied ... so as to afford protection to domestic production".[19] Thus, the legitimacy of internal taxes and regulations should be determined primarily on the basis of their purpose (*aims*) and the implications for the marketplace (*effects*). The important question becomes whether domestic regulations have a bona fide regulatory pur-pose, and whether their effect on the conditions of competition is to create a protective advantage in favour of domestic products.

Hudec sees two advantages of this approach over the traditional "like product" test based on competitiveness. First, the *aim and effects* approach consigns the metaphysics of "likeness" to a lesser role in the analysis, and instead makes the question of violation depend primarily on the two most important issues that separate bona fide regulation from trade protection: the trade effects of the measure, and the bona fides of the alleged regulatory purpose behind it. Second, by making it possible for the issue of regulatory justification to be considered at the same time that the issue of violation itself is being determined, the *aim and effects* approach avoids the premature dismissal of valid complaints on grounds of un-likeness alone.[20]

If the *aim* of a regulation was deemed to be a sufficient criterion for discriminating between products, there would be a degree of automa-ticity in the application of national treatment. This follows from the logic that, if the aim of a regulation is not to protect a domestic producer, then presumably it serves a useful purpose from the point of view of the gov-ernment imposing the regulation; it is therefore a bona fide regulation. Thus, the intention of a measure can be established by looking at its pro-tective intentions, but also in terms of a sovereign government claiming that the intentions behind the regulation are legitimate. The determina-tion of protective intent requires investigating the other side of the coin by determining legitimacy. This has the potential to place the WTO judi-cial system in a difficult situation.

Resort to the *aims and effects* test raises at least one other important consideration. Does it render the exceptions option under Article XX redundant? That is, if Panels and the Appellate Body were required to consider the regulatory purpose of a measure (its *aim*) when deciding the issue of violation under Article III, all of the regulatory justifications provided in Article XX would already have been considered and disposed of in the first-stage determination of violation. There would be no reason to conduct the same inquiry again under Article XX.

Hudec argues that these issues "go to the very core of the WTO's policing function over domestic regulatory policy – *in some respects the most important element of its legal character*".[21] They are clearly of crucial importance for sustainable development. With his typical wisdom and pragmatism, Hudec is quick to rationalize the situation. In his view, it may be the very sensitivity of this area that explains the choices made by the Appellate Body thus far. The policing activity of the WTO intrudes upon domestic regulatory sovereignty and leaves the WTO legal institutions exposed to damaging criticism from national governments. Recognizing this very exposed position, the Appellate Body may well have concluded that the safest refuge from political criticism was to stay as close as possible to the shelter of the legal texts accepted by governments. In other words, in order to prosper in the long run, it is necessary first to survive the short run.

If products are like – and not differentiated on the basis of the aims of the regulation – and one product is discriminated against vis-à-vis another, then resort to the GATT Article XX exceptions is available. This is a tougher course of action for several reasons. Under Article XX, while accepting the legitimacy of the policy objective, what is required is proof that the regulation is both *necessary* and *related to* the environmental or other national objective. Both these terms are open to interpretation on a case-by-case basis. Should likeness of product be determined on the basis of regulatory intent in the context of national treatment, or as an exception under Article XX? The answer to this question is crucial in terms of determining the role of the WTO in restraining national policy options in the area of sustainable development. A WTO dispute settlement case relating to the import of asbestos is exemplary in demonstrating the pragmatism and ingenuity of the Appellate Body.

Asbestos is a product that is potentially hazardous to health; it is a highly toxic material, exposure to which poses significant threats to human health.[22] However, owing to its resistance to high temperatures and chemical attack, it is widely used in industrial and other commercial applications. The French government, which had previously imported large amounts of asbestos, adopted a Decree that provided for an origin-neutral ban on asbestos fibres and products containing asbestos fibres. Canada, the largest exporter of asbestos in the world, brought the dispute to the WTO, arguing that its asbestos products were discriminated against: they were *like products* when compared with those used as substitutes in France. The Canadian view was that the French prohibition resulted in less favourable treatment for Canada's like (asbestos) products and that national treatment was therefore violated.

What was never in doubt in this case was that the asbestos fibres in question constituted a risk to human health. Their carcinogenic nature has been acknowledged since 1977 by international bodies such as the International Agency for Research on Cancer and the World Health Organization.[23] Accordingly, France's health policies were never in question. The argument advanced by Canada in this respect was that, although it recognized the health risk associated with the use of asbestos, controlled usage could avoid health-related risks and, if this course of action were followed, their exported goods were like French substitutes. There was thus de facto discrimination against a like product.

The first question addressed by the Panel was whether asbestos fibres and products were like the substitute. The second step was to establish whether, if the two products are like, the measure does accord like imported products less favourable treatment than it accords like domestic products. As noted, the term "less favourable treatment" expresses the general principle, in Article III:1 of the GATT-1994, that internal regulations "should not be applied ... so as to afford protection to domestic production". If there is "less favourable treatment" of the group of like imported products, there is "protection" for the group of like domestic products.

The Panel concluded that a *risk* criterion should not be taken into account when examining the properties, nature and quality of the product, or when examining other criteria of likeness. The Panel found that the health, safety or other concerns that led regulators to apply different treatment to products may be taken into account in the analysis *only* under Article XX, *not* in the analysis under Article III:4 of the GATT-1994. The European Communities argued that this misconstrues the relationship between Articles III:4 and XX of the GATT-1994, requires the likeness of two products to be determined solely on the basis of commercial factors, and entails a serious curtailment of national regulatory autonomy. The argument was that, if non-commercial aspects may be considered only under Article XX, then the list of policy purposes provided for under Article XX is unduly limited and places a serious constraint on national autonomy.

The Panel said that, with respect to the relationship between national treatment and the Exceptions provision, introducing a health criterion into the analysis of "likeness" would nullify the effect of Article XX(b). This would lead to unpredictability as regards the scope of national treatment and would imply that likeness of products requires complex scientific analysis (under Article III) for which Panels have no special expertise. Since Article XX was specially designed to balance the interest of promoting international trade against legitimate societal interests, Article XX was a more appropriate framework than Article III for taking account of these types of consideration.

Would the failure to consider the health factors constitute a curtailment of national regulatory autonomy in the context of national treatment? It has been argued that it would. The reasoning is that the list of policy measures provided for in Article XX is finite and limited. In fact, only 10 policy goals are listed in Article XX as justifying measures that deviate from other provisions of the WTO. The argument is that there are far more policy goals that should provide a justification for non-conforming WTO measures than those listed in Article XX.[24]

The reasoning of the Panel was that the object and purpose of Article III is to provide equality of competitive conditions for imported and domestic products, and the four traditional criteria of "likeness" all relate to the state of commercial competition between products. The Panel was of the view that the "dangerousness" of products is unrelated to commercial competition and "dangerousness" is not a factor to be considered in determining "likeness". This then leaves the "aims and effects" approach out in the cold.

The Appellate Body was of the view that the health risks associated with a product may be pertinent in an examination of likeness. Its approach, however, was quite ingenious. It considered that the health risks associated with asbestos *could* be evaluated under the competitiveness criteria of physical properties, consumer tastes and habits. More specifically, it considered that asbestos is a product that competes in the marketplace with its substitutes but, because of the health risk involved, it is implausible that it would really compete. For the Appellate Body, the products were not like products; because of health considerations, they would not compete in the market. The competitiveness criteria were maintained, as was attaching importance to the aim of the regulation.

Evaluating evidence relating to the health risks arising from the physical properties of a product does not prevent a measure that is inconsistent with Article III:4 from being justified under Article XX(b). The Appellate Body noted, in this regard, that different inquiries occur under these two very different Articles. Under Article III:4, evidence relating to health risks may be relevant in assessing the competitive relationship in the marketplace between allegedly like products. The same, or similar, evidence serves a different purpose under Article XX(b); namely, that of assessing whether a member has a sufficient basis for adopting or enforcing a WTO-inconsistent measure on the grounds of human health.

Under the Exceptions Article, the issue is whether the import restrictions imposed by France could be considered to be "necessary" in terms of Article XX(b). The traditional approach in terms of GATT and WTO jurisprudence is to treat a measure as necessary only if no alternative measure less inconsistent with the GATT could *reasonably* be employed to achieve the policy objectives.

Whether a more consistent measure is reasonably available is not a decision that rests on hard evidence. According to the Appellate Body, it requires a "weighing and balancing process ... [C]omprehended in the determination of whether a WTO-consistent alternative measure" is reasonably available is the extent to which the alternative measure "contributes to the realization of the end pursued".[25] In this respect, the Appellate Body made clear how flexible it is likely to be in this weighing and balancing process: "[t]he more vital or important [the] common interests or values" pursued, the easier it would be to accept as "necessary" measures designed to achieve those ends.[26]

In the *EC-Asbestos* case, the objective pursued with the measure in question was the preservation of human life and health through the elimination, or reduction, of the well-known and life-threatening health risks posed by asbestos fibres. For the Appellate Body, this value is both "vital and important in the highest degree". The remaining question, then, is whether there is an alternative measure that would achieve the same end and that is less restrictive of trade than a prohibition. This then begs the question of whose responsibility it is to decide whether the objective pursued is vital and important, and whether there is a need to resort to an alternative measure. Because it is the Appellate Body that ascribes the degree of importance in terms of what is "vital and important", it has carved out for itself a mammoth task in considering regulatory objectives across approximately 150 countries with very different levels of economic development, social norms and priorities with respect to the environment and public health, and perceptions of what is vital and important.

Extraterritoriality and coercion

The situation might well arise where a government wishes to differentiate between imports of identical products according to their source because of the manner in which one of them was produced in the country of export. This is *origin-specific* discrimination. It could be achieved, for example, through a licensing process resulting in the quantitative limitation of the imports produced by a production process in an exporting country. Perhaps this process was considered unacceptable to the importing country because it emitted large amounts of greenhouse gases. In terms of the objectives of many groups – such as environmental or human rights activists – an appropriate justification for imposing a quantitative restriction on an imported good is to prohibit the import of a product produced in an environmentally unacceptable manner or without respect for core labour standards. To consume such a product is anathema to such groups.

The issues surrounding these matters arouse strong emotions. Should imported eggs be *banned* if they were laid by hens kept in battery cages rather than by free-ranging hens? Are these eggs like products? What about imported fur products, banned because wild animals are caught in steel-jawed leg traps? And how about food products derived from genetically modified organisms, which are banned even when they are indistinguishable from non-modified products? Should imported carpets be banned if made by children under the age of 12? Should the banning of shrimp caught in a manner that harms endangered turtles be acceptable?

The imposition of quantitative restrictions on either imports or exports is a violation of the general prohibition on quantitative restrictions provided for under Article XI of the GATT-1994. To the extent that a discriminatory measure targets one or more countries, it violates the MFN obligation. An important issue immediately presents itself. Governments are free to regulate products and processes within their own borders and to regulate imports if they are damaging to their own public health or environment. But what about environmental damage outside the country imposing the quantitative restriction? Is this legal under GATT/WTO law, and, if an exception is sought, what would be the ruling?

Whether such action is justifiable is a matter for interpretation by Panels and the Appellate Body. Much to the disapproval of public interest groups, the traditional interpretation has been that trade measures relating to environmental and other standards should be taken only with respect to the fauna and flora and natural resources within the country taking the action. The implications are clear. Countries are free to adopt whatever regulations they wish within their own borders to reflect standards related to sustainable development, but they cannot restrict trade on the grounds that countries that are the source of the imports do not apply the same standards domestically.

The experiences of Panels and the Appellate Body in both the GATT and the WTO throw useful light on the issues involved and the degree of discretion available in the interpretation of such rules. In the following, I concentrate on two environment cases at the GATT and WTO. As both are well documented, only those aspects that are relevant for present purposes will be explored.

The Tuna-Dolphin *case*

The *Tuna-Dolphin* case is far from recent.[27] Although the report was never adopted, it was a landmark case and provides a useful indication of the thinking of trade officials at the time (see chapter 2). Comparing the logic of the case with the *Shrimp-Turtle* case a decade later (see below) provides useful insights into the evolution of the WTO dispute settlement process with regard to matters of critical importance for sustainable development.

The very brief facts of this case are that the United States claimed that the Mexican tuna caught using purse seine-nets resulted in the incidental kill of dolphins. Mexico appealed on the grounds that the embargo applied by the United States on tuna imported from Mexico was a violation of the prohibition on quantitative restrictions. The Panel ruled in favour of Mexico on the basis of two points of importance for present purposes. Mexico argued that domestic products were "like products" with respect to imported tuna products, because the process of production (in the capture) was not apparent in the final product (i.e. the tuna). Thus, the US regulation was inconsistent with the "like product" interpretation in the GATT. Second, a measure regulating a product could not legally discriminate between domestic and imported products solely on the basis of the production process outside the borders of the country taking the action.

The United States argued that tuna caught according to the two different methods were not like products because of the distinction between regulations affecting the production of the product in the United States. The production method was considered unlawful by US law, therefore the sale of the product was unlawful. The United States also noted that US regulations relating to the catch of tuna were clearly related to the process and not to the product. The comparison made under the US regulations was whether the production methods of another harvesting nation were comparable to those of the United States.

The Panel argued that, under GATT rules, the United States was obliged to provide Mexican tuna (as a product) with treatment no less favourable than that accorded to US tuna (also as a product), regardless of how the tuna itself was harvested. The tuna caught by Mexican fishermen was the same product (tuna) but caught by another means. The Panel also observed that, although GATT members could adopt GATT-inconsistent measures for the protection of the environment or the conservation of exhaustible natural resources, it was not clearly spelled out in the Agreement whether the resources being protected could fall outside the jurisdiction of the party adopting the environmental controls. To address this issue, the Panel inspected the drafting history of Article

XX, and came to the conclusion that the drafters intended it to be applied only to the jurisdiction of the country taking the action.

Although the report of the Panel was not adopted by GATT member countries, its ruling was a red flag to environmental groups, which saw trade rules as an obstacle to environmental protection. As a result, there was a call for the WTO to modify its interpretation of like products, to provide a justification for discriminatory action according to production methods, and to modify its interpretation of extraterritoriality under the Exceptions provision.

The Shrimp-Turtle *case*

The *Shrimp-Turtle* case was the first environment case dealt with by a WTO Panel and Appellate Body.[28] The brief facts are that India, Malaysia, Pakistan and Thailand brought a joint complaint against a ban imposed by the United States on the importation of shrimp. Under US legislation, wild-caught shrimp could not be imported into the United States if they did not meet US standards regarding the protection of sea turtles. Because of the guidelines of the regulation, this meant that the United States required shrimp trawlers in the exporting countries to install a "turtle excluder device" in their nets when fishing in areas where there existed a significant likelihood of encountering sea turtles: countries wishing to export their shrimp products to the United States had to impose the same requirement on their fishermen.

The United States claimed that its measures were justified under Article XX(b) and (g) and that these provisions did not contain any jurisdictional limitations in terms of the location of the resources to be conserved. The complainants argued, to the contrary, that Article XX(b) and (g) could not be invoked to justify a measure applying to animals outside the jurisdiction of the member enacting the measure. This then was a quite different approach from that of the *Tuna-Dolphin* cases. The issue was not one of like products and regulatory intent, and therefore of product- and non-product-related production processes. The issue was whether the application of trade restrictions to meet environmental objectives outside the jurisdiction of the country imposing the sanctions could be justified under the Exceptions provisions of the GATT-1994.

Shrimp-Turtle *and sustainable development*

The *Shrimp-Turtle* case is instructive when looking at the role of the WTO in sustainable development for a number of reasons. The most important reason is that it is the only case brought to the WTO where specific mention is made by a Panel or the Appellate Body of sustainable development. Further, the Appellate Body ruling is particularly interesting when seen in the context of the 1992 United Nations Conference on Environment and Development and the Rio Principles. According to Principle 15 of the *Rio Declaration*, "Unilateral actions to deal with environmental challenges outside the jurisdiction of the importing state should be avoided. Environmental measures addressing trans-boundary or global environmental problems should, as far as possible, be based on an international consensus."[29] Philippe Sands has usefully pointed out that this text does not endorse a blanket prohibition on unilateral actions that address environmental challenges outside the jurisdiction of the state taking the trade measures: the requirement that such actions "should be avoided" is different from actions "shall be prohibited". Also, such actions "should, as far as possible, be based on international consensus". Thus, an international consensus is desirable but not a prerequisite. Sands notes that Principle 15 points "to the permissibility of unilateral measures that address environmental challenges outside the jurisdiction of the state taking the measure – including but not limited to trade measures – where a consensus amongst interested states has been sought but not necessarily achieved".[30] To what extent is the Appellate Body ruling an implementation of the principles contained in Principle 15 of the *Rio Declaration*?

A further matter of importance for the WTO – sustainable development link is that the WTO legal process was ruling on a matter that is so clearly on the sustainable development agenda – namely, the conservation of endangered species. This should remove any doubt that sustainable development is clearly on the WTO agenda. In doing so, the Appellate Body decision made clear the importance for the WTO of the lack of effective environment agreements in some areas. Although an agreement existed for trade in endangered species, it did not address the situation where trade is restricted in order to conserve an endangered species.

Another important consideration in this respect is the number of cross-references in the Appellate Body report to other international agreements. The largely uncharted waters of the relationship between "soft" environmental law and "hard" WTO law were an important element in the overall decision. In an earlier case (*EC-Hormones*), and with respect to the Precautionary Principle, for example, the Appellate Body noted that "[t]he status of the precautionary principle in international law continues to be the subject of debate among academics, law practitioners, regulators and judges.... We consider, however, that it is unnecessary, and probably imprudent, for the Appellate Body in this appeal to take a position on this important, but abstract, question."[31] The Precautionary Principle had not yet "crystallized" to become a general principle of law. Finally, the controversy of how far the authority of the WTO legal

process should extend in taking decisions that are of critical importance from a policy perspective – that is, without negotiation between
governments – is clearly apparent in the proceedings of this case. The
process and outcome are in stark contrast to the manner in which the
link between fish stocks – also a depletable natural resource – and fisheries subsidies is being negotiated between governments. In common
with the negotiation of fisheries subsidies in the Special Session of the
Rules Committee (see chapter 3), the question must inevitably be posed
of whether the WTO legal processes are best suited to deal with these
matters.

Threat to the trading system

The Panel concluded that the US ban could not be justified under Article
XX, because allowing such a ban would undermine members' autonomy
to determine their own policies and thus would provide a threat to the
multilateral trading system. This is an interesting concept introduced by
the Panel and not found in any WTO legal texts. Because of this threat,
the Panel did not find it necessary to examine whether the US measure
was covered by paragraphs (b) and (g) of Article XX. The logic of the
Panel was that the object and purpose of the WTO Agreements did not
encompass measures where a member conditioned access to its market
on the adoption of conservation policies by the exporting member. For
the Panel, what was at stake was not the urgency of protecting sea turtles,
because all the parties agreed that sea turtles needed to be protected.
What was important was that the measure in question was unilateral in
nature, and there was no existing MEA to deal with the situation.[32] On
these grounds it could not be considered a legitimate exception from
WTO obligations.

The Appellate Body ruled against the Panel, and noted that, although
maintaining the multilateral trading system is a pervasive premise underlying the WTO Agreements, it is neither a right nor an obligation, nor is
it an interpretative rule that can be employed in the appraisal of a measure to protect the environment. Instead of looking into the object and
purpose of just the chapeau of Article XX, the Panel had looked into
the object and purpose of the whole of the GATT-1994 and the WTO
Agreements, and thereby interpreted the object and purpose of the
Head Note in an overly broad manner. Thus, "[t]he task of interpreting
and applying the chapeau is ... essentially the delicate one of locating
and marking out a line of equilibrium between the right of a Member to
invoke an exception under Article XX and the rights of the other Members under varying substantive provisions (e.g. Article XI) of the GATT
1994 ... The location of the line of equilibrium, as expressed in the chapeau, is not fixed and unchanging; the line moves as the kind and the

shape of the measures at stake vary and as the facts making up specific cases differ."[33] Clearly, there is considerable discretion for the Appellate Body in determining the moving line of equilibrium, and according to which circumstances.

The view of the Appellate Body was not received well in the Dispute Settlement Body. A number of interventions argued that, indeed, "maintaining, rather than undermining, the multilateral trading system is necessarily a fundamental and pervasive premise underlying the WTO Agreement". Thailand reasoned that it had brought the *Shrimp-Turtle* dispute to the WTO "not so much for its economic interest, but as a matter which involved a fundamental principle of the multilateral trading system ... [T]he application of unilateral and extraterritorial measures was unacceptable and incompatible with the multilateral trading system ... [A] delicate balance of rights and obligations among Members, could be undermined and weakened by such measures. Under the multilateral trading system, no country could impose unilaterally its trade policies on other trading partners through a restrictive embargo."[34] For countries such as this, the case was indeed about maintaining, rather than undermining, the multilateral trading system.

Exhaustible natural resources

The Appellate Body was required to determine if the import restriction by the United States was a measure to conserve an exhaustible natural resource, thereby qualifying for consideration under the Exceptions Article. For the Appellate Body, the issue was whether a living creature should be considered to be an exhaustible natural resource. This interpretation is of importance for future environment-related disputes; could sanctions be applied to the exports of countries emitting excessive greenhouse gases since cool air is an exhaustible natural resource?[35] Answering this question also has important territorial implications. One country's greenhouse gas emissions might well cause sea levels to rise and flood another country.

The Appellate Body ruled that the sea turtles constituted an exhaustible natural resource and that the US measure qualified for provisional justification under Article XX(g). In reaching this conclusion, "soft" law was important. The Appellate Body acknowledged the importance assigned by the international community to bilateral or multilateral action to protect living natural resources. Importantly, it drew attention to the explicit recognition by WTO members of the objective of sustainable development in the Preamble of the WTO Agreement. Its conclusion was that it is too late in the day to suppose that Article XX(g) of the GATT-1994 may be read as referring only to the conservation of exhaustible mineral or other non-living natural resources. The Appellate Body referred to a number of related international treaties (see chapter 6) and held that, in line with the principle of effectiveness in treaty interpretation, measures to conserve exhaustible natural resources, whether living or non-living, fall within Article XX(g).

The Head Note

The Appellate Body did not rule directly against the United States on the grounds of extraterritoriality, but rather ruled that the measure was applied in a manner that amounted to unjustifiable and arbitrary discrimination between countries where the same conditions prevailed. Nevertheless, it did rule that justification existed for a measure to be taken to conserve exhaustible resources beyond the jurisdiction of the importing country. The error by the United States in this respect was the failure to attempt to negotiate an agreement to deal with the problem.

Although non-product-related processes and extraterritoriality were not directly addressed, the ruling is significant in this respect. Such cases do not, in principle, create rigid precedents, but there can be little doubt they do set the pattern for future rulings. The Appellate Body has on occasion scolded Panels that have not ruled in the light of earlier Appellate Body reports. In this instance, it would appear that the manner in which the shrimp were harvested was a crucial element in the conditional acceptance by the Appellate Body of trade restrictions designed to change a policy beyond a member's own territory. However, views among WTO members differ with respect to the interpretation of the ruling as well as to the role of the Appellate Body when ruling on such matters (see below).

The view of governments

As far as the United States was concerned, it is "of considerable significance that the Appellate Body had not accepted the complainants' argument that some sort of jurisdictional limitations would prevent the use of Article XX(g) with respect to the measures in question".[36] Thailand, the other complainants and other countries took a very different view. They charged that the ruling was on a "fundamental and impermissible alteration of the present balance of the rights and obligations of Members under the WTO Agreement.... The right to discriminate based on like products had not been negotiated in the Uruguay Round. The Appellate Body, upon its own will, had altered the balance of rights and obligations under the WTO Agreement."[37] In the view of India, if "the present decision of the Appellate Body were deemed applicable to all future measures, then the door would open to unilateral measures aimed at discrimination based on non-product related production methods".[38]

In the view of the Appellate Body, however, "[p]erhaps the most conspicuous flaw in this measure's application related to its intended and actual coercive effect on the specific policy decisions made by foreign governments, Members of the WTO".[39] It considered that "it is not acceptable, in international trade relations, for one WTO Member to use an economic embargo to require other Members to adopt essentially the same comprehensive regulatory program, to achieve a certain policy goal, as that in force within that Member's territory, without taking into consideration different conditions which may occur in the territories of those other Members".[40] The flaw was in requiring the *same* conservation strategy in the exporting country as was required in the importing country. The flaw was not the requirement to adopt equivalent measures in terms of their effect on the conservation of turtles in areas outside the jurisdiction of the importing country. This distinction is critical.

The United States revised its guidelines and argued that it had responded to the requirement to attempt to negotiate an agreement on further conservation to be in conformity with the ruling of the Appellate Body.[41] There was, however, a further challenge because Malaysia claimed that the United States should have negotiated *and* concluded an international agreement on the protection and conservation of sea turtles before imposing an import prohibition. The Appellate Body rejected Malaysia's contention that avoiding "arbitrary and unjustifiable discrimination" under the chapeau of Article XX required not only negotiation but also the conclusion of an international agreement on the protection and conservation of sea turtles.

Implications

In the *Shrimp-Turtle* case, the Appellate Body did not interpret the meaning of extraterritoriality, like products, or product- and non-product-related production processes. Nevertheless, these issues were at the heart of the ruling. There is no doubt that the manner in which the shrimp were harvested was critical in the ruling, as was the fact that the Appellate Body ruled even though the turtles were living in waters outside the jurisdiction of the United States. Has something changed?

It may be that the case is an important precedent, but the circumstances are almost unique. According to Philippe Sands, the circumstances were very special. In particular, the necessary conditions were that the state taking the measure must have a legitimate interest in the resource it is seeking to protect (i.e. the resource might be migratory and therefore a shared resource); the resource concerned must be the subject of international measures to protect it from endangerment; and the state taking the measure must have exhausted prior diplomatic efforts to enter into an agreement with the state that is the subject of the measures.[42] In Sands' view, the Appellate Body had (successfully) identified values that were recognized by the international community: that a resource is shared (community value), that protective measures are required because the conservation of the species is recognized as a desirable objective (conservation value), and that a consensual approach is desirable (consensus/cooperation value). The last of the values was not in place and there was therefore a need to cooperate to create an intergovernmental agreement.

This commentary is much along the lines of what Hudec has less formally described as a "seat-of-the-pants judgment" by the Appellate Body. He observes that, in circumstances where discretion is required in interpreting unclear text, most tribunals decide the case as best they can by making a "seat-of-the-pants judgment" about whether the defendant government is behaving correctly. Once the tribunal comes to a conclusion about who should win, it fashions an analysis – in terms of the criteria it has been asked to apply – that makes the case come out that way. So long as the tribunal gets it right most of the time – that is, decides its cases according to the larger community's perception of right and wrong behaviour – the decisions tend to be accepted. Hudec speculates that, in future cases, GATT/WTO tribunals are likely to adopt the "aim and effects" approach. Indeed, it is his guess that most previous like product decisions by GATT Panels have been based, consciously or unconsciously, on an intuitive application of the same criteria. In this, Hudec contends, Panels applying the traditional "like product" test were already being guided by seat-of-the-pants application of the aim and effects approach.[43]

The *Shrimp-Turtle* ruling may sound like a rather successful experience, but there are a couple of caveats. The decision was not well received in the Dispute Settlement Body. Two points are important here. First, as already noted, it requires only one WTO member to vote for the report of the Appellate Body or of the Panel for it to be adopted. Second, adopting such a report is an all or nothing affair. A winning party may officially voice and record its dissatisfaction in the adoption process, but it is unlikely to reject the report in its entirety if there are aspects that it disagrees with that are subsidiary to the main finding. John Jackson notes another caveat. While applauding the *Shrimp-Turtle* decision, he advances the slippery slope argument, first by summarizing in his own words the last paragraph of the *Tuna-Dolphin* case: "We recognise that there is a problem about how the environment and the process question relate and how process characteristics should be applied in this context. We don't think it's appropriate for us in our role as a panel or judicial tribunal to solve that. This really should be solved by negotiators in a variety of formats."[44]

This sentiment is reflected in the comments of a number of WTO members which have argued that the Appellate Body extended its authority beyond that granted to it under the WTO Agreement. The DSU limited the jurisdiction of the Appellate Body to issues of law covered in Panel reports and to legal interpretations developed by Panels. It prohibited the Appellate Body from adding to, or diminishing, the rights and obligations provided for in the covered Agreements. A number of countries have argued – in a disapproving manner – that there has been an "evolutionary" interpretative approach adopted by the Appellate Body, which had given a new interpretation to certain DSU provisions and overstepped the bounds of its authority by undermining the balance of rights and obligations of members.[45] The question is what to do about it.

One approach is to maintain the status quo. This line of reasoning is that, although some interpretations may be controversial, in broad measure the system is working well. This is particularly so if consideration is given to the fact that the WTO Agreements deal with vast amounts of commercial activity that is both diverse and conducted between countries at very different levels of development and with different backgrounds. Further, legal precedents do not exist for many of the rules and concepts in the WTO Agreements and, since they contain a large amount of "constructive ambiguity", someone, at some stage, has to make a decision. Controversy over interpretation is therefore to be expected. Although ascertaining the regulator's purpose is not always an easy task, those supporting the status quo note that, in their view, Panel members and, even more, Appellate Body members are actually likely to be just the right sort of people to review determinations concerning "purpose". They are not infallible, but they are people of wide "political" experience, and many cases can be resolved by a commonsense appreciation of the content and context of the regulation.[46]

At the other end of the spectrum is the possibility that the legal interpretations are quite out of line with the majority view in the WTO, an organization where consensus rules the day. Here the thought is that, although survival may appear to be an achievement, it is made possible only by the reverse consensus rule. In this respect, it is argued that it is instructive to read the summary records of the Dispute Settlement Body in conjunction with the Panel and Appellate Body reports at the time of their adoption. This is the litmus test of the sentiment of members. The harsh reality is that members have spoken with considerable annoyance on a number of occasions when reports have been adopted. In the *Shrimp-Turtle* case, examples are provided in the way in which the receipt of *amicus* briefs was handled and the de facto acceptance of unilateral measures that are not arbitrary and discriminatory. But, then again, it may be that the comments made by dissatisfied members in the Dispute Settlement Body are "huffing and puffing" for the benefit of sectors of the home community that would have liked to see some aspects of the discussion pan out differently. Maybe the process and rulings are acceptable after all.

The key question from a policy perspective is whether governments wish to continue with the current approach. In that context, the negotiated and transparent outcome in dealing with fisheries subsidies is interesting (see chapter 3). In this instance, there was complete transparency, with all country positions on the table for public interest groups to see (and lobby outside the WTO). The situation was similar in the treatment of access to affordable medicines and the negotiated outcome in terms of reaching a consensus on how to proceed. This too could be compared to a hypothetical challenge in the dispute settlement process. The bigger question is what should be settled through legal interpretation, what should be negotiated, where the dividing line is, and who draws it. For some the WTO legal processes have clearly overstepped the mark.[47]

According to Hudec, the eventual political acceptability of the WTO's policing function over domestic regulatory measures will continue to depend, as in the past, not on the persuasiveness of the legal standards being applied but on the ability of WTO tribunals to find the right answers in these cases; in other words, their ability to know when to prohibit those regulatory measures viewed as illegitimate by the larger community, and when to let pass those measures that the community views as bona fide regulation. If the answers are largely right, the "occasional absurdity" of the legal rationale will probably not matter.

What is also important in this respect is the role of "soft" law in Appellate Body rulings. Sands says that, in giving effect to the Appellate Body approach, it is necessary to identify international values, such as community, conservation and consensus. The Appellate Body drew on a collection of international instruments, some of which are intended to have legal effects, others of which are not.[48] The approach gives considerable width to "soft" law, and its use requires a reconsideration of the traditional sources of international law. The approach is sensitive because it necessarily interjects a subjective element, in terms of the process both of determining which instruments or acts may be relevant, and then of determining what weight, if any, to give to them. It also raises the question of the relationship between soft and hard law. The subjectivity of the approach does not necessarily de-legitimize the function, so long as one is clear about what is actually happening. In this regard, the background and representativeness of the members of the adjudicating body become a key element in determining the legitimacy of the approach, and the process of identifying the individual members of the adjudicating body becomes especially significant.

Conclusions

The president of WWF International has observed that the *Shrimp-Turtle* dispute illustrates that formal WTO dispute settlement, because of its adversarial nature, may not be the best means to resolve disputes of this kind. He suggested that WTO members should explore the establishment of multi-stakeholder consultative processes in which relevant facts could be put on the table by all interested parties from governments, non-governmental organizations, industry, academia and local communities.[49] In fact, the Dispute Settlement Understanding formally creates the option for parties to the potential dispute to request the good offices of the Director-General of the WTO to engage in consultations to settle the dispute. Such a consultative process could assist in providing the countries involved with an opportunity to consider a range of policy instruments suitable to resolve any trade-related environmental issue that may have arisen.

Should agreement not be reached, a possible approach – which would require no textual changes to WTO Agreements – would be for the Director-General, in collaboration with his counterpart in the relevant MEA in terms of the subject matter being contested, to hold consultations jointly with the governments concerned.[50] To meet the criticisms of lack of transparency confronting the WTO in these matters, there could also be public hearings involving all interested parties. In this respect, it is worth noting that, in the *Shrimp-Turtle* case, the good offices of the Director-General were not sought.

This course of action would not be an obligation imposed on disputing parties, but it would constitute an alternative available to them. If it was resisted on the grounds that a public hearing would delay the settling of a dispute that could be urgent from an environmental perspective, it could be counter-argued that the absence of a formal procedure would expedite the process of bringing the parties together informally. And, if there were no definitive outcome, presumably the consultations under the good offices of the Director-General would not be required.

Even if there were not a positive outcome in terms of a clear decision, this process would be totally transparent – something that is sought by many non-governmental organizations. The possibility of providing inputs from technical experts is another advantage. And although the more formal WTO dispute settlement process would be avoided if the mediation were successful, the normal WTO channel of dispute settlement would still remain open. No country's rights and obligations would be affected in this process, but it could be argued that the technical information provided could eventually influence the conclusion of the Panel or the Appellate Body, if the process went that far. Yet it is hard to argue that additional factual information is a handicap if a well-informed decision is the ultimate objective.

The question could also be posed of what is so special about environmental disputes that merits an approach such as this. The answer is: Nothing. The process is equally applicable to all potential disputes if the defending and complaining countries agree. Indeed, such a process could be carried out by an MEA outside the WTO if the idea was not adopted by the WTO.

Some have argued that Article XX should be interpreted to permit the application of trade restrictions on imports from countries that do not participate in multilateral agreements protecting the global commons. One response is that to assume that the members of the WTO have already expressed in Article XX their consent to the imposition of trade sanctions against them in the framework of a multilateral agreement that they have not accepted is to leave the realm of interpretation and enter that of law-making.[51]

Consequently, it is not surprising that WTO members express a strong preference for the adoption of international standards by all members and the use of multilateral agreements in non-trade domains to facilitate the task in this respect. Who sets the environmental standards, who enforces them and is there to be a role for the WTO and its dispute settlement process in legitimizing the imposition of discriminatory trade measures? Answering these questions goes a long way to defining the future limits of the WTO in global environmental governance. These are the subjects addressed in chapters 5 and 6.

Notes

1. It is restated in Article III that taxes should not be applied to *like products* in a manner designed only to protect domestic producers. As far as *non-like products* are concerned, it is added that a tax would be inconsistent with national treatment in cases where directly competitive imported products were not taxed in a similar manner to domestic products. The legal text relating to taxes differs from that relating to regulations, leading to a number of interesting questions.
2. There is no restatement – as in the case of taxes – that regulations should not be applied in a manner designed only to protect domestic producers. Similarly, there is no reference to a regulation being inconsistent with national treatment in cases where directly competitive imported products are not regulated in a similar manner to domestic products. It seems that the drafters wished to treat national treatment with respect to taxes and regulations differently, but without clear guidelines as to how to do this. This has been left to interpretation.

3. These observations were made by the Appellate Body. See *European Communities – Measures Affecting Asbestos and Asbestos-Containing Products* [*EC-Asbestos*], Appellate Body Report, WT/DS135/AB/R, and Panel Report, WT/DS135, adopted 5 April 2001, para. 92.

4. For a discussion of "treatment no less favourable", "so as to afford protection" and "like products", see Frieder Roessler, "Diverging Domestic Policies and Trade Integration", in Jagdish Bhagwati and Robert H. Hudec (eds), *Fair Trade and Harmonisation: Prerequisites for Free Trade?*, Vol. 1, Cambridge, MA: MIT Press, 1997, chapter 1.

5. For the history of all Article XX exceptions cases, see WTO, *Analytical Index*, Geneva: WTO Secretariat, 2003. For a comprehensive study documenting all the Article XX environment cases in the GATT and the WTO, see WTO, *GATT/WTO Dispute Settlement Practice Relating to GATT Article XX Paragraphs (b), (d) and (g): Note by the WTO Secretariat*, Geneva: WTO Secretariat, WT/CTE/W/203, 8 March 2002.

6. This chapter does not describe all aspects of the dispute settlement process in the WTO. This has been done at length in other excellent tomes. See, in particular, WTO, *Analytical Index*.

7. See Claude Martin, "Trade, Environment and the Need for Change", in Gary P. Sampson (ed.), *The Role of the WTO in Global Governance*, Tokyo: United Nations University Press, 2001, pp. 137–154.

8. Third parties are members who are not directly involved in the launch of a dispute, but who participate in the proceedings because they have a substantial interest in the matter. A mere interest in the proceedings is not enough. Members wishing to become third parties must show that they have a trade interest at stake. Third parties may appear before the Panel; they may also make written submissions. In turn, they receive the submissions to the first Panel meeting of the parties in dispute. Third parties may not appeal against Panel reports or decisions. In cases where a third party considers that the subject of a dispute has adverse effects on it, it may resort to the normal dispute settlement procedures. Where possible, the original Panel hears this submission also.

9. See also Daniel C. Esty, "Environmental Governance at the WTO: Outreach to Civil Society", in Gary P. Sampson and W. Bradnee Chambers (eds), *Trade, Environment and the Millennium*, 2nd edn, Tokyo: United Nations University Press, 2002, pp. 119–144.

10. See GATT, *Working Party Report on "Border Tax Adjustments"*, Geneva: GATT, L/3464, 2 December 1970. For a comprehensive discussion of the report, see WTO, *Taxes and Charges for Environmental Purposes: Border Tax Adjustment*, Geneva: WTO Secretariat, WT/CTE/W/47, 2 May 1997.

11. See the GATT, *United States – Taxes on Petroleum and Certain Imported Substances*, Panel Report, BISD 34S/136, 17 June 1987, para. 5.2.5.

12. For a discussion see WTO, *Report of the Committee on Trade and Environment to Singapore Ministerial Conference*, Geneva: WTO Secretariat, WT/CTE/1, 12 November 1996.

13. WTO, *Taxes and Charges for Environmental Purposes: Border Tax Adjustment*.

14. Such taxes include consumption taxes on capital equipment, auxiliary materials and services used in the transportation and production of other taxable goods (e.g. taxes on advertising, energy, machinery and transport).

15. See GATT, *Working Party Report on "Border Tax Adjustments"*, para. 18.

16. WTO, *Japan – Alcoholic Beverages*, Appellate Body Report, WT/DS8,10,11/AB/R, adopted 1 November 1996, p. 114, fn 58.

17. This example and question are presented in Donald H. Regan, "Regulatory Purpose and '*Like Products*' in Article III:4 of the GATT (with Additional Remarks on Article III:2)", *Journal of World Trade*, Vol. 36, 2002, pp. 443–478.

18. Robert E. Hudec, "GATT/WTO Constraints on National Regulation: Requiem for an

'Aim and Effects' Test", 1998; reprinted in Robert E. Hudec, *Essays on the Nature of International Trade Law*, London: Cameron May, 1999, pp. 359–395.

19. Ibid., p. 371.
20. This second improvement has the added advantage of bringing Article III analysis in line with the analytical framework of the Sanitary and Phytosanitary Measures and Technical Barriers to Trade Agreements, both of which had adopted a one-stage test of violation in which the question of regulatory justification is treated simultaneously with the issue of protective trade effects. These Agreements are addressed in the next chapter.
21. Hudec, "GATT/WTO Constraints on National Regulation", p. 381, emphasis added.
22. *EC-Asbestos*, Appellate Body Report and Panel Report.
23. *EC-Asbestos*, Panel Report, para. 8.188.
24. Roessler, "Diverging Domestic Policies and Multilateral Trade Integration".
25. *Korea – Measures Affecting Imports of Fresh, Chilled and Frozen Beef*, Appellate Body Report, WT/DS161/AB/R, WT/DS169/AB/R, adopted 10 January 2001, fn 49, paras. 166 and 163.
26. Ibid., para. 162.
27. GATT, *United States – Restrictions on Imports of Tuna [Tuna-Dolphin]*, DS 21/R, circulated 3 September 1991, not adopted.
28. *United States – Import Prohibition of Certain Shrimp and Shrimp Products [Shrimp-Turtle]*, Panel Report, WT/DS58/R, circulated 15 May 1998, and Appellate Body Report, WT/DS58/AB/R, circulated 12 October 1998. See also Lorand Bartels, "Article XX of GATT and the Problem of Extraterritorial Jurisdiction: The Case of Trade Measures for the Protection of Human Rights", *Journal of World Trade*, Vol. 36, No. 2, 2002, pp. 353–403.
29. Report of the United Nations Conference on Environment and Development, Annex 1, *Rio Declaration on Environment and Development*, Rio de Janeiro, 3–14 June 1992, Principle 15.
30. Philippe Sands, "'Unilateralism', Values and International Law", *Environmental Journal of International Law*, Vol. 11, No. 2, 2000, p. 296.
31. *European Communities – Measures Concerning Meat and Meat Products [EC-Hormones]*, WT/DS26/AB/R, WT/DS48/AB/R, adopted 16 January 1998, para. 123.
32. Because there was no trade in turtles in this case, the Convention on International Trade in Endangered Species could not be resorted to.
33. *Shrimp-Turtle*, Panel Report, para. 159.
34. WTO, *Minutes of Meeting of the Dispute Settlement Body*, Geneva: WTO Secretariat, WT/DSB/M/50, 14 December 1998, p. 1.
35. See GATT, *United States – Taxes on Petroleum and Certain Imported Substances*, Panel Report, BISD 34S/136, 17 June 1987.
36. See WTO, *Minutes of Meeting of the Dispute Settlement Body*, WT/DSB/M/50, p. 11.
37. Ibid., p. 4.
38. Ibid., p. 10.
39. *Shrimp-Turtle*, Appellate Body Report, para. 161.
40. Ibid., para. 164.
41. Ibid., para. 5.24.
42. Sands, "'Unilateralism', Values and International Law", pp. 303–307.
43. Hudec, "GATT/WTO Constraints on National Regulation".
44. John H. Jackson, "Comments on Shrimp/Turtle and the Product/Process Distinction", *Environmental Journal of International Law*, Vol. 11, No. 2, 2000, pp. 291–302.
45. See comments by Malaysia, India, Pakistan and others in WTO, *Minutes of Meeting of the Dispute Settlement Body*, WT/DSB/M/50.
46. Regan, "Regulatory Purpose and '*Like Products*' in Article III:4 of the GATT".

47. For a well-researched and instructive explanation of this process, coupled with some constructive proposals on how to proceed in the future, see Claude E. Barfield, *Free Trade, Sovereignty, Democracy: The Future of the World Trade Organisation*, Washington D.C.: American Enterprise Institute Press, 2001.
48. Sands, "'Unilateralism', Values and International Law", p. 301.
49. See Martin, "Trade, Environment and the Need for Change".
50. This proposal is further elaborated in Gary P. Sampson, *Trade, Environment and the WTO: The Post Seattle Agenda*, Washington D.C.: Overseas Development Center and Johns Hopkins University Press, 2000.
51. Roessler, "Diverging Domestic Policies and Trade Integration".

5

WTO Agreements and standards

Introduction

With the passage of time, the importance of standards and their potential impact on international trade have increased in tandem with incomes and public awareness about the protection of public health and the environment and other matters of economic and social concern. One outcome of this has been a growth in mandatory technical regulations, voluntary standards, and conformity assessment procedures to verify the conformity of products and processes with technical regulations. With more sophisticated standards, the complexity of regulations has also increased, along with the opportunity for these to be used for protectionist purposes. Further, as conventional trade barriers such as tariffs and quotas are progressively reduced, the risk that countries will resort to standards and regulations for purely protectionist purposes may well increase. Because standards may be designed to undermine market access concessions and create unnecessary obstacles to trade, there is an undisputed role for the World Trade Organization (WTO) in protecting market access concessions. However, defining precisely what that role is raises many complex issues. Thus, the question has been put of whether free trade requires the adoption of common standards across trading partners. Is harmonization of standards a precondition for open markets?

One important consideration is that standards will differ across countries for very good reasons. Physical conditions will differ, meaning different absorptive capacities for air pollution, different effects from water run-off on levels of artesian water basins, and different implications of timber cutting for deforestation and desertification. However, even if physical conditions are identical across countries, and the same risks to the environment are present, societies will still wish to manage these risks differently.[1] From a trade policy perspective, to accommodate this reality means providing for the autonomy of governments to adopt legitimate measures necessary to meet their national requirements, while ensuring that these measures are not disguised restrictions on trade. But which measures are legitimate and who decides on legitimacy? Of course, if all countries adopt the same standards and measures, there should be no controversy over legitimacy. Here lies the attraction (recognized in WTO Agreements) of countries adopting common international standards. But the reality is that international standards do not exist to meet all situations, and international standards do not meet the needs of all countries.

The key WTO Agreements dealing with standards are the Agreement on Technical Barriers to Trade (TBT) and the Agreement on Sanitary and Phytosanitary Measures (SPS). Neither Agreement obliges countries to adopt minimum standards. They do, however, create rules that are to be respected to ensure that market access rights are not undermined through regulations that are disguised restrictions on trade. They also recognize that, for many reasons, common standards, far from being barriers to trade, work to promote trade.

The plurilateral 1979 Agreement on Technical Barriers to Trade – also called the Standards Code – was one of the outcomes of the Tokyo Round of multilateral negotiations and was an important step in dealing with standards that could be unnecessary non-tariff barriers to trade. This Code permitted signatories to introduce regulations to fulfil legitimate objectives, including the protection of human, animal or plant health, the protection of the environment, animal welfare, religious considerations, and national security motives. With the growing importance of standards in trade, it was thought important to refine the Standards Code in the Uruguay Round and create an expanded and clearer set of rules. The outcome was the WTO Agreement on Technical Barriers to Trade.

Prior to the entry into force of the WTO, members could impose and maintain GATT-inconsistent measures necessary for the protection of human, animal and plant life or health under the Exceptions provision (Article XX) of the GATT. Given the increasing complexity of SPS measures, it was thought that, in the absence of clearer and more detailed rules, governments might well resort to SPS measures to shield domestic industries from competition and to frustrate attempts to liberalize trade in agriculture. The objective was to flesh out Article XX(b) and to establish a new, comprehensive set of norms for the adoption and maintenance of SPS measures. The Sanitary and Phytosanitary Agreement emerged from the Uruguay Round.

Both the TBT and SPS Agreements seek to strike a balance – to avoid *unnecessary* trade-restricting measures while recognizing the sovereign right of governments to adopt whatever standards are appropriate to fulfil legitimate objectives. But striking this balance is not a simple task and difficult questions quickly emerge. In this chapter, I discuss the relevant background to the two Agreements and review how domestic policy alternatives relating to the application of standards – often of primary importance for sustainable development – are circumscribed. As in chapter 4, I examine the extent to which discretion is available in the WTO legal processes in the interpretation of a number of key terms. The focus is the identification of some policy considerations that may be important in the context of sustainable development.

Sanitary and Phytosanitary Measures

All countries maintain measures to ensure that food is safe for consumers and to prevent the spread of pests or diseases among animals and plants.[2] Sanitary (human and animal health) and phytosanitary (plant health) measures apply to domestically produced food or local animal and plant diseases, as well as to products coming from other countries. Although such measures may by their very nature result in restrictions on trade, all governments accept that such trade restrictions may be necessary. However, measures introduced for health reasons can be very effective protectionist devices and, because of their technical complexity, a particularly deceptive and difficult barrier to challenge. The aim of the Agreement on Sanitary and Phytosanitary Measures (SPS) is to maintain the sovereign right of any government to provide the level of health protection it deems appropriate, but to ensure that these sovereign rights are not misused for protectionist purposes and do not result in unnecessary barriers to international trade.[3]

What is particularly important in this respect is that the SPS Agreement explicitly recognizes members' sovereign rights to take appropriate national measures, bringing an important change to how SPS measures are dealt with compared with GATT practices. WTO members now have the *right* to take origin-specific SPS measures necessary for the protection of human, animal or plant life or health without seeking a justification under the Exceptions Article XX(b). As a consequence, the burden of proof is on the complaining member to prove that the measure does not comply with the SPS Agreement. However, the SPS Agreement does not compel a member to accept any particular level of protection – higher or lower – than the one it has chosen, even if a lower level of protection would result in less trade restriction. It provides national authorities with a framework to develop their domestic policies and set their own standards, which normally include substantial safety margins as a precautionary measure. However, in order to be consistent with the WTO, once a government has determined its appropriate level of sanitary and phytosanitary protection it should not choose a measure that is more stringent and trade restrictive than necessary. Thus, the evaluation of risk is important in determining the measure, whose effects should be proportional to the risk.

Very different conditions prevail across countries and require different SPS measures to deal with them. The SPS Agreement addresses this problem via the use of *harmonized* SPS measures based on international standards developed by the relevant international organizations. There is a presumption of consistency with the SPS Agreement for such standards, which offers considerable encouragement for members to make their SPS measures conform with international standards. Another important consideration is that members have the right to use SPS measures that result in a higher level of protection than would be achieved by measures based on international standards. This option is significant in that it recognizes members' right to choose their own level of SPS protection – an important principle in the SPS Agreement.

Although harmonization around international standards is encouraged, adoption of these standards is not mandatory. The choice of a level of protection is viewed as a sovereign decision and accorded substantial deference in the SPS Agreement.[4] Thus, the SPS Agreement defines international standards, guidelines and recommendations to be those set by the Codex Alimentarius Commission in the area of food safety; the International Office of Epizootics in the area of animal health; the International Plant Protection Convention in the area of plant health; and other relevant international organizations open for membership to all WTO members. Each of these organizations follows its own procedures in setting standards on the basis of standard scientific information from risk assessments. These standards are in fact *voluntary*; they do not become *mandatory* by being specified in the SPS Agreement.[5] Importantly, a government is not obliged to adopt an international standard that leads to a level of health protection higher or lower than it deems to be appropriate, and, in reality, international standards are often higher than the national requirements.

The specific mention of non-consensus-based standards in the WTO as a justification for the adoption of standards presents an interesting precedent. It introduces a degree of flexibility into a consensus-based organization where consensus may be difficult to achieve, places decisions in the hands of experts, and deflects potential criticism of the WTO processes and decisions elsewhere. There is a strong incentive for countries to harmonize their standards because, although the standards are not explicitly mandatory, by adopting them the WTO member is presumed to be in full compliance with the SPS Agreement.

Although WTO members have the right to choose higher levels of protection than are provided for in international standards, there is a balancing obligation. The SPS Agreement calls for such measures to be based on scientific data. If a country does not adopt an international standard because of its own specific requirements – or because a standard simply does not exist – it must conduct its own risk assessment and determine its *acceptable level of risk* and provide *sufficient scientific evidence* of the existence of the risk. This raises a number of issues relating to interpretation.

By applying only to sanitary and phytosanitary measures, the SPS Agreement has extended the reach of WTO disciplines well beyond those of the GATT-1947. This has important implications. One classic example relates to a 1989 ban by the European Communities (EC) on meat products treated with hormones in order to promote growth. The European Communities maintained that the human consumption of hormone-treated beef had carcinogenic effect. Prior to the entry into force of the SPS Agreement, the European measure could not be challenged under the GATT because the only applicable GATT obligation was national treatment. If the regulation was origin neutral but more burdensome for the United States exporters – de facto discrimination – it would have had to be shown that the aim of the measure was to provide protection to domestic producers (see chapter 4).[6] Under the SPS Agreement, members are required to ensure that any sanitary or phytosanitary measure is applied only to the extent *necessary* (a familiar GATT term, which is open to interpretation) to protect human, animal or plant life or health, is based on scientific principles, and is not maintained without *sufficient scientific evidence* (a new term found in the SPS Agreement). The requirement of "sufficient scientific evidence" is now crucial for determining the necessity of contested SPS measures.

Thus, not surprisingly, the first test to which the SPS Agreement was put was indeed the *EC-Hormones* case. In this instance, the Appellate Body ruled that there was insufficient scientific evidence for the European Communities to maintain its ban on imports. In this context, it is important that insufficient scientific evidence does not preclude governments from acting with precaution and taking provisional measures while waiting for the conclusive results of scientific analyses. Following the scare in 1996 relating to bovine spongiform encephalopathy ("mad cow disease"), and in the absence of sufficient scientific evidence, several emergency bans were introduced in the European Communities.

In the *EC-Hormones* case, however, the European Communities had categorized its SPS measure as final, rather than provisional, and as such was relying on the Precautionary Principle outside the framework of the SPS Agreement. The Directive was a definitive regulation, which appealed to the Precautionary Principle as a general customary rule of international law, or at least a general principle of law, applicable to the interpretation of the scientific disciplines in the SPS Agreement. The Precautionary Principle is, of course, central to a number of multilateral environment agreements (see chapter 6). The European Communities was restricting the importation of hormone-treated beef when scientific risk assessments could not take account of the fear of society about the potential risk involved. In fact, the Appellate Body did not reach any conclusion on whether the Precautionary Principle had crystallized to become a general principle of law,[7] but it noted that, although the Agreement allows members to adopt provisional SPS measures, this is a qualified exemption that should not be read in an overly broad and flexible manner. Whereas the Appellate Body was prepared to consider both "hard" and "soft" law in forming its judgement in the *Shrimp-Turtle* case, it was not prepared to consider the Precautionary Principle in the same manner in the *EC-Hormones* case.

Apart from the provisional application of measures, a number of aspects of the Precautionary Principle are apparent in different forms in the provisions and interpretation of the SPS Agreement.[8] As noted, the Agreement explicitly recognizes the right of members to establish their own appropriate level of sanitary protection, which may be higher (i.e. more precautionary) than that in existing international standards. Also, the view of the Appellate Body is that responsible, representative governments commonly act from *perspectives of prudence and precaution* where risks of irreversible, e.g. life-terminating, damage to human health are concerned.[9] Often rulings are relevant. In the *EC-Asbestos* case, the Appellate Body noted "that it is undisputed that WTO Members have the right to determine the level of protection of health that they consider appropriate in a given situation".[10]

Indeed, the rights of members to determine the level of protection they want, and to act with prudence on the basis of minority opinion, have been recognized by the Appellate Body. A responsible and representative government may act in good faith on the basis of what, at a given time, may be a *divergent* opinion coming from qualified and respected sources. In justifying a measure under Article XX(b) of the GATT-1994, "a Member may also rely, in good faith, on scientific sources which, at that time, may represent a divergent, but qualified and respected, opinion. A Member is not obliged, in setting health policy, automatically to follow what, at a given time, may constitute a majority scientific opinion."[11] Further, the more serious the risks, the easier it will be to prove "sufficient scientific evidence". In the *EC-Asbestos* case, the Appellate Body ruled that the more vital or important the common interests or values pursued, the easier it would be to accept as necessary measures designed to achieve those ends (see chapter 4).[12]

There is also flexibility because risks can be managed in alternative ways. Although measures should not be more trade restrictive than required to achieve their appropriate level of protection, this is a restriction on the choice of measure, not on the level of protection. Further, a measure is more trade restrictive than required only if there is another SPS measure that is *reasonably available*, achieves the member's chosen level of sanitary protection, and is *significantly less trade restrictive* than the contested measure. Thus, WTO members have the prerogative to set their own level of protection and cannot be required to lower it even if less trade-restrictive alternatives exist. That the available alternative measure be significantly less trade restrictive means that a small difference in the trade impact of the two measures is not sufficient to oblige a member to adopt the alternative measure.

Technical Barriers to Trade

The Uruguay Round Technical Barriers to Trade (TBT) Agreement addresses mandatory regulations and voluntary standards other than those covered by the SPS Agreement.[13] It also addresses conformity assessment procedures. The Agreement states that no country should be prevented from taking measures necessary for the protection of human, animal, and plant life or health, of the environment, or for the prevention of deceptive practices, at the levels it considers appropriate.[14] The list of legitimate policy goals is open-ended. In pursuing these objectives, the Agreement takes into account divergences of taste, income, geography and other factors between countries, and thereby accords flexibility in the preparation, adoption and application of national technical regulations.

Like the SPS Agreement, the TBT Agreement is designed to achieve an important balance between avoiding unnecessary obstacles to trade while ensuring that members retain sufficient regulatory autonomy to achieve their domestic policy goals. An excessively restrictive application of the TBT Agreement would undermine members' pursuit of legitimate policy interests, whereas a loose application could mean that technical regulations might be used for protectionist purposes, and the gains members have achieved through progressive rounds of tariff reductions might be lost.

The Agreement draws a distinction between standards and technical regulations, on the basis of compliance and enforcement. If mandatory regulations are not complied with, then a product cannot be sold in a given market. Standards, on the other hand, are voluntary, and no product can be stopped at the border or refused access to the domestic market because of non-compliance with standards. However, imports that do not comply with voluntary standards but are allowed into the market may be shunned by consumers, so that the standards have the same effect as mandatory regulations. Adherence to standards may be a precondition for acceptability by consumers.[15] For this reason the Code of Good Practice for the Preparation, Adoption and Application of Standards – an Annex to the TBT Agreement – is potentially important in dealing with standards that are in effect trade restrictions. Through the Code, most of the principles applied by the TBT Agreement to technical regulations apply to standards. All governmental and non-governmental standardizing bodies, at the national and regional levels, are invited to accept to Code.

Like the SPS Agreement, the TBT Agreement encourages WTO members to use internationally recognized standards or conformity assessment guides as a basis for their own regulations and procedures. Their use is presumed not to constitute an unnecessary barrier to trade. Nevertheless, like the SPS Agreement, the TBT Agreement acknowledges that there are good reasons for mandatory regulations and voluntary standards to differ between countries. Unlike the SPS Agreement, the TBT Agreement does not require sufficient scientific evidence to justify a technical regulation that differs from an international standard, although, in verifying that measures are no more restrictive than necessary, scientific evidence may be called for.

Technical regulations must not be more trade restrictive than necessary to achieve a policy goal and fulfil a legitimate objective. The concepts of "necessary" and "legitimate objective" are crucial in the interpretation of the Agreement. As noted above, a non-exclusive list of legitimate objectives is cited in the Agreement.

The concept of necessity has not been interpreted through legal proceedings involving the TBT Agreement. Its interpretation will, however, most probably be influenced by past experience with the GATT-1994 and the General Exceptions Article XX. Past jurisprudence indicates that a measure can be considered "necessary" only if there is no alternative measure consistent with the GATT, and which a government could "reasonably" be expected to employ to achieve its legitimate objective. The term "reasonably" will also be influenced by past experience. In this respect, the Appellate Body has found that a determination of whether a

WTO-consistent alternative measure is reasonably available requires a "weighing and balancing process" in which an assessment is made about whether the alternative measure "contributes to the realization of the end pursued".[16] As noted earlier, the more "vital or important" the common interests or values pursued, the easier it would be to accept the measures designed to achieve those ends as "necessary".[17]

The relevance of the TBT Agreement for sustainable development is clear. The largest number of technical regulations and standards are adopted with a view to protecting the environment or human safety or health. An important empirical question is to what extent these technical regulations differ from international standards, and for what reasons. Some evidence can be gathered from the fact that, under the TBT Agreement, technical regulations are to be notified if they differ from international standards and have an important effect on international trade. As part of the notification process, the objective of the measure must be identified. One way of approaching the question of the extent to which technical regulations differ from international standards and for what reasons is to examine the notifications that have been made to the WTO Secretariat under various WTO Agreements. Although far from all technical regulations are notified to the Secretariat, the data are nevertheless instructive.

There were 2224 notifications under the various WTO Agreements in 2000.[18] Of these, 651 were under the TBT Agreement, 15.6 per cent of which identified protection of the environment as the main – or one of the main – purposes for notifying. Interestingly, the share of total notifications for environmental purposes more than doubled between 2000 and 2004. The principal areas where regulations differed from international standards included waste management, energy efficiency, providing for environmental management systems, eco-taxes, and soil, water and air pollution.[19]

Does it matter that so many environmental standards differ? The answer is both yes and no. Ostensibly the problems are limited because there has been only one dispute panel addressing whether the obligations of the TBT Agreement have been breached. Nevertheless, one-third of the requests for consultations under the Dispute Settlement Understanding cite a violation of the TBT Agreement. Yet, by the stage of the Panel process, references to the TBT Agreement have been dropped[20] because other general WTO obligations that have been well tested in other disputes can be cited instead (including national treatment and most favoured nation treatment). Testing the TBT Agreement is perhaps avoided given the lack of precedent and possibly unpredictable outcomes.

The TBT Agreement provides for both national treatment and MFN treatment, and it requires that imported products are to be accorded treatment no less favourable than that accorded to *like products* of national origin in respect of technical regulations and voluntary standards. However, domestic regulations may well apply to both the product and the manner in which it was produced. In the context of these Agreements, the question needs to be addressed of whether the importing country can require the same process requirements of the importers as of national producers. If process regulations and standards (such as labelling relating to life-cycle production) are covered by the Agreement, then the disciplines of the Agreement apply.[21] Some members are presumably of the view that this is the case, because they have notified certain process-related regulations, including eco-labelling schemes.[22] If the notification obligations apply – as would the national treatment and MFN obligations – imports would have to meet the same process requirements as domestically produced goods.

To say the least, uncertainty surrounds whether or not the TBT Agreement extends to process-related technical regulations and standards. The controversy turns on the ambiguous definitions of "technical regulations" and "standards". For the Agreement, a technical regulation is defined as a document that lays down product characteristics, or their related processes and production methods, and with which compliance is mandatory. A standard is a document that provides for characteristics of products or related processes and production methods, and with which compliance is not mandatory.

In the case of technical regulations, "related" should be read as "incorporated in" the final product. Thus, mandatory regulations apply to products when there is evidence of the process in the final product. If carbon residues are apparent in products that were produced with an energy-intensive process, then this process is *related to* the product and the production method, and therefore can be the object of a technical regulation. If there are no carbon residues, then this cannot be specified as part of the regulation (e.g. for labelling purposes). Of course, governments can require whatever regulation they wish for the purposes of domestic production. This is consistent with the notion of like products, with likeness not being determined by production methods.

The question that has led to controversy relates to the definition of standards, compared with that of technical regulations. In the case of the definition of technical regulations, there is specific reference to "their" related processes and production methods. This is absent in the definition of standards. Does the absence of "their" mean that standards that relate only to the processes that produced the good – and are not a characteristic of the final product – are covered by the Agreement and therefore subject to its disciplines? The WTO Secretariat conducted an exhaustive inquiry into the negotiating history of the coverage of the TBT Agreement. It concluded that, for mandatory regulations, the situation is clear. If the production method is *related* to the product, it is apparent in the product that emerges from the production process and can be specified as a technical regulation. Similarly, standards based on processes and production methods (PPMs) that are evident in the final characteristics of a product are clearly covered by the TBT Agreement. They are therefore subject to the requirement of being applied in conformity with the disciplines of the Agreement. Importantly, the study concluded that standards based on production processes that are unrelated to a product's final characteristics are *probably* not covered by the TBT Agreement.[23] What are the implications of this conclusion? Problems could arise in those situations where process-based standards are covered by the TBT Agreement but are inconsistent with it, or where they are not covered by the Agreement and are inconsistent with GATT-1994 rules (such as national treatment).

The provisions of the GATT and WTO are considered by many to be arcane and unnecessarily complicated, with textual differences that are feverishly discussed but are of little practical significance. It is not at all difficult to sympathize with this view. Nevertheless, in the final analysis, the answers to the questions posed above are critical for WTO acceptability of regulations that relate to sustainable development. Eco-labelling provides a good example. Eco-labels are normally voluntary standards that apply not to the physical characteristics of the product but rather to the production process – the manner in which tuna are harvested or tropical timber is logged, rather than the quality of the tuna or the hardness of the wood. Are they subject to the disciplines of the TBT Agreement, and, if so, what are the implications? Is this a good thing or a bad thing – and from whose perspective?

One presumption could be that, if process-based standards were covered by the TBT Agreement, they would be consistent with it as long as the other obligations of the Agreement were met. Many developing countries resist this approach. They argue that, even if standards based on unincorporated production processes were covered by the TBT Agreement, they should be considered as actionable under other GATT rules because this would be inconsistent with the GATT/WTO interpretation of "like products". Any other interpretation would mean that preferred domestic production standards – via, for example, labelling requirements – were being imposed extraterritorially, which would be an infringement of national sovereignty. The developing countries' concern is a systemic one. If process-based standards are considered to be covered by the TBT Agreement – which has advantages, such as greater transparency of the schemes and their notification – this creates a precedent for the acceptability of non-product-related production methods from a WTO perspective. This is something that most – if not all – developing countries wish to avoid (see also chapter 3).[24]

If voluntary and mandatory process-based standards are not covered by the TBT Agreement and are actionable under the GATT-1994, this has far-reaching practical implications, particularly for regulations based on the life-cycle approach. The very *raison d'être* of such schemes is to distinguish between products according to the manner in which they have been produced (i.e. in an environmentally friendly or unfriendly manner). The view of the TBT Committee is that labelling is an important market-based and positive response to many health and environmental problems. And WTO members have specifically acknowledged the positive aspects of eco-labelling schemes.[25] However, an ongoing and important practical manifestation of the potential problems relating to interpretation has emerged in recent meetings of the TBT Committee, where it has been argued that labelling products derived from genetically modified organisms is inconsistent with the WTO interpretation of like products. The United States and Canada have expressed concern over the EU regulation on the labelling of products containing genetically modified soya or maize. The European Union requires foodstuffs and food ingredients containing traces of modified DNA or protein to be labelled as "produced with genetically modified soya/maize". The United States and Canada argued that such labels were unnecessary technical barriers to trade since no scientific reason exists to differentiate foodstuffs produced with genetically modified crops. The United States also questioned the feasibility of developing reliable and commercially practical tests for detecting DNA or protein resulting from genetic modification.

Conclusion

Risk management can open the door to abuse and create arbitrary and unjustified restrictions on trade and commerce. The avoidance of unjustified and discriminatory barriers to trade is central to WTO Agreements and disciplines. The challenge facing WTO members in implementing the various Agreements is to provide the necessary flexibility for governments to pursue whatever domestic policies they think are appropriate, without the associated measures being used as disguised or unnecessary barriers to trade. This difficult task has already led to a great deal of controversy in the WTO. Matters are further complicated by the fact that not only is scientific evidence inconclusive in some instances, but public perceptions of certain risks and how they should be managed can differ considerably between WTO member countries.

What is certain is that the WTO should not be the arbitrator on matters well outside the realm of conventional trade policy considerations without this position being agreed to in advance. It is not reasonable to expect to find solutions requiring multilateral agreement in the case of disputes involving food safety or public health that cannot be settled bilaterally. Nor should the problem be relegated to a dispute settlement process in which trade officials take decisions on a de facto basis that will almost by definition (because there is no agreement at the national level) be unpopular with large parts of the public. The way to deal with the problem must be discussed in the context of policy choices relating to the use of the Precautionary Principle. Where scientific evidence alone does not make the policy choices clear, there must be a coherent approach.

A closely related problem concerns the condition under which a WTO member can legally label a product according to how it was manufactured. When preferences differ between consumers for products that are physically the same but produced differently, should consumers be free to differentiate through reference to product labels? WTO rules apply to labelling. The situation may arise where the application of WTO rules means that goods about which some public interest groups are highly suspicious are traded freely because of a lack of scientific evidence to prove they are harmful. At the same time, through a WTO ruling that a proposed labelling scheme is illegal, these groups may be denied what they consider to be a possible solution. From the public perspective, the WTO could be seen as the source of the problem and blocking the solution at the same time. Labelling is increasingly likely to be an issue for goods with enormous commercial value. The WTO rules on labelling are quite unclear and should be clarified as a priority. The uncertainty that surrounds their application will bring unpredictability to commercial operations – the very thing the WTO was designed to avoid.

Notes

1. Standards will differ across countries for both objective and subjective reasons. Countries have not only different production functions, but also different utility functions and indifference curves, and therefore different priorities for internalizing externalities.
2. These sanitary and phytosanitary measures can take many forms, such as requiring products to come from a disease-free area, inspection of products, specific treatment or processing of products, the setting of allowable maximum levels of pesticide residues, or permitted use of only certain additives in food.
3. For a detailed description, see WTO, *Sanitary and Phytosanitary Measures*, WTO Agreement Series No. 4, Geneva: WTO Secretariat, 1998. For a useful analysis of the SPS Agreement, see UNCTAD, *Course on Dispute Settlement – SPS Measures*, UNCTAD series on Dispute Settlement No. 3.9, Geneva: UNCTAD Secretariat, 2003.

4. "The right of a Member to establish its own level of sanitary protection under Article 3.3 of the SPS Agreement is an autonomous right and not an 'exception' from a 'general obligation' under Article 3.1." *European Communities – Measures Concerning Meat and Meat Products [EC-Hormones]*, WT/DS26/AB/R, WT/DS48/AB/R, adopted 16 January 1998, para. 172.

5. The Codex does not represent a consensus-based standard for minimum residue levels of growth-promoting hormones, since it was adopted by a vote of 33–29, with 7 abstentions.

6. Steve Charnovitz, "The World Trade Organization, Meat Hormones and Food Safety", *International Trade Reporter*, 15 October 1998, and Steve Charnovitz, "Improving the Agreement on Sanitary and Phytosanitary Standards", in Gary P. Sampson and W. Bradnee Chambers (eds), *Trade, Environment, and the Millennium*, 2nd edn, Tokyo: United Nations University Press, 2002, pp. 207–234.

7. The Appellate Body in *EC-Hormones* stated, "The status of the precautionary principle in international law continues to be the subject of debate among academics, law practitioners, regulators and judges.... We consider, however, that it is unnecessary, and probably imprudent, for the Appellate Body in this appeal to take a position on this important, but abstract, question." *EC-Hormones*, para. 123.

8. Similar "expressions" of the Precautionary Principle exist in the TBT Agreement and in Article XX of the GATT.

9. *EC-Hormones*, para. 123.

10. *European Communities – Measures Affecting Asbestos and Asbestos-Containing Product [EC-Asbestos]*, Appellate Body Report and Panel Report, WT/DS135, adopted 5 April 2001, para. 148.

11. Ibid., para. 178.

12. Ibid., para. 162.

13. For a useful and insightful overview of the TBT Agreement, see UNCTAD, *Course on Dispute Settlement – Technical Barriers to Trade*, UNCTAD series on Dispute Settlement No. 3.10, Geneva: UNCTAD Secretariat, 2003.

14. Thus, the Agreement applies to a diverse range of measures, many of which may be health or environment related. Examples include the labelling of cigarettes to indicate that they are harmful to health, and regulations intended to ensure that animal or plant species endangered by water, air and soil pollution do not become extinct. Regulations may be adopted requiring that endangered species of fish reach a certain length before they can be caught, that paper and plastic products are recycled, or that the levels of motor vehicle emissions are limited.

15. For example, some consumers may shun an energy-intensive air-conditioning system that has not met a voluntary standard for energy consumption. Most technical regulations and standards are aimed at protecting human safety or health. Examples abound: requirements that motor vehicles carry reflective devices to prevent road accidents; labelling requirements for drugs and alcoholic beverages; electric insulation requirements; car emission standards; limits on the use of certain dyeing and tanning materials.

16. *Korea – Measures Affecting Imports of Fresh, Chilled and Frozen Beef*, Appellate Body Report, WT/DS161/AB/R, WT/DS169/AB/R, adopted 10 January 2001, paras. 166 and 163.

17. Ibid., para 162.

18. See WTO, *Provisions of the Multilateral Trading System with Respect to the Transparency of Trade Measures Used for Environmental Purposes and Environmental Measures and Requirements That Have Significant Trade Effects: Note by the Secretariat*, Geneva: WTO Secretariat, WT/CTE/W/195, 20 June 2001.

19. By way of comparison, 32 of the 133 notifications under the Subsidies and Countervailing Measures Agreement were environment related, covering programmes such as waste management, incentives for pollution control, and environmental subsidies for pollution prevention. In the case of the Agreement on Agriculture, 40 of the 229 notifications related to environment measures, including domestic support for research, payments for soil conservation, promotion of the sustainable use of natural resources, and payments for environmentally friendly wine-growing methods.

20. The complaint by Canada lodged against France relating to asbestos standards – *EC-Asbestos* – is an example.

21. Thus, a standard relating to fuel for a motor vehicle would not take into account the process used to produce the fuel unless the characteristics of the product were affected. Mineral fuels and ethanol can have the same standards with respect to chemical composition. The fact that one is the product of a biological process is relevant only if the chemical composition of the fuel is affected.

22. Eco-labelling schemes are usually voluntary programmes under which a label is awarded to environmentally friendlier products based on an environmental assessment of all phases of a product's life cycle, including production, use and disposal.

23. The Secretariat also noted that, towards the end of the Uruguay Round negotiations, some delegations proposed changing the language contained in the "definitions" in Annex 1 of the Agreement to make it unambiguous that only PPMs related to product characteristics were to be covered by the Agreement. Although no participant is on record as having opposed that objective, at that late stage of the negotiations it did not prove possible to find a consensus on the proposal. See WTO, *Negotiating History of the Coverage of the Agreement on Technical Barriers to Trade with Regard to Labelling Requirements, Voluntary Standards and Processes and Production Methods Unrelated to Product Characteristics*, Geneva: WTO Secretariat, WT/CTE/W/10, 29 August 1995.

24. For a discussion of these points and other aspects of the relationship of eco-labelling to the TBT Agreement, see Doaa Abdel Motaal, "The Agreement on Technical Barriers to Trade, the Committee on Trade and Environment, and Eco-Labelling", in Gary P. Sampson and W. Bradnee Chambers (eds), *Trade, Environment, and the Millennium*, 2nd edn, Tokyo: United Nations University Press, 2002, pp. 267–286.

25. In its conclusions and recommendations to the 1996 Singapore Ministerial Conference, the Committee on Trade and Environment stated: "Well-designed eco-labelling schemes/programmes can be effective instruments of environmental policy to encourage the development of an environmentally conscious consumer public." WTO, *Report of the Committee on Trade and Environment*, Geneva: WTO Secretariat, WT/CTE/1, November 1996.

6

MEAs, the WTO and sustainable development

Introduction

Since its establishment, one of the most actively discussed topics in the World Trade Organization (WTO) has been the relationship between its provisions and the use of trade measures in multilateral environment agreements (MEAs). The debate has centred on the possibility of a conflict arising over trade-related measures in MEAs – namely, their potential inconsistency with WTO rules – and how conflict in these rules could be avoided or dealt with.[1]

In broad perspective, it could be argued that no real problem exists. Only a small proportion of MEAs contain trade provisions, and no trade dispute has arisen in the WTO over their use. It is also argued that the WTO rules already provide for WTO-inconsistent trade measures to be taken to protect the environment, and the existing architecture of the WTO is adequate to deal with any potential problems. The counter-argument runs along the lines that uncertainty over the relationship between the two sets of rules is increasingly affecting MEA negotiations, and that this uncertainty unnecessarily exacerbates tensions between MEAs and the WTO. Additional concerns are that the objectives of some MEAs are frustrated by WTO rules. For example, the definition of patents in the WTO Agreement on Trade-Related Intellectual Property Rights (TRIPS) is seen by some to be at variance with the objectives of the Convention on Biological Diversity – on the rights of indigenous peoples; on the transfer of environmentally sound technology; and, to the extent that patents apply to life forms, on loss of biodiversity.

Although there is disagreement about the extent of the problem, there is no disagreement among WTO members that MEAs are the best way to coordinate policy action to tackle global and trans-boundary environmental problems. WTO member governments do not want the WTO to become an environment policy-making organization or environmental standards enforcement agency. Indeed, most WTO members are of the view that WTO rules permit governments to adopt whatever trade measures they wish to protect their domestic environment. When it comes to environmental problems beyond their borders, the expectation is that governments will agree to – and enforce – environmental regulations through regional or international environment agreements and not unilateral coercion through WTO-inconsistent measures.

Because the WTO and MEAs represent two different bodies of international law, it is important that the relationship between them be coherent and fully understood by all concerned. This is not, it is argued, the case at the moment. Given the importance of the global trade and environment regimes, any clash over the application of rules agreed to among nations would have unfortunate ramifications for both regimes. In my view, to remove this possibility, and to avoid the WTO being the arbiter of environmental disputes, any WTO-inconsistent measures should be clearly spelled out and agreed to by the parties to a broad-based multilateral environment agreement. Disagreement over the legality of MEA measures should then be dealt with by the compliance mechanism in the MEA itself and should not be left to interpretation by a WTO dispute Panel or the Appellate Body. For this to be a reality, there should be *effective* MEAs with a number of characteristics. If measures are to be taken for environmental purposes, then the type of measure and the circumstances in which it may be taken should be carefully spelled out, there should be broad-based support in terms of country membership, and the MEA should have a robust dispute settlement system or compliance mechanism. My argument is that effective MEAs – so defined – are critical to avoid environmental disputes gravitating towards the WTO and inhibiting the smooth functioning of the WTO itself.

Prior to the Ministerial Meeting in Doha in 2001, there was an active debate in the Committee on Trade and Environment (CTE) on the relationship between the WTO and MEAs, which culminated in ministers launching negotiations on the relationship between existing WTO rules and specific trade obligations set out in multilateral environment agreements. The negotiations are to be limited in scope to the applicability of existing WTO rules among parties to the MEA in question. There are also to be negotiations on the procedures for regular information exchange between MEA secretariats and the relevant WTO committees and on the criteria for the granting of observer status. That negotiations are called for places the relationship between WTO rules and MEAs on a higher plane of importance than discussions in the CTE.

This renewed interest in MEAs is perhaps a reaction to the commercial, political and social importance of some recent MEAs that could well have an impact on trade. The Framework Convention on Climate Change and the Kyoto Protocol provide good examples. There is also concern that the lack of clarity between WTO and MEA rules has led to confusion in the negotiation of some MEAs. The point has been made that the negotiations surrounding the Cartagena Protocol on Bio-safety, for example, proved to be difficult "precisely because of the lack of clarity with regard to the relationship of the Protocol to the WTO".[2] The renewed interest could also be due to high-profile trade and environment disputes that have come to the WTO in recent times (see chapter 4), and the recognition that they probably never would have arisen had an effective MEA been in place. An additional consideration is that the debate in the WTO has been enriched with a large amount of useful work being undertaken by reputable non-governmental organizations (NGOs), intergovernmental institutions and academics.[3]

The outline of this chapter is as follows. First I address why it is important to have clarity in MEAs when trade-related measures are provided for, as well as the consequences of any lack of clarity. A discussion of the options already available for trade-related environmental measures to be considered as exceptions to WTO rules can be found in chapter 4. In this chapter, I explore the more direct relationship between MEAs and exceptions. A review of recent experience in the WTO dispute settlement process illustrates how, in the course of settling disputes, the existence of MEAs can be beneficial to the WTO legal process. I then advance a number of policy proposals with a view to avoiding, and eventually dealing with, future disputes. The chapter closes with some policy considerations.

Unclear and inconsistent measures

At the most fundamental level, the potential problems surrounding the inconsistency of measures found in trade and environment agreements fall into just two groups. The first group covers trade-related measures taken by a party to an MEA against another party, and where the measure is *not specifically provided for* in the MEA itself. On the other hand, it is "justified" by the party taking the measure as necessary to achieve the objectives of the environment agreement. The necessity of this measure may be challenged by the party against which the measure is taken. In this case, both parties could be members of the WTO and the measure could violate WTO rights and obligations. This could lead to a dispute as to the legitimacy of the measure in terms of either the MEA or the WTO.

It seems reasonable that such a dispute should be pursued under the dispute settlement procedures of the MEA. In this respect, it would be helpful if MEA parties stipulated from the outset that they intended trade disputes arising out of the implementation of the obligations of the MEA to be settled under the MEA's provisions. It could be argued that this approach could help ensure the convergence of the objectives of MEAs and the WTO, while safeguarding their respective spheres of competence, thus overcoming problems arising from overlapping jurisdictions.

This, however, requires the MEA to have an effective compliance mechanism. As with the Dispute Settlement Understanding of the WTO, MEAs emphasize the avoidance of disputes. They include provisions to increase transparency through the collection and exchange of information, coordination of technical and scientific research, and collective monitoring of implementing measures, as well as consultation provisions. Most of the MEAs with trade-related provisions also contain mechanisms for resolving disputes, but these lack the power of the WTO dispute settlement process.[4] In the absence of an effective dispute settlement system in the MEA, the dispute could gravitate to the WTO. It has been suggested on numerous occasions in the CTE that there would be value in strengthening MEA dispute settlement mechanisms. This, of course, is outside the terms of reference of the CTE. If the measure is challenged in the WTO, trade officials have the task of determining if the measure if necessary to achieve the objectives of the environment agreement – a task that neither trade officials nor environmentalists think should fall to the WTO.

The second group of problems relates to WTO-inconsistent measures that are *specifically provided for* in an MEA and taken by a party to the MEA against a non-party. A problem may then present itself if the measure is against a WTO member that challenges the legitimacy of the measure in the WTO dispute settlement process. The party to the MEA may seek an exception for the WTO-inconsistent measures under Article XX and cite the existence of the MEA as a justification for the measure. However, the defending country might not have joined the MEA expressly because it does not agree with its provisions.

Dealing with this group of problems involves a decision by the WTO dispute settlement process about the importance to ascribe to the existence of the MEA. This is not easy. In fact, even the ostensibly simple first step of determining what is an MEA, much less which ones are important, has led to only very general definitions in the WTO, which have proved to be of little help in determining which MEAs should be assigned special importance. Definition apart, however, the likelihood of a positive decision on the necessity of the measure is presumably enhanced if the goals of the environment agreement are accepted globally in a broad-based MEA to which most, and preferably all, WTO members belong. In fact, most proposals relating to the relationship between WTO and MEA rules are based on the notion that, subject to specific conditions being met, certain trade measures taken pursuant to MEAs should benefit from special treatment under WTO provisions. This approach has been described as creating "an environmental window" in the WTO. However, determining what is an acceptable MEA from the perspective of receiving greater WTO acceptability when taking WTO-inconsistent measures has proved to be a far from simple task.

In both the cases described above, the WTO finds itself in the role of an arbiter in environment matters – a role WTO member governments have specifically stated that they do not wish to assume. In both instances, effective MEAs with precise language, broad-based membership and a robust dispute settlement process would avoid environmental matters of this nature finding their way onto the WTO agenda. If WTO members have agreed to forgo their rights not to be discriminated against when certain agreed conditions prevail, it is difficult to see how questions of inconsistency could arise.

Clarity of measures

To appreciate the potential importance for the WTO of the lack of specificity in the provision of trade measures in an MEA, it is perhaps instructive to look at a real-world situation. The United Nations Framework Convention on Climate Change (FCCC), which entered into force on 21 March 1994, is particularly instructive in this respect because the parties to the FCCC formally recognize that measures taken to address climate change problems have the potential to be used for trade protectionist purposes. In fact, in wording borrowed from the GATT-1994, the Climate Change Convention specifically states that measures taken to combat climate change, including unilateral ones, should not "constitute a means of arbitrary or unjustifiable discrimination or a disguised restriction on international trade".[5]

The Climate Change Convention does not provide for any specific trade-related measures to deal with the environment. However, in achieving the objectives of the Convention, a wide variety of measures will be taken that may well affect the costs of production of traded goods and therefore the competitive position of producers in the world market. Examples include energy, carbon and other taxes; mandatory and voluntary standards; subsidies for environmentally friendly production processes; labelling and certification schemes; and the sale and transfer of emission permits within or between groups of countries. Offsetting measures will be called for by those whose competitive position is adversely affected by cheaper imports not subject to the same measures in the country of origin, and border tax adjustment problems could arise (see chapter 4). All of these measures have potential implications for the WTO: they may violate WTO rules, or, at the least, some of the most contentious aspects of WTO concepts and rules may be pushed onto centre stage.

The Convention is – as its name indicates – a framework only, and specific provisions on the nature of the commitments by parties and legal instruments (such as compliance procedures) are elaborated in subsequent protocols. The Kyoto Protocol, for example, contains a commitment for industrial countries to reduce their collective emissions of greenhouse gases to at least 5 per cent below 1990 levels by 2008–2012. The Protocol has entered into force following ratification by 55 countries that accounted for at least 55 per cent of carbon emissions in 1990. Although the future of the climate change agreements looks uncertain, the ratification by Russia in May 2004 has ensured their entry into force.

The Kyoto Protocol provides for mechanisms through which parties can implement their emissions commitments. The signatories may take measures to promote the "progressive reduction or phasing out of market imperfections, fiscal incentives, tax and duty exemptions and subsidies in all greenhouse gas emitting sectors that run contrary to the objective of the Convention and application of market instruments". This is certainly very much in line with the WTO objective of the progressive removal of trade restrictions and distortions and, more particularly, with the discussion in the CTE of the need to remove restrictions and distortions that might adversely affect both trade and the environment; namely, the win–win scenarios discussed in chapter 3. The Protocol provides further formal assurance that the intention is to avoid the use of trade-distorting measures. As with the FCCC itself, the Kyoto Protocol does not provide for any trade measures; in fact, parties are to strive to implement policies and measures "in such a way as to minimise adverse effects … on international trade".[6]

Notwithstanding these general assurances, the Kyoto Protocol also states that each party, "in achieving its quantified emission limitation and reduction commitments … [and] in order to promote sustainable development, shall implement and/or further elaborate policies and measures in accordance with its national circumstances". These include vague objectives (in terms of acceptable measures) such as the enhancement of energy efficiency in relevant sectors, the protection and enhancement of sinks, and the promotion of sustainable forms of agriculture. Parties are to develop their national response strategies to reduce emissions, and impose environmental taxes that may well apply directly to production processes. Environmental charges and taxes are increasingly used for the pursuit of national environment policy objectives and for "internalizing" domestic environmental costs. Chapter 4 explores how WTO rules discipline the way in which governments impose internal taxes and charges on traded goods, either on imported products or when rebated on exports. When the international competitiveness of products is affected by such taxes, it would be surprising if there was not domestic pressure for them to be rebated. As I noted in chapter 4, the rebating of such taxes is one of the most sensitive areas of unresolved legal interpretation of WTO rules.

I pointed out in chapter 4 that taxes levied directly on products because of their physical characteristics are eligible for tax adjustment under WTO rules. In the case of imports, this could be the imposition on imported products of equivalent domestic taxes – domestic taxes, for example, on the same imported coal and petroleum. As far as exports are concerned, taxes could be rebated if they were levied on the product at the domestic level – for example, domestic taxes on exported coal and petroleum. This same understanding does not, however, extend to taxes paid in the process of producing the good (i.e. according to its life cycle); for example, domestic taxes applied to processes, such as indirect taxes levied because of the energy consumed or the carbon emitted in the production process.[7] Thus, a domestic tax can be applied legitimately to imported fuel, but a tax cannot be applied on the energy consumed in producing an imported ton of steel. In short, under existing WTO rules and jurisprudence, "product" taxes and charges can be adjusted at the border but "process" taxes and charges probably cannot. Since environmental taxes and charges are at least as much process oriented as product oriented, WTO rules have caused concern about the competitiveness implications for domestic producers.

This distinction also has implications for WTO obligations relating to subsidies. The rebate of taxes in one country, if it is not permitted in another, can have the same effect from a commercial perspective as a subsidy. Different views have been expressed on the likely treatment under the Agreement on Subsidies of a rebate for exported products of indirect environmental taxes on processes that are not incorporated into the characteristics of the product.

Another important consideration is that the Technical Barriers to Trade (TBT) Agreement provides flexibility by recognizing that priorities with respect to the environment differ between countries and that this can be fully reflected in domestic regulations. Therefore, it permits the adoption of different regulations by WTO members. This could relate to the amount of energy used in the production of a good, or the level of carbon emissions within national borders. If a country chose not to adopt a certain technical regulation that had an important effect on emissions reduction, this might give it a certain cost advantage over competitors in the world market. This raises a number of issues. First, the importing country cannot apply technical regulations to the processes outside its own borders. Such regulations can apply to domestic processes, but not to processes in other countries. Further, the labelling of imports with respect to production methods is certainly controversial in the WTO.[8] As noted, there is also a subsidy issue. If a country did not invoke exacting standards with respect to an energy-intensive production process, for example, would this not constitute a subsidy to the country with the lower process standards?

Where MEAs have clearly mandated the parties to take specific action against each other in agreed circumstances, the normal rules of international law and treaty interpretation would provide little room for a party to such Agreements to contest the legality of the measures on WTO grounds. If the agreed solution involves a loss of rights under the WTO (e.g. being discriminated against on the grounds of production methods) then, providing all WTO members agree to forgo those rights, it is difficult to see where there could be a problem. If measures taken to meet the objectives of the MEA are not clearly provided for in the MEA itself – both what is and what is not permitted in terms of measures to meet the objectives of the MEA – the issues to be settled may well gravitate to the WTO and could include some of the most sensitive WTO legal ambiguities.

Inconsistent measures

In general terms, measures to protect the environment can be taken by WTO members even if this means a violation of WTO rights and obligations. However, a waiver or an exception has to be sought for such measures. In the case of a waiver, this has to be with the approval of WTO members; if the measure is challenged and an exception is sought, rather strict conditions will be imposed.

Waivers

In special circumstances, a waiver can be granted to a WTO obligation, subject to approval by at least three-quarters of WTO members. This could provide a measured, case-by-case response to non-conforming measures taken for environmental purposes. It might also apply to a more general waiver, such as special treatment for all measures specifically provided for in certain MEAs. Although this process may appear attractive, it has not received general support from either trade or environment officials. There are a number of reasons for this: a waived obligation is time limited and must be renewed periodically; and a trade measure applied pursuant to a waiver could still be challenged in WTO dispute settlement on the grounds of non-violation, nullification or impairment of WTO rights.

The waiver approach could be modified to make it more attractive for environmental purposes. Provision could be made for a special "multi-year" waiver for trade measures applied pursuant to MEAs. All such measures taken under MEAs would be eligible for a waiver, provided they met specified criteria. A "negative vetting" approach could be adopted whereby the waiver would be automatically renewed if no new developments affected the exceptional circumstances that justified it in the first place. Specific trade measures contained in existing and future MEAs, whether among parties or against non-parties, could also be granted a waiver on a case-by-case basis subject to non-binding guidelines. The waiver would be extended annually until its termination, as long as the WTO requirements we met and the "exceptional circumstances" referred to in that provision covered the specific trade measures included in certain MEAs.

Since WTO members vote on waivers, presumably there would be little resistance to a waiver being accepted if there were broad-based support for the MEA, and as long as there was effective coordination between different parts of national administrations. Nevertheless, given the legal certainty sought by environmentalists, resort to any test of voting on a waiver in the WTO would probably fail to provide MEA negotiators with the required degree of security or predictability in their negotiations. Even worse, it might be seen to entail the WTO passing judgement on other international legal instruments.

Exceptions

Exceptions to WTO rules for environmental purposes are provided for in the GATT-1994 Exceptions Article (Article XX). In this Article, non-conforming measures can be taken for environmental purposes if they are necessary to protect human, animal, or plant life or health (Article XX(b)), or if they relate to the conservation of exhaustible natural resources and are made effective in conjunction with restrictions on domestic production or consumption (Article XX(g)). If at least one of these conditions is fulfilled, then the remaining requirement is specified in the

Head Note to Article XX: that the measures not be applied in an arbitrary or unjustifiable manner in order to discriminate between countries where the same conditions prevail or constitute a disguised restriction on international trade. These exceptions are discussed in detail in chapter 4.

Guidance from disputes

Some insight can be obtained in addressing the interface between MEAs and the WTO by looking at recent Panel and Appellate Body rulings. Importantly, the most informative case is one where an MEA was not in existence – the *Shrimp-Turtle* case.[9]

In that case, the Appellate Body had to determine whether a living creature should be considered to be an exhaustible natural resource. The Appellate Body ruled that, in the light of contemporary international law, living species, which are in principle renewable, "are in certain circumstances indeed susceptible of depletion, exhaustion and extinction, frequently because of human activities". In taking this decision, the existence of an MEA was critical. Because "all of the seven recognised species of sea turtles are listed in Appendix 1 of the Convention on International Trade in Endangered Species of Wild Fauna and Flora (CITES)", the Appellate Body concluded that the five species of sea turtles involved in the dispute constituted "exhaustible natural resources" within the meaning of Article XX(g) of the GATT-1994.[10]

This raises the question of the link between "hard" and "soft" law in determinations by the Appellate Body, which invoked a host of international instruments to support its conclusions. Philippe Sands has noted that five instruments are referred to in support of the view that concerted and cooperative efforts are needed to exhaust diplomatic efforts before a state may act unilaterally. Of these, two are not – and do not purport to be – legally binding (the *Rio Declaration* and *Agenda 21*), one is a convention that the United States has signed but declined to ratify (the Convention on Biological Diversity), another is a convention that none of the five states involved in the case has even signed (the Convention on the Conservation of Migratory Species of Wild Animals), and the fifth is a convention with which none of the four Asian states has any associations (the Inter-American Convention for the Protection and Conservation of Sea Turtles). According to Sands, these instruments of international law – soft and hard, binding and not – illustrate the extent to which the judicial function (at least within the WTO context) has departed from formal positivism. "The tribunal has not limited its function as being to identify mechanically a norm and then apply it, but rather to divine the existence of one or more international values that may then be invoked to assess the permissibility of particular behaviour."[11]

As noted in the discussion of the *Shrimp-Turtle* case in chapter 4, the Appellate Body ruled against the measure taken by the United States to restrict imported shrimp, on the grounds that it was applied in a manner that amounted to a means not just of unjustifiable discrimination but also of "arbitrary" discrimination between countries where the same conditions prevail. This, it was concluded, was contrary to the requirements of the Head Note of the GATT Exceptions Article. Thus, the absence of an MEA to associate turtle protection with trade measures proved critical. The Appellate Body found that the failure to establish an environment agreement as an instrument of environmental protection policy had resulted in discriminatory and unjustifiable unilateralism. The Appellate Body ruled against the United States because of its failure to engage the complaining countries, as well as other members exporting shrimp to the United States, in serious, across-the-board negotiations with the objective of concluding bilateral or multilateral agreements for the protection and conservation of sea turtles, before unilaterally enforcing the import prohibition against the shrimp exports of those members.[12]

Innovative approaches

The view commonly expressed in the CTE is that amending the Exceptions Article XX would open a debate and entail the risk that the whole Article – which is viewed as the balanced result of long negotiations – would have to be reconsidered. However, a number of innovative ideas have emerged that capture some of the concerns discussed above but fall short of a textual change to the Exceptions Article.[13]

In order to make sure that specifically mandated trade measures taken pursuant to MEAs are recognized as being necessary and justified under WTO rules, a proposal has been made to "reverse the burden of proof" when seeking an exception from WTO rules to protect the environment.[14] The proponents of this approach draw a parallel with the WTO Sanitary and Phytosanitary Agreement and the Technical Barriers to Trade Agreement, where the country challenging a measure would have to prove that the measure imposed by the other party did not meet the conditions of the Exceptions Article. Therefore, a trade measure provided for by an MEA should benefit from a presumption of WTO conformity: that is, it is "necessary" to protect the environment, it is not arbitrarily or unjustifiably discriminating, and it is not a disguised restriction on international trade. The conditions such MEAs must fulfil to be able to avail themselves of such presumptions would have to be agreed to;

inter alia, these criteria should ensure that the MEAs are supported by all interested parties and that their provisions concerning trade-related measures are drafted precisely. In this respect, there are a number of important practical issues. For example, if a country chose not to accept a certain standard, who would judge the appropriateness of that decision? The country might not adopt the more rigorous standard because it finds the scientific evidence unconvincing, it has a high absorptive capacity for the environmental damage concerned, or it has other social and economic priorities.

One way for parties to an agreement to clarify their intentions vis-à-vis other agreements has been recognized in the Vienna Convention as the "savings" clause. If all parties to a negotiation are clear that no conflict is intended, they could agree to reflect this in a savings clause. The formal insertion of such a clause could be an effective way of preventing governments from changing their intentions and of avoiding disputes from arising at the WTO. However, agreeing on a savings clause is not always a simple matter, as the negotiation of the Bio-safety Protocol – which addresses the concerns raised by the trans-boundary movement of living modified organisms – made clear. Much has been asked about the potential incompatibility between WTO rules and the Protocol. The case has been made that conflicts over potential inconsistencies during the negotiation of the Bio-safety Protocol clearly highlighted the need for a savings clause to clarify the basic parameters of the agreements. However, the text that emerged from the Montreal negotiations does not appear to clarify matters at all. It states that "this Protocol shall not be interpreted as implying a change in the rights and obligations of a party under any existing international agreement". This in itself would appear clear enough – WTO rights and obligations stay in tact. The following paragraph, however, states that "the above recital is not intended to subordinate this Protocol to other international agreements". This reads that WTO rights and obligations do not stay in tact.

Another approach to avoid disputes should not be beyond the competence of governments, given the existing knowledge about the trade provisions of MEAs, their objectives, and WTO rules to ensure that no formal dispute should arise between the provisions of the MEAs and WTO rules. A number of steps could be taken, however, to increase the likelihood of avoiding an environmental dispute finding its way to the WTO.

It should be possible to enhance transparency, dialogue and cooperation between MEAs, relevant international organizations and the WTO from the initial stage of negotiation of an MEA to its implementation. This cooperation could contribute to dispute avoidance if it involved an exchange of information, mutual participation in meetings, access to documents and databases, and briefing sessions, as necessary. It has been proposed in the CTE that a guide containing WTO principles could be compiled by the WTO Secretariat, and could be used by MEA negotiators in their consideration of proposed trade measures. Cooperation agreements between the WTO and MEA institutions have also been suggested that would provide for the WTO Secretariat to respond to requests for technical information about relevant WTO provisions. Another proposal is for the establishment of an informal mechanism for dialogue to discuss and exchange information on trade and environment issues.[15] This could involve, *inter alia*, the United Nations Environment Programme, the WTO and MEA Secretariats, the members of the WTO and parties to the environment agreements, as well as NGOs and industry. Such a mechanism would allow interested parties to develop a better understanding of trade- and environment-related issues, in a forum that is not mandated to negotiate rules but rather is aimed at preventing conflict and improving cooperation and coordination amongst policy makers.

It would seem important that representatives of both the environment and trade ministries are present in MEA negotiations to ensure that MEAs utilize only those trade measures that are necessary for the protection of the environment, and that do not constitute a means of arbitrary or unjustifiable discrimination or a disguised restriction on international trade. In fact, newer MEAs, such as the Prior Informed Consent Convention or the Cartagena Protocol on Bio-safety, explicitly refer to the principle of mutual supportiveness, and have involved both trade and environment officials.

In this manner, environmental standards for agreed production and process methods and products could be established within the context of the MEA. If there are grounds for discrimination in trade because of the characteristics of what is being traded (endangered species) or how a product is produced (carbon-emitting production processes), the appropriate standards should be established through agreement by the appropriate experts. There should be no objection to this approach. In fact, because this procedure would relieve the WTO of many concerns relating to difficult concepts such as "like products" and "non-product-related production methods", it is not surprising that WTO members, as well as Panel and Appellate Body reports, have strongly promoted the use of multilateral or other agreements to deal with these matters.

Improving coherence

It is widely believed by WTO members that improved policy coordination at the national level between trade and environment policy officials can contribute to eliminating policy conflicts at the international level between trade and environment. Lack of coordination has, in the past, contributed to the negotiation of conflicting agreements in trade and environmental forums. In addition, it is widely recognized that multilateral cooperation in the form of MEAs constitutes the best approach for resolving trans-boundary (regional and global) environmental concerns. MEAs provide a safeguard against unilateral attempts to address environmental problems (such as with the tuna/dolphin dispute in which the United States acted unilaterally). Unilateral solutions are often discriminatory and involve the extraterritorial application of values and environmental standards. The UN Conference on Environment and Development in 1992 clearly endorsed consensual and cooperative multilateral environmental solutions to global environmental problems. Such solutions reduce the risks of arbitrary discrimination and disguised protectionism, and reflect the international community's common concern and responsibility for global resources.

In order to ensure consistency between the different bodies of law, it would seem appropriate to create a "framework" within which MEAs can operate more effectively in order for environmental problems to be dealt with outside the WTO. In developing such a framework, the first order of business must be to reach consensus on the standards according to which there can be discrimination in trade for products that are physically the same. This can and has been done in a variety of MEAs. Few would disagree about the need for restrictions on trade in stolen goods and that they should be regulated in a discriminatory fashion, even if the physical form of the goods is the same. But few would argue that solutions to these sorts of problems are within the competence of the WTO.

The critical question is, if an exception is sought for a non-conforming measure in the WTO, what support should be given to the government seeking the exception because of the existence of the MEA. The answer is very clear: it depends. What the framework should contain is a procedure whereby this question is addressed on a multilateral basis with the involvement of both the trade and environment communities; it should not be left in the hands of panellists in the WTO dispute settlement process or the Appellate Body. In fact, the decision could be taken through a public debate and disclosure of all the relevant facts.

At the most fundamental level, what is required is a coherent approach to the formulation of trade and environment policies at both the national and multilateral levels. This is true with respect to addressing not only agreements that may have inconsistent rules, but also those that are inconsistent in their approaches to meeting their objectives. Some would cite as examples the treatment of patents in the TRIPS Agreement, the protection of indigenous peoples' rights in the Convention on Biological Diversity, and the treatment of precaution in the SPS Agreement and the Biodiversity Convention. Greater coherence between multilateral trade and multilateral environment agreements could be best achieved in a future round of negotiations by establishing a negotiating group to examine the question. Such a group was established in the Uruguay Round. The so-called FOGS (Functioning of the GATT System) Group produced a Ministerial Declaration on the Contribution of the World Trade Organization to Achieving Greater Coherence in Global Economic Policy-making. This Declaration served as the basis for the comprehensive and formal agreements that were struck between the WTO, the World Bank and the International Monetary Fund to guide them in their future collaboration. The policy discussion in this context is found in chapter 12.

Conclusion

Although the range of potential conflicts between MEAs and the WTO Agreements is somewhat circumscribed, questions will continue to arise when the provisions of an MEA are unclear as to the action they mandate, even among the parties to it, or in situations where the parties to an MEA are applying trade measures against a non-party. Change in WTO rules and processes to accommodate the concerns of environmentalists will not come easily and certainly not outside the context of a new round of broad-based multilateral negotiations. The WTO is a consensus-based organization and many WTO members see no need for change in this respect. Notwithstanding that, eventual conflict between the rules of MEAs and the WTO remains a real possibility, and a collision between regimes as important as those protecting the environment and the trading system should certainly be avoided.

In order to operate in a credible and efficient manner, the WTO needs effective, broad-based and consensus-driven MEAs that include all interested WTO members. If WTO-inconsistent measures are provided for in the MEA, they should be clearly defined and enforced by a robust dispute settlement system within the MEA itself. If the political will of the international community falls short of what is necessary to agree on MEAs with these characteristics, a heavy price will be paid. Trade-related environmental disputes will gravitate to the WTO, because no alternative mechanism will be available to deal with them. In the absence of a world government to settle global environment problems, and with a division of responsibilities among different international organizations, we are confronted with a problem of global governance. It should not be beyond the capabilities of the world's leaders to decide on what is to be the role of the WTO in the coming years.

Notes

1. For a useful description of the relevant measures in MEAs, see WTO, *Matrix on Trade Measures Pursuant to Selected MEAs: Note by the Secretariat*, Geneva: WTO, WT/CTE/ W/160, 19 September 2000.
2. See WTO, *Clarification of the Relationship between the WTO and Multilateral Environmental Agreements – Submission by Switzerland*, Geneva: WTO Secretariat, WT/CTE/ W/168, 19 October 2000.
3. See, for example, Duncan Brack, "Multilateral Environment Agreements and the Multilateral Trading System", in Gary P. Sampson and W. Bradnee Chambers (eds), *Trade, Environment, and the Millennium*, 2nd edn, Tokyo: United Nations University Press, 2002, pp. 321–352.
4. For a useful comparison of dispute procedures and compliance mechanisms more generally in the WTO and MEAs, see WTO, *Compliance and Dispute Settlement Provisions in the WTO and in Multilateral Environmental Agreements*, Geneva: WTO Secretariat, WT/CTE/W/191, Joint Note by the WTO and UNEP Secretariats, June 2001.
5. See Article 3.5 of the Framework Convention on Climate Change.
6. Both quotations in this paragraph come from the Kyoto Protocol, Article 2.
7. Other such taxes include consumption taxes on capital equipment, auxiliary materials and services used in the transportation and production of other taxable goods (e.g. taxes on advertising, energy, machinery and transport).
8. See Doaa Abdel Motaal, "The Agreement on Technical Barriers to Trade, the Committee on Trade and Environment, and Eco-Labelling", in Gary P. Sampson and W. Bradnee Chambers (eds), *Trade, Environment, and the Millennium*, 2nd edn, Tokyo: United Nations University Press, 2002, pp. 267–286.
9. *United States – Import Prohibition of Certain Shrimp and Shrimp Products* [*Shrimp-Turtle*], Appellate Body Report, WT/DS58/AB/R, 12 October 1998.
10. Ibid., para. 128.
11. Philippe Sands, "'Unilateralism', Values and International Law", *Environmental Journal of International Law*, Vol. 11, No. 2, 2000, p. 2301.
12. *Shrimp-Turtle*, para. 166.
13. See WTO, *Clarification of the Relationship between the WTO and Multilateral Environmental Agreements – Submission by Switzerland*. This view is also expressed by the European Union in WTO, *Resolving the Relationship between WTO Rules and Multilateral Environmental Agreements, Submission by the European Community*, Geneva: WTO Secretariat, WT/CTE/W/170, 19 October 2000.
14. See WTO, *Resolving the Relationship between WTO Rules and Multilateral Environmental Agreements, Submission by the European Community*.
15. See WTO, *The Relationship between the Provisions of the Multilateral Trading System and Trade Measures for Environment Purposes Including those Pursuant to Multilateral Environment Agreements, Communication from New Zealand*, Geneva: WTO Secretariat, WT/CTE/W/162, 10 October 2000.

7

Biotechnology, sustainable development and the WTO

Introduction

Biotechnology, or the use of living organisms to make or modify products, has flourished in one form or another since prehistoric times. When human beings realized that they could plant and improve their own crops through seed selection, they learned to use biotechnology. The first animal breeders, noticing that different physical traits could be either magnified or lost by mating appropriate pairs of animals, engaged in the manipulations of biotechnology. Activities such as baking bread, brewing alcoholic beverages, producing serum and vaccines for human or animal health, or cross-breeding food crops or domestic animals have been practised by human society since the beginning of recorded history, although an understanding of the scientific principles behind fermentation and crop improvement practices has come only in the past hundred years. Nonetheless, the early, crude techniques, even without the benefit of sophisticated laboratories and automated equipment, were a true practice of biotechnology.

Public interest in biotechnology has increased greatly in recent years. This change in sentiment has come with the development of modern techniques made possible with the advance of knowledge regarding genetic and molecular structures. Genetic engineering now permits scientists to change the characteristics of living organisms by transferring genetic information from one organism into another that is too distantly related to permit natural cross-breeding. It is this transfer of genetic information across the boundaries of species that has led to the most vocal public reaction.

Numerous issues relating to the regulation of modern biotechnology arouse strong feelings among many people. Some of this concern is related to the unknown. There are fears that the release of living genetically modified organisms (GMOs) into the environment might have deleterious consequences for Mother Nature. There are concerns that the development of genetically modified crops would create a monoculture that could put food security and traditional agricultural crops at risk. There are also fears about the consumption of food derived from GMOs that could damage public health. Other concerns relate to equity considerations: it is argued that developing countries rich in genetic material are not adequately rewarded when this resource is tapped by the biotechnology industry and marketed by companies from the developed world. Then there are ethical considerations. Some question whether it is proper to provide for the patenting of life in the form of micro-organisms. Some life-saving drugs produced by modern biotechnology are expensive and out of reach for impoverished people. Is this inevitable as pharmaceutical companies recoup the costs of past research and prepare the ground for new life-saving initiatives, or are excessive profits derived from exclusive marketing rights that come with the ownership of patents?

As governments engage in the process of regulating biotechnology, it is apparent not only that different countries have different concerns, but that opinions differ widely within countries. The liberal views of countries such as the United States and Canada toward GMO food products, for example, are in stark contrast to the view of a number of European countries, which are hostile to the cultivation and import of genetically modified organisms and products derived from them. As a result, countries are far from agreement on the risks associated with biotechnology, and they differ widely on the appropriate precaution in managing these risks. The life of regulators is further complicated by the fact that much of the science surrounding GMOs is unclear.

What is clear, however, is that biotechnology is a vast area of current and potential commercial application, whose regulation will certainly affect many facets of everyday life.[1] From an international trade perspective, WTO rules have the potential to influence national regulations and international treaties that address the results of genetic engineering in many ways. A review of this interaction sheds light on the question of why the WTO has moved onto centre stage in regulatory areas that would not normally be considered part of traditional trade policy.

It seems to me that, as far as the WTO is concerned, GMO-related issues present themselves under three different headings. First, there are

market access considerations, because a number of WTO Agreements
have as their objective providing the freedom for governments to regulate as they see fit, while avoiding unnecessary barriers to trade. How
is it possible to regulate trade in living modified organisms destined for
release into nature when there are vastly different concerns about the
environmental consequences of doing so? Are trade-restricting domestic
regulations relating to food products derived from GMOs protectionist
in their intent or based on rational public concerns over health? What
international standards would create the presumption of acceptability
should a dispute come the WTO, and who would create and enforce such
standards?

This then raises the second set of issues, which relate to coherence
across different treaties: are the WTO Agreements supportive of other
multilateral agreements dealing with various aspects of biotechnology?
The Agreement on Sanitary and Phytosanitary Measures (SPS), for example, defers to standards established in other international agreements
in determining the legitimacy of SPS measures (see chapter 5). How does
the SPS Agreement interface, if at all, with the Cartagena Protocol on
Bio-safety – an international treaty dealing specifically with the cross-
border movement of living GMOs? In a different domain, providing for
the patenting of micro-organisms – under the WTO Agreement on
Trade-Related Intellectual Property Rights (TRIPS) – has implications
for the preservation of biodiversity and rewarding indigenous peoples
for their genetic resources. Are the objectives of the Convention on Biological Diversity (CBD) best met through the TRIPS patenting regime?

Third, there are issues relating to equity and ethical considerations.
Given the patenting obligations of the TRIPS Agreement, how can affordable medicines arising from biotechnological research be accessed
by poor people while rewarding pharmaceutical companies for past research? The TRIPS Agreement provides for the patenting of micro-
organisms and therefore life forms. What are the religious, ethical and
other considerations involved in patenting life forms for commercial
purposes – or any other purposes for that matter? In both instances, central questions include what is life worth, who should own it and who
should pay for preserving it? Matters such as these understandably
arouse emotions in many quarters.

The objective of this chapter is to present a case study of how the
WTO, with its expanded Uruguay Round mandate, finds itself at the
centre of controversial issues involving non-traditional trade concerns.
Technical developments since the completion of the Uruguay Round
could not have been foreseen by negotiators at the time, and this has considerable policy implications. I pay specific attention in the following to
the TRIPS Agreement, the SPS Agreement, the Technical Barriers to

Trade (TBT) Agreement and the Committee on Trade and Environment (CTE).

Market access: Health and the environment

Scientists have provided numerous examples of both the positive and the negative implications of using modern biotechnology to facilitate and improve plant species. Among the positive outcomes are the development of plants characterized by increased drought and pest resistance and possible survival in saline water. There are also potential negative consequences.[2] Moreover, it is argued that herbicide-resistant crops will entrench the dependence of agricultural production on capital- and energy-intensive chemical inputs, further narrow the genetic base employed for agricultural purposes, and increase farmers' dependence on specific agricultural supply firms.

As far as human health is concerned, potential benefits include the production of more nutritious fruits, vegetables and cereals; processed foods that are healthier; foods that help fight disease; fewer allergenic proteins in nuts and pulse crops; rice that can help fight anaemia and blindness; and foods that can be used to deliver vaccines and medicines. But, as is the case for improving plant species, there are potentially negative consequences. It is argued, for example, that with the current state of knowledge there is no way of predicting the effects of the insertion of genes into the genome, or the effects on human health of genetic modification with respect to the development of unknown toxic and allergenic components.

Viewed from a policy perspective, these concerns are manifested in the assessment and management of risk. Risk assessment is the scientific determination of the relationship between cause and effect in situations where adverse effects can occur. Risk management, on the other hand, is the process of identifying, evaluating, selecting and implementing measures to reduce risk. Managing risk entails ascertaining what constitutes an acceptable level of risk and then setting the necessary standards by which the risk can be managed appropriately. In this process of risk management, the lives of regulators – as well as of trade officials – would be greatly simplified if all countries adopted the same standards through international agreement with respect to goods that enter international trade. This, however, is not the case. Thus, the problem arises of whether standards are devised, and other measures taken, with the intent of limiting market access or responding to well-founded and scientifically justified concerns.

Because WTO Agreements have as their objective the avoidance of the use of technical regulations as unnecessary impediments to trade, one of the major challenges facing WTO members is to provide the necessary flexibility for governments to pursue whatever domestic policies they think are appropriate in the regulation of GMOs and their products, without the associated measures being used as disguised barriers to trade. This is not easy, particularly as different perceptions exist as to the appropriate degree of precaution in assessing and managing risks. Here the Precautionary Principle enters the picture. It is based on the premise that in some cases – particularly where the costs of action are low and the risks of inaction are high – preventive action should be taken, even without full scientific certainty about the problem being addressed. More formally, and according to the *Rio Declaration*, "[i]n order to protect the environment, the precautionary approach shall be widely applied by States according to their capabilities. Where there are threats of serious or irreversible damage, lack of full scientific certainty shall not be used as a reason for postponing cost-effective measures to prevent environmental degradation."[3] In practice, this gives governments a fair amount of discretion in setting environmental policy. It responds to the gap between banning a product or procedure until science has proved it is harmless and not banning it until science has proved that there is a real risk.[4]

The relative weight assigned to science and societal choice in the determination of standards – or how "precautionary" regulations should be – underpins much of the possible future disagreement over the legitimacy of standards relating to genetically modified products within the context of dispute settlement in the WTO. As will be seen below, the weight given to scientific evidence creates the potential for an important lack of coherence between some multilateral agreements, such as the Bio-safety Protocol,[5] on the one hand, and the SPS Agreement or the TBT Agreement, on the other.

As outlined in chapter 6, the Sanitary and Phytosanitary Measures Agreement addresses governmental measures applied to protect humans or animals from food risks and diseases, and to protect the country from the spread of pests. In this respect its purpose is to determine what might be considered a legitimate measure in terms of being no more trade restrictive than required to achieve domestic objectives. In the absence of international standards relating to these products, each country must conduct its own risk assessment and determine its "acceptable level of risk". Thus, the Agreement explicitly recognizes members' sovereign right to take appropriate national measures and provides national authorities with a framework to develop their domestic policies and set their own standards. These commonly include substantial safety margins as a precautionary measure. However, in order to be consistent with the WTO, once a government has determined its appropriate level of sanitary and phytosanitary protection it should not choose a measure that is more stringent and trade restrictive than necessary. Evaluating this is important in determining the measure, whose effects should be proportional to the risk.

In terms of its scope of application, the SPS Agreement applies to measures to protect human or animal life from risks arising from additives, contaminants, toxins or disease-causing organisms in their food; human life from plant- or animal-carried diseases; animal or plant life from pests, diseases or disease-causing organisms. It also applies to measures to prevent or limit other damage to a country from the entry, establishment or spread of pests. Although the SPS Agreement might appear to be relevant with respect to the cross-border movement of living GMOs and food derived from them, this is not clear. The Agreement applies to measures to protect animal or plant life or health, but these measures relate to the entry, establishment or spread of pests, diseases, disease-carrying organisms or disease-causing organisms. Can living GMOs be considered to be any of these? At first blush at least, a reasonable answer would appear to be in the negative. But what if a measure were taken that would restrict the importation of a living GMO on the grounds that it could reduce the resistance of crops to pests and therefore damage a country from the "entry, establishment or spread of pests". Is this within the scope of the SPS Agreement? It would indeed be a difficult case for the dispute settlement process of the WTO to deal with.

Chapter 5 also describes the TBT Agreement and its application to technical regulations, voluntary standards and conformity assessment procedures. The Agreement specifies that technical regulations should not be prepared, adopted or applied with the effect of creating unnecessary obstacles to international trade. For this purpose, the Agreement requires that technical regulations must not be more trade restrictive than necessary to fulfil a legitimate objective, taking account of the risks that non-fulfilment would create. Such legitimate objectives include: national security requirements; the prevention of deceptive practices; and the protection of human health or safety, animal or plant life or health, or the environment. In assessing such risks, relevant elements for consideration include the available scientific and technical information, related processing technology, or the intended end-uses of products.

The two Agreements have some common elements, including basic obligations for non-discrimination and similar requirements for the advance notification of proposed measures. However, many of the substantive rules are different. For example, both Agreements encourage the use of international standards. However, under the SPS Agreement the only justification for not using such standards for food safety and animal/plant health protection are scientific arguments resulting from an assessment of the potential health risks. Under the TBT Agreement, in contrast, governments may decide that international standards are not appropriate for other reasons, including fundamental technological problems or geographical factors.

Moreover, under the TBT Agreement, governments may introduce regulations such as the labelling of products when necessary to meet a number of objectives, such as national security or the prevention of deceptive practices. WTO members acknowledge, in principle, the positive aspects of labelling schemes, whose intention is to provide consumers with information about the manner in which goods have been produced in order for them to identify products that may carry risks for public health or the environment. When preferences differ between consumers for non-scientific reasons with respect to products that are physically the same (or "like products"), then one approach is to permit consumers to differentiate through reference to product labels. However, members also point to the risks of abuse and impediments to trade of labelling schemes and the TBT Agreement requirement.

Furthermore, there is no consensus on the coverage of the Agreement for standards and regulations relating to the processes that produced the product (see chapter 5). This is not an issue if the method of production is "incorporated" into the product (i.e. the production method is evident in the product itself), but what if the biotechnological process that was involved in the production is not evident in the final product? Would a labelling scheme that requires the labelling of products derived from genetically modified organisms be considered WTO inconsistent on the grounds that GMO-derived products are "like" non-GMO products when there is no evidence of the genetic modification in the final product? The manner in which this debate is resolved will have major practical implications in a number of areas of considerable commercial significance; both voluntary and mandatory labelling schemes are covered by the TBT Agreement and the WTO will find itself in the centre of the debate.

Another consideration is that the TBT Agreement recognizes that no country should be prevented from taking measures necessary for the prevention of deceptive practices, subject to the requirement that these measures do not discriminate between countries and are not a disguised restriction on international trade. Would the failure to notify consumers of the biotechnological production of foods be tantamount to an infringement of the TBT Agreement on the grounds of deception?

In past meetings of the TBT Committee, the United States and Canada expressed concern over a European Union regulation on the labelling of food products containing or derived from genetically modified soya or maize. The European Union requires foodstuffs and food ingredients containing traces of modified DNA or protein to be labelled as "produced with genetically modified soya/maize". The United States and Canada have argued that such labels are unnecessary technical barriers to trade since no scientific reason exists to differentiate between foodstuffs produced with genetically modified crops and "normal" maize/ soya. The United States also questioned the feasibility of developing reliable and commercially practical tests for detecting DNA or protein resulting from genetic modification, especially at very low thresholds. The European Commission also proposed that *all* GM foods should be labelled, including foods derived from but no longer containing GMOs, such as highly refined products (e.g. maize or soya oil) where the original GMO content is removed during the production process. These rules have been approved by the EU governments and the European Parliament, and have entered into force. They are under challenge, the issue at stake being whether GMOs are "like" other products.[6]

At the request of the United States, Argentina and Canada, a Panel was established in August 2003 on the European Union's procedures for the approval and marketing of biotechnology products.[7] The three complainants claim that the suspension of considering/granting biotech product approvals, as well as several national marketing and import bans, are inconsistent with a number of provisions in the TBT Agreement and the SPS Agreement, including being more trade restrictive than necessary and lacking scientific justification based on risk assessments. The complainants also claim that the approval procedures are inconsistent with national treatment, which requires governments to treat "like" foreign and domestic products in the same way. The argument is that genetic modification does not make products fundamentally different from their non-GMO counterparts and no approval processes or controls other than those applicable to conventional crops should apply to GMOs.[8]

Under which Agreement should disputes related to genetically modified organisms be dealt with? Regulations that address microbiological contamination of food, set allowable levels of pesticide or veterinary drug residues, or identify permitted food additives fall under the SPS Agreement. Some packaging and labelling requirements, if directly related to the safety of the food, are also subject to the SPS Agreement. Most measures related to human disease control come under the TBT Agreement, unless they concern diseases that are carried by plants or animals (such as rabies). In terms of food-labelling requirements, nutritional claims and concerns, quality and packaging regulations are generally not considered to be sanitary or phytosanitary measures and hence are normally subject to the TBT Agreement.

Coherence with other treaties

The WTO and the Bio-safety Protocol

With respect to the trans-boundary movement of GMOs, it would seem sensible that a multilateral agreement be negotiated to ensure consistent regulations at the global level. In fact, such a treaty was foreseen in the Convention on Biological Diversity, which provides for the establishment of biosafety-related regulations to "control the risks associated with the use and release of living modified organisms resulting from biotechnology which are likely to have adverse environmental impacts that could affect the conservation and sustainable use of biological diversity, taking also into account the risks to human health". The CBD broadened the traditionally applied concept of "genetically modified organisms" by adopting the term "living modified organisms" (LMOs).

The Cartagena Protocol on Bio-safety was negotiated under the auspices of the United Nations, agreed to in March 2001, and adopted under the auspices of the CBD. It was the first international legal instrument to deal with biotechnology, and it has been agreed to by 129 countries. At the most fundamental level, the Cartagena Protocol can be viewed as a trade agreement; and it is certainly the most important multilateral environment agreement (MEA) from a commercial trade perspective. Whereas the Cartagena Protocol addresses trade-related GMO topics from the perspective of conserving biodiversity, many WTO members that trade in GMO products see GMO regulation as an unnecessary trade barrier. At the domestic level, individual WTO members are under pressure, and the Protocol was sure to be controversial from the outset.

The Cartagena Protocol covers some common ground with the SPS Agreement. Both the Protocol and the SPS Agreement address the ability of countries to restrict the importation of products in order to protect the environment from possible adverse effects; both provide for the use of precautionary measures; and both require the use of scientific risk assessment. The Protocol resulted from intensive and protracted negotiation in which particular emphasis was placed on avoiding any inconsistencies with WTO rules.

The centre-piece of the Protocol is the Advance Informed Agreement (AIA) procedure whereby prior notification and consent are required for the export and import of LMOs. The AIA procedures incorporate the principle that states have sovereign rights to control the transfer, handling and use of LMOs, including the right to refuse the importation of LMOs. A central question throughout the negotiation of the Protocol was whether it should cover only those classes of LMOs that are released into the environment, or also LMOs that are intended for direct use as food or feed or for processing. Although it was agreed that both classes of LMOs would fall under the Protocol's scope, the AIA provisions apply only to LMOs that are intended for introduction into the environment. The AIA procedure is to be based on risk assessment carried out in a scientifically sound manner. The lack of agreement among the parties on the nature and extent of the risk associated with the release of LMOs is highlighted in differing approaches to the degree of precaution that is considered appropriate in the management of risk. As far as LMOs for food, feed or processing are concerned, a clearing-house mechanism has been created to provide a link between national authorities whereby products exported for food, feed or processing are to be notified to the other party within 15 days. The information to be provided should include details about the producer and the LMO as well as a risk assessment report. The importing party may make its own decision on the import of the product according to its own domestic regulatory regime for GMOs. Both these procedures have the potential seriously to affect trade flows.

After establishing that parties could take a precautionary approach to restricting imports of LMOs, the challenge now remains to put into practice the principle of precaution. The potential conflict between the rules of the WTO and the Bio-safety Protocol has been under discussion in the CTE and was given further impetus with the agreement to negotiate the relationship between the WTO and MEAs in the Doha Development Agenda. Whether there are WTO-inconsistent measures in the Bio-safety Protocol seems to be answered in the affirmative, at least as far as the treatment of precaution in the SPS Agreement is concerned.[9] For example, although both the Protocol and the SPS Agreement formally provide the right to resort to precaution in the absence of sufficient scientific evidence, this is not necessarily considered to be a provisional measure in the case of the Bio-safety Protocol – whereas in the SPS Agreement it is.

Because the Protocol does not yet have a compliance mechanism, any dispute between WTO members would be dealt with under the WTO dispute settlement process. This could raise fundamental questions about the relevance of the Protocol in a WTO dispute if the disputants are not both parties to the Protocol. The United States – which accounts for three-quarters of the world's agricultural biotechnology crops – is not a member of the Protocol and, even if it chooses to abide by the rules, it is not bound by them. A further question is whether the Protocol and the Precautionary Principle should be conceived of as customary international law in future years by the WTO dispute settlement process. In effect, the WTO would be deciding on the interpretation of precaution.

The WTO and the Biodiversity Convention

Many of the poorest people in the world live in areas where a large part of the world's biological diversity survives. In addition, the traditional knowledge of these communities relates to the use of their biological resources as medicines, foodstuffs and other goods. There has been extensive commercial use of the knowledge and biological resources of indigenous peoples in a variety of sectors such as pharmaceuticals, agriculture, horticulture, personal care and cosmetics.[10] Indeed, without indigenous knowledge, many products in these sectors would not exist today. Traditional knowledge has long been considered to be the common heritage of humanity, where laws regulating access to genetic resources did not exist.

The Convention on Biological Diversity (CBD) was negotiated under the auspices of the United Nations Environment Programme and entered into force in 1993. Its objectives are the conservation of biological diversity, the sustainable use of its components, and the fair and equitable sharing of the benefits arising out of the utilization of genetic resources. The Convention is based on the notion that, in accordance with the principles of international law, states have the sovereign right to exploit their own resources pursuant to their own environmental policies, and the responsibility to ensure that activities within their jurisdiction and control do not cause damage to the environment.

The fact that the CBD acknowledges that genetic resources have a commercial, economic and scientific value, and entitles parties providing access to such resources to receive benefits on mutually agreed terms, means that intellectual property rights are central to the Agreement and should influence the distribution of benefits flowing from their use.[11]

There are, however, a number of legal and practical issues concerning the relationship between the CBD and the TRIPS Agreement. The CBD introduced the notion of intellectual property rights as a strategy for conserving biodiversity by granting countries sovereign rights over their resources, and the TRIPS Agreement acknowledges the ownership and exclusive use of inventions (not discoveries) to ensure a time-bound monopoly over the use of the invention. The term of patent protection is 20 years from the filing date.

According to the TRIPS Agreement, inventions in all fields of technology, whether products or processes, are patentable provided that they are new, involve an inventive step and are capable of industrial application. Owing to these requirements, the intellectual property "system" is seen to be biased against the interests of developing countries – it precludes the granting of patents for many inventions or discoveries that constitute the traditional knowledge of indigenous people. Moreover, it is argued that the patenting of seeds, herbs and traditional processes without reward to developing countries is "bio-piracy" and robs the developing world of rightful profits.

Addressing this issue raises a number of questions. In most traditional communities, knowledge is acquired over time, being passed from one generation to the next, and keeps evolving and changing in character. Therefore, it is difficult to establish when such knowledge was actually discovered and when it entered the public domain. Also, because traditional knowledge has been handed down through generations, entire communities are involved in its evolution. Who is the inventor? The problem is further complicated in cases where the same indigenous knowledge is used by different communities in various parts of the world.[12]

Although developing country governments could enact strong laws to regulate the conditions under which corporations access domestic resources, few have the legislation in place or the expertise to create it. Additionally, in many instances, patent examiners in developed countries are not aware of the innovations already made by native peoples and therefore grant patents to developed country corporations in error. However, expense and lack of expertise preclude developing country citizens from challenging patents issued in error.[13]

Because national access laws have proved to be inadequate to prevent intellectual property rights being granted in situations where the genetic material has been illegally used without authorization, or incorporated into an invention emanating from another national jurisdiction, several developing countries have been pressing for mechanisms to protect traditional knowledge. They are also seeking recognition for regimes that aim to regulate access to genetic resources in order to prevent bio-piracy, as well as to reap benefits from the use of traditional knowledge or genetic resources in patented products. Thus, the Doha Development Agenda instructs the Council for TRIPS "to examine, *inter alia*, the relationship between the TRIPS Agreement and the Convention on Biological Diversity, the protection of traditional knowledge and folklore, and other relevant new developments raised by Members".[14]

Ethical and other considerations

Patenting life forms

It is important to note that the TRIPS Agreement makes no reference to biotechnology. However, Article 27.3(b) of the Agreement does provide for the patenting of micro-organisms and of non-biological and microbiological processes for the production of plants and animals. Views differ greatly – on ethical, religious and other grounds – about the appropriateness of patenting and owning life forms. Many individuals regard genetic engineering as a qualitatively different technology from traditional plant-breeding or animal husbandry techniques.[15] They hold that the species barrier is a boundary set by God or nature, that species have an inherent integrity, and that the violation of this status is an act of extreme arrogance on the part of human beings.

An animal, plant or micro-organism owes its creation ultimately to God, not human endeavour. It can not be interpreted as an invention or a process, in the normal sense of either word. It has a life of its own, which inanimate matter does not. In genetic engineering, moreover, only a tiny fraction of the makeup of the organism can be said to be a product of scientists. The organism is still essentially a living entity, not an invention. A genetically modified mouse is completely different from a mouse trap.[16]

Graham Dutfield – an Oxford researcher – usefully draws attention to the work of Arthur Kornberg (a Noble Prize laureate) and his pioneering research on DNA synthesis; his view is that "the most rational understanding of life" is "its reduction to the molecular details of chemistry". This conceptualization of life is essentially chemical, embodied in – and promoted through – the discourse of biotechnology. It is undoubtedly appealing to those who esteem modern science for its progressiveness and rationality. Dutfield notes that this way of imaging life provides a basis for arguments for extending protectable subject matter to micro-organisms, plants and animals. He argues that it has played a significant role in the evolution of patent law in various countries from the 1980s, and ultimately of the global regime too.[17]

Access to affordable medicines

According to James Orbinski, the president of Médecins sans Frontières writing shortly after having accepted the Nobel Prize on behalf of his institution: "The failure of market forces, the failure of governments to regulate these or substitute for them, and the lack of a clear global public health policy have caused the current inhumane, mostly silent and wholly unacceptable catastrophe that lack of access to health care and essential medicines represents. The WTO, by design or by default, is at the heart of this issue."[18]

The point at issue from the multilateral perspective is how to ensure that patent protection for pharmaceutical products does not prevent people in poor countries from having access to medicines, while at the same time maintaining the patent system's role in providing incentives for research and development. To deal with this issue, the TRIPS Agreement contains flexibility provisions. In particular, governments can issue compulsory licences to allow a competitor to produce the product or use the process under licence, but only under certain conditions aimed at safeguarding the legitimate interests of the patent holder. An additional flexibility relates to parallel importing.[19] Countries' laws differ on whether they allow parallel imports. The TRIPS Agreement simply states that governments cannot bring legal disputes to the WTO on this issue. Importantly, in situations of national emergency or other circumstances of extreme urgency, compulsory licensing and government use without the authorization of the right holder are allowed (although subject to conditions protecting the legitimate interests of the right holder). The scope and duration of such use are limited to the purpose for which it was authorized, which is non-assignable and predominantly for the supply of the domestic market.

Although the flexibility provisions may appear clear cut, some governments – in particular in African countries – were unsure of how they would be interpreted should a dispute arise, and how far their right to use them would be respected. Thus, a clarification was crafted in the form of a special Declaration on TRIPS and Public Health at the Doha Ministerial Conference in November 2001. According to the Doha Declaration, public health should take precedence over commitments undertaken with respect to intellectual property rights. In affirming that the TRIPS Agreement "can and should be interpreted and implemented in a manner supportive of WTO Members' right to protect public health and, in particular, to promote access to medicines for all" (para. 4), members confirmed that the TRIPS Agreement has room for flexibility at the national level, namely with regard to the determination of the grounds for compulsory licensing and the admission of parallel imports. This can be read to mean that a failure to make use of the available flexibilities would run counter to the spirit and purpose of the TRIPS Agreement, especially in the light of the recognized gravity of the problems. In the Declaration, members also agreed to extend exemptions on pharmaceutical patent protection for least developed countries until 2016.

An important issue quickly emerged. The "flexibilities" of the TRIPS accord, as they relate to government-sanctioned non-voluntary use of a patent for domestic production, may in practice be of little use except for the few countries that have the capacity to produce the products in question. The issue arises because Article 31(f) of the TRIPS Agreement states that products made under compulsory licensing must be "predominantly for the supply of the domestic market". This has a direct impact on countries that can manufacture drugs – by limiting the amount they can export when the drug is made under compulsory licence. And it has an indirect impact on countries unable to make medicines and therefore wanting to import generic products. It would be difficult for them to find countries that can supply them with drugs made under compulsory licensing because exports may not be provided for in the agreement between the pharmaceutical company and the licence holder. Thus, Article 31(f) is a general rule that limits exports when the product is manufactured under a compulsory licence.

Moreover, although the TRIPS Agreement clearly permits imports – both where the product is off patent in the importing country and where the government overrides the patent rights under compulsory licensing provisions – the difficulty for the importing country is to find a source. To address this situation, paragraph 6 of the Doha Declaration on TRIPS reads: "We recognize that WTO Members with insufficient or no manufacturing capacities in the pharmaceutical sector could face difficulties in making effective use of compulsory licensing under the TRIPS Agreement. We instruct the Council for TRIPS to find an expeditious solution to this problem and to report to the General Council before the end of 2002."

After almost a year of discussion, the TRIPS Council considered a draft Decision in the form of a waiver permitting countries that can make drugs to export them under compulsory licence to countries that cannot manufacture them. The waiver would last until the TRIPS Agreement was amended. It would include provisions on transparency (which would give a patent owner some opportunity to react by offering a lower price) and on special packaging and other methods to avoid the medicines being diverted to developed country markets. An annex would describe what a country needs to do in order to declare itself unable to make the pharmaceuticals domestically.

The draft Decision received very wide support, but there was no consensus. It was particularly opposed by the United States, arguing, *inter alia*, that the Decision was too open-ended on the range of diseases it would cover. The United States was also concerned that the Decision did not go far enough in preventing the medicines from being diverted to the wrong markets. Developing countries too had concerns, mainly about what they considered to be burdensome conditions, such as on transparency and preventing the medicines being diverted to the wrong markets.

However, in 2003, an agreement was reached in the General Council for the implementation of paragraph 6. The Decision takes the form of an *interim* waiver, which allows countries producing patented products under compulsory licence to export the products to eligible importing countries, provided that a compulsory licence has also been granted in the importing country and that various other conditions are met. The waiver is set to last until the TRIPS Agreement is amended.

It has been argued that the conditions established in both the text of the Decision and the Statement for allowing exports of patented medicines are hardly compatible with the idea of an "expeditious" solution: in order to qualify for importing drugs under this mechanism, 12 exacting steps must be followed.[20] The argument continues that, in view of the multiple conditions required for its application, such a complex and burdensome system is largely symbolic and is unlikely to lead to any significant increase in the supply of medicines for the poor.

Food security

As noted, under the TRIPS Agreement members are required to provide patent protection for micro-organisms, non-biological and microbiological processes, and plant varieties. Environmentalists have expressed concern about the effect of intellectual property protection for genetically modified plant varieties, even though their long-term environmental impacts have not been established. The concern here is that the prevailing policy framework enhances incentives to develop seeds that will have a large potential demand. The focus of seed company research will therefore be on high-value crops, leading to decreased crop diversity. It is also argued that the creation of trans-genetic plants with built-in resistance to herbicides could lead to ecological damage with the release of these crops into the wild. The threat to food security comes from protection for innovations associated with the development of new plant varieties, which limits the type and number of seeds available to farmers, decreases crop resistance, and increases the likelihood of food shortages and, possibly, famine.

However, what is important to consider here is that intellectual property protection does not confer the legitimate right otherwise to regulate products. If a product receives intellectual property protection, this does not mean that it has been approved for production, use or marketing. In terms of patent protection for plant varieties, for example, the right holder cannot automatically produce, use or market the plant variety. The same is true of the granting of a patent on a pharmaceutical product; it does not grant an immediate right to market a drug. Rather, a separate review of the drug's safety is typically required before it is introduced widely to the public.

On the other hand, an argument in favour of intellectual property protection of plant varieties is that it could have positive effects on food security by providing incentives for farmers to produce new, improved plant varieties. It also protects local farmers, plant breeders or scientists by providing exclusive rights to their innovations. It is argued that biotechnological innovations hold out the promise dramatically to increase crop yields and viability in developing countries. Whereas conventional plant-breeding techniques involve extensive trial and error, scientists using biotechnology are able to transfer specific traits through direct manipulation of the genome of a plant. Biotechnology has also allowed for the development of new technological solutions in the field of agriculture, including frost-inhibiting bacteria, pesticide resistance and enhancement of the disease resistance of livestock. It is argued that research in this area would be greatly limited if an appropriate system of intellectual property protection was not in place.

Conclusions

Although many regard the current provisions of the WTO to be sufficient and effective in dealing with circumstances surrounding trade in all products, some hold the view that biotechnology is sufficiently unique to require existing provisions to be further clarified and/or elaborated so that they may apply effectively and in a predictable and transparent manner. It is argued that the current lack of certainty works to undermine the realization of the full potential of biotechnology by the world's producers and consumers.

To a number of governments, it appears timely for the WTO to engage in a collective exercise aimed at establishing how trade and investment in biotechnology are covered by existing WTO provisions and whether these provisions constitute a sufficiently effective regime from the WTO's perspective. Because a number of existing WTO Agreements are of particular relevance to biotechnology, it would be difficult for this exercise to be conducted effectively by any one Committee. Instead, a Working Party could be established that would have a fact-finding mandate to consider the adequacy and effectiveness of existing rules, as well as the capacity of WTO members to implement these rules effectively. The Working Party would bring a number of benefits to WTO members, including: providing a transparent process with a common focus and time-frame for preparatory, fact-finding work building on work already under way at the national level in several WTO members; providing information for those WTO members not currently engaged in such exercises at the national level; and serving to identify constraints on the full implementation by members of WTO-consistent regulatory systems for biotechnology.

In very practical terms, a number of important considerations emerge from the policy perspective. What minimum degree of scientific validation is required for a trading partner to be obliged to accept as legitimate a standard relating to a product of biotechnology? What is the role of "precaution" if there is insufficient scientific evidence to establish a standard relating to GMOs but the potential consequences to society of not setting such a standard are substantial? What weight should be given to irrationality (in the sense of a lack of firm evidence), which may be exhibited in any society when establishing national standards based on national preferences?

The technical nature of these questions means they deserve consideration in specialized bodies outside the WTO that can draw up the appropriate standards. Since social and ethical considerations are involved, developing a means to deal with matters such as precaution in the WTO should not be left to negotiators working according to briefs that reflect only national interests. What is at stake is maintaining the effective operation of the multilateral trading system while dealing with concerns that go far beyond conventional trade policy. At the moment, such questions are being addressed with respect to a variety of WTO Agreements and it is far from clear how they should be handled.

Notes

1. According to *Agenda 21*, biotechnology "promises to make a significant contribution in enabling the development of, for example, better health care, enhanced food security through sustainable agricultural practices, improved supplies of potable water, more efficient industrial development processes for transforming raw materials, support for sustainable methods of afforestation and reforestation, and detoxification of hazardous wastes". United Nations, *Report of the United Nations Conference on Environment and Development*, New York: United Nations, A/CONF.151/26 (Vol. II), August 1992, Chapter 16, para. 1. *Agenda 21* also calls for more support to be given to the positive contribution that biotechnology may provide in the area of public health. Since the discoveries of the 1960s, biotechnology has been applied to seemingly intractable health issues, determining which genes are responsible for creating or enabling disease processes, how these genes control these processes and what might be done to stop them. See UNDP, *Human Development Report*, New York: United Nations, 2001.
2. For many examples, see A. H. Zakri and M. Taeb, "Prospects and Problems of Biotechnology in Sustainable Development, Institute of Advanced Studies, United Nations University", Invited address at the 6th International Conference on Technology Policy and Innovation (ITPI Kansai 2002), 12–15 August 2002, Kyoto, Japan.
3. See the report of the United Nations Conference on Environment and Development, Annex 1, *Rio Declaration on Environment and Development*, Rio de Janeiro, 3–14 June 1992, Principle 15. The principle has already secured its place in a number of international agreements. The Convention on Biological Diversity, for instance, states that, "where there is a threat of significant reduction or loss of biological diversity, lack of full scientific certainty should not be used as a reason for postponing measures to avoid or minimise such a threat".
4. For an elaboration, see European Commission, *Guidelines on the Application of the Precautionary Principle*, Directorate General XXIV, HB/hb D(98), Brussels: European Commission, 17 October 1998.
5. See Gary P. Sampson, "Risk and the WTO", in David Robertson and Aynsley Kellows (eds), *Globalisation and the Environment: Risk Assessment and the WTO*, Cheltenham: Edward Elgar Publishers, 2000, chapter 2.

6. See Matthew Stilwell and Brennan Van Dyke, *An Activist's Handbook on Genetically Modified Organisms and the WTO*, Geneva: Centre for International Environmental Law, March 1999. The authors note that other tests could be applied more appropriately to determine whether GMO and non-GMO products are "like". The traditional WTO test for determining the likeness of products looks at: (1) consumers' tastes and habits; (2) the products' physical characteristics and end-uses; and (3) the products' properties, nature and qualities.

7. The three countries had filed separate complaints but agreed that a single Panel would hear all cases. According to the US Panel request, the measures affecting biotech products are: (a) the suspension by the European Union of consideration of applications for, or granting of, approval of biotech products; (b) the European Union's failure to consider for approval applications for specific biotech products; and (c) national marketing and import bans maintained on specific products by EU member states.

8. Australia, China, Chile, Colombia, El Salvador, Honduras, New Zealand, Norway, Peru, Thailand, Uruguay and Chinese Taipei have reserved their third-party rights.

9. See Barbara Eggers and Ruth Mackenzie, "The Cartagena Protocol on Biosafety", *Journal of International Environmental Law*, Vol. 3, No. 3, 2000.

10. For a useful discussion, see S. Prakash, "Towards a Synergy between Biodiversity and Intellectual Property Rights", *Journal of World Intellectual Property*, Vol. 2, No. 5, September 1999.

11. It could be argued that intellectual property rights and the protection of biodiversity are conceptually unrelated. However, since the Biodiversity Convention establishes the right of national governments to control access to genetic resources, and intellectual property rights provide a possible mechanism for controlling the use of information relating to genetic resources, the link is made through the Convention.

12. See Graham Dutfield, *Intellectual Property Rights, Trade and Biodiversity*, London: IUCN and Earthscan Publications, 2000, p. 41.

13. Ibid.

14. See WTO, *Doha Declarations: The Doha Development Agenda*, Geneva: WTO Secretariat, 2001, para. 19.

15. Scientists and others have objected to any procedure that changes the genetic composition of an organism. Critics are concerned that some of the genetically altered forms will eliminate existing species, thereby upsetting the natural balance of organisms. There are also fears that recombinant DNA experiments with pathogenic micro-organisms may result in the formation of extremely virulent forms that, if accidentally released from the laboratory, might cause worldwide epidemics. Some critics cite ethical dilemmas associated with the production of transgenic organisms.

16. Statement by the Church of Scotland cited in Graham Dutfield, "Biotechnology, Patents and the Life Science Industry", mimeo, September 2000, and referenced in D. Bruce and A. Bruce, *Engineering Genesis – The Ethics of Genetic Engineering in Non-Human Species*, London: Earthscan, 1998.

17. Dutfield, "Biotechnology, Patents and the Life Science Industry".

18. See James Orbinski, in Gary P. Sampson (ed.), *The Role of the WTO in Global Governance*, Tokyo: United Nations University Press, 2001, p. 239.

19. In this case, the original patent holder (in Country A) grants a licence to produce and market the patented product (in Country B), and the licence holder (in Country B) then sells the product cheaply – without the permission of the patent owner (in Country A) – to a purchaser in a third country (in Country C).

20. Carlos Correa, "Access to Drugs under TRIPS: A Not So Expeditious Solution", *Bridges*, Vol. 8, No. 1, January 2004.

8

Trade in services and sustainable development

Introduction

The General Agreement on Trade in Services (GATS) is considered by many to be one of the major successes of the Uruguay Round of multilateral trade negotiations. It extends internationally agreed rules and commitments, broadly comparable with those of the General Agreement on Tariffs and Trade (GATT), into a huge and still rapidly growing area of international trade. Also, because of how trade in services is defined for the purposes of the Agreement, a large share of trade in services takes place inside national borders (for example, through the commercial presence of foreign service providers). Thus, the requirements of the Agreement have a considerable potential influence on national domestic laws and regulations. As such, the GATS holds the potential greatly to change the global patterns of investment, production and consumption in services: telecommunications services, transport services (air, maritime and inland), financial services (banking, insurance and security trading), professional services, tourism, construction and engineering, and many others. These services include medical and hospital services and other areas of public health, and infrastructural services such as the supply of water, electricity and public utilities generally. It is not surprising that the GATS has provoked a great deal of interest – and anxiety – on the part of those concerned with sustainable development. In fact, any doubts about the concern of some with respect to the GATS and sustainable development should be dispelled by the conclusions of developmental non-governmental organizations. One such organization approvingly cites a comprehensive review which concludes that the GATS could "have devastating effects on the ability of governments to meet the needs of their poorest and most powerless citizens".[1]

In broad outline, the Uruguay Round services package resembles that for goods. A central set of rules was to a great extent directly modelled on the GATT and relies on many of the same principles. Supplementary agreements – some in the form of Annexes to the GATS, others embodied in Ministerial Decisions – deal with specific sectoral and other issues. And national schedules, one for each WTO member, set out commitments not to impose greater restrictions on the supply of services than are specified in the schedules. Whereas obligations under the GATT can to a great extent be understood by reference only to the general rules set out in its Articles, the GATS obligations of each member depend significantly on what commitments it has undertaken and therefore are specifically inscribed in its own schedule.

One factor that will mitigate against the full realization of the potential of the GATS is that it is not an easy Agreement to work with. It consists of 29 complex Articles that elaborate the concepts, obligations and procedures on which the Agreement is based. There are also eight Annexes, which bring further specificity to sectoral considerations as well as the movement of persons, and in some instances modify the application of the concepts contained in the Agreement. Of nine additional Attachments, eight are Ministerial Decisions on a variety of subjects ranging from the environment to dispute settlement procedures. There is also an Understanding on how some governments may wish to negotiate liberalization in financial services. All in all, the GATS is far from "user friendly".

Further, each member country not only adopts the texts but also undertakes commitments to liberalize trade in services in a vast variety of sectors and subsectors. These liberalization commitments are selective with respect to the sectors concerned and the limitations and restrictions that may be placed on service suppliers. In addition, there are specific measures in different sectors that importing governments are not prepared to subject to most favoured nation treatment. That is to say, members retain the right to discriminate between service suppliers according to their country of origin.

The difficulty in working with the Agreement in large measure relates to the complexity of the subject matter, but also is a reflection of the fact that the Agreement was heavily negotiated. For example, various provisions are unclear and the obligations themselves, as contained in the Agreement, are not organized in an analytical fashion. Further, although some of the concepts have familiar-sounding names for those acquainted with the GATT and related Agreements, these familiar-sounding concepts have different meanings and implications when applied to trade in services. The word "trade" itself, for example, has a totally different meaning in terms of the Services Agreement compared with the GATT and other merchandise-related Agreements. For example, trade in services may well take place with nothing crossing the border.

A further example of the complexity of the Agreement comes from the manner in which liberalization commitments are undertaken and recorded. Specific commitments are undertaken in individual sectors and subsectors as specified by governments; limitations and conditions may then be legally placed on the commitments themselves depending on how the service enters international commerce (i.e. the means by which the service is supplied) and the restrictive measures the importing country may wish to maintain. There is no parallel in any other multilateral, plurilateral or bilateral Agreement dealing with international commerce of any kind. Indeed, only time will tell the extent to which the legally binding commitments inscribed in the schedules that transcribe the legal undertaking will stand up in a court of law.

The objective of this chapter is to describe in general terms the relevant characteristics of the GATS that permit a balanced discussion of the criticisms that have been levelled at it. Only in this manner can the contribution or otherwise of the Agreement to sustainable development be correctly evaluated. The outline of the chapter is as follows. After describing the background to the Agreement, I discuss its architecture, drawing attention to the added complexity brought by its complicated structure. I then examine the scope of application of the Agreement and comment on the nature of the obligations contained in the Agreement. A number of concerns have been raised in connection with the implications of the Agreement – particularly for developing countries. I address these and identify policy considerations.

Background

The approach of developing countries to negotiations on services prior to the Uruguay Round is legendary; most actively resisted the idea of negotiations and the remaining few were unconvinced at best.[2] From an academic perspective, this should come as no surprise. In the development literature of the past half-century, the role ascribed to the services sector – if indeed there was a role at all – has at best been a passive one. Its contribution to economic growth has traditionally been relegated to a stage of economic development rather than a driving force behind it. Famous growth economists – Allan Fisher, Walt W. Rostow and Colin Clark –

espoused a theory in which the process of development consisted of three main phases: first, the pre-industrial phase; second, the industrial phase, where manufacturing plays the dominant role with a shift from agriculture to industry; and, third, the post-industrial stage, in which the economy becomes a service economy. Viewed in this perspective, a well-functioning services sector was considered as a symptom rather than a source of economic development.[3] Times have changed. A viable services sector is now considered to be a precondition for economic growth and a crucial ingredient for sustainable development.

From a negotiating perspective, the scepticism of developing countries was well placed.[4] The early options in terms of an outcome were a modification of the text of the GATT itself to include references to services at various agreed places in the Articles. This was resisted because there was no guarantee that applying traditional GATT concepts – such as non-discrimination and transparency – to trade in services would be to the benefit of developing countries. Another option was an addendum to the GATT along the lines of Part IV, something that history had proven to be of limited usefulness (see chapter 9). Another alternative was to have a stand-alone Code on Trade in Services with a limited number of signatories and provisions that were best endeavour in nature. A plurilateral agreement of this type – it was proposed – could be modelled on some of the Codes of the Organisation for Economic Co-operation and Development (OECD). Most importantly, however, developing countries saw little to gain and much to lose because their potential services exports came in the form of labour-intensive services or labour itself, and there was little likelihood of expanded export opportunities given the prevailing level of unemployment in OECD countries. At the same time, a services agreement could lead to investment flows to areas of strategic importance to developing countries that they might not be well placed to receive.

Subsequently, however, there was a radical change in the thinking of developing countries, for a number of reasons. First, the effective provision of infrastructural services – such as health, education, local communications and local transport – came to be seen as a priority for developing countries' own national economic development. A carefully negotiated and balanced agreement could assist in achieving this goal. Second, there was a realization that these and other services – maritime transport, freight insurance, marketing, distribution and international finance – are vitally important in determining developing countries' export supply capacity of goods. More international competition could result in better-quality and less expensive services of this nature. Third, there are services of interest to developing countries that were currently traded (exported and imported) or could be exported (or replace imports) if they did not face trade barriers; these include tourism, international transport and certain off-shore labour-intensive services. Further, there was the general orientation in a number of key developing countries towards adopting more outward-oriented development strategies in both goods and services. Concessions could be obtained elsewhere as a result of this liberalization. Finally, and most importantly, the developing countries realized that, by negotiating effectively in an area in which they were not the *demandeurs*, they could achieve a paradigm different from the GATT – development could be an integral part of whatever agreement emerged. They were correct in this respect.

As the negotiations proceeded, developing countries' goal to use the Agreement to extract commitments to increase their participation in world trade started to take form. The key elements included commitments to transfer technology, to improve their access to distribution channels and information networks, and to ensure liberalization in services sectors of export interest to them, including labour-intensive services. Very importantly, developing countries sought the flexibility to pursue their own development priorities, opening fewer sectors, liberalizing fewer types of transactions, and extending market access in line with their development situation.

In fact, developing countries were remarkably successful in shaping the agenda and setting the pace in Uruguay Round negotiations on services. Some 20 developing countries not only took a very high profile in the Group of Negotiations on Services (GNS) – the group established to negotiate trade in services in the Uruguay Round – but were largely responsible for the architecture of the Agreement itself. A number of institutional considerations were important in this respect.

For almost the duration of the Uruguay Round the GNS had a developing country chairperson, and developing countries devoted their best resources to the negotiating process. No formal or informal meetings were convened by the chairperson unless all developing country interests were covered by those present. In fact this pattern was established at the start of the Uruguay Round negotiations by an important manoeuvre on the part of developing countries. They had insisted that the negotiations on services be placed on a completely separate track from other agenda items of the Uruguay Round. The reason for this strategy was to ensure that concessions could not be asked of developing countries in the area of services in exchange for concessions of interest to them in the area of goods trade. One specific example is that developing countries were not prepared to open their services markets in exchange for developed country "concessions" in the form of a phasing out of the Multi-fibre Arrangement. This Arrangement, which quantitatively restricted the exports of developing countries, was construed as a derogation from the normal workings of the GATT. Developing countries correctly insisted that nothing should be paid to return a derogation to normalcy.

An additional factual point of some interest is that, unlike other aspects of the negotiation process, the services negotiations were never derailed by being caught up in a total blockage of the negotiating process, as occurred, for example, in agriculture and thus all negotiating groups dealing with goods at the Montreal and Brussels Ministerial Meetings. Negotiations progressed steadily on a separate track with compromises being found to accommodate the above concerns within the services negotiations themselves.[5]

As the negotiations progressed, however, it was clear that the GATS was destined to be a framework agreement establishing the concepts, principles and rules of the Agreement, with specific and legally binding commitments registered in national schedules – rather like with trade in goods. Very little was demanded of signatory countries at the outset. The lack of ambition in this respect is not surprising. No countries – developing or developed – were enthusiastic about committing themselves to far-reaching general obligations in the framework agreement when so little was known about the implications of their application in sectors of strategic importance to their economies. As far as the specific commitments were concerned, how far a country wished to go in committing itself to market-opening obligations was – according to the architecture of the Agreement – a national choice and something to be negotiated. In addition, although all countries, including least developed countries, were obliged to have a national schedule containing commitments for individual sectors, this was considered by many (and particularly by least developed countries) to be little more than a formality. Many countries did little more than bind something less than the status quo in terms of committed openness in a limited number of sectors.

Contrary to the accusations of some critics, developing countries in large measure secured what they were looking for in the negotiations. First, the Agreement is a multilateral framework of principles and rules for trade in services within which there can be progressive liberalization of trade in services. This principle is important for developing countries and they insisted on its inclusion. What it translated into was that, at the time of signing the Agreement, few commitments were required and, at the insistence of developing countries, additional commitments would come only progressively with time. Second, developing countries were not restricted at the time of joining the Agreements when introducing new regulations to meet national policy objectives. What was important here was the recognition that, given the asymmetries in the development of services regulations in different countries, there was a particular need for developing countries to have the appropriate regulations in place before considering liberalization. Third, there was a commitment for developing countries to take a fuller part in world trade in services, particularly through strengthening the capacity, efficiency and competitiveness of their own domestic services. Further, contrary to what is sometimes argued, the GATS does not oblige – or even encourage – any country to privatize or deregulate its services sectors. Finally, a real attraction of the Agreement for developing countries was that it provided them with the possibility of imposing restrictions and limitations on the presence of foreign service providers to ensure that they respected domestic regulations. As in goods trade, this was available through the use of scheduled and legally enforceable commitments – an option not open to developing countries under bilaterally negotiated deals with more powerful trading countries (or companies) where they might be pressured unfairly. Importantly, non-respect of obligations on the part of foreign service providers was to be actionable under the WTO dispute settlement provisions.

In the final stages of the Uruguay Round, there was considerable difficulty in closing off the total package of what had been negotiated. The Round was an all-or-nothing affair, so the services outcome had to be accepted along with all the other components. Services negotiations were no exception in terms of difficulty of adoption. However, this was not due to an unwillingness on the part of developing countries. It was entirely a result of resistance by developed countries because of the difficulties they had in undertaking commitments in a number of other sectors, such as maritime transport and audiovisual services, and their lack of satisfaction about the adequacy of market openings in the financial and telecommunications services.

It is odd that the GATS Agreement is savagely criticized by a number of developmental non-governmental organizations (NGOs), when developing countries see it as a major achievement of the Uruguay Round. One contributing factor to this apparent anomaly may be a perception that countries – particularly developing countries – are obliged to undertake more commitments under the Agreement than is the case. Another closely linked consideration may be that it is thought that the scope of application of the Agreement is broader than it actually is, with correspondingly fewer possibilities to make exceptions or to revoke earlier commitments. Another contributing factor could be that some consider the Agreement not to be development oriented and not to be supported by developing countries. A further possibility is a false perception that developing countries were somehow duped in these negotiations. This was not the case and it is offensive and patronising to say so. Developing countries undertook commitments in areas where they wished to. The GATS is very much a bottom–up agreement in which few obligations are undertaken at the outset and additional obligations are undertaken according to national preferences. If countries are bullied into undertaking more commitments than they should because of powerful trading partners, it makes little sense to criticize the Agreement on these grounds. The bullying would take place in any event. The great advantage of this Agreement is that negotiations are carried out in a transparent manner, the results are written into transparent schedules, along with the limitations and restrictions placed on foreign suppliers, and the limitations and restrictions are legally binding irrespective of the power of the foreign supplier.

Important concepts in the Agreement are unclear and critics tend to look for uncharitable interpretations. This lack of clarity may be owing to the fact that no comprehensive history of the services negotiations has been written to date. In the same vein, the lack of clarity that characterizes some of the text comes as no surprise for those engaged in the negotiation of this Agreement. It is the result of the legendary penchant of GATT/WTO members to resort to constructive ambiguity in the drafting process. When agreement is not reached on a particular aspect of the negotiation, clever drafting can be a way for each of the negotiators to report back to their capital that the national position is covered. The ambiguous drafting means that different meanings are ascribed to the same terms, in the hopes that it will never be necessary to seek clarification at a later stage through dispute settlement or through interpretation via a more inclusive process.

The architecture of the GATS: Its complexity

At the outset of the Uruguay Round, there was some concern that numerous international agreements and institutions already exist to do with services: the International Telecommunications Union, the International Civil Aircraft Organization, the International Tourism Organization and the International Maritime Organization are examples. Was there a need for yet another institution to be dealing with the same subject matter? The answer to this was in the affirmative for two reasons. First, the terms of reference of the Uruguay Round negotiations were to liberalize trade in services *progressively*. This was not in the mandate of any of the existing institutions. Second, the negotiations were to deal with government measures affecting trade in *all services sectors*. The terms of reference were unique in the sense that they were not sector specific and no services sector was a priori excluded.

The GATS consists of 29 Articles made up of six parts. An opening section sets out the scope and definition of the Agreement. Part II, the longest, deals with general obligations and disciplines; that is, with rules that apply, for the most part, to all traded services and all members. Part III sets out rules that relate to the specific commitments negotiated between governments and recorded in schedules. The counterpart to services schedules in the case of trade in goods is national tariff schedules. Part IV provides for the future negotiation of specific commitments and rules relating to the schedules themselves. Part V covers institutional provisions and Part VI deals with final provisions. There are supplementary agreements – some in the form of Annexes to the GATS, others embodied in Ministerial Decisions – that deal with specific sectoral and other issues. And there are national schedules, one for each WTO member, which set out commitments not to impose greater restrictions than are specified on the supply of services by other members.

Not only is the GATS a complex agreement, but its contents (concepts, principles, rules, rights and obligations) are not organized in a particularly analytical fashion – reflecting the protracted and difficult negotiating process that created it. Although similarities with the GATT exist in the sense that the GATS relies on many of the same principles, these have very different meanings in the context of trade in services. Understanding of the Agreement can perhaps be facilitated, however, if the rights and obligations it contains are grouped in terms of two broad sets of obligations.

The first comprises general obligations, which are compulsory and generic in coverage. They are compulsory in the sense that they apply to all WTO members and are non-negotiable. They are generic in the sense that that they apply to all measures covered by the Agreement. They set the floor in terms of the commitments undertaken when WTO members joined the Agreement – or join through the process of accession to the WTO. It will be argued that they are non-onerous and sensible. In any event, they are considered to be neither contentious nor unreasonable for the signatory countries, and therefore are not under critical review within the WTO.

The second set of obligations is voluntary in the sense that they apply only to sectors and subsectors where governments have chosen to go beyond the compulsory and generic obligations mentioned above. If they have taken this option, it is because they consider it to be in their national interests.[6] These sectors are inscribed in a positive list that identifies the economic activities where specific commitments have been undertaken. As far as the specific commitments are concerned, there are again two types of obligations. The first are both compulsory and generic in nature: they apply in the same way to all the sectors where specific commitments have been undertaken (i.e. they are generic) and they are non-negotiable (i.e. they are compulsory). The second set of voluntary commitments comprises obligations that are tailor-made for each of the committed services on the positive list. They do not have to be undertaken, they are negotiable (i.e. they are not compulsory), and therefore they may be different for each sector or subsector (i.e. they are not generic).

It is these commitments that establish the degree of market openness for individual countries via the binding of existing or improved market access. As with tariffs and the GATT, they are contained in schedules, which are legally binding and an integral part of the Agreement. Unlike the GATT, however, specific commitments are subject to limitations and conditions imposed on foreign service providers and in this sense they are tailor-made. This feature of the Agreement is particularly attractive to developing countries because a government can legally register the conditions to be respected by the foreign service supplier. Further, and of critical importance to developing countries, any service activity that is not inscribed in the schedule is subject only to the first set of obligations – the compulsory obligations that apply to all measures affecting trade in services. As will be reasoned below, these are minimal to say the least.

The scope of the Agreement: Measures affecting trade in services

A critical starting point for a review of the GATS is the wording that defines its scope of application, which is one of the most troublesome aspects of the Agreement for many of its critics. It is important to note that the forefathers of the Agreement never meant it to apply to trade in services per se, and indeed it does not. The objective is to apply the obligations of the Agreement to measures – in fact, any measure affecting trade in services. As a result of this approach, three critical questions immediately presented themselves for negotiators:
• What measures are relevant for the purposes of the GATS?
• What is trade in services for the purposes of the Agreement?
• What is a service?
These questions will be addressed in turn.

Measures: What is a measure?

The definition of what constitutes a measure is particularly far-reaching; "measures by Members" means any measure, whether in the form of a law, regulation, rule, procedure, decision, administrative action, or any other form. The definition is thus open-ended. As in the case of the GATT, the reach of this definition goes beyond central governments to include measures taken by regional and local governments. Members are required to do their best to ensure that subnational governments observe GATS obligations and commitments. The definition also extends to the measures of non-governmental bodies exercising powers delegated to them by governments. There is, however, a carve out: measures relating to services supplied "in the exercise of governmental authority" are not covered. These are defined as services (such as central banking and social security) that are supplied "neither on a commercial basis, nor in competition with one or more service suppliers". Clearly, many public services are not provided on a commercial or a competitive basis and are therefore not subject in any way to the GATS.[7] However, some are. In virtually all countries, the public provision of services – for example, education, public utilities and health – coexists with private sector provision. Many governments recognize that ensuring the universal availability and quality of these essential services is among their primary responsibilities. They undertake commitments to allow domestic – and in some cases foreign – suppliers to provide education or health services in their markets, on condition that they respect domestic regulations. Most countries strictly regulate such activities, irrespective of whether they are supplied by local or foreign firms or by the government itself.

Critics' principal concern here would appear to be that the foreign provision of these services could constitute an encroachment on national sovereignty and undermine domestic regulations. A number of points are important in this respect. For those government services that are supplied on a commercial or competitive basis, the coverage of the activity means that only the compulsory obligations apply. As will be seen, these could not be considered an encroachment on national sovereignty. Second, additional obligations are undertaken because the government chose to do so. Third, and most importantly, if governments do admit foreign suppliers in these areas, these suppliers are obliged to operate in accordance with domestic regulations and the restrictions and limitations written into the national legally binding schedules. These restrictions and limitations are transparent and are legally enforceable through the WTO dispute settlement system. As noted, this is far superior to negotiating bilaterally with powerful transnational corporations. A further point is perhaps that there is nothing in the Agreement that requires – or even encourages – publicly provided services (e.g. health, education, public utilities) to be privatized. Additionally, if governments make no specific commitments on these sectors – and undertake only the general obligations of the Agreement – they are free to maintain both public and private monopoly suppliers.

The reality is that governments have indeed undertaken commitments with respect to government services supplied on a commercial basis in the area of education and health services.[8] They have not, however, engaged in a privatization of public healthcare or education systems. They most certainly have not compromised domestic regulations; indeed, they have enforced the same standards on foreign suppliers as on nationals for the protection of the public. A number of governments have also imposed additional requirements on foreigners beyond those required of national service suppliers.

Trade in services: What is it?

The GATT does not define trade in goods. Perhaps it is obvious because international trade takes place when merchandise crosses the border. In the case of services, the components of a cross-border definition of trade in services would be, for example, postal services, voice telephony and telefax services. Such a definition would, however, exclude a vast array of services where international transactions do indeed take place. Services are, by their nature, perishable and therefore supplied and consumed at the time of fabrication (a barber cutting hair or a portfolio manager providing advice), which means that the cross-border movement of the service is not involved. Rather, the physical presence of the service supplier is required in the importing country, or the physical presence of the service consumer in the exporting country. In these instances, for an international transaction to take place, the supplier of the service may have to move to the location of the receiver (fields in one country cannot be ploughed by tractors in another), or the receiver of the service may have to move to the point of supply to consume the service (the Taj Mahal cannot be shipped to Paris, and the Eiffel Tower cannot be shipped to Agra).

In the early stages of the Uruguay Round negotiations, there were differing views about the dividing line between trade and investment in services. Developing countries had successfully opposed launching fully fledged negotiations on investment, and were sensitive to the risk of services negotiations delivering an investment agreement through the back door. If the Agreement was to encompass services provided through the establishment of the service providers, it would indeed be tantamount to creating a multilateral agreement on investment in services. Another concern was that a number of developed countries were arguing that the Services Agreement should establish a right to investment. Resistance was finally overcome through agreeing that there were various ways of providing services internationally, some of them being alternative means to reach the same end; that conditions and limitations could be placed on any foreign commercial presence, which ensured that investment would not be considered a right in the Agreement; and that horizontal limitations could be placed on all foreign services suppliers (such as through a required approval for establishment from the national foreign investment review body), which assured developing countries that investment could be appropriately regulated (see below).

Thus, the definition of trade in services was to be based on the means by which services were supplied internationally.[9] Four modes of supply were identified: cross-border movement of the service; consumption abroad of the service; the commercial presence in the consuming country of the service supplier; and the presence of natural persons in the importing country to supply the service. The notion of modes of supply has largely shaped the principles and rules embodied in the GATS, as well as the specific commitments written into the schedules. An analysis of the definition helps in appreciating the special problems and regulatory issues that arise in negotiating the liberalization of the international trade in services. Each mode has its own peculiarities.

First, the service itself may cross the border from the territory of one member to that of another (for example, an international telephone call). This mode of supply corresponds with the normal form of trade in goods. It is in many ways the most straightforward form of trade in services, because it resembles the familiar subject matter of the GATT, not least in maintaining a clear geographical separation between seller and buyer.

Second, the service consumer of one member may move across a border to consume a service supplied by another member in its own territory. This mode of "consumption abroad" is, in the words of Article I of the GATS, the supply of a service "in the territory of one Member to the service consumer of another Member". Typically, this will involve the consumer travelling to the supplying country, perhaps for tourism or to attend an educational establishment. Another example of consumption abroad would be the repair of a ship or aircraft outside its home country. Like cross-border supply, this is a straightforward form of trade which raises few problems since it does not require the service supplier to be admitted to the consuming country for work purposes.

Third, a large proportion of service transactions require that the provider and the consumer be in the same place. In such instances, there is a need for the presence of a service supplier of one member in the territory of the consumer of another member through a form of commercial establishment (for example, a commercial presence to sell retail banking services in the importing country). This mode of supply raises the most difficult issues for host governments and for GATS negotiations because rules governing commercial presence are very different from those on tariffs and other border measures.

Fourth, the movement of natural persons may involve the movement of persons to establishments where the supplier has a permanent commercial presence or the natural persons may be providing services as independent individuals. For example, a surgeon may move to work in a hospital where a commercial presence has been established or may be temporarily visiting another country to perform a specialized operation. An Annex to the GATS makes it clear, however, that the Agreement has nothing to do with individuals looking for employment in another country, or with citizenship, residence or employment requirements. Even if members undertake commitments to allow natural persons to provide services in their territories, they may still regulate their entry and stay, for instance by requiring visas, as long as they do not prevent the commitments from being fulfilled.

This wide definition of trade in services makes the GATS directly relevant to policy areas that traditionally have not been touched upon by multilateral trade rules.[10] Access regulations for the supply of professional activities are an example, as are investment regulations relating to the foreign presence of a foreign bank branch and the prudential concerns that this may involve. In short, regulations affecting foreign investment are directly relevant to the supply of a service through the establishment of commercial presence, and certain restrictions on the temporary movement of personnel are relevant through the presence of natural persons required to supply a service.

Services: What are they?

The last in the trio of questions that confronted negotiators concerned the sectoral coverage of services for the purposes of the Agreement. The answer to this question is complicated because there is no natural scientific definition of a service. Services differ radically according to the economic or social function they provide and the production function and factors of production that produce them. There are no economic characteristics that are common to all services. In national accounts, services are grouped together as residuals and in the International Monetary Fund balance of payments statistics they are referred to as invisibles. These terms are unhelpful when defining economic activities for the purposes of negotiations.

In a typically pragmatic GATT tradition, and after considerable debate, the Group of Negotiations on Services simply requested the GATT Secretariat to draw up a provisional list of what it considered to be services sectors based on empirical observation. As a result, in 1991 the Secretariat produced what has proven to be a classic document, which served to identify the scope of application of the GATS in terms of sectoral coverage.[11] The basis of this classification is the United Nations Central Product Classification (CPC) system, which identifies 11 basic service sectors, plus a twelfth category for miscellaneous services: business (including professional and computer) services; communication services; construction and related engineering services; distribution services; educational services; environmental services; financial (insurance and banking) services; health-related and social services; tourism and travel-related services; recreational, cultural and sporting services; transport services; and other services not included elsewhere. These sectors are subdivided into some 160 subsectors or separate service activities. As an example, the tourism category breaks down into subsectors for: hotels and restaurants; travel agencies and tour operators; and tourist guide services.

The nature of the obligations

As noted at the outset, the obligations of the GATS fall into two broad categories.

General obligations

Part II sets out the general obligations and disciplines that apply irrespective of whether a service has been scheduled. The most important general obligation is most favoured nation (MFN) treatment, which is also a key obligation in the GATT-1994 and other WTO Agreements. It requires members to grant services and service suppliers of any other member the most favourable treatment granted to like services and service suppliers of any other country. This obligation guarantees that any liberalization will be extended to all members. Although it does not, by itself, require any particular degree of market openness, it does ensure unbiased competition among trading partners. It is certainly attractive for developing countries, which fought hard in the Uruguay Round negotiations to have MFN as a compulsory and general obligation rather than negotiated for each service category.

For both developed and developing countries, a number of sectors were characterized by preferential arrangements at the time of the negotiations. For example, all countries had preferential arrangements in their air transport sectors, a number of developing countries had preferential cargo-sharing arrangements for their maritime service sectors, and some developed countries had preferential arrangements in their maritime and audiovisual sectors. To gain acceptance of the concept at the time of negotiation, it was agreed that any member was permitted to maintain a measure inconsistent with the general MFN requirement in the form of an exemption.[12] The exemptions could be taken either at the time of entry into force of the Agreement or at the time of accession to the WTO.

The result was that more than 70 WTO members specified services activities in a list of MFN exemptions. These exemption lists are governed by conditions set out in a separate Annex to the GATS that makes clear that no new exemptions can be granted, at least not by this route, and that future requests for non-MFN treatment can be met only through WTO waiver procedures. Although some exemptions are subject to a stated time limit, some members have indicated that their intended duration was indefinite. For those that are not, the Annex provides that in principle they should not last longer than 10 years (that is, not beyond 2004), and that in any case they are subject to negotiation in future trade-liberalizing rounds. The listed exemptions were reviewed in the Council for Trade in Services prior to the end of 1999 to see whether they were still needed.

Given the sensitive and strategic nature of many of the domestic regulations that relate to service activities, it is not surprising that governments took care not to undertake general commitments that would unduly limit their flexibility to meet national policy objectives. The right to regulate is one of the fundamental premises of the GATS – as it is in all the WTO Agreements – and is specifically acknowledged as such. The objective of the GATS is to liberalize measures affecting trade in services, to regulate in a non-discriminatory manner, but not to deregulate services activities. Members are free to introduce new regulations in order to meet national policy objectives and, given the asymmetries in the degree of development of services regulations in different countries, the particular need of developing countries to exercise this right is acknowledged.

Thus, the general obligations relating to domestic regulations are modest, to say the least. In this respect, the Council for Trade in Services was instructed via the text of the GATS to develop disciplines, through appropriate bodies, that may be necessary to ensure that regulatory measures are based on objective and transparent criteria, such as competence and the ability to supply the service; are not more burdensome than necessary to ensure the quality of the service; and, in the case of licensing procedures, are not in themselves a restriction on the supply of the service.

A failure to recognize the legitimate qualifications of a service supplier from another country – in terms of meeting the minimum domestic standards to deliver a service – can be an effective means to deny the possibility to supply a service. For this reason, the GATS urges members to recognize the educational or other qualifications of service suppliers of other countries. It allows governments to negotiate agreements among themselves for mutual recognition of such qualifications, provided other countries with comparable standards are given a chance to join. Qualifications requirements are not to be applied in a way that discriminates between countries or constitutes a disguised restriction on trade in services, and should be based wherever appropriate on internationally agreed standards. Both the Technical Barriers to Trade Agreement and the

Sanitary and Phytosanitary Measures Agreement have the same recognition of the importance of international standards. WTO members are also committed by the GATS to work in cooperation with intergovernmental and non-governmental organizations towards the establishment and adoption of common international standards for the practice of services, trades and professions. This does not mean, however, that the WTO itself should play any role in the formulation of standards or the development of criteria for recognition.

As noted earlier, it was crucial for developing countries that development considerations, in the form of the increasing participation of developing countries, were an integral part of the Agreement. According to the GATS, this is to be facilitated through negotiated specific commitments relating to the strengthening of their domestic services capacity and their efficiency and competitiveness, *inter alia*, through: access to technology on a commercial basis; the improvement of their access to distribution channels and information networks; and the liberalization of market access in sectors and modes of supply of export interest to them. It is in the making of specific commitments and the provisions surrounding them that this obligation is to be implemented.[13] Thus, unlike Part IV of the GATT-1994, in which the commitments undertaken with respect to developing countries are best endeavour in nature, the GATS provides the possibility for commitments by developed countries to be inscribed in their schedules, thereby rendering them mandatory. One of the principal stumbling blocks in the Doha Development Agenda is how to meet the agreed need to make best endeavour special and differential treatment provisions mandatory in the case of goods trade.

The GATS provisions on general and security exceptions are, as in the GATT, preceded by a Head Note that makes the right of a member to adopt or enforce measures for the purposes listed subject to the condition that they not be applied as a means of "arbitrary or unjustifiable discrimination between countries where like conditions prevail, or as a disguised restriction on trade in services". The list that follows includes legitimate policies similar to those that apply to trade in goods, such as the protection of public morals and human, animal or plant life or health. Others are particularly applicable to services, such as the protection of individual privacy in the handling of personal data and equitable and effective taxation.

Work on two provisions of the GATS – safeguards and subsidies – was unfinished at the end of the Uruguay Round and remains so. With respect to safeguards, until the completion of the continuing negotiations, a member may modify or withdraw a specific commitment if it can show the Council for Trade in Services that the action is necessary, in spite of the normal rule that such commitments cannot be changed for three years. With respect to subsidies and the possible need for countervailing duties, it is recognized that subsidies can distort trade in services, and the Agreement provides that a member adversely affected by another member's subsidy may request consultations that will be accorded sympathetic consideration. The absence of further GATS provisions on subsidies does not mean that, under the general rules, WTO members are entirely free to use them to assist only their domestic service suppliers. The obligation of national treatment would normally mean that certain foreign suppliers would also be entitled to receive any subsidies given to a competing domestic supplier. Many countries have in fact specifically excluded this possibility by stating in their schedules of services commitments that certain subsidies will not be available to foreign suppliers.

One general obligation of the GATS that has no GATT counterpart relates to anti-competitive practices of private enterprises. This is a pioneering clause in a multilateral trade agreement because it recognizes that certain business practices of service suppliers may restrain competition and thereby restrict trade in services. Members agree to consult on such practices, when so requested by another member, and to exchange information with a view to eliminating them.

There may be different, and perfectly legitimate, motivations for the existence of monopoly suppliers. However, services supplied by monopolies often constitute inputs to other service activities: obvious examples are telecommunications, financial services and transport. The GATS does not prohibit the maintenance of monopoly or exclusive rights to supply a service, but each member is required to ensure that any monopoly acts in a manner consistent with that member's obligations. For example, if a telecommunications monopoly allows interconnection to suppliers of value-added telecommunications, it should do so on the basis of MFN treatment.

General obligations for scheduled services

Although there are general obligations that apply to all measures that affect trade in all services (as discussed above), there are also general obligations that apply only to scheduled services, but nevertheless to *all* scheduled services. Others are tailor-made for the specific scheduled services activity and are described below. In the case of domestic regulations, there are obligations that apply to all measures irrespective of whether they are scheduled or not (as discussed above), but in the same Article there are obligations relating only to scheduled sectors. This is one of the features of the GATS that adds to its complexity.

Where authorization is required for the supply of a service on which a specific commitment has been made, the applicant for the authorization must be informed within a reasonable period of time of the decision or status concerning the application. The objective is to ensure that, for all sectors where specific commitments have been undertaken, laws, regulations and administrative guidelines are administered in a reasonable, objective and impartial manner. Thus, the focus is on the administration of measures, not on their substance. The main purpose is to ensure that foreign service suppliers are not discriminated against or unduly impeded in their activities by arbitrary or biased administration. Also, in all sectors where specific commitments have been undertaken, licensing and qualification requirements and technical standards should not be used to nullify or impair the specific commitments.

Scheduled services: Negotiable obligations

All schedules conform to a standard format, being divided into "horizontal" and "sector-specific" sections. The horizontal section contains limitations that apply to all sectors included in the schedule. These often refer to particular modes of supply, notably commercial presence and movement of natural persons. The purpose of having such a section is to avoid repeating the same entry in relation to each sector contained in the schedule. The extent of any sector-specific commitment is tempered by the horizontal entries. For each sector inscribed in the schedule, there must be an indication of the status of the four modes of supply and any restrictions or limitations on market access or national treatment.

With respect to market access, each member is to give no less favourable treatment to the services and service suppliers of other members than is provided in its schedule of commitments. This provision makes it clear that service commitments resemble those in a GATT schedule in at least one very important respect: they are binding and set out the minimum treatment of the foreign service or its supplier.[14] These commitments do not affect the right to regulate services, and a country may undertake no commitment at all if it so wishes. It may place limitations on the access to its markets of foreign service providers, but these limitations do not relate to domestic regulation and foreign suppliers are subject to conditions and qualifications indicated in the national treatment section of the schedule.

National treatment is stated in terms very similar to the GATT's Article III, but is limited to commitments listed in the schedule. As in the case of market access, the requirement that any limitations on national treatment be specified in the schedule gives these limitations the same character as a GATT-bound tariff: the stated conditions or qualifications represent the minimum treatment that may be given. The limitations placed on national treatment are important in terms of countries maintaining their autonomy in the regulation of the services provision. Discrimination is specifically provided for, whereas in Article III of the GATT-1994 it is prohibited. The reason lies in the nature of trade in services. Non-discrimination in the form of national treatment for goods does not necessarily lead to free trade, because foreign goods can be controlled by border measures. In the case of services, national treatment means free trade if no regulatory advantage can be offered to the national supplier. This gives considerable flexibility to the local authorities in discriminating against foreign services or maintaining complete discretion with respect to such discrimination by not scheduling the sector at all. Not surprisingly, the manner in which national treatment is handled in the GATS holds particular attraction for developing countries because they may impose on foreign service providers any conditions they wish. They may insist on the employment of locals if the service provider has a commercial presence, the training of local understudies, the transfer of technology and technical expertise, the use of local services in foreign-owned hotels, and writing these requirements into their schedules to make them legally enforceable.

The GATS and developing countries

One of the most significant differences from the GATT-1994 is that the GATS provides for the increasing participation of developing countries but links it to the negotiation of specific commitments. As discussed in chapter 9, one of the principal criticisms by developing countries is that most of the provisions of the GATT-1994, the Enabling Clause and other WTO Agreements are of a best endeavour nature. This is not the case with the GATS Agreement. As noted above, when developing countries provide access to their markets for foreign service suppliers, they are to attach to it conditions aimed at increasing their participation in trade in services (Article XIX:2). There is recognition in the Agreement that an efficient public telecommunications network is critical for service suppliers to be internationally competitive. Thus, developing countries are free to place conditions on access to their public telecommunications transport networks and services in order to strengthen the domestic telecommunications infrastructure.[15]

The provisions relating to the increasing participation of developing countries are designed to improve the supply capacity of developing countries rather than afford preferential market access or exempt them from obligations. In fact, unlike in the Enabling Clause, no preferential market access is provided for. Nevertheless, in negotiating specific commitments, appropriate flexibility is provided for individual developing countries to open fewer sectors, liberalize fewer types of transactions, and progressively extend market access in line with their development situation.

One of the many defining characteristics of the GATS is that it obliges signatories to enter into successive rounds of negotiations with a view to achieving a progressively higher level of liberalization of trade in services. This requirement has no counterpart in the GATT or in the other Uruguay Round agreements (except, to a more limited extent, the Agreement on Agriculture). Although the GATS sets the objective of achieving a progressively higher level of liberalization, members are under no formal obligation to undertake any given level of specific commitments. Each member must have a national schedule of commitments, but there is no rule about how extensive it should be. Some least developed members have made commitments only on tourism, for example, and in general there is great variation in the coverage of schedules, reflecting national policy objectives and levels of economic development. There is agreement among all governments that in the new round of negotiations the freedom to decide whether to liberalize any given service and the principle of progressive liberalization will be maintained.

However, liberalization of services trade should not be confused with deregulation. Many service industries must and will remain carefully regulated in the public interest. The GATS makes a distinction between trade barriers that distort competition and restrict access to markets on the one hand, and regulations that are necessary to pursue public policy objectives and ensure the orderly functioning of markets on the other hand. For example, restrictions on the number of suppliers of a certain service or discrimination against foreign suppliers are considered barriers to trade in services and may be subject to negotiation in future rounds. On the other hand, requiring compliance with technical standards or qualifications requirements that aim at ensuring the quality of the service and the protection of public interest is a legitimate form of domestic regulation. The Agreement does not restrict the ability of governments to maintain and develop such regulations. It also recognizes the particular need of developing countries to develop appropriate regimes to regulate services.

Access commitments undertaken under the GATS, and the ensuing gains in transparency and predictability, are a powerful means of encouraging foreign direct investment in key services such as telecommunications, finance and transport. In turn, the productivity effects associated with such investments tend to be enhanced by improved access to state-of-the-art technology and expertise. They are likely to benefit not only the sectors directly concerned, but a wide range of related industries. Specific commitments should be undertaken in such a way as to help developing countries to strengthen their domestic services capacity, and to provide access in sectors and modes of supply that are of export interest to them.

Withdrawing commitments

An important practical consideration is that circumstances may well arise in which a government may wish to take back something it has given in past negotiations. GATS commitments, like tariff bindings, are not irreversible. There are three ways in which a country can modify, or even withdraw, a commitment if it finds that to be necessary.

First, any commitment may be withdrawn or modified after it has been in force for three years. As under the Safeguards Agreement of the WTO or Article XVIII of the GATT-1994, compensation may need to be negotiated with members whose trade is affected. This means replacing the commitment withdrawn with another market opening of equivalent value. This process is similar to the renegotiation of tariff bindings under the GATT, which has been in use for over half a century.

Second, where it is necessary to act to protect major public interests, including safety, human, plant or animal life or health, national security or public morals, the General Exceptions in Article XIV of the GATS can be invoked. Under this provision, a member may take a measure that does not conform with its GATS obligations if the intention is to pursue a legitimate policy objective. It has its parallel in Article XX of the GATT-1994.

Third, under the WTO Agreement, governments may seek a temporary waiver from any obligation. In addition, negotiations are now in progress under the GATS on the question of developing an Emergency Safeguard Measure, whose purpose would be to permit the suspension of a commitment in the event of damage or the threat of damage to a domestic industry. It is also possible for a government to suspend commitments in the event of serious balance of payments difficulties.

GATS Annexes and Ministerial Decisions

Eight Annexes are attached to the GATS, along with eight Ministerial Decisions adopted in Marrakesh on the same day that the GATS was signed, plus an Understanding on Financial Services. These are all important with respect to the GATS rules. Two of the most important and permanent Annexes are on MFN exemptions and the Movement of Natural Persons. The other permanent Annexes concern four specific sectors of trade in services: air transport; financial services; telecommunications; and maritime transport services.

The Annex on Movement of Natural Persons Supplying Services is of particular importance to developing countries. It deals with the temporary movement of natural persons who supply services in the territory of another member. It is made clear that the Agreement does not apply to measures regarding citizenship, residence or employment on a permanent basis, or to people who travel abroad looking for work. As a result, the Agreement applies only to the stay in a foreign country of natural persons supplying services. The Annex also states that members may regulate the entry of natural persons into their territory and impose border controls, provided that such measures are not applied in such a manner as to nullify or impair the benefits accruing to any member under the terms of a specific commitment.

Movement of natural persons constitutes the fourth mode of supply identified in Article I of the GATS. As a result, it does not constitute a sector per se. Most members of the WTO have covered movement of natural persons in the horizontal section of their schedule of specific commitments. At the end of the Uruguay Round, because developing countries were dissatisfied with the commitments made for this mode of delivery of services, in which they felt they had particular competitive strengths, it was agreed to resume negotiations after the end of the Uruguay Round with the aim of achieving higher commitments. The Decision on Negotiations on Movement of Natural Persons provided for an extended period of negotiations, stating their objectives and establishing a negotiating group.[16]

Constraints on domestic policy

The most frequent concern is that the GATS circumscribes the policy options available to governments adopting domestic regulations. This is neither the intention nor the effect of the Agreement. With respect to the more onerous obligations, it is presumed that it is a sovereign right of governments to act in accordance with what they perceive to be in their national interests and to undertake only commitments seen to be in their national interest. To deny this right would be to circumscribe national sovereignty itself. In this respect, it is important that, as with the GATT-1994, when commitments are undertaken by governments, they are taken not with respect to the policy objective they are pursuing but with respect to the measure itself. If this were not the case, policies relating to public utilities, education and medical care would be reviewed, affecting the right of governments to set levels of quality, safety, price or any other policy objectives. This would be totally unacceptable to any government. In reality, governments are free to establish the regulations they see fit. A foreign supplier that failed to respect the terms of its contract or any other regulation would be subject to the same sanctions under national law as a national company, including termination of the contract. A GATS commitment provides no shelter from national law to an offending supplier. A related consideration is that services supplied in the exercise of governmental authority are outside the scope of the Agreement, and no disciplines that might be developed on domestic regulations would apply to them. This is discussed in an earlier section of this chapter.

A more specific concern relates to the GATT-like language paralleling that found in other agreements such as the Agreement on Technical Barriers to Trade – namely, that regulatory measures should not constitute unnecessary barriers to trade in services. The fear is that some policy options could be circumscribed by the requirement that certain measures adopted to achieve a policy objective are not necessary.

This requirement needs to be placed in its proper context, in that it appears only once in the GATS, in relation to the requirement for the Council for Trade in Services to develop rules to prevent requirements on qualifications for service suppliers, technical standards or licensing from being unnecessary barriers to trade. These disciplines are to ensure that qualifications requirements and procedures, technical standards and licensing requirements are based on objective and transparent criteria, such as competence and the ability to supply the service; are not more burdensome than necessary to ensure the quality of the service; and, in the case of licensing procedures, are not in themselves a restriction on the supply of the service. It is instructive to look briefly at the first – and probably the only – Agreement to be drawn up in this context. It relates to technical standards, qualifications and licensing requirements for accountancy services. In this Agreement, professional qualifications will not be under review, nor will the Agreement provide for the setting of standards. The objective of the Agreement is to increase transparency – namely, access to information about regulations, standards and procedures for licensing or obtaining qualifications – and to ensure that applicants are treated with fairness and are given a chance to compete on an equal footing. This is a major concern of developing countries. Importantly, although it was not clear in the text of the GATS, it has been agreed by governments that the accountancy disciplines – which will come into force at the end of the current round of negotiations – will apply only to countries that make commitments on accountancy services.

The interpretation of "necessary" in the GATS – should it ever be required – would presumably be influenced by GATT and WTO jurisprudence. Here past history reveals that, if two or more measures exist that can achieve the same objective, the measure with the least restrictive impact on trade should be chosen – as long as it is reasonably available. It is the measure, not the policy, that is reviewed, meaning that governments do not compromise the level of quality or consumer protection they are seeking to achieve through the regulation in question. As in other WTO Agreements, it is for governments to choose the level of protection they want to achieve (for instance when regulating for the protection of public health or the environment), and this prerogative is not open to challenge. Also, as spelled out in some detail in chapter 4, if two or more measures exist that can achieve the same objective, WTO jurisprudence has revealed that it is not necessarily the measure that is the least restrictive that need be chosen, because it must also be reasonably available. In any event, governments will have to show that they are employing least-trade-restrictive practices only if asked to justify a specific regulation in the event of a dispute with another government. It does not mean that governments would have to compromise the policy objective they are seeking to achieve through the regulation in question. Finally, recent rulings by the Appellate Body have indicated that whether a more consistent measure is reasonably available is not a decision that rests on hard evidence but is reviewed on a case-by-case basis.[17] This introduces a great deal of flexibility for measures retaliating to protect vital and important interests and values.

There has been no challenge to any measure of domestic regulation under the GATS since it came into existence. At the most fundamental level, interpreting the obligations of the GATS, the disputes process will recognize that all governments are sovereign, and within their own jurisdictions they can reserve the right to act in any way they wish – even to the extent of banning foreign trade altogether. Like all WTO Agreements, the GATS is an agreement to abide by a set of multilaterally agreed rules and therefore entails some surrender of sovereignty. So do other international agreements.

Conclusions

A number of other lessons can be learned from the history of the negotiation of the GATS. For example, had more attention been paid to past experience at the time of the negotiation of the Multilateral Agreement on Investment (MAI) at the OECD, what seems to be generally perceived as a fiasco might well have been avoided in my view. Negotiating an international agreement with a limited number of countries and expecting to apply the agreement to countries not part of the original negotiating process was seen not to work in the case of services.

The Draft Framework Agreement on Services was prepared by OECD member countries and brought to the GNS in 1987. Not only was it rejected by developing countries at the GNS, it went close to derailing the process entirely. This was a matter not of substance but of process. In fact, many of the concepts that eventually became part of the GATS were to be found in the OECD Draft Framework. Similarly, problems relating to whether commitments should be based on a positive or negative list approach had emerged in the GNS well before the MAI discussions were even started. Moreover, the sectors that were to prove to be problem areas in the MAI had already emerged as such in the GNS discussions – in particular, audiovisual and maritime services. And, in terms of where commitments were to be made and the nature of scheduling, virtually all options had already been explored in the services negotiations: a top–down approach, a bottom–up approach, a hybrid approach (as eventually adopted in the GATS), and sectoral exemptions.

In fact, the list of lessons that could have been learned from the services negotiations is long. Unfortunately, the history of the Uruguay Round services negotiations has never been written because this was not the wish of governments at the time. In fact, most of the key meetings took place in open-ended informal sessions in the presence of the chairperson – precisely to avoid the taking of summary records. One policy conclusion that emerges is that an effort should be made to record the history of these negotiations – or at least to create a documentary history – because much is to be learned in terms of a rich experience.

Another lesson comes from the nature of the negotiations. The text of the GATS is notoriously complex, and at the time of the negotiations little was known in terms of the implications of the application of the proposed concepts, principles and rules to such diverse economic activities as civil aviation, audiovisual services and construction services. Little – if any – empirical research had been conducted by the academic community on many of these sectors, and some of the core concepts (such as trade in services, national treatment and modes of delivery) were in their early stages of discussion in the academic community.

Most importantly, however, the GATS text is the result of many years of intense negotiation. There are many reasons for this. As spelled out in earlier parts of this chapter, many of the terms are not clear – a product of constructive ambiguity – and the manner in which they would be interpreted in Panel and Appellate Body rulings is a mystery. The unpredictability of the outcome is increased in the absence of an authoritative negotiating history. Furthermore, apart from the normal division of interest groups (e.g. developed versus developing), many diverse sectoral interests had to be accommodated. Parts of the text evolved semi-independently of others. For example, the Financial Services Annex was very much in the hands of treasury and Reserve Bank officials, and tele-communications negotiations were thought by telecommunication regulators to be too important to be left to trade officials.

This was well known at the time of the negotiations. In fact, for most of the latter part of the negotiations, there was a proposal (whose origins lay with the Mexican delegation) for the resulting text of the GATS to be reviewed after a period of time had elapsed to ensure it was coherent and effectively fulfilling the intentions of negotiators. What was left to be decided in the negotiations was whether the review would be after a period of three or five years. In the hectic closing off of the negotiations, this, along with one or two other sensible proposals, seems to have been lost along the way.

It would be useful to reconsider this proposal and even to rewrite the GATS in a far more analytical and user-friendly manner. This could be done by governments collectively, and they could correspondingly sign off on what they considered to be a faithful – albeit more usable – set of concepts, principles and rules, along with the rights and obligations and scheduling procedures. Desirable as this might be, it will of course never happen. It would require the approval by all WTO members of new texts and this would simply never be forthcoming. However, this does not mean that it should not be done. Those with a comprehensive knowledge of the GATS and its origins could prepare such a version. Although it would not be a legally binding document, it could serve numerous useful purposes – not least by providing factual material that might help to guide (and, more importantly, avoid) future disputes, rather than leaving the task of interpretation to those who may have little idea of the original intentions of the negotiators.

Much can also be learned from the GATS in terms of the role of developing countries in the process of negotiation of the Agreement as well as its substance. As noted above, developing countries were recalcitrant negotiators to say the least. They were seen by some among the developed countries to be foot-draggers and obstructionists, unnecessarily retarding the negotiations by seeking answers to irrelevant questions before agreeing to proceed. Tensions frequently ran high. One such example related to the paucity of statistics on international services transactions and its link with the definition of trade in services. It was argued by developing countries that, in the absence of a minimum of statistics being available on trade in services, it was impossible to define trade in services, because the commercial boundaries of what was being defined were unknown. What was needed was comprehensive statistical information. On the other hand, how could statistics on trade in services be gathered without it being defined? Although this and many other concerns of developing countries were seen to be obstructionist, and indeed may have been moves to gain time (and information) to formulate negotiating positions, they were nevertheless crucial questions that had to be addressed in order to have a robust agreement.

As far as the process is concerned, developing countries proved to be well-informed and effective negotiators, with the United Nations Conference on Trade and Development playing a key role in this. Here too there is a policy conclusion: insisting on a developing country chairperson of the GNS for almost the entire duration of the Uruguay Round certainly contributed to the confident approach developing countries took in the negotiations. As noted, there were no problems for developing countries in closing off the negotiations, and having kept them on a separate track added to this.

A constructive role for development NGOs would be to provide developing countries with the support they need to reap the maximum benefits of the GATS. This could be done by monitoring the process itself; focusing on the development-related provisions of the GATS to see how they can be more usefully implemented; using their local knowledge to see where there are bottlenecks in the services sectors of developing countries; and seeing what conditions should be attached to the foreign presence and scheduled in order to maximize the usefulness to the developing country.

Notes

1. See OXFAM, *Rigged Rules and Double Standards: Trade, Globalization and the Fight against Poverty*, Oxford: OXFAM, 2002, p. 224.
2. The concerns of developing countries in the early stages of the negotiations can be found in Gary P. Sampson, "Uruguay Round Negotiations on Services: Issues and Recent Developments", in Detler Dicke and Ernst-Ulrich Petersmann (eds), *Foreign Trade in the Present and a New International Economic Order*, Switzerland: University of Fribourg Press, 1988, pp. 274–287. See also, Gary P. Sampson, "Comments on International Trade in Services", in R. Baldwin et al. (eds), *Europe–US Trade Relations*, National Bureau of Economic Research, Chicago: University of Chicago Press, 1987.
3. In other development literature the services sector has played no role at all. The traditional growth models based on macroeconomic variables (aggregate demand, investment and savings) ignored the services sector. Theories of import substitution normally considered only manufactured goods. Input–output models and linear programming models rarely, if ever, specified the services sector. Indigenous development models based on the notion of autonomous development, collective self-reliance and related concepts neglected the services sector.
4. See Gary P. Sampson, "Developing Countries and the Liberalisation of Trade in Services", in John Whalley (ed.), *Rules, Power and Credibility*, Ontario: University of Western Ontario Press, 1988, chapter 7.
5. Having said that, it would be naïve to consider that "corridor deals" were not done outside the formal and informal negotiations conducted under the chairperson of the GNS.
6. The extent to which this flexibility is freely exercised by developing countries is contested by some critics of the Agreement who perceived pressure from more powerful

governments on behalf of transnational corporations. I shall argue in what follows that this is an empirical question; it is unfair to level this as a criticism of the Agreement as such – rather it is a mismatch of negotiating strength of developing country governments vis-à-vis more powerful counterparts. The understanding of the Agreement itself is that developing countries are expected to liberalize fewer sectors and types of transactions in line with their development situation. In practical terms, the commitments of developing countries are in general far less extensive than those of more industrialized countries.

7. An issue of interpretation could arise only if a specific measure had been challenged in dispute settlement and were to be defended on the ground that it applied only to services supplied in the exercise of governmental authority, the conclusion being that it was outside the scope of the GATS.

8. As of February 2001, around one-third of WTO members had made commitments on education or health, sectors that many would regard as essentially functions of the state.

9. The first articulation of this definition is to be found in Gary P. Sampson and Richard H. Snape, "Identifying the Issues in Trade in Services", *The World Economy*, Vol. 8, No. 2, June 1985.

10. An important consideration for the purposes of the Agreement is that the four modes of supply are not mutually exclusive. In some instances, the same service may be sold internationally according to more than one mode of supply. In the examples given above, a medical operation can take place through the movement of the surgeon to the country of the patient, or vice versa. Naturally, businesses seek to carry out their international transactions according to their preferred mode of supply.

11. GATT, *Services Sectoral Classification List: Note by the Secretariat*, Geneva: GATT Secretariat, MTN.GNS/W/120, 10 July 1991.

12. Apart from services specified in individual MFN exemption lists, the only permitted departure from MFN treatment under the GATS is among countries that are members of regional trading arrangements. The GATS rules on "Economic Integration" (in Article V) permit any WTO member to enter into an agreement to further liberalize trade in services only with the other countries that are parties to the agreement, provided the agreement has "substantial sectoral coverage", eliminates measures that discriminate against service suppliers of other countries in the group, and prohibits new or more discriminatory measures.

13. Developed countries are also to establish contact points to facilitate developing country access to information related to their respective markets concerning: commercial and technical aspects of the supply of services; the registration, recognition and obtaining of professional qualifications; and the availability of services technology.

14. There are six forms of measure affecting free market access: limitations on the number of service suppliers; limitations on the total value of services transactions or assets; limitations on the total number of service operations or the total quantity of service output; limitations on the number of persons who may be employed in a particular sector or by a particular supplier; measures that restrict or require supply of the service through specific types of legal entity or joint venture; and percentage limitations on the participation of foreign capital, or limitations on the total value of foreign investment.

15. See paragraph 6 of the Annex on Telecommunications in the GATS.

16. WTO, *Decision on Negotiations on Movement of Natural Persons*, Geneva: WTO Secretariat, adopted by Ministers in Marrakesh on 15 April 1994. Another important Decision was for the Committee on Trade and Environment to carry out a work programme on the relationship between environmental measures and trade in services.

17. *Korea – Measures Affecting Imports of Fresh, Chilled and Frozen Beef*, WT/DS161/AB/R, WT/DS169/AB/R, Appellate Body Report, adopted 10 January 2001, paras 166 and 163.

9

Special and differential treatment and sustainable economic development: Substance and process

Introduction

A precondition for the successful conclusion to the Doha Development Agenda, launched at the Ministerial Meeting in Qatar in 2001, is for all countries to be convinced that it is in their interests to sign on to the outcome of the negotiations. Of the almost 150 countries needed to join the consensus, two-thirds are developing countries. It is crucial for them that the legal framework that emerges from the negotiations contains the right sort of disciplines and flexibility to ensure they can implement their appropriate development strategies. The questions that follow naturally are: what is an *appropriate* development strategy for developing countries; what are the *proper* measures to implement this strategy; and, therefore, what are the right sorts of *legal flexibilities and constraints* that the system should provide? The economic and institutional issues that have to be dealt with in addressing these questions are many and varied.

Although the original General Agreement on Tariffs and Trade (GATT) contained special provisions for developing countries, the vision was for one global system of trade rules – developing countries were to be full players. The situation radically changed in the decades following the creation of the GATT, with provisions characterized by the acceptance of infant industry protection, flexibility in the use of balance of payments measures, non-reciprocity in trading tariff concessions, and preferential market access for manufactured exports.

In their past attempts to create the right legal framework, GATT members adopted the premise that *equal treatment of un-equals is unfair*. The legal flexibility they created constituted the core of what came to be known as *special and differential treatment*, with its withdrawal being described as *graduation*. For many, the logic was clear. Just as poor people pay lower taxes in a country where progressive income taxes are levied, underdeveloped countries pay less in their membership to the GATT and more as they develop. During the first half-century of the GATT – and now the first decade of the World Trade Organization (WTO) – different stages in dealing with legal flexibility for developing countries can be clearly identified. Prior to the conclusion of the Uruguay Round, each round of negotiations was marked by the extension of the legal freedom granted by the GATT rules to developing countries. Although the Uruguay Round involved a considerable turnaround in approach, it certainly did not slow down the growth of special provisions.

Today, there are 155 specific provisions specially crafted for developing countries in the WTO Agreements. Why have so many provisions been added over recent years? This is a result of negotiations by developing countries to secure more legal flexibility under the GATT, the wider reach of the WTO Agreements, and the changing nature of commitments undertaken by all WTO members. Now, special and differential provisions come in many forms: some are directed to increasing trade opportunities, others are aimed at safeguarding the interests of developing countries, others provide for flexibility in the implementation of commitments, some permit the use of otherwise WTO-unacceptable policy instruments, and some relate to the granting of technical assistance. The provisions are both mandatory and non-mandatory. A large number are considered completely useless by developing countries or excessive by developed countries.

But do these provisions sit comfortably with the policy prescriptions now advanced by development economists? Have the prescriptions of the past half-century been the right ones? Has there been a change in approach under the WTO to special and differential treatment based on a different view of development? Do the current provisions relating to developing countries contribute to their integration into the multilateral trading system or do they retard it? In fact, has the greater integration of developing countries into the world trading system via an expanded share of world trade lost its traditional meaning? Has it been replaced by the progressive adoption of all WTO obligations by all members? Are we back to the original vision of the GATT of six decades ago with one system for all? What have we learnt on this journey?

Answering these questions entails looking at the evolution of the legal flexibilities provided for developing countries over the past half-century, and at the parallel thinking of economists about what were prescribed as the *right* development strategies. There are of course excellent tomes describing the evolution of special and differential treatment for developing countries in the GATT.[1] Similarly, there are numerous academic and more popular discourses debating the link between trade and development. The important question for this chapter, however, is whether the GATT and WTO provide the right sort of legal framework to accommodate the right sort of development strategies.

In this respect, we currently have a unique opportunity to address this question. The Doha Development Agenda is under way and special and differential treatment provisions are on the negotiating table. WTO negotiators have been mandated by their ministers to render these provisions more *precise, operational and effective* by converting *best endeavour provisions* into *mandatory ones*.

Although this chapter is concerned with the *substance* of development strategies and legal flexibility, it also addresses *process*. The process of improving special and differential treatment provisions pre-dates the creation of the WTO, and most would agree that the results have been meagre at best. Thus, the process itself provides an interesting case study. Its usefulness is underscored by the fact that in general terms, although the time- and resource-consuming aspects of many negotiations and their limited outcome are frequently lamented, the nature of such processes is rarely documented. In the absence of such information, it is difficult to advance prescriptions for improvement.[2]

A word of clarification is required about the title of this chapter and the link between the WTO and the development of developing countries. As has been emphasized throughout this book, there are different perceptions of sustainable development. Few would deny that economic development is a key element of sustainable development, but many are quick to point out that economic development is not an end in itself; it is a contributor to sustainable development. Thus, different aspects of economic development have been emphasized in the context of sustainable development. Amartya Sen acknowledges the importance of economic development but identifies freedom as both the primary end and principal means of development.[3] For the Brundtland Commission, as discussed in earlier chapters, economic development is a means to provide for the care and nurturing of the environment for future generations. The *Human Development Report* of the United Nations Development Programme stresses that, although growth in gross domestic product per capita is a vital component of the development process, there are numerous other indictors of development. This chapter specifically addresses the link between economic growth and sustainable development, focusing on the provisions needed in order for developing countries to extract the maximum benefits from the multilateral trading system, which is considered to be an important component of economic development, and eventually of sustainable development. Other chapters in the book deal in more detail with the environment, social considerations and other key elements of sustainable development.

Accommodating import substitution

In the early years of the GATT, the policies advocated by economists were clear. Developing countries depended heavily on commodity exports, and owing to their decline, coupled with low price and income elasticities, free trade would entail a continuing dependence on commodity exports. This dependence would mean perpetual poverty. Export pessimism was the name of the game. To grow, countries needed to accumulate capital, and this could not be done with a workforce in agriculture with negative marginal returns. In such circumstances, capital could not be imported; the domestic production of manufactured goods was required. The policy prescription was clear. According to Hollis B. Chenery, Economic Adviser to the President of the World Bank from 1970 to 1972, and later World Bank Vice President for Development Policy: "Industrialisation consists primarily in the substitution of domestic production of manufactured goods for imports."[4]

The belief was that developing countries could foster development by heavily protecting and producing for the domestic markets, and substituting domestic production for imports. Externalities were expected to flow from the creation of these new industries, so, for many economists, subsidies were thought to be justified. Because the new industries were infants (in the sense that low-cost producers already existed abroad), temporary intervention was required to start production and then reach a stage where costs became competitive as the scale of production increased. Often little thought was given to the fact that domestic markets were small in size and the scope simply did not exist to benefit from economies of scale by supplying only a domestic market. Import substitution policies required high levels of border protection – both tariffs and quantitative restrictions – and an absence of reciprocity in trade-liberalizing negotiations. External disturbances were considered synonymous with development, so import restrictions would be required for balance of payments purposes. Similarly, with internationally uncompetitive domestic production in a number of sectors, subsidies would be needed – in particular export subsidies.

Because the GATT legal system was based on the removal of quantitative restrictions, the reduction and binding of tariffs, reciprocity in trade liberalization and the elimination of subsidies, import substitution policies required considerable legal flexibility.[5] This came in the form of GATT Article XVIII, entitled "Governmental Assistance to Economic Development". It provided a clear recognition of the need for this legal flexibility. GATT members recognized "that special governmental assistance may be required to promote the establishment, development or reconstruction of particular industries or branches of agriculture, and that in appropriate circumstances the grant of such assistance in the form of protective measures is justified". Interestingly, however, they also recognized "that an unwise use of such measures would impose undue burdens on their own economies and unwarranted restrictions on international trade, and might increase unnecessarily the difficulties of adjustment for the economies of other countries".

Article XVIII was completely redrafted in a GATT Review Session held in 1955 to give it more precision and clarify the extent of the legal flexibility accorded to developing countries. The Review brought three key changes, all of which were important in accommodating import substitution policies. First, there was an acceptance that protective measures taken in accordance with Article XVIII were not derogations from the GATT but legitimate measures to promote economic development. Second, less stringent requirements were introduced with respect to justifying balance of payments restrictions. Third, there was recognition that developing countries were not required to offer full reciprocity in tariff reduction negotiations.

More specifically, Section A of Article XVIII provided for the withdrawal or modification of negotiated concessions to promote the establishment of a particular industry in order to raise the general standard of living. This process is subject to notification and negotiation with those GATT members with which concessions had been negotiated, or which have a substantial interest in it. In Section C, there is provision for developing countries to deviate from the provisions of the GATT (except Articles I, II and XIII) if governmental assistance is required to promote the establishment of a particular industry but no measure consistent with the other provisions is practicable to achieve that objective. In short, as a result of the Review Session, Sections A and C of Article XVIII – the infant industries clauses – allowed developing countries to modify or withdraw concessions included in their schedules and to impose quantitative or other restrictive measures to protect infant industries.

Section B recognized that countries in "their early stages of development" experience balance of payments difficulties when undergoing rapid development. Developing country members were therefore permitted to control the general level of imports by restricting the quantity or value of imports, with the proviso that restrictions did not exceed the level required "to forestall the threat of, or stop, a serious decline in monetary reserves" or, where the member had inadequate reserves, to achieve a "reasonable rate of increase" in reserves. Provision was made for developing countries to act selectively and give priority to certain categories of imports deemed "more essential" in light of development policies while imposing import restrictions. There were provisions for consultations every two years with GATT members for developing countries maintaining restrictions for balance of payments reasons. Thus, Section B permitted the use of selective quantitative restrictions in situations where balance of payments problems arose, its disciplines on the use of restrictions being less stringent than those for developed countries in GATT Article XII. A further result of the Review Session was that the prohibition on the use of export subsidies on manufactured products was accepted only by developed countries, providing a de facto additional legal flexibility for developing countries.[6]

There are perhaps two useful observations that can be made at this stage. The first is that this form of special and differential treatment was very easy to give. It required only that developed countries provide legal freedom to developing countries. Bob Hudec has summarized this situation well: "Once it had been conceded, as a matter of principle, that legal freedom constitutes 'help' to developing countries, the future was virtually fixed.... As a consequence, developed–developing country relations for the next forty years began and ended on the same note – 'more help is needed'.... Granting legal freedom to other countries is an easy concession to give, for it requires neither domestic legislation nor the use of other legal powers by the grantor countries. It is possible to 'give' merely by doing nothing."[7] In a similar vein, a report presented to the Director-General of the GATT in 1985 by an Eminent Persons Group on World Trade concluded that special and differential treatment in the past had encouraged the "tendency to treat them [the developing countries] as being outside [the trading system]". They were also of the view that developed countries had, by granting preferences to developing countries, relieved themselves of their share of responsibility "for action in more essential areas".[8]

Second, special and differential treatment was destined to be generic, in the sense of being applicable to all developing countries. Anne Krueger, in her Presidential Address to the American Economic Association, remarked that early trade and development theories and policy prescriptions were based on some widely held stylized facts and premises about developing countries. These, she says, were "a mixture of 'touristic' impressions, half-truths and misapplied policy inferences".[9] The result was that in the early years of the GATT, although there was a belief that development economics warranted a separate discipline, the common features that characterized developing countries meant they were to be treated in a *generic* way. Of course, there was a recognition of the differences in resource endowment and other features of developing countries, but acknowledged differences were thought to be overwhelmed by the common characteristics of underdevelopment. Thus, in terms of the new Article XVIII, the characteristics of countries to which the flexibilities were to be applied were not defined, nor were the eligible countries identified by name. They were simply referred to in Article XVIII as economies that can sustain only "low standards of living" and are in "the early stages of development". This language was clearly open to interpretation.

By the end of the 1950s, the number of developing countries that were members of the GATT had greatly increased – 34 developing countries joined in the 1960s. The majority were recently independent countries in Africa; by acceding to the GATT they were complementing their political independence with a move for economic independence. In addition, 1961 saw the launching of the first United Nations Development Decade, together with attempts to establish a global trade organization within the United Nations system. The result was the creation of the United Nations Conference on Trade and Development (UNCTAD). This coincided with the launching of the Kennedy Round (1964–1967) of multilateral trade negotiations (MTN), the sixth round of such negotiations held under the auspices of the GATT.

The coming into existence of UNCTAD provoked the members of the GATT to demonstrate more concretely their commitment to the development of developing countries. The original idea was to redraft Article XVIII, but, as events unfolded, the negotiated text that emerged from this exercise was considered to be sufficiently lengthy to be added to the GATT as a new Part IV entitled "Trade and Development". It entered into force in 1966 and marked the beginning of another stage of legal flexibility for developing countries. It provided a supplementary basis for commitments and actions by (developed) contracting parties for expanding the trade of developing countries, and consolidated the orientation of the GATT towards addressing matters relating to trade and development.

However, Part IV added nothing to the legal relationship between developed and developing countries, particularly in the sense of according lower levels of obligations for developing countries. In reality, the text of Part IV contrasts with that of other GATT Articles, being both vague and non-binding; in fact, its non-mandatory nature characterizes many other (best endeavour) commitments relating to economic development in the GATT. This has long been lamented by developing countries and is very much on the negotiating agenda today – converting best endeavour provisions of both the GATT-1994 and the WTO Agreements into mandatory obligations is a central part of the Doha Development Agenda. Part IV of the GATT has been specifically targeted by many developing countries in this respect (see below).

In fact, the new Part IV deals mainly with the *behaviour* of developed countries towards developing countries. This difference in orientation was based on a premise that had gained considerable support at the time; namely, that special and differential treatment for developing countries should relate not only to internal measures (e.g. permitting developing countries to protect domestic producers) but also to external measures (e.g. the exports of developing countries should receive a better treatment in the markets of the developed countries). Although best endeavour in nature, Part IV does formalize – in rather legal-sounding language – that developed countries do not expect reciprocity for removing tariffs and other barriers to the trade of developing countries. This was generally seen at the time as a major achievement for developing countries. The question of developed countries granting preferences to developing countries, as well as preferences among developing countries, was also addressed at the time, and, as no agreement was reached on this matter, work continued after the adoption of Part IV.[10]

The Committee on Trade and Development (CTD) was established in November 1964 to supervise the implementation of the new Part IV of the GATT. Its terms of reference were, *inter alia*, to keep under continuous review the application of the provisions of Part IV and to consider proposals and to make appropriate recommendations. As such, the CTD has regularly reviewed developments in international trade affecting developing countries and monitored the implementation of commitments undertaken with respect to the avoidance of new restrictions and the removal or reduction of existing barriers. With the changing nature and scope of the Uruguay Round Agreements, the role of the CTD was greatly intensified.

Changing policy prescriptions

From a substantive point of view, a strong case can be made that there should be special provisions for countries with underdeveloped infrastructures, a heavy dependence on a few exports, and many other shared and country-specific characteristics. How to craft these provisions – both legal flexibilities and constraints – in order to best serve the interests of the countries themselves requires a good understanding of the link between trade policies and economic development. In this sense it is important to identify both the *sources* and the *symptoms* of the difficulties confronted by developing countries in order to define the flexibilities. Here a closer look at import substitution policies is instructive.

Import substitution policies have been severely criticized on many fronts. It is claimed that they are now dead and buried and therefore will not be returned to.[11] Interestingly, however, the grounds on which they are rejected differ quite considerably. One view is that the *micro* intervention that accompanied import substitution policies led first to resource misallocation and then to disturbances in the form of *macro* balance of payments difficulties and debt. One stylized version of the story runs as follows.

With the protection of import-competing industries via high tariffs and quantitative restrictions, resources are pulled out of export industries. The situation is worsened by low commodity prices and low income and price elasticities, and further exacerbated by the protection in developed country markets of semi-manufactures and labour-intensive goods such as textiles, clothing and footwear. A lack of foreign exchange, coupled with demand for capital goods as part of the normal growth process, means that the production of import-competing goods is further promoted. Substitution for imports necessitates ambitious development plans that add to aggregate demand. In conventional Keynesian terms, if additional aggregate demand is not properly managed, high rates of inflation will follow. If nominal exchange rates are fixed – which they were at the time of import substitution policies – this leads to a depreciation of the real exchange rate, thereby subsidizing the manufacturing sector and taxing the agricultural sector for commodity-exporting countries. A deficit on the external account follows. The end result is that balance of payment crises are frequent and there is chronic indebtedness. Thus, the source of the problem that should be addressed, it is argued, is the import substitution policies.

Others see the source of the problem at the macro level: "what eventually drove many import substituting countries to ruin were not so much micro economic inefficiencies, but macro economic imbalances and the inability to correct them."[12] The reasoning is that, although import substitution may well lead to resource misallocation and inefficiency, it does not necessarily result in macroeconomic disturbance. The *starting point* for the economic disturbance is an overvalued exchange rate leading to a trade deficit. If balance of payments difficulties arise and persist, foreign exchange reserves run low. In a crisis, the government may be forced to devalue the currency. But, before being driven to this, it may try to redress the balance by restricting imports or encouraging exports, in a typical mercantilist fashion. The selective application of import restrictions provides preference to some industries over others – just as import substitution does. Import-competing industries would be candidates for trade protection, and subsidies are required to reduce the reliance on imported goods, with a worsening of the fiscal deficit.

In this scenario, although trade protection can be damaging from a resource misallocation perspective, the sustained budget deficits do not come from trade measures and industrial subsidies. They come from an excess of aggregate demand over aggregate supply and the use of micro policies where macro polices are needed. Imbalance on the internal and external accounts should be rectified by expenditure *changing* through reduced aggregate demand by and expenditure *switching* between importable goods and exportable goods via a devaluation, but the easy option is to resort to quantitative restrictions to reduce imports selectively.

It is interesting that, decades after the demise of import substitution policies and with all the information now available, their impact is still debated. This serves to mark a relevant point; namely, how difficult it is clearly to identify the relationship between trade policy and economic growth and stability. It also serves to exemplify the difficulty in designing the legal flexibility needed to accommodate the right policies. In this respect, it has been argued that the GATT failed miserably in its early decades because the flexibility it offered was absolutely counterproductive: it was the de facto legitimization of the wrong policies.

That the GATT, the upholder of an open international trading system would allow an "exception" for developing countries shows how deeply entrenched were the views supporting import substitution. It is arguable that the very existence of this exception not only legitimised developing countries' inner oriented trade policies, but also removed pressures that might otherwise have been brought to bear earlier for them to adopt trade and payments regimes more conducive to economic growth.... [How] could it happen that a profession, for which the principle of comparative advantage was one of its key tenets, embraced such protectionist policies?[13]

Perhaps some guidance as to the source of the problem can be gleaned by reviewing which GATT flexibilities developing countries turned to: balance of payments protection or infant industry protection. The first deals with a macro disturbance and the second with micro intervention. In carrying out this exercise, it is somewhat surprising, particularly given the criticism levelled at the infant industry protection provisions of the GATT by those favouring outer-oriented development strategies, that there have been only four instances in the past 60 years when an infant industry justification for protection has been sought in the GATT or the WTO. Cuba, Haiti and India all received approval for restrictions on a single product for infant industry reasons in the first years of the GATT, and Ceylon for a variety of products in 1952. There have been no further approvals since that date.[14] On the other hand, release from GATT obligations owing to balance of payments problems has been frequently resorted to by developing countries. In the early 1950s, 9 of the 14 developing country members of the GATT were restricting imports for balance of payments reasons, and the pattern continued for some decades.

Does this tell us that the flexibility required by developing countries related to balance of payments difficulties rather than the accommodation of import substitution policies through infant industry protection? Unfortunately, the answer is not clear. Developing countries had a preference for the flexibility provided by Article XVIII:B for a number of reasons. One has always been – and remains – that the use of the infant industry provisions requires authorization in the form of prior approval by other members, as well as provision for the payment of compensation for affected trading partners in the form of additional concessions. If compensation is not paid, the developing country faces the temporary suspension of a substantially equivalent concession. On the other hand, developing countries encountering balance of payments difficulties faced much less stringent requirements, and were free to apply trade restrictions selectively on an industry-specific basis, ostensibly for balance of payments purposes.[15]

This introduces other points that are relevant for what follows. Governments will naturally turn to the least onerous flexibilities available to pursue their own policy choices, even if the provisions were not designed for the problem at hand. Further, whereas support for import substitution policies may be considered *passé* in the academic community, demands for more flexibility for developing countries wishing to invoke infant industry protection are certainly not. In the context of the Doha Development Agenda, developing countries have argued that, because of the onerous compensation and other requirements relating to infant industry protection, and the real threat of suspension of concessions on the part of the developed countries, these provisions have little or no practical effect for those seeking to promote infant industries.[16] The associated proposal in the Doha Development Agenda is to render more usable the flexibilities available for infant industry protection. This position is held by a number of developing countries.

There are many reasons for the demise of the import substitution approach.[17] They include: the abandonment of the notion that countries would forever specialize in the production of commodities if comparative advantage prevailed; agreement that there were no consistent means of determining which industries will mature beyond infancy; widespread rent-seeking as a by-product of protection promoted by intervention at the industry level; the inability clearly to identify, much less quantify, externalities that were to come from infant industry protection; the prevalence of over-pricing and under-invoicing associated with the protection of domestic industries; and the development of effective rates of protection, domestic resource costs, cost–benefit analysis and other tools that quantified the high costs of import substitution policies. Moreover, experience showed that many infant industries moved directly to geriatric status without passing through adulthood.

However, one of the most potent forces in changing perceptions was the remarkable success of a number of newly industrializing countries (NICs) in Asia when pursuing what were seen to be the antithesis of import substitution policies. The enthusiasm of the economics profession for import substitution policy was replaced by the export-orientation policies of the NICs, or what could be described as export substitution; namely, policies directed towards the substitution of exports for the domestic consumption of domestically produced goods. The NICs' success seemed to give real-world validation to what appeared to be a very different approach to the link between trade policy and development. But the success of this policy required, above all, access to the markets of the developed countries and, depending on the case in hand, domestic measures to promote exports. Greatly improved access to developed country markets had important implications for a number of developing countries.

Since the early 1980s, the average annualized growth of trade of developing countries as a whole has been faster than that of both world trade and the trade of developed countries. But differences between and within developing country regions are very pronounced. For instance, over this period, annual average growth in Asian trade was 12 times faster than African trade (excluding South Africa). Within Africa, annual average growth in trade ranged from a high of 12 per cent to a low of minus 21 per cent.

Developing countries in East and South East Asia have steadily increased their trade over the past 40 years, sustaining high rates of economic growth and bringing dramatic declines in their rate of poverty. They could not have achieved this if they had not found growing markets for their exports and if they had not taken advantage of technological advances and foreign know-how available in an increasingly globalized world. Countries in sub-Saharan Africa, by contrast, have grown too slowly to raise per capita incomes or to reduce their rate of poverty. It is no coincidence that their trade has not prospered and that their share of world markets has fallen.

Like the import-substituting governments, the NICs were actively intervening in their economies, and those that were GATT members could also take advantage of the legal flexibility provided for in the GATT.[18]

But the policy prescriptions of the NICs differed from those of the import-substituting countries. Intervention in the NICs was characterized by uniform export incentives and an assurance of stability in the exchange rate.[19] Although these countries did not necessarily aim at free trade, and industrialization was indeed being pursued, it was industrialization for both the domestic and export markets through intervention of another type – more neutral in nature and directed to both removing obstacles to exports and promoting them. Paradoxically for those NICs that were GATT members, it was precisely the legal flexibility that permitted them to pursue their development strategies of import restriction and export promotion that led to their export-oriented success.[20] In other words, they too were interventionist and free to use the legal flexibility that existed at the time.

A further factor was that the export-oriented countries benefited enormously from the improved access to developed country markets that came with the various rounds of GATT trade-liberalizing negotiations. Even though East Asian countries were not major players in the negotiating process, and notwithstanding restrictions on some of their principal manufactured exports (such as textiles, clothing and other products), their share in the trade of manufactured goods increased greatly through most favoured nation (MFN) concessions and, in some cases, the benefits that flowed from the Generalized System of Preferences (see below). In fact, the current US dollar value of developing country merchandise export earnings increased by a factor of nearly 69 in the period between the creation of the GATT (1948) and the establishment of the WTO (1995).

The end result was that, for a number of economists and policy makers, the East Asian experience provided a final blow to the notion that a developing country could achieve industrialization only through import substitution. The properties thought to be common to all developing countries that led to economic disturbances and stagnant or negative growth rates were now thought by mainstream economists to be those of import substitution regimes rather than perceived common characteristics based on "touristic impressions".

Where does all this leave us today? Does it help us in answering the question of what is the right degree of flexibility for implementing the right policies? The experience of developing countries is instructive. There are those that took advantage of the GATT flexibilities available to them, intervened in various ways and were successful (East Asian NICs). Others used the flexibilities and failed (a number of Latin American countries). How were some countries (the East Asian governments) able to avoid the rent-seeking activities that typically accompanied intervention to implement import substitution policies? Most importantly, this gives substance to the now frequently posed question about the appropriateness of a generic approach to providing special and differential treatment to developing countries when creating legal constraints and flexibilities.

Export orientation

The next stage in the evolution of legal flexibility came with the Tokyo Round of multilateral trade negotiations (launched in 1973) and reflected the growing interest of developing countries in export expansion. An important outcome was the Enabling Clause, which created a permanent legal basis for special and differential treatment in terms of non-reciprocal tariff preferences accorded under the Generalized System of Preferences (GSP).[21] Additionally, acceptance of the Codes that emerged from the Tokyo Round dealing with non-tariff barriers was not mandatory, which led to automatic flexibility because most developing countries chose not to adopt them.[22] Tariff preferences and, subject to approval, non-tariff preferences among developing countries in the framework of regional or global trade arrangements were also provided for, as was additional special treatment for least developed countries. Moreover, developing countries sought, and obtained, a further relaxation of existing procedures relating to restrictions for balance of payments purposes.

Importantly, the Enabling Clause introduced into the GATT system – for the first time and in clear terms – the notion of phasing out legal flexibility as the level of development increased.[23] Developing countries were expected to improve "their capacity to make contributions or negotiated concessions or take other mutually agreed action" with the progressive development of their economies. It was observed at the time that this should be "conceived of as a dual principle. It should include not only the phasing *out* of more favourable treatments in the market of developed countries but also the phasing *in* of developing countries' compliance with the generally prevailing rules of the international trading system based on a balance of rights and responsibilities."[24]

Discussions on the need for a new round of trade negotiations started in the GATT as early as 1981. It was felt that many problems had not been solved in the Tokyo Round and that the GATT multilateral trading system was at risk. Areas of considerable importance to developing countries, such as agriculture and textiles, were being dealt with on a de facto basis outside GATT rules, and developing countries' exports, both traditional and non-traditional, were increasingly subject to anti-dumping and countervailing duties. Export restraint arrangements relating to textiles and clothing had received GATT legal cover as a sectoral derogation from MFN treatment in the form of the Multi-fibre Arrangement (MFA). Prospects for improved market access through agricultural trade liberalization were almost non-existent. On the other hand, developed countries were not only seeking solutions to their own long-standing problems, such as those in the areas of agriculture and textile trade, but also aiming to bring three new areas of commercial activity under GATT disciplines – trade in services, intellectual property rights and investment measures.

There were also systemic concerns because the period after the Tokyo Round was characterized by limited membership of the Tokyo Round Codes, a negative special and differential treatment for agriculture and textiles, and a proliferation of what has been described as contingent protection through the use of anti-dumping measures, voluntary export restraints (VERs) and other measures.[25] This resulted in a perception that the balance of rights and obligations had been lost, a balance that member countries thought should be restored. Thus, at the GATT Ministerial Meeting of September 1986 in Punta del Este, Uruguay, ministers agreed to launch the Uruguay Round of multilateral trade negotiations. The compromise texts on which the Punta del Este Declaration was based were co-authored by Colombia and Switzerland, providing a first indication that participation by developing countries in the Round would increase.

As in the 1960s, the period of the Uruguay Round (1986–1994) saw the number of member countries of the GATT increase substantially; 29 developing countries joined during this period. Their motivation differed from that of countries joining in the 1960s. It could be argued that it was no longer a question of establishing independence, but rather a recognition of global interdependence, a need to have a voice in the trading system and the possibility of benefiting from the continuing expansion of world trade.

Coinciding with the Uruguay Round was the emergence of the so-called "Washington Consensus" and what now seems to form the basis for the thinking of most mainstream economists about the appropriate policies for development purposes.[26] It was reasoned that the set of policy reforms that most officials in Washington thought would be good for developing countries could be summarized in the following propositions: fiscal discipline; a redirection of public expenditure priorities toward fields offering both high economic returns and the potential to improve income distribution, such as primary health care, primary education and infrastructure; tax reform (to lower marginal rates and broaden the tax base); interest rate liberalization; a competitive exchange rate; trade liberalization; liberalization of inflows of foreign direct investment; privatization; and deregulation (to abolish barriers to entry and exit, and to secure property rights).

Although support for these policy prescriptions has not been unanimous, much of the contemporary policy discussion can be understood by using the term "Washington Consensus" as a reference point.[27] For instance, it has been suggested that there now exists an "Augmented" Washington Consensus,[28] which adds to the items listed above: corporate governance; anti-corruption; flexible labour markets; WTO Agreements; financial codes and standards; "prudent" capital account opening; non-intermediate exchange rate regimes; independent central banks and inflation targeting; social safety nets; and targeted poverty reduction. Clearly, the debate continues about the Washington Consensus – its definition, its successes and failures, and whether it even exists.

But does the Washington Consensus determine the appropriate trade strategies and offer guidance for the requisite legal flexibilities in the WTO? In broad terms, the approach to trade policy within the policy package has in many instances been identified simply as *trade liberalization* or *free trade*. Although this gives an orientation, what does it translate into in terms of practical policy prescriptions? Here views are at variance, even in very broad terms. They largely turn on differing opinions about the relationship between trade liberalization and economic development. There are those who doubt the existence of a positive link. It has been remarked that "theoretical complications could be side-stepped if there were convincing evidence that in practice trade liberalisation systematically produces improved economic performance. But even for this relatively uncontroversial policy, it has proved difficult to generate unambiguous evidence." The point is that "even the simplest of policy recommendations – *liberalise your trade* – is contingent upon a large number of judgement calls about the economic and political context in which it is being implemented".[29] Thus, if the trade policy element is trade liberalization, there are a number of important but less general considerations: should it be complete liberalization; what if there are other market imperfections; what are the income and resource distribution implications of liberalization; what should be done about lost tariff revenues; and is liberalization politically sustainable?

Importantly, as has been stressed throughout this book, trade policy can no longer be thought of in terms of tariffs and quantitative restrictions. If trade policy is to find a place in the Washington Consensus, intellectual property rights, agricultural policy, financial services, telecommunications, special and differential treatment, and many other crucial policy areas need to be considered. What are the *appropriate* policies within the context of the entirety of the WTO Agreements when implementing the Washington Consensus?

The WTO Agreements

As a result of the Uruguay Round (1986–1994) and the greatly extended reach of the WTO, a change in approach to legal flexibilities was required. Not just border measures – tariffs and quantitative restrictions – but completely new areas were now addressed in WTO Agreements; in particular, trade in services and intellectual property rights. These trade agreements raised new policy questions for developing countries: how much foreign commercial presence should there be in the domestic financial services and telecommunications sectors; should domestic markets be opened to foreign suppliers of medical and educational services; what changes would be required in terms of domestic legislation and procedures to fulfil commitments in the Agreement on Trade-Related Intellectual Property Rights (TRIPS); and how could the onerous notification requirements be met with existing resources? Similarly, changes in rules relating to certain sectors – agriculture and textiles – presented additional policy choices: how to adjust to the loss of assured markets in MFA importing countries with the removal of quantitative restrictions; how to deal with the domestic situation in agriculture with eventual improved market access for exporting countries and more expensive food for net importing countries; how to respond to the removal of export subsidies and to new disciplines on other subsidies.

Prior to the Uruguay Round, the frequently stated objective of increasing developing countries' participation in world trade (as monitored by the GATT Committee on Trade and Development) was considered to be a concept that could be quantified in terms of the changing share of developing countries in world trade. With the Uruguay Round, however, the phrase "increasing participation of developing countries in world trade" (which appears regularly in the WTO Agreements) acquired a new meaning. The general approach in the negotiations was that developing countries should adopt broadly the same liberalization policies as developed countries. Thus, *increasing participation* was to be measured in terms of the extent of developing countries' *adoption of legal obligations* in the Uruguay Round Agreements rather than being absolved from these obligations. Given the changed nature and coverage of the obligations to be met, this was clearly a more demanding task.

As the Uruguay Round negotiations evolved, developing countries proved to be more and more active in all areas. They were conscious of the lack of success of earlier approaches to special and differential treatment and they recognized the need to respond to the changing nature of the commitments they were now undertaking. Although there is no hard evidence to support the contention, it would appear that developing countries recognized that non-reciprocity and the legal freedom they had been accorded in the past had not functioned to their advantage; by having nothing to offer, and in the absence of benevolent negotiating parties, they had nothing to gain except statements of general principle. Instead of being faced with a *fait accompli* for which an exemption had to be sought, developing countries lent support to the notion that a multilateral trading system based on a uniform set of strengthened rules and disciplines with global application would work in their favour, and that the smaller and weaker countries needed a credible set of enforceable rules as much as, or even more than, larger countries did. A further consideration is that many developing countries were autonomously adopting trade liberalization measures,[30] and they saw the Uruguay Round as an occasion to gain recognition for domestic reform, acquire reciprocal market access for liberalization measures, and lock in domestic policy reform by undertaking binding commitments in the GATT.

A crucial and defining characteristic of legal flexibility in the Uruguay Round (compared with previous rounds of multilateral trade negotiations) was that its outcome was a single undertaking. In order to join the WTO, countries were obliged to accept all the Uruguay Round Agreements. Similarly, all members were obliged to assume acceptable binding market access commitments in *all* the areas of goods, services and intellectual property rights, thus addressing some developed countries' long-standing complaints concerning free-riding by some developing countries.

As regards benefits accruing to developing countries as a result of the negotiations, a number of the Uruguay Round Agreements are in themselves of particular importance. As noted, rules relating to agricultural trade have been less operational and effective than those for industrial goods, and the rules governing trade in textiles and clothing have been a de facto derogation from GATT-1947 disciplines. This was no longer the case with the Uruguay Round Agreements. Further, the Agreement on Safeguards had as its objective eliminating the need for export restraint arrangements, which had worked to the disadvantage of developing countries. The disciplines contained in the Agreements on Subsidies and Countervailing Measures and on Anti-Dumping were strengthened and clarified; developing countries had frequently found themselves on the receiving end of restrictive measures and were adversely affected through the inappropriate use of procedures contained in earlier arrangements.[31] The Agreement on Trade-Related Aspects of Investment Measures (TRIMS), which was highly controversial at the beginning of the Uruguay Round negotiations, represented a compromise between developed countries' requests and developing countries' concerns; as did the Understanding on Balance-of-Payments Provisions of the GATT-1994.

Because the GATT-1947 is still part of the total outcome of the Uruguay Round (albeit revised as the GATT-1994 – see below), existing provisions relating to special and differential treatment remain. It could be argued, however, that these are now of little operational significance, a fact that has led developing countries to negotiate for their strengthening in the Doha Round. As outlined above, much of the special treatment offered to developing countries in the GATT-1947 related to non-reciprocity in negotiations to liberalize trade. This flexibility has been overtaken by the events of the Uruguay Round, as tariffs have been significantly reduced and bound, and the General Agreement on Trade in Services (GATS) has its own provisions in this respect. Further, vague commitments in Part IV of the GATT-1947 have been replaced by more precise commitments vis-à-vis developing countries in the various WTO Agreements, which, although providing developing countries with some flexibility in the implementation of the various obligations, do not absolve them from their eventual adoption.

The GATT-1947 has been modified through the Uruguay Round negotiations (and emerged as the GATT-1994) in such a way as to increase the discipline on the use of some of the flexibilities available to developing countries. The use of restrictions for balance of payments purposes provides a good example. Although Article XVIII:B, which was used and sometimes abused by developing countries, still remains in the GATT-1994, the Understanding on Balance-of-Payments Provisions represents a fundamental change. It requires preference to be given to price-based measures (e.g. import surcharges), as opposed to quantitative restrictions, which were legally permitted by GATT Article XVIII:B. It subjects the use of quantitative restrictions to more stringent rules, such as the need to provide justification for their use and a commitment to phase them out progressively. The Understanding reinforces the original intention of restrictive measures being neutral and applied only to control the overall level of imports – i.e. they should be applied across the board rather than selectively. It also clarifies that, at least in cases where the Balance-of-Payments Committee has not reached any clear conclusion on the consistency of the measures with the GATT-1994, recourse to dispute settlement remains open.

The Doha Development Agenda

During the Uruguay Round, developing countries agreed to accept binding disciplines in areas that formerly were optional (for example, subsidies, anti-dumping and technical barriers to trade), as well as new obligations in intellectual property, services and investment-related measures. The payoff for this was to be the combination of greater market access for agricultural goods and textiles and more operational and effective provisions relating to special and differential treatment. The improved market access would come through flexibility in the implementation of rules, the expanded provision of technical assistance, and preferential market access.

One of the concerns expressed by developing countries has been that the commitments undertaken towards them are largely best endeavour in nature and unenforceable under the newly strengthened dispute settlement procedures. In the developing countries' view, not only should there be additions to the existing 155 special and differential provisions, but the existing provisions should be modified and in some cases rendered mandatory to better confer the benefits of their original intent. But what are the appropriate means to strengthen special and differential provisions and make them more *precise, effective and operational*; and, indeed, which provisions are relevant in this respect?

Developing countries have also sought to review the implementation of the various Agreements. Although, in conventional terms, implementation is thought of as the extent to which the various WTO members have fulfilled their obligations, developing countries chose to view work on implementation as a means of addressing what they saw as imbalances in the Uruguay Round Agreements. They argued that the implementation of the Agreements – or the lack of it – had not provided them with the promised gains. This was owing to a number of factors. Developed countries had failed to implement certain commitments, practical difficulties were encountered by developing countries themselves in implementing obligations (e.g. fulfilling notification requirements), and some Agreements had turned out to be unbalanced when put into operation. From a negotiating perspective, developing countries argued that, because they had already offered concessions for Agreements that proved to be unbalanced, there was no question of further concessions to redress imbalances in the future. In other words, any discussion of implementation was not on the negotiating agenda. For the developing countries, the system was not delivering the goods, it needed to be changed, and these changes should not be brokered through a process based on reciprocity. On the other hand, developed countries were of the view that meeting such demands meant changing the balance of rights and obligations contained in the Agreements concerned. This, in their view, required negotiation among WTO members and an exchange of concessions.

There is a fundamental question to be addressed here. In the view of developed countries, there may be some derogations for particular countries at lower (read "specified") levels of development for a certain period of time. However, they argue that the debate cannot progress in the absence of a predetermined criterion for eligibility for certain flexibilities. This debate is central to the resolution of the most significant substantive controversies on special and differential treatment. Some developed and developing countries have expressed sympathy for the need to establish a system of development thresholds and trade performance targets to guide the application of rules and their flexibilities or modulations; others are against it. These will be discussed below.

It is against this backdrop that the Doha Development Agenda is taking place, along with consideration of 88 proposals advanced by developing countries.[32] The rather excruciating and time-consuming nature of this process, together with its meagre outcome, constitutes an excellent case study. It has led to frustration on the part of developing countries, which certainly contributed to the collapse of the Ministerial Meeting in Cancún, Mexico, in 2003. Comments are made on the process in the following section, but the details are described in the appendix to this chapter.

The Work Programme on Special and Differential Treatment

After considerable pressure on several fronts, it was agreed at the Ministerial Meeting in Doha, Qatar, in November 2001 to launch the Doha Development Agenda. Today, there are very few developing countries that are not members of the WTO or in the process of acceding to it.[33] The Ministerial Declaration emerging from Doha was complemented by the Ministerial Decision on Implementation-Related Issues and Concerns, which was the outcome of the work pursuant to the Geneva Ministerial Meeting in 1998 (see below).[34]

The Doha Ministerial Declaration reaffirmed that "provisions for special and differential treatment are an integral part of the WTO Agreements" and directed that "all special and differential treatment provisions shall be reviewed with a view to strengthening them and making them more precise, effective and operational". The Decision on Implementation-Related Issues and Concerns instructed the Committee on Trade and Development to identify those special and differential treatment provisions that were already mandatory in nature and those that were non-binding in character, to identify those that should be made mandatory, and to report to the General Council with recommendations for a decision by July 2002. The Committee was also to examine additional ways in which special and differential treatment could be made more effective and to report to the General Council with recommendations for a decision by July 2002. Furthermore, the Implementation Decision instructed the Committee to consider how special and differential treatment could be incorporated into the architecture of the WTO rules. These were impossible deadlines (see the appendix).

As noted, reviewing special and differential provisions has been part of the standard terms of reference of the Committee on Trade and Development since the early 1960s, so, at the time of the launching of the Doha Development Agenda, a vast amount of work had already been undertaken. This was specifically noted as a basis for further work.[35] However, although much work had been done, there was an important new element with potentially far-reaching implications; namely, governments were to identify which provisions should be made mandatory.

For special and differential treatment to be incorporated into the architecture of the WTO rules, for it to be made more effective and operational, and for non-mandatory provisions to be made into mandatory ones, answers to many questions are required. What sort of special and differential treatment best meets the needs of developing countries? Are there generic provisions that relate to all developing countries or must special treatment be differentiated according to the countries concerned? Given the very different nature of the Agreements, what is the specific form the various provisions could take? And if *differentiated* treatment is the best alternative, what would be the criterion for granting it, and how can the political opposition of developing countries as a group to selective and differentiated treatment be addressed?

The answer to this last question is complex and politically charged. In one form or another it permeates many aspects of the Doha Development Agenda as well as the daily workings of the WTO. The political sensitivity stems from the fact that, if there is a formal realization of the different needs of developing countries for legal flexibility, there is also a formal recognition not only of *graduation* but also of the creation of classes of developing countries other than the current "developing" and "least developed" distinction. Many developing countries see this as an attempt to fragment their collective strength in negotiations and they resist it staunchly.

Policy considerations

Although some ambiguities remain, past experience clearly demonstrates that there is a statistically close association between expanded trade and economic growth, and that poverty is reduced when per capita incomes rise.[36] Obviously policy in other areas also matters and will influence how much the poor benefit from growth. Similarly, empirical results show that trade policies characterized by openness – including a competitive exchange rate and reasonably low tariffs – are more favourable to growth than are policies of protection. There is no support in the data for restrictive, protectionist trade policies by developing countries.

There are two caveats. The existence of open external markets and of open trade policies does not guarantee success in trade-based economic growth. Other factors are crucially important, such as human resources, investment, sound macroeconomic policy and low corruption. The poor, too, have no guarantee of participation in the fruits of trade-based growth. Some are vulnerable to the changes brought by shifts in external market demand and by altered policies. No policy of trade reform is complete without an assessment of the costs of adjustment for the poor and without anticipatory measures to facilitate the transition. The pace of reform should be such as to minimize the frictional costs without losing the gains from efficiency and growth.

These conclusions set the scene for today's debate. Developing countries are right to seek better access in foreign markets for their exports. They are right when they undertake judicious and well-planned reforms to open their markets and encourage investment. However, to take full advantage of the opportunities that world markets offer, they also need to pay attention to the gamut of other factors – human resources, policies, laws, administration – that contribute to a successful enterprise economy.

Preferences

With a growing acceptance that outer-oriented countries do better than closed ones, it is not surprising that improved market access has been a very high priority on the negotiating agenda of developing countries. The important question is how to ensure that the process of trade liberalization and the strengthening of trade rules in both goods and services continues, and that the countries benefiting from it are far more broadly based. The potential is certainly there in both agricultural and non-agricultural market access negotiations because the wider ambitions of the Doha Development Agenda (in particular, the inclusion of the Singapore issues) have now been narrowed. The Doha Development Agenda has been converted into what is in operational terms a *market access* round of negotiations. No country is denying the usefulness of improved market access. But what is the role of special and differential treatment in promoting improved market access for developing countries?

Under the Generalized System of Preferences, developed countries discriminate in favour of qualifying developing countries by granting non-reciprocal tariff reductions below most favoured nation rates for certain products. As noted above, this exception to MFN treatment was authorized through a 10-year waiver in 1971 and given permanent legal status in 1979 through the Enabling Clause of the Tokyo Round Agreements.[37] However, the potential for GSP schemes to yield benefits is somewhat modest. Average GSP rates are 3.7 per cent in the United States, 4.5 per cent in the European Union, 5.4 per cent in Canada and 5.7 per cent in Japan. This means that they are only 1–2 percentage points lower than the corresponding average applied MFN rates. Recent Trade Policy Reviews of other major providers of GSP preferences show that the differentials between MFN and GSP rates are considerably smaller for sensitive sectors, such as agriculture and textiles and clothing, both of which are frequently excluded from GSP and other unilateral preferences.[38]

The operation of the GSP has been frequently criticized by developing countries in the Trade Policy Review Mechanism. Specific concerns include the fact that items of particular export interest for developing countries are not eligible for GSP benefits, or are only partially included in the schemes; some schemes contain binding ceiling quotas on certain products; some schemes are highly skewed in terms of both the number of main beneficiaries and the range of products included; imports under preferences are subject to emergency safeguards or zero-duty quotas, which have negative effects on preference schemes; exports have been progressively excluded from a number of GSP schemes as they reach the competitiveness criteria defined by GSP-granting countries; sector and country graduation is contrary to the principles of non-discrimination and non-reciprocity that underpin the GSP; the consequent uncertainty of access is a major concern to the countries affected; linking the benefits to non-trade issues, such as environmental and social (labour) standards, as well as intellectual property rights and the fight against drugs, curtails the benefits under the scheme and introduces elements of discrimination and reciprocity.

This last point is particularly important in the context of sustainable development: namely, can preferences be used as a carrot or stick for groups of developing countries in relation to respect for core labour standards, the environment or controls on the production and trafficking of drugs?[39] As far as developed countries are concerned, it is politically difficult not to punish countries that are not pursuing policies considered worthy of recognition and reward. On the developing country side, this represents discrimination, coupled with trade diversion to what are considered by the importers to be problem countries, when the countries suffering from trade diversion may well have fought hard to overcome just those problems. For example, by using preferences as a carrot for drug-trafficking countries, trade is diverted away from those countries that do not have such problems or that have fought hard to avoid them. Most important of all is the systemic issue. As developing countries see it, they fought hard to acquire non-reciprocal preferences, and now those preferences are being modified on a unilateral basis. Further, classes of developing countries are being created not only on economic grounds but according to other predetermined standards in the importing countries.

This system consideration came to a head on 5 March 2002, when India requested consultations with the European Union concerning the conditions under which the Union accords tariff preferences to developing countries under its current GSP scheme.[40] India considered that EU tariff preferences for combating drug production and trafficking and protecting labour rights and the environment create undue difficulties for India's exports to the European Union. In particular, they nullify or impair the benefits accruing to India under the MFN provisions of the GATT-1994 and the Enabling Clause.

The WTO Panel ruled that the Enabling Clause was an exception to MFN and not an autonomous right existing in parallel with MFN. Taking into account the "exceptions" nature of the Enabling Clause, and the related GATT objective and purpose of "elimination of discrimination in international commerce", the Panel found that the term "non-discriminatory" in the Enabling Clause requires that *identical tariff preferences be provided to all developing countries without differentiation, except for the implementation of a prior limitation.*

The Appellate Body reversed the Panel finding.[41] It concluded that the Enabling Clause allows for differentiation among categories of beneficiaries of preference schemes in certain circumstances in order to address the special development, financial or trade needs of particular developing countries. In this regard and also taking into account the Preamble of the WTO Agreement, which states that there is a need to ensure that developing countries secure a share in the growth of international trade commensurate with the needs of their economic development, the Appellate Body found that the term "non-discriminatory" in the Enabling Clause does not prohibit developed country members from providing different tariff preferences to products originating in different beneficiary countries. Rather, the term "non-discriminatory" requires that *identical treatment is available to all similarly situated beneficiaries that have the same development, financial and trade needs.* The Appellate Body also found that the phrase "developing countries" referred to in the Enabling Clause does not mean *all* developing countries.

A number of developing countries claimed that the purpose of the Enabling Clause was *specifically* to transfer benefits from developed to developing countries.[42] The following arguments were articulated at the meeting of the Dispute Settlement Body at the time of adoption of the Appellate Body report. Developing countries had never consented to forgo their MFN rights between themselves. The Appellate Body ruling meant that developing countries' MFN rights were being deprived by judicial fiat as a result of this decision. As to the Appellate Body's interpretation, which would now allow discriminatory preferences to be given to similarly situated beneficiaries based on broadly recognized standards as set out in multilateral instruments adopted by other international organizations, it was argued that there is absolutely no legal basis in the WTO for tying the particular needs of certain countries to selective tariff pref-erences solely for these countries. Moreover, the use in the WTO of concepts from other organizations without the consent of the membership of the WTO was unacceptable. As a result, the legal responsibility for establishing categories of developing country members to be accorded special treatment under WTO law had always been with the entire WTO membership through the negotiation of waivers. Only the membership as a whole can approve a (selective) preferential scheme under conditions that maintain an overall balance of rights and obligations. Panels and the Appellate Body do not have the means to ensure that compensation is granted to those excluded from, and adversely affected by, the special preferences. In allowing for the establishment of new subcategories of countries beyond the three categories recognized by the membership (i.e. developed, developing, least developed), the Appellate Body had acted as a de facto legislator.

Domestic considerations

The picture that emerges from empirical studies is that, although there are many influences bearing on economic growth (including technological change, macroeconomic stability, and rapidly declining transport and communication costs), liberal trade policies generally promote higher economic growth. However, economic growth does not ensure increased welfare for all sectors of the economy. Consequently, it is generally recognized that a broader measure of living standards than economic growth is needed. This would take account of improvements in life expectancy, literacy and other social indicators as well. Nevertheless, the evidence suggests that liberal trade policies have contributed not only to the substantial global economic growth experienced during much of the twentieth century, but also to increased living standards and welfare generally. Trade liberalization has the potential to improve the performance of other aspects of domestic markets, helping them to function better, resources to be allocated more efficiently, and additional income to be generated from trade as exports expand. Yet trade liberalization by itself is not sufficient to address the various economic (or other) problems that afflict people in developing countries, particularly those in the least developed nations. Indeed, the literature suggests that policies aimed at strengthening internal institutions and markets and alleviating transitional hardships should accompany trade liberalization.

As Amartya Sen has remarked, the global economy has brought prosperity to many different areas of the globe. A few centuries ago, pervasive poverty and "nasty, brutish and short" lives dominated the world, with only a few pockets of rare affluence. In overcoming that penury, both modern technology and economic interrelations are important, and the economic predicament of the poor across the world cannot be reversed by withholding from them the well-established efficiency of international trade and exchange, and the social as well as economic merits of living in open rather than closed societies.[43]

But has trade liberalization been a burden for developing countries? An enquiry by the WTO Secretariat could not uncover any information indicating that any developing country has had difficulty in implementing tariff cuts according to its schedules of concessions. Further, there are no statements to that effect in the relevant WTO Committees. In addition, a survey of the WTO Trade Policy Reviews of developing countries reveals that adjusting to tariff liberalization has not been a problem. Perhaps this is because WTO tariff concessions undertaken by developing country members under Article II of the GATT-1994 have generally been implemented over a longer or extended time-frame compared with developed countries. Furthermore, should members have difficulty in implementing WTO tariff concessions, they can renegotiate these concessions under Article XXVIII procedures, which are available to all WTO members and are commonly utilized for such purposes.[44]

Additionally, the number of developing country members relying on balance of payments restrictions has declined sharply. There has been improved economic management of trade and fiscal deficits and surpluses, and a growing recognition that restrictive trade measures can inhibit the structural change required to resolve balance of payments problems. Since the beginning of the Uruguay Round in 1986, 12 countries considering themselves as "developing" have disinvoked, or given undertakings to disinvoke, balance of payments exceptions.[45] At the time of creation of the WTO, only five developing countries were in active consultation with the WTO Committee on Balance-of-Payments Restrictions.[46] All but one (Bangladesh) have phased out their restrictions.

However, the decline in the use of balance of payments restrictions has been coupled with a renewed interest in the rarely used infant industry provisions: Sections A and C of Article XVIII. The flexibility provided for in these provisions has now assumed a new significance for a number of countries as circumstances have changed. First, balance of payments justifications for industry protection no longer provide a means to protect infant industries. Second, because developing countries have bound many of their tariffs (although their applied rates are frequently lower), they do not have the same flexibility to increase tariffs for individual industries. Third, many more developing countries are members of the WTO compared with the GATT, and the earlier flexibility that came with non-membership of the GATT no longer exists. Fourth, there are countries that clearly wish to maintain their autonomy in "picking the winners" or identifying industries that they consider warrant support for reasons not accounted for by the market. This approach shares many of the characteristics of import substitution policies, and therefore suffers from many of their defects. These include an inability to determine in any consistent manner which industries will mature beyond infancy and become "winners", and the potential for rent-seeking as a by-product of protection, whether it be for the purposes of subsidizing the winners or substituting for imports.

According to UNCTAD, reform of Sections A and C of Article XVIII is "particularly desirable because "the compensation requirements are so onerous that they are likely to nullify the very intent of the article, which is to allow developing countries to promote new industries".[47] Additionally, it has been argued that certain less developed economies – particularly those with limited human resources and overburdened administrations – lack the administrative capability to impose safeguards or anti-dumping and/or countervailing duty measures, which are seen as selective "protective measures" available to developed countries. Therefore, acting in accordance with WTO rules greatly restricts the flexibility of developing countries in protecting individual industries.

Yet, even if greater flexibility in infant industry protection were to be available for some African and least developed countries, it is most unlikely that self-declared developing countries at an advanced stage of development (Taiwan, Singapore, Korea) would be included. Nor would countries with advanced and competitive sectors such as biotechnology (India and Brazil), computer software programming (India) or textiles, clothing, footwear and other manufactured goods (China).

The same is true of Part IV of the GATT-1994, where the conversion of best endeavour texts to binding commitments is sought from developed countries. For example, the African Group of countries has proposed making Part IV mandatory.[48] If this happened, the implications would be that the developed countries would, *inter alia*, be *obligated* to ensure a rapid and sustained expansion of developing countries and a share in the growth in international trade commensurate with the needs of their economic development. Developed countries would also be obliged to provide the maximum market access to products of export interest to developing countries, to take measures to stabilize and improve conditions in world markets for developing countries' products, and to assist in the diversification of their economies. Although this might be an option available to Botswana, it would certainly not be available for Korea.

Differentiated treatment

The track record of the Doha Development Agenda is such that the views of developed and developing countries are a long way apart on how much legal flexibility to create and who gets it. According to major developed countries, all special and differential treatment provisions should be seen as steps towards a common system of rights and obligations.[49] This raises the broader question of whether preferential treatment, except for least developed countries, should still be provided on a universal non-discriminatory basis for all developing countries.[50] As noted, from a legal perspective it has been argued that discriminating between developing countries in according preferential treatment constitutes non-compliance with the Enabling Clause.

Although many developing countries insist on generic special and differential treatment, developed countries argue that, as long as such provisions remain available to *all* developing countries irrespective of their individual level of development, there will be severe limits on any significant departure from multilateral commitments. Another argument is that WTO rules already provide recourse to non-universal treatment, including through waivers, for developing countries with individual needs that require preferential treatment. If there is to be legal flexibility, it should be temporary and reflect the specific capacities, limitations or needs of each developing country in a specified area. The reasoning continues that the legal flexibility should be regularly reviewed and cease to apply as soon as the problem it was designed to compensate for no longer exists. On the developing country side, their national submissions have revealed that, of the almost 90 proposals to modify the legal flexibility, a very large number were looking for greater flexibility to implement policies thought to be in their national interest.

Neither group of countries denies that developing countries require flexibility in certain circumstances, but the important questions are who decides which obligations will benefit from legal flexibility, what should be the nature of that flexibility (e.g. in terms of the transition period), and who should decide when the flexibility should be terminated? One thing is clear for developed countries – major developing countries should not be permitted to make such choices on a unilateral basis.

One suggestion has been for WTO members to agree to a criterion according to which they could distinguish between developing countries for the purposes of granting special and differential treatment. This may relate to various economic, institutional and other characteristics of the country concerned – one of which could be gross domestic product per capita. In the absence of such an agreed criterion, and with each developed country unilaterally deciding the countries to which it would accord special and differential treatment, what would prevail would, by default, be a type of à la carte approach and totally unacceptable to developing countries. It is argued that this is not realistic, would be far too time consuming to develop, and would lead to the lowest common denominator in terms of ambitions.[51] Several developing countries have also favoured tailoring special and differential treatment provisions to individual circumstances. One relevant example relates to transition periods. The African Group has argued that, in the WTO Agreements, transition periods are particularly arbitrary, when in fact they should be designed to ensure that the period of flexibility is adequate to carry out institutional change in a particular country.[52] This should be established by determining broad parameters tailored to take into account the individual circumstances of each country in question. What underpins much of the disagreement, however, is the lack of clarity as regards the countries that can benefit from legal flexibility.

Least developed countries

There are many proposals to deal with the special situation in least developed countries.[53] Many of the specific proposals revolve around making duty- and quota-free access to all LDC exports mandatory and avoiding the erosion of preferential margins under GSP schemes. For instance, if MFN tariff reductions result in such erosion (and thus loss of competitiveness), "the LDCs affected would require compensatory or adjustment support measures in the trade, financial and technological fields to mitigate adverse effects on their export earnings as well as enable them to cope with increased global competition",[54] and developed countries should bind the preferences they grant under their GSPs. The measures proposed in this respect include the elimination of all internal and border constraints inhibiting the full utilization of existing preferential access; support for diversification efforts, including the elimination of all tariff peaks and tariff escalation affecting semi-processed and processed products; debt relief and facilitation of technology transfers; removal of non-tariff barriers to all LDC exports; and temporary financial compensation for a fall in export earnings in the case of products whose share in the total export earnings of an LDC exceeds 50 per cent.

In addition, it has been proposed that LDCs should always be entitled to extensions for their transition periods as they may require and that technical assistance should aim among other things to remove any supply-side constraints to benefits under all WTO Agreements, such as benefits of market access opportunities and development of domestic productivity. Rules of origin requirements should be realistic and flexible to match the industrial capacity of least developed countries, and existing special and differential treatment provisions under WTO Agreements should be improved in an effective manner with a view to ensuring that duty-free access is not nullified by non-tariff measures. In addition, LDCs should not be required, under structural adjustment programmes imposed by the World Bank or the International Monetary Fund, to take liberalization measures that are inconsistent with their development, trade and financial needs.[55]

The broad thrust of these proposals is that acceptance of the greater obligations of the WTO legal system comes as a result of economic development and should not be seen as an input into it. However, if (as claimed) accepting WTO obligations promotes economic development, this begs the question of why those most in need of provisions to promote economic development should not be obliged to adopt them. Why are particular measures good for Ghana and Ivory Coast but bad for Bangladesh and Botswana, when the difference between them in terms of underdevelopment, at least with respect to regions in the countries concerned, is minimal? It is hard to rationalize that there is something magical in the cut-off point of a gross domestic product of US$600 per annum. Why is one development strategy appropriate for all members of one group of countries but not the other?

Expectations and the process

As noted above, in 50 years of GATT history, the only significant additions to GATT law and practice responding to the concerns of developing countries were modifications to Article XVIII, the addition of Part IV, and the Enabling Clause. According to the instructions that emerged from the Doha Ministerial Decision on Implementation of November 2001, *all* special and differential treatment provisions were to be reviewed with a view to strengthening them and making them more *precise*, *effective* and *operational*. This is a truly massive task by any measure, and could be thought of as a challenge with a 10-year time horizon. Yet the Committee on Trade and Development was expected to complete the task and report to the General Council with clear recommendations in just eight months – by July 2002. How could this be possible, given the number of provisions and their very different objectives, whose nature affects different countries differently? Developing countries responded to the challenge as they had been encouraged to, by coming forward with 88 proposals. The Committee on Trade and Development was also to report to the General Council on changing *non-mandatory provisions into mandatory ones*, with clear recommendations for a decision, by July 2002. Such changes affect the rights and obligations of different countries differently, come through modifying Agreements, Decisions or agreed Interpretations, and require consensus on the part of all members. This too was a clearly impossible task. Not surprisingly, three deadlines were missed, the mandate was moved to the General Council, and the Ministerial Meeting in Cancún in 2003, where agreement was to be struck, failed. The animosity and frustration of developing countries with the lack of progress reached new highs, and certainly contributed to the collapse of Cancún.

A further consideration is that, in the Ministerial Decision on Implementation, ministers instructed the work of the Committee on Trade and Development to take "fully into consideration" previous documentation of the Secretariat. The one document specifically referred to describes the nature of special and differential provisions and how they have been implemented, and classifies them according to whether they are mandatory or best endeavour. This amounted to 207 pages of legal texts and commentaries for all WTO members to be reviewed over the 12 months from November 2001.[56] This document was to be read in conjunction with its earlier versions, which added another 158 pages.[57] The amount of important material to be analysed was vast, placing an unreasonable burden on all small and under-resourced delegations.

However, this is not all in terms of the material to be reviewed by small country delegations both in Geneva and in capitals. The Special Session of the Committee on Trade and Development met formally 15 times between March 2002 and February 2003. This generated 250 pages of summary records to be reviewed and reflected upon if serious negotiating positions were to be formulated. And this formal work pales into insignificance when compared with the unknown number of informal meetings and non-papers discussed with – or without – the involvement of the chairperson. Then there were the 88 proposals from individual countries and groups of countries to consider. These were frequently highly complex from a legal perspective and potentially important from an economic point of view.

These demands on the time and resources of the Secretariat and delegations occurred against the backdrop of parallel processes in the Implementation Review Mechanism of the General Council, the Trade Negotiations Committee, the 40 standing bodies of the WTO (for example, the Regional Trade Agreements Committee, Accession Working Parties and the Trade Policy Review meetings). Further, there was the dispute settlement process to service, and the negotiations surrounding the review of the Dispute Settlement Understanding. This Herculean task was to be carried out along with the more conventional meetings associ-

ated with the negotiating agenda for the Doha Development Agenda –
arguably one of the most complex and ambitious in the history of trade
negotiations – which took place in the Special Sessions of other negotiating groups. This was a tall order for all countries – and in particular for
least developed countries that do not even have a physical presence in
Geneva. No wonder that, in the absence of any meaningful outcome,
frustration reached breaking point in Cancún. In his report to the General Council, the chairperson of the Committee on Trade and Development specifically mentioned the difficulties for members associated with
the large number of Agreement-specific proposals, "the complexity and
potential implications of some of the proposals, the need to examine individually the legal and practical implications, and a shortage of time, as
factors that prevented them from being able to engage in more than a
preliminary consideration of many of the proposals".[58]

Striking a balance

A number of WTO Agreements are considered to be unbalanced and
weighted against the interests of developing countries. This view is supported by some non-governmental organizations, which advance the proposition that WTO rules are "rigged" against developing countries. Exploring whether there is a lack of balance raises complex questions.

With rounds of negotiations, such as the Uruguay Round, it is understood by negotiators that, in the final analysis, the important consideration is whether or not the *totality* of the outcome is acceptable to each
of the countries involved. "What is lost on the swings is made up on the
roundabouts", and trade-offs between Agreements are more than common. Viewed in this context, it could be argued that each individual
Agreement need not necessarily be balanced within itself. To claim at a
later stage that an Agreement should be rebalanced because it was not
fair in the first place is not to play according to the rules of the game.
These are tough rules, which it may not be possible to defend in the future, and it is an unsatisfactory situation for public interest groups that
have a particular interest in a particular Agreement.

The TRIPS Agreement constitutes a useful example. It was already
considered unbalanced by some developing countries at the time of its
adoption. It was apparently traded off against the assured phasing-out of
the Multi-fibre Arrangement – something that never should have been
paid for because it was itself a derogation from GATT rules. According
to one ambassador who took a high profile as a spokesperson for developing countries in the TRIPS and other Uruguay Round negotiations:
"At the end of the day, it was the assessment of developing countries
that they needed the multilateral trading system, based on principles of

non discrimination much more than developed countries, and if inclusion of TRIPS in the system was the price to pay for that, they would have to pay it."[59]

There are more lessons to be learned from the TRIPS Agreement. Experience gained in its implementation shows that the promised flow of technology to developing countries that was anticipated at the time of signing has not eventuated. Additionally, a number of the obligations accepted as part of the total undertaking (such as notification requirements) have been more onerous than expected. More generally, whereas a particular Agreement may have been thought to be balanced on paper – or even tilted positively in favour of some countries at the time of adoption – this may not have been the experience in practice. Thus, there is a call for rebalancing some Agreements.

Further, many developing countries have argued that best endeavour provisions have not been honoured as anticipated. The mandate given by ministers to review mandatory and non-mandatory provisions envisaged the possibility of making changes, especially for non-mandatory provisions that have not proved to be of value. Deciding on the criteria for converting best endeavour provisions to mandatory ones has not been a simple task. A first question is process related: where should such proposals be addressed – in the Trade Negotiations Committee; the Special Session of the Committee on Trade and Development; the Special Sessions of other negotiating groups; in the regular technical (or non-negotiating) committees servicing specific agreements (e.g. the Technical Barriers to Trade Committee); the Implementation Review Mechanism of the General Council; or elsewhere?

Some argued that a number of proposals to create mandatory obligations were under consideration within various WTO bodies and could be best addressed in terms of the ongoing negotiations – more specifically, in the Special Sessions created for negotiating purposes. Others argued that the proposals should be dealt with outside the negotiating process, being non-negotiable for the reasons described above. One possibility was to deal with them within the various technical committees, such as the Sanitary and Phytosanitary and Technical Barriers to Trade Committees, which had the necessary technical expertise to deal with them effectively. However, sending proposals to the technical committees would, in the view of some, minimize their importance as they became lost in the daily activities of these committees. An additional issue was the need to ensure complementarity and coordination between the work of the Special Sessions dealing with the negotiations and the work of other bodies – both those that were usually attended by experts in technical areas, as well as those undertaking negotiations in areas on which proposals were also before the Special Session.

Interpreting or modifying Agreements

The various special and differential provisions under review are very different in legal terms. For instance, some provisions concern transition times in implementing obligations. Others relate to specific exceptions to rules to which developing countries may have recourse if they so choose, to technical assistance, to safeguarding the interests of developing countries, as well as to positive actions to be undertaken in favour of developing countries. In addition, individual WTO Agreements contain different types and combinations of special and differential treatment, reflecting, in part at least, their specific characteristics. For instance, Agreements that require considerable investment in capacity-building for their implementation may also include provisions relating to technical assistance and transition time periods.

This raises the questions of what would constitute a clear recommendation for decision, in which forums the proposals should be considered (see above), what criteria would be used for distinguishing which provisions were mandatory and which were non-mandatory, and how to strengthen them and make them more precise, effective and operational. In reality, for example, a non-mandatory provision that is honoured may prove to be more effective than a mandatory provision that is ignored.

The WTO Secretariat proposed two ways to convert non-mandatory provisions into mandatory ones. The first was to amend the provisions of the WTO Agreement in question.[60] This would involve replacing the term "should" with "shall", while leaving the rest of the provision unchanged. The alternative route – preferred by most delegations – was a clarification via Guidelines, Decisions or Interpretations. The shortcoming here was that, according to GATT jurisprudence, an authoritative Interpretation can be used only to confirm that the relevant provisions are, in fact, meant to be mandatory in nature. Only the Ministerial Conference or the General Council has the authority to adopt Interpretations of the provisions of a WTO Agreement, and these must be taken by a three-fourths majority of the members. This too could be difficult to achieve. Others were of the view that the debate on mandatory versus non-mandatory provisions was enough in itself, because it served the purpose of making existing special and differential treatment provisions more operational.[61] Such a discussion would not, of course, convert non-mandatory provisions into mandatory ones.

New mechanisms: Monitoring and a framework

In their submissions, a number of developing countries stressed that the concept of special and differential treatment underwent a dramatic transformation in the Uruguay Round Agreements, from recognizing the special problems faced in the course of economic development to dealing with the problems faced in the implementation of the Agreements. These countries argued that, as a result, it was assumed that the level of development had no relationship with the level of rights and obligations under the multilateral trading system; the same policies could be applicable for countries at various levels of development. This they considered to be a dramatic erosion of special and differential treatment. To improve the situation, they proposed to institutionalize and rationalize the adoption and application of special and differential treatment in the various WTO Agreements by elaborating a framework or umbrella agreement on special and differential treatment to ensure a more coherent and effective approach. Special and differential treatment should be mandatory and legally binding through the dispute settlement system of the WTO and, in any future WTO Agreements, there should be an evaluation of how these Agreements facilitate attainment of the developmental targets set out in the United Nations Millennium Declaration.[62] Particular attention was given to this proposal because it was singled out in Doha by ministers in the Implementation Declaration.

A proposal was also made for an Annual Special Session of the General Council on the participation of the least developed countries in the multilateral trading system.[63] LDCs proposed that the agenda of such an annual session could encompass (i) the implementation of the Decision on Measures in Favour of Least-Developed Countries and its overall objectives in favour of least developed countries; (ii) a review of the implementation of the specific special and differential provisions included in the WTO Agreements, Decisions and Declarations; and (iii) an overall review of special and differential treatment.

The African Group was of the view that a strong Monitoring Mechanism should be established.[64] Among its main functions would be (i) the regular evaluation of the utilization and effectiveness of the special and differential treatment provisions, with a view to ensuring that the provisions are duly utilized and any problems arising are effectively addressed, and (ii) the provision of a framework for initiating and considering recommendations that the Committee on Trade and Development could make to members on the best manner to utilize special and differential treatment provisions. There has been general support for the idea and some agreement that the Mechanism should monitor the implementation and utilization of special and differential provisions; that WTO Committees should keep special and differential treatment as a standing or regular item on their agenda; and that the General Council could consider, probably on an annual basis and possibly in Special Session, the Mechanism's report on the implementation and utilization of special and differential treatment provisions.

However, there were still some important areas of difference, including on the institutional structure of the Mechanism and the timing of its coming into force. The general view was that it should be an open-ended body. Some members felt that the monitoring of special and differential treatment should be carried out by the regular CTD or by the CTD in dedicated sessions, whereas other members were of the view that a Sub-Committee of the CTD should be established for this purpose.

Influencing the process

The growing stake of developing countries in the world economy has both strengthened their claim for a role in its management and increased their confidence in asserting that claim. Historically, the poorest developing countries have been slow to assert themselves in the GATT and the WTO. In both institutions, every member country formally enjoys an equal say in the development of consensus decision-making – a feature that offers less powerful countries some leverage to achieve their aims, particularly in creating groups to claim a common cause for common good. Until recently, the developing countries' strategy appears to have been largely defensive. They have sought to ensure "special and differential treatment" in trade agreements and a series of concessions and exceptions from certain internationally agreed disciplines on the grounds that they were at a lower level of development than other WTO members.[65] Recent developments, particularly the assertive role manifested by the Group of Twenty, the African Group and the Least Developed Country Group, may have put an end to this defensive approach.

Another recent development is a shifting of position by some developing countries to the extent that they have become the *demandeurs* for tighter discipline – on agriculture, textiles, services and anti-dumping, for example. Trade can no longer be seen as a trilateral affair involving North America, Europe and Japan, nor should it be seen in a North–South context; it is now firmly a multilateral affair that is becoming increasingly global as China and others adopt the multilateral disciplines.[66] And the influence of developing countries will only grow, as seen with the formation of the Group of Twenty led by India, Brazil and South Africa and including China. Besides, countries from regional blocs such as MERCOSUR (the Southern Cone Common Market comprising Argentina, Brazil, Paraguay and Uruguay) or the Association of South East Asian Nations (which includes Brunei, Indonesia, Malaysia, the Philippines, Singapore and Thailand) will have, either individually or collectively, increasing bargaining power within the WTO system.

Conclusion

Many questions remain unanswered with respect to how best to deal with the needs of developing countries in terms of both process and substance. It is clear that the process has been unmanageable from the start. How can a process that is expected to result in close to 150 governments reviewing 155 special and differential treatment provisions on the basis of almost 90 national submissions be realistically reviewed? How can the dozens of best endeavour provisions be evaluated with a view to rendering them mandatory and incorporating them into the architecture of WTO rules in just a few months, when in the 50 years of GATT history there were only two such changes in rules? Is the lack of satisfactory results because the national submissions do not provide the necessary elements, or because the large number of submissions makes the process unmanageable? Are the countries that are advancing proposals not doing the necessary homework for them to be fully understood by their colleagues from other countries? Are developed countries unsympathetic and obstructionist in their approach? Where are trade-offs to be made with other areas in the negotiations if that is the only way to advance the substance? What are the responsibilities that developing countries need to undertake themselves? Are *all* members showing sufficient flexibility in their negotiating positions or are they coming to negotiations to restate pre-established positions? How can the politically driven insistence of developing countries to be treated as a group in the GATT – and now the WTO – be dealt with when it is increasingly clear that differentiated treatment holds the key? Is the issue too complex to be dealt with in the rough and tumble of the negotiating process?

Special and differential treatment was accepted within the GATT as an integral part of the rules-based multilateral trading system. Whereas in the early years of the GATT the preferred treatment was based on a belief that developing countries can foster development by heavily protecting domestic industries, producing for the domestic markets and substituting for imports, there has been a dramatic change over the past half-century. Now, special and differential treatment is found in many forms in the WTO legal texts, with the common characteristic that it is to be provided in a manner consistent with the trade, financial and development needs of developing countries. In addressing the issue of what is the appropriate legal flexibility given the needs of developing countries, the crucial question is whether it provides them with the necessary flexibility to implement their *appropriate* development strategies. Thus, a logical starting point in creating legal flexibility is to have a clear vision of what is the appropriate development strategy. But what is the appropriate development policy; who decides what is appropriate; what domestic policy space is required to implement it; what legal flexibility is required; and what is the nature of the measures that are best suited to achieve the desired result?

The bottom line is that the importance of special and differential treatment within the WTO legal system lies in the fact that it is the mirror-image of not only the physical, institutional and other characteristics of the country in question, but also what is considered to be the proper development strategy of developing countries within the context of the WTO. With the advent of the Uruguay Round, "increasing the participation of developing countries" became synonymous with developing countries forgoing legal flexibility and undertaking more commitments in relation to trade liberalization. The negative connotations surrounding the term "graduation" will increasingly be replaced by a more positive approach in which the reduction of legal flexibility is traded for increased discipline, improved market access through greater competitiveness, and a negotiated reduction in remaining trade barriers. This will be coupled with a new role for developing countries in the multilateral trading system as the guardians of openness, resisting moves by more developed countries to invent and apply new trade barriers.

What is increasingly apparent is that each country is unique. From a substantive perspective, the simple reality is that the term "developing countries" masks very different levels of development and, as a consequence, the divergent negotiating positions that have emerged within developing countries as a "group". The relevance of any development model is inextricably linked to a wide variety of country characteristics, including natural resource endowments, cultural heritage, characteristics of leadership, and institutional and other arrangements. Successful reforms are those that package sound economic principles around local capabilities, constraints and opportunities. Since these local circumstances vary, so do the reforms that work. An immediate implication is that growth strategies require considerable local knowledge.

In this chapter, I have argued that, although special treatment is appropriate for developing countries, it should be special and *differentiated* treatment that depends on the circumstances in the particular country. The challenge is to find the flexibilities that are appropriate for these circumstances. This is a daunting task that deserves better than the fragmented treatment it has received over the past decade and more.

Appendix

The process

The process of discussing special and differential treatment provisions in the WTO has been both long and resource intensive. Even prior to the entry into force of the WTO, the GATT Committee on Trade and Development decided to review the Uruguay Round Agreements, Legal Instruments and Ministerial Decisions that specifically refer to developing countries. In order to provide background to the discussion, the Secretariat prepared a document that summarized each of the relevant provisions under four headings: those that recognize developing countries' interests; those that require developing countries to meet fewer obligations; those that provide a longer time-frame for the implementation of certain obligations; and those that provide for technical assistance.[67] Provisions classified under the heading of "Recognition of Interests" are those that are of a best endeavour nature or that request members, within their own trade policy, to grant a more favourable treatment to developing country members. This categorization was later expanded, and is dealt with in more detail below. Work also proceeded on evaluating the increasing participation of developing countries in the world trading system based on the presumption that increased participation in world trade meant an increase in the share of a country in world trade.[68] It is important to note that the provisions applied to all *self-designated* developing countries.

With the creation of the WTO in 1995 came the WTO Committee on Trade and Development. Its terms of reference included a review of the impact of the results of the Uruguay Round on developing countries and their participation in the multilateral trading system. It was also mandated to consider measures and initiatives to assist in the expansion of their trade and investment opportunities. What is important for present purposes is that the Committee was to review annually the application of special provisions in the multilateral trade agreements and related Ministerial Decisions in favour of developing country members, and to report to the General Council for appropriate action.[69] This led to an extended period of comprehensive analytical reporting by the WTO Secretariat on various aspects of special and differential treatment.

In 1996, and to advance its review in the light of preparations for the Singapore Ministerial Conference, the CTD sought written contributions on progress in the implementation of provisions in favour of developing countries from both members and the WTO bodies with responsibility for monitoring the WTO Agreements. The first substantive debate took place in September 1996 in the run-up to the Singapore Ministerial Meeting. The CTD also held discussions on ways to implement the Decision on Measures in Favour of Least-Developed Countries, which had emerged from the Uruguay Round.[70]

The outcome of the Ministerial Meeting in December 1996 was quite general: ministers recalled that the WTO Agreements embodied provisions conferring differential and more favourable treatment for developing countries, and acknowledged the fact that developing country members had undertaken significant new commitments, both substantive and procedural. A Plan of Action for Least Developed Countries was adopted, including provisions "for taking positive measures, for example duty-free access, on an autonomous basis, aimed at improving their over-all capacity to respond to the opportunities offered by the trading system ... and enhancing conditions for investment and providing predictable and favourable market access conditions for least developed country products".

At the Second WTO Ministerial Meeting in Geneva in 1998, ministers drew attention to the importance of the "full and faithful *implementation* of the WTO Agreement and Ministerial Decisions". They indicated that at the Third Ministerial Meeting in Seattle they would pursue their "eval-uation of the implementation of individual agreements and the realiza-tion of their objectives". They recalled that, according to the Marrakesh Agreement Establishing the World Trade Organization, the WTO was to provide "a framework for the *implementation* of the results of such nego-tiations, as may be decided by the Ministerial Conference". They decided to establish a process under the direction of the General Council in which the work programme on implementation would encompass recom-mendations concerning "the issues, including those brought forward by Members, relating to implementation of existing agreements and decisions".

At a meeting of the CTD in November 1998, the Secretariat was in-structed to undertake a review of the practical difficulties in the imple-mentation and use of special and differential provisions.[71] This was to be conducted on the basis of a questionnaire completed by members and information available in the Secretariat. The Secretariat summarized the replies by members and compiled the relevant statements in the vari-ous Councils or Committees. In more general terms, issues relating to the state of play in the implementation of the various WTO Agreements were heavily debated in preparation for the Seattle Ministerial, and the Draft Declaration destined for the ill-fated Seattle meeting contained a comprehensive reproduction of the various proposals. The chairman pre-pared, on his own responsibility, a draft set of recommendations to min-isters in Seattle. It did not include all of the detailed amendments on an earlier draft, which amounted to approximately 300 pages. Neverthe-less, the final draft text ran to 34 pages and contained many of the pro-posals relating to implementation.[72] These proposals were of course not adopted in Seattle.

An Implementation Review Mechanism was created by the General Council in May 2000 in pursuance of the Declaration of the May 1998 Ministerial Meeting in Geneva. Under this framework, the General Council, meeting in Special Sessions, was called on to assess existing difficulties with the implementation of WTO Agreements, to identify ways to resolve them, and to take decisions for appropriate action. This process was to be completed not later than the Fourth Session of the Ministerial Conference in Doha in November 2001. There were more than 90 developing country national submissions to the Implementation Review Mechanism calling for a modification in the application – and in some cases the substance – of certain WTO rules.[73] As noted, the intention of these submissions was to right the imbalances that developing countries perceived had prevented them from reaping expected benefits in the implementation of the Uruguay Round Agreements. The changes sought frequently overlapped with those proposed in the special and differential treatment review conducted in the Committee on Trade and Development. The debates in both committees were largely similar.[74]

In the context of the Implementation Review Mechanism, on 31 July 2001 the chairperson of the General Council requested the CTD "to review all special and differential treatment provisions in the WTO Agreements and report to the General Council by 30 September 2001 on how they could be operationalised and further enhanced". As a result of this request, the chairperson of the CTD held informal consultations, and the Secretariat continued to update the earlier information it had collected, along with comments and statements made in the many bodies overseeing the WTO Agreements.[75] These, together with subsequent documentation, contained a great deal of useful information.[76] As far as the source material is concerned, the Secretariat had identified the special and differential provisions in both the Uruguay Round Agreements and other WTO legal instruments. The provisions that had earlier been divided into four categories were now grouped under six headings.

(i)   There are 14 provisions across four Agreements and one Decision aimed at **increasing the trade opportunities of developing country members**. They are often couched in "best endeavour" language and occur the least frequently. The key questions here are the extent to which these provisions have contributed to increasing developing countries' trade opportunities, how this may be assessed, and, if they have not made such a contribution, what may be done.

(ii) There are 47 provisions contained in 13 WTO Agreements and 2 Decisions under which WTO members agree to **safeguard the interests of developing countries**. These provisions concern either actions to be taken or actions to be avoided by members. More than half of them are mandatory. The main questions here are whether the provisions have led to the safeguarding of developing country interests, and whether the actions to be taken can be specified concretely and monitored and their implementation objectively measured or evaluated.

(iii) There are 50 provisions across 10 Agreements that provide for **flexibility of commitments and use of policy instruments** by developing countries. These provisions relate to exemptions from disciplines that apply to the membership in general; exemptions from commitments applying to all members in general; or a reduced level of commitments by developing countries compared with all members. They figure largely in Agreements where WTO rules have extended beyond traditional GATT-type border measures. In almost all cases, flexibility takes the form of individual provisions that members may or may not choose to exercise.

(iv) There are 19 provisions contained in 8 Agreements that provide for **transitional time periods** for exemptions from disciplines that are otherwise generally applicable. Some transition time periods in different Agreements have elapsed and some include modalities through which an extension might be sought. Transition time periods were an innovation of the Uruguay Round reflecting a recognition that the process of implementation and the accompanying reforms could give rise to transitional costs: those that relate to the need for human and institutional capacity, and those of a political economy nature requiring structural adjustment following liberalization.

(v) There are 14 provisions across 6 Agreements and 1 Decision dealing with **technical assistance** for developing countries. These are found predominantly in Agreements that require significant levels of capacity for their implementation. The provision of technical assistance can thus be closely linked with transition time periods in facilitating the implementation of certain WTO Agreements.

(vi) There are 24 provisions across 7 Agreements and 3 Decisions relating to **least developed country members**. These provisions, which apply exclusively to the LDCs, all fall under one of the other five types of provision.

The Doha outcome and beyond

At the Ministerial Conference in Doha in November 2001, the Declaration launching the Doha Development Agenda was adopted, along with a Decision on Implementation-Related Issues and Concerns. The latter was the outcome of the work pursuant to the Geneva Ministerial Meeting in 1998.

The Doha Ministerial Declaration reaffirmed that "provisions for special and differential treatment are an integral part of the WTO Agreements" and directed that "all special and differential treatment provisions shall be reviewed with a view to strengthening them and making them more precise, effective and operational".[77] It must have been clear to negotiators at the time that, by introducing the objective of reviewing provisions for special and differential treatment *with a view to strengthening them and making them more precise, effective and operational*, they were employing language that would be particularly difficult to interpret and would certainly lead to proposals that would be impossible to agree on. The CTD was to report to the General Council with clear recommendations for a Decision by July 2002 – an obviously impossible task in a period of barely eight months.

As far as the manner in which implementation concerns were dealt with in the Doha Declaration itself, ministers stated that "[w]e agree that negotiations on outstanding implementation issues shall be an integral part of the Work Programme we are establishing" (para. 12). This text also caused problems, leading to considerable disagreement over what was under negotiation. One view was that all issues – including those listed in the *Compilation of Outstanding Implementation Issues Raised by Members* – were subject to negotiations. The second was that it applied only to the issues for which the Doha Ministerial Declaration provided a specific negotiating mandate.

The Doha Ministerial Declaration provides two procedural tracks for dealing with the negotiations (para. 12). When a specific negotiating mandate is given in the Declaration, that item is to be addressed in the relevant negotiating body established by the Trade Negotiations Committee (TNC). The second procedural track provides for other outstanding implementation issues of the Decision on Implementation and for items without a specific negotiating mandate in the Declaration. On this track, relevant WTO bodies were to address these issues as a matter of priority and report to the TNC by the end of 2002. Thus, a related contentious issue is whether other outstanding implementation issues would be discussed – not negotiated – in regular WTO bodies. As a result, a deadlock emerged at the end of 2002, and the job of finding a way around the impasse was given to the TNC. The chairperson of the TNC announced in July 2003 that discussions on certain implementation issues would resume, with some continuing under the auspices of the TNC and others returning to subsidiary bodies for further technical work.

As far as the Doha Decision on Implementation is concerned, out of approximately 95 points raised by members in the lead-up to the Seattle Ministerial, roughly 40 are touched upon in the Doha Decision on Implementation and nearly 50 in the *Compilation of Outstanding Implementation Issues Raised by Members*; another is found in the TRIPS and Public Health Declaration and a few have disappeared. A few are simply omitted. As far as implementation and special and differential treatment are concerned, the Committee on Trade and Development was handed a

mammoth task, because it was mandated to identify those special and differential treatment provisions that are already mandatory in nature and
those that are non-binding in character. Having done this, it was to report
to the General Council with clear recommendations for a Decision by
July 2002 – another clearly impossible task.

The deadlines of July 2002 were obviously completely unreasonable.
The important question is, why were they set? There are a number of
possible explanations. One was developing countries' desire to assign an
urgency to the task. This was a natural outcome of their frustration at
that time and extended efforts on many fronts to virtually no effect.
Also, in the view of some developing countries the Doha Development
Agenda was to make effective the results of previous negotiations. This
required changes in rights and obligations but, because developing countries thought nothing should be paid for righting past wrongs, July 2002
was chosen as being far removed from, and unrelated to, the proposed
end of the Development Agenda negotiations. There was to be no last-
minute trade-off as the Round came to a close. As will be seen below,
unrealistic deadlines were to become par for the course.

The mandate to strengthen the provisions and make them more precise, effective and operational was pursued in the Committee on Trade
and Development meeting in Special Sessions.[78] As part of the process
it was necessary to distinguish between mandatory and non-mandatory
provisions. The Secretariat conducted the background work on the basis
of the language employed in the various texts of the Agreements. The
working hypothesis was that mandatory provisions use "shall" language
and non-mandatory provisions use "should" language.[79] Subsequent documentation added information on whether the provisions required the
achievement of a certain result (obligations of result) or engagement in
a certain conduct (obligations of conduct), or whether they stipulated
that the obligations of members were to be taken individually or collectively.[80] The Secretariat also identified whether the commitments provided for positive actions in terms of expanding trading opportunities,
safeguarding interests or providing technical assistance.[81]

Despite intensive discussions, little progress was made and the deadline of reporting to the General Council with "clear recommendations"
by July 2002 was missed. The General Council instructed the Special Session of the Committee on Trade and Development to "proceed expeditiously to fulfil its mandate" and extended the deadline for the Special
Session to December 2002. After a series of informal consultations in
September 2002, the Special Session adopted an intensive indicative work
programme so as to fulfil the mandate given by the General Council.[82]

Agreement was not struck by the new deadline of December 2002. The
General Council agreed to further extend the deadline for the Special

Session to February 2003. At this meeting, members remained divided in their views, to such an extent that the General Council was unable to adopt a Report from the Committee on Trade and Development requesting the General Council to "clarify" the relevant Doha mandates and to suspend further work on the issue until the General Council had provided guidance.[83] An important issue was that a large number of developing countries[84] preferred not to submit to the General Council a meagre crop of recommendations on a handful of provisions; it was preferable in their view to clarify the scope of the ministerial mandate. A number of developed countries,[85] in contrast, were of the view that it was better to "harvest" the 12 specific proposals on which there was agreement, and to forward the rest of the proposals to the appropriate negotiating (or other) WTO bodies.

A lack of clarity prevailed. No new deadline had been set, and no decision had been taken on where Agreement-specific proposals should be discussed, or whether to continue work toward an "early harvest" of at least some of the proposed changes. After a three-month pause, the General Council returned to the question at its May 2003 session. Despite the inconclusive nature of those discussions and the lack of agreement on the need to clarify the mandate, in typical GATT/WTO fashion an imaginative solution was found so that the work could continue: the chairperson of the General Council proposed to grapple with the issues by consulting on the basis of a three-tiered structure. He produced a 55-page "approach" paper that grouped 88 developing countries' proposals into three categories.[86] In effect, the disagreement over the need to clarify the text was settled and the process moved from the Special Session to the General Council. The failure to reach agreement at the Ministerial Meeting in Cancún meant that another deadline had been missed and an important opportunity lost.

Re-launching the Doha Development Agenda

The outcome of the Cancún Ministerial Meeting was that ministers instructed negotiators to continue with a December deadline for re-launching the Doha Development Agenda. The breakthrough eventually came in July 2004. The General Council reaffirmed that provisions for special and differential treatment are an integral part of the WTO Agreements. It recalled ministers' decision in Doha to review all special and differential treatment provisions with a view to strengthening them and making them more precise, effective and operational, and once again instructed the Committee on Trade and Development in Special Session to complete the review of all the outstanding Agreement-specific proposals expeditiously and to report to the General Council, with clear recommendations for a Decision, by July 2005. The Council further instructed the CTD, within the parameters of the Doha mandate, to address all other outstanding work, including on the cross-cutting issues, the Monitoring Mechanism and the incorporation of special and differential treatment into the architecture of WTO rules.

The Council also instructed all WTO bodies to which proposals in Category II (issues on the second procedural track) had been referred to complete consideration of these proposals expeditiously and to report to the General Council, with clear recommendations for a Decision, as soon as possible, and no later than July 2005. In doing so these bodies were to ensure that, as far as possible, their meetings did not overlap, so as to enable full and effective participation by developing countries in these discussions.

Concerning implementation-related issues, the General Council reaffirmed the Doha Ministerial Declaration and the Decision on Implementation, instructed the various WTO bodies to redouble their efforts to find a solution, and requested the Director-General to continue his consultative process. The deadline of July 2005 was established for the Council to take appropriate action.

With respect to the market access negotiations, special attention should be paid to the specific needs and concerns of developing countries, including addressing their supply-capacity constraints, assuring food security, facilitating their rural development, and rewarding them for prior unilateral liberalization. Thus, special provisions should apply on the one hand to assist developing countries to obtain more effective market access for their exports and, on the other, to allow them the freedom to implement active policies to stimulate competitiveness and thereby take advantage of market access opportunities. The sentiment among most developing countries is that developed countries have not delivered on their side of the bargain.[87]

Notes

1. One remarkably insightful volume was by Bob Hudec. See Robert E. Hudec, *Developing Countries in the GATT Legal System*, London: Gower, for the Trade Policy Research Centre, 1987, p. 18.
2. It should be noted, however, that the dividing line between process and substance is a thin one. This chapter also has an appendix, which documents some of the specifics of the negotiating process.
3. Amartya Sen, *Development as Freedom*, New York: Anchor Books, 1999. Sen argues that development should be a process that expands the freedom people enjoy or removes the obstacles to freedom that leave people with little choice and few opportunities. He defines freedom as escape from the indignities of poverty, illiteracy, ill-health

and early mortality. It is liberty from political tyranny, the possession of political rights and civil liberties, the absence of racial, ethnic, sexual or religious discrimination, and the availability of social and economic opportunities and the capability to take advantage of them.

4. Cited in Anne Krueger, "Trade Policy and Economic Development: How We Learn", *American Economic Review*, Vol. 87, No. 1, 1997, p. 3.

5. Of the original 23 contracting parties of the GATT, 10 were developing countries: Brazil, Burma, Ceylon, Chile, China, Cuba, India, Pakistan, Syria and Lebanon. Within the first few years, China (by then the Taiwan government), Lebanon and Syria withdrew. Four more developing countries acceded in the Annecy negotiations in 1949: the Dominican Republic, Haiti, Nicaragua and Uruguay. Indonesia became a contracting party in 1950 on achieving independence; Peru and Turkey negotiated their entry during the Torquay Round negotiations of 1951. By the end of the Torquay Round negotiations, the total developing country membership stood at 14.

6. Article XVIII (*bis*) also stated that multilateral negotiations were to be conducted on "a basis which affords adequate opportunity" to take into account, *inter alia*, "the needs of less-developed countries for a more flexible use of tariff protection to assist their economic development and the special needs of these countries to maintain tariffs for revenue purposes" and "all other relevant circumstances, including fiscal, developmental and strategic and other needs".

7. See Hudec, *Developing Countries in the GATT Legal System*, p. 18. For an overall commentary, see C. Michalopoulos, *Developing Countries in the WTO*, London: Palgrave Macmillan, 2001.

8. See *Meeting the World Trade Deadline*, Report of the Eminent Persons Group on World Trade [the Lambsdorff Report], July 1990, p. 31. This Group included the then GATT Director-General, Peter D. Sutherland.

9. Krueger, "Trade Policy and Economic Development: How We Learn", p. 3.

10. Between 1966 and 1971, the GATT members granted three waivers along these lines: Australia was permitted to offer preferences for developing countries on a specific list of products; all developed contracting parties were free to introduce schemes in favour of developing countries under the Generalized System of Preferences; 16 developing countries were allowed to exchange concessions among themselves.

   In parallel to the initiatives relating to preferences, developing countries pursued efforts to obtain special treatment in the area of dispute settlement. The principal outcome in this respect was that, in the case of developing countries, a consensus was not required for the establishment of the Panel, and time limits for the dispute settlement procedures were established as a way of preventing excessive delays.

11. According to Krueger, there is no question of "going back" to the earlier thinking and understanding of import substitution. Krueger, "Trade Policy and Economic Development: How We Learn", p. 2. And, according to Rodrik, "[v]ery few policy analysts think that the answer is to go back to the old style import substitution initiatives". Dani Rodrik, *Growth Strategies*, Cambridge, MA: National Bureau of Economic Research, Working Paper 10050, 2003, p. 29.

12. Rodrik, *Growth Strategies*, p. 12.

13. Krueger, "Trade Policy and Economic Development: How We Learn", p. 5.

14. In the 1960s and 1970s, a number of the import-substituting countries were not in fact members of the GATT, so the question of the legal flexibility to protect individual industries is not relevant.

15. Indeed, as the Secretary of the Balance of Payments Committee has remarked, in practical terms "it has at times been difficult to differentiate genuine balance-of-payments safeguards measures from import restrictions to protect infant industries." See Karen

McCusker, "Are Trade Restrictions to Protect the Balance of Payments Becoming Obsolete?", *INTERECONOMICS*, March/April 2000, p. 90.

16. This view is advanced by the delegation of India in WTO, *Preparations for the 1999 Ministerial Conference, Proposals Regarding Article XVIII:A and C of the General Agreement on Tariffs and Trade 1994 in Terms of Paragraph 9(a)(i) of the Geneva Ministerial Declaration: Communication from India*, Geneva: WTO Secretariat, WT/GC/W/ 363, 12 October 1999.

17. They have been usefully described in Krueger, "Trade Policy and Economic Development: How We Learn", p. 3.

18. Taiwan did not join until 2001 but Malaysia had joined in October 1957, Korea in April 1967, Singapore in August 1973, Thailand in November 1982, and Hong Kong in April 1986.

19. Anne Krueger, "Trade Policy and Economic Development: How We Learn", pp. 1–22.

20. According to Rodrik, when "Taiwan and South Korea decided to reform their trade regimes to reduce anti-export bias, they did this not via liberalisation (which would have been a Western economist's advice), but through selective subsidisation of exports". Rodrik, *Growth Strategies*, p. 15.

21. The formal title of the Enabling Clause is "Differential and More Favourable Treatment, Reciprocity and Fuller Participation of Developing Countries". See GATT, *The Texts of the Tokyo Round Agreements*, Geneva: GATT Secretariat, 1986.

22. These Codes cover technical barriers to trade, government procurement, subsidies and countervailing duties, customs valuation, import licensing, anti-dumping duties, bovine meat, dairy products, and civil aircraft.

23. The graduation principle was nevertheless implied in Article XVIII, which imposed different disciplines on contracting parties in "early stages of development" and on those "in the process of development".

24. See Isaiah Frank, "The 'Graduation' Issue for LDCs", *Journal of World Trade Law*, July–August 1979, pp. 289–302.

25. See, for example, Brian Hindley, "Safeguards, VERs and Anti-Dumping Action", in *The New World Trading System*, Paris: OECD, 1994.

26. The term was coined by John Williamson, "What Washington Means by Policy Reform", in *Latin American Adjustment: How Much Has Happened*, Washington, DC: Institute for International Economics, 1990.

27. The "Washington Consensus" is often seen as synonymous with "neo-liberalism" and "globalization" and, as Williamson has commented, "there are people who cannot utter the term without foaming at the mouth". John Williamson, *Did the Washington Consensus Fail? Outline of Remarks at CSIS*, Washington, DC: Institute for International Economics, 6 November 2002.

28. Dani Rodrik, "The Economics of Export Performance Requirements", *Quarterly Journal of Economics*, Vol. 102, 1987, pp. 633–650.

29. Rodrik, *Growth Strategies*, p. 12.

30. See GATT, *List of Liberalization Measures*, Geneva: GATT Secretariat, MTN.GNG/ MA/W/10/Rev.2, 14 December 1993, which lists 38 developing countries that undertook autonomous liberalization measures over the period September 1986 – December 1993.

31. Out of a total of 1,133 anti-dumping investigations during the period 1 July 1985 to 30 June 1992, exports from developing countries were subject to 468 investigations, exports from developed countries to 552 investigations and exports from economies in transition to 113 investigations. See GATT, *Overview of Developments in International Trade and the Trading System, Note by the Secretariat*, Geneva: GATT Secretariat, C/RM/OV/4, 3 May 1993.

32. WTO, *General Council Chairman's Proposal on an Approach for Special and Differential Treatment*, Geneva: WTO, Job 03/68, 1 April 2003.

33. Countries that are not members of the WTO include Middle Eastern countries (Iran, Iraq, Lebanon, Libya, Syria and Yemen), European and Asian transition economies (Bosnia and Herzegovina, the Federal Republic of Yugoslavia, Tajikistan and Turkmenistan), a few low-income African countries (Equatorial Guinea, Eritrea, Liberia and Somalia), Afghanistan, North Korea, West Bank and Gaza, and several, mostly small, island economies (Bahamas, Bermuda, Cayman Islands, Comoros, Federated States of Micronesia, Kiribati, Marshall Islands, São Tomé and Príncipe).

34. WTO, *Draft Ministerial Declaration*, Geneva: WTO, WT/MIN(01)/DEC/W/1, 14 November 2001.

35. The following document was specifically referred to in this context: WTO, *Implementation of Special and Differential Treatment Provisions in WTO Agreements and Decisions: Note by Secretariat*, Geneva: WTO Secretariat, WT/COMTD/W/77/Rev.1, 21 September 2001.

36. T. N. Srinivasan and Jagdish Bhagwati, "Outward-orientation and Development: Are the Revisionists Right?", in Deepak Lal and Richard Snape (eds), *Trade, Development and Political Economy*, Basingstoke: Palgrave, 2001, pp. 3–26.

37. Recently, the "Quad" (the United States, the European Union, Japan and Canada) and other industrialized countries have passed legislation providing improved, if not duty-free, access for LDCs for almost all products. More specifically, the United States enacted the African Growth Opportunities Act (AGOA) in May 2000 and the European Union enacted the Everything But Arms (EBA) scheme in March 2001. Under AGOA, 38 African countries currently qualify for preferential treatment; in order to qualify for AGOA, the country must already be eligible for GSP treatment. AGOA extends GSP for eligible sub-Saharan African countries until 1 September 2008.

38. Rohini Acharya and Michael Daly, *Selected Issues Concerning the Multilateral Trading System*, Discussion Paper No. 7, Geneva: WTO, 2004.

39. WTO, *Financing of Losses from Preference Erosion: Note on Issues Raised by Developing Countries in the Doha Round Communication from the International Monetary Fund*, Geneva: WTO, WT/TF/COH/14, 14 February 2003.

40. *European Communities – Conditions for the Granting of Tariff Preferences to Developing Countries*, WT/DS246, December 2003.

41. *European Communities – Conditions for the Granting of Tariff Preferences to Developing Countries*, Appellate Body Report, WT/DS246/AB/R, 7 April 2004.

42. WTO, *Dispute Settlement Body: Minutes of Meeting*, Geneva: WTO, WT/DSB/M/167, 27 May 2004. India, Brazil, Paraguay, Thailand, the Philippines, Malaysia and Mexico all expressed deep concerns on this issue.

43. Amartya Sen, *Global Doubts as Global Solutions*, ABC Radio National Alfred Deakin Lectures, Melbourne, 15 May 2001, p. 4.

44. Cited in WTO, *Implementation of Special and Differential Treatment Provisions in WTO Agreements and Decisions: Note by Secretariat*, WT/COMTD/W/77/Rev.1.

45. In chronological order, Greece, Portugal, Republic of Korea, Argentina, Brazil, Peru, Colombia, Egypt, Israel and South Africa have disinvoked, and Turkey and the Philippines have given undertakings to phase out remaining measures by end-1996 or (the Philippines) end-1997.

46. Bangladesh, India, Nigeria, Pakistan and Tunisia.

47. See UNCTAD, *Trade and Development Report 1999*, Geneva: UNCTAD Secretariat, 1999, p. 132.

48. WTO, *Special and Differential Treatment Provisions, Joint Communication from the African Group*, Geneva: WTO, TN/CTD/W/28, 14 February 2003, and WTO, *Remarks of*

the United States Delegation in the Committee on Trade and Development Special Session on Special and Differential Treatment, Geneva: WTO Secretariat, TN/CTD/W/9, 28 June 2002.

49. See, for example, WTO, *Committee on Trade and Development – Special Session – Approach to Facilitate Deliberations on the Agreement-Specific S&D Proposals – Communication from the United States*, Geneva: WTO, TN/CTD/W/27, 13 February 2003; WTO, *Committee on Trade and Development – Special Session – The WTO Work Programme on Special and Differential Treatment – Communication from the European Communities*, Geneva: WTO, TN/CTD/W/26, 11 December 2002.

50. The discussions on this issue are reflected in the discussions of the Special Session of the CTD. See, for example, WTO, *Minutes of the Meeting of the Special Session of the CTD*, Geneva: WTO Secretariat, TN/CTD/M/4, 14 June 2002.

51. See WTO, *Committee on Trade and Development – Special Session – The WTO Work Programme on Special and Differential Treatment, Communication from the European Communities*.

52. See WTO, *Special and Differential Treatment Provisions, Joint Communication from the African Group*, and WTO, *Remarks of the United States Delegation in the Committee on Trade and Development Special Session on Special and Differential Treatment*.

53. For the principal proposals see WTO, *Special and Differential Treatment Provisions: Joint Declaration by the Least-Developed Countries*, Geneva: WTO, TN/CTD/W/4, 24 May 2002.

54. WTO, *Special and Differential Treatment Provisions: Joint Declaration by the Least-Developed Countries*, Geneva: WTO, TN/CTD/W/4Add1, 1 July 2002, p. 3.

55. WTO, *Special and Differential Treatment Provisions: Joint Declaration by the Least-Developed Countries*, Geneva: WTO, TN/CTD/W/4.

56. See WTO, *Implementation of Special and Differential Treatment Provisions in WTO Agreements and Decisions: Note by Secretariat*, WT/COMTD/W/77/Rev.1, plus its four addendums.

57. See WTO, *Implementation of WTO Provisions in Favour of Developing Country Members: Note by the Secretariat*, Geneva: WTO, WT/COMTD/W/35, 9 February 1998; WTO, *Concerns Regarding Special and Differential Treatment Provisions in WTO Agreements and Decisions: Note by the Secretariat*, Geneva: WTO Secretariat, WT/COMTD/W/66, 16 February 2000; and WTO, *Implementation of Special and Differential Treatment Provisions in WTO Agreements and Decisions: Note by Secretariat*, Geneva: WTO, WT/COMTD/W/77, 25 October 2000.

58. WTO, *Committee on Trade and Development: Report of the Chairman to the General Council*, Geneva: WTO, TN/CTD/3, 26 July 2002, p. 3.

59. See B. K. Zutshi, "Bringing TRIPS into the Multilateral Trading System", in Jagdish Bhagwati and Mathias Hirsh (eds), *The Uruguay Round and Beyond: Essays in Honour of Arthur Dunkel*, Berlin: Springer-Verlag, 1998, p. 48. Many Indian software and bio-tech companies strongly support the TRIPS Agreement, and Indian exports of textiles and clothing continue to benefit from the removal of the MFA.

60. No such amendment has been made since the entry into force of the WTO Agreement.

61. WTO, *Remarks of the United States Delegation in the Committee on Trade and Development Special Session on Special and Differential Treatment*.

62. WTO, *Preparation for the Fourth Ministerial Session of the Ministerial Conference: Proposal for a Framework Agreement on Special and Differential Treatment; from Cuba, Dominican Republic, Honduras, India, Indonesia, Kenya, Malaysia, Pakistan, Sri Lanka, Tanzania, Uganda and Zimbabwe*, Geneva: WTO, WT/GC/W/442, 19 September 2001.

63. WTO, *Special and Differential Treatment Provisions: Joint Declaration by the Least-Developed Countries*.

64. WTO, *Monitoring Mechanism for Special and Differential Treatment Provisions: Proposal of the African Group in the WTO*, Geneva: WTO, TN/CTD/W/23, 11 December 2002.

65. For an elaboration, see Peter Sutherland, John Sewell and David Weiner, "Addressing Global Governance in the WTO", in Gary P. Sampson (ed.), *The Role of the WTO in Global Governance*, Tokyo: United Nations University Press, 2001, pp. 81–112.

66. This is not a new phenomenon. As stated in the Lambsdorff Report in 1990, the principle of multilateral obligations, adopted in the Uruguay Round, provides the solution to the "present, more one-sided approach, [which] risks destroying the ideal of a single multilateral trading system". See *Meeting the World Trade Deadline*, Report of the Eminent Persons Group on World Trade, July 1990.

67. GATT, *A Description of the Provisions Relating to Developing Countries in the Uruguay Round Agreements, Legal Instruments and Ministerial Decisions: Note by the Secretariat*, Geneva: GATT Secretariat, COM.TD/W/510, 2 November 1994.

68. GATT, *Developing Countries and the Uruguay Round: An Overview. Note by the Secretariat*, Geneva: GATT Secretariat, COM.TD/W/512, 10 November 1994.

69. WTO, *Draft Program of Work for 1995*, Geneva: WTO Secretariat, WT/COMTD/W/2, 30 March 1995.

70. WTO, *Implementation of Uruguay Round Provisions in Favour of Developing Country Members: Note by the Secretariat*, Geneva: WTO Secretariat, WT/COMTD/W/16, 27 August 1996.

71. See WTO, *Concerns Regarding Special and Differential Treatment Provisions in WTO Agreements and Decisions: Note by the Secretariat*.

72. WTO, *Preparation for the 1999 Ministerial Conference, Ministerial Text: Revised Draft*, Geneva: WTO Secretariat, JOB(99)/5868/Rev.1, 19 October 1999.

73. These issues are listed in WTO, *Compilation of Outstanding Implementation Issues Raised by Members*, Job(01)/152/Rev.1, 27 October 2001.

74. See WTO, *Implementation-Related Issues and Concerns: Note by the Secretariat*, Geneva: WTO Secretariat, WT/MIN(01)/W/10, 14 November 2001.

75. As contained in WTO, *Implementation of Special and Differential Treatment Provisions in WTO Agreements and Decisions: Note by Secretariat*, WT/COMTD/W/77; and WTO, *Special and Differential Treatment: Implementation and Proposals: Note by the Secretariat*, Geneva: WTO Secretariat, WT/COMTD/W/85, 14 May 2001.

76. See WTO, *Implementation of Special and Differential Treatment Provisions in WTO Agreements and Decisions: Note by Secretariat*, WT/COMTD/W/77/Rev.1.

77. WTO, *Doha Declarations: The Doha Development Agenda*, Geneva: WTO Secretariat, 2001, para. 44.

78. The first meeting of the Special Session was held in March 2002, after which 14 formal meetings and a very large number of informal meetings were held during the year. The Special Session received 30 submissions during the course of 2002.

79. Some provisions were excluded from this exercise. It was considered that the distinction between "mandatory" and "non-mandatory" did not apply to provisions relating to flexibility in the implementation of commitments or the use of policy instruments, or to some provisions relating to least developed countries (specifying levels of flexibility and transition time periods that developing countries may choose to exercise should they so wish). See WTO, "Implementation of Special and Differential Treatment Provisions in WTO Agreements and Decisions: Mandatory and Non-Mandatory Special and Differential Treatment Provisions", *Note by the Secretariat*, Geneva: WTO Secretariat, WT/COMTD/W/77/Rev.1/Add.1, 21 December 2001.

80. WTO, "Implementation of Special and Differential Treatment Provisions in WTO

Agreements and Decisions: A Review of Mandatory Special and Differential Treatment Provisions", *Note by the Secretariat*, Geneva: WTO Secretariat, WT/COMTD/W/77/Rev.1/Add.2, 21 December 2001, and WTO Secretariat, "Implementation of Special and Differential Treatment Provisions in WTO Agreements and Decisions: Non Mandatory Special and Differential Treatment Provisions in WTO Agreements and Decisions", *Note by the Secretariat*, Geneva: WTO Secretariat, WT/COMTD/W/77/Rev.1/Add.3, 4 February 2002.

81. WTO, "Implementation of Special and Differential Treatment Provisions in WTO Agreements and Decisions: Information on the Utilisation of Special and Differential Treatment Provisions", *Note by the Secretariat*, Geneva: WTO Secretariat, WT/COMTD/W/77/Rev.1/Add.4, 7 February 2002.

82. As a result, the Special Session of the Committee on Trade and Development met eight times during this period, when 12 submissions were received from members. These addressed a range of issues such as the Enabling Clause, the Monitoring Mechanism and the "way forward" (both to December 2002 and the Cancún Ministerial), and provided responses to questions raised during the consideration of proposals. Five of the meetings were scheduled as close as possible to meetings of other WTO bodies, in order to utilize the expertise in those bodies, and were dedicated to discussions on the Agreement-specific proposals that had been made in those areas.

83. Although industrialized countries had not formally opposed this clarification request at the CTD, they told the General Council at the December meeting that the mandate was in fact clear but that developed and developing countries disagreed on the substance of the proposals on the table. The General Council "took note" of the debate and decided to revert to this issue at its next meeting in May.

84. Bangladesh (on behalf of least developed countries), Kenya (on behalf of the African Group), India, Pakistan, Cuba, Egypt, China and Paraguay.

85. Australia, Canada, the European Union and the United States.

86. WTO, *General Council Chairman's Proposal on an Approach for Special and Differential Treatment*.

87. WTO, *Committee on Trade and Development – Special Session – Approach to Facilitate Deliberations on the Agreement-Specific S&D Proposals – Communication from the United States*; WTO, *Committee on Trade and Development – Special Session – The WTO Work Programme on Special and Differential Treatment – Communication from the European Communities*; WTO, *Committee on Trade and Development – Special Session – The WTO Work Programme on Special and Differential Treatment – Some EU Ideas for the Way Ahead – Communication from the European Communities*, Geneva: WTO, TN/CTD/W/20, 20 November 2002.

10

Changing importance and perceptions of the WTO

Introduction

The World Trade Organization (WTO) has extended its reach far beyond that of the General Agreement on Tariffs and Trade (GATT). Its importance in international economic and political affairs has increased dramatically and public interest has heightened accordingly, often negatively. One reason for the expression of adverse public sentiment has been a lack of understanding about what the WTO can and does do. The reasons for this are many, not the least being the non-transparent workings of the GATT, which were carried over into the operations of the WTO. Although matters have greatly improved in this respect, there is still more to do, and WTO members at the Ministerial Meeting in Doha, Qatar, in 2001 emphasized that they will "continue to promote a better public understanding of the WTO and to communicate the benefits of a liberal, rules-based multilateral trading system", particularly "through the more effective dissemination of information and improved dialogue with the public".[1] There are also, however, an increasing number of interest groups that have a detailed and comprehensive knowledge of the WTO. One pervasive worry is that the WTO has extended its reach too far.

This raises a number of policy-related questions. What precisely does "too far" mean? Does it relate to subject matter, the nature of the regulations the WTO enforces, its country membership, the non-trade issues that are gravitating towards it, or some other feature of its operations? In addition, "too far" in whose eyes – the 150 governments that have set its parameters or the public interest groups that find its role intrusive in national affairs? Or has its reach been extended not by design but unwillingly or unwittingly by governments themselves? For example, have major issues gravitated towards the WTO on a de facto basis, or have the implications of the Agreements it is now responsible for turned out to be more far-reaching than originally foreseen?

The objective of this chapter is to address the implications of a more important WTO in terms of how it is perceived by the public. Before passing judgement on whether the WTO has extended its reach too far, it is useful first to ask how and why its importance has increased. However, answering this question is far from straightforward because the reasons are many and varied and some are more obvious than others. I then discuss the different roles that can be ascribed to the WTO, particularly in terms of the criticisms levelled at it. What is really being criticized when it is charged that the WTO is non-democratic, non-transparent and not accountable to its proper masters (namely, the public at large)? And are these criticisms justified? I identify and address the criticisms and suggest how to deal with them.

The increased importance of the WTO

One obvious reason for the WTO being more important than the GATT is the expanded role of trade rules in both domestic and global affairs. This has come about for a variety of reasons. First, there has been a dramatic increase in both the value and volume of world trade since the creation of the GATT, and therefore in the amount of commercial activity to which the rules apply.[2] Not only that, because world trade has grown more rapidly than world production in almost every year since the Second World War, it is an arithmetic truism that countries now trade a far greater share of their domestic production than they did half a century ago. The world average of trade as a share of national production is now 26 per cent, meaning that one way or another WTO rules are relevant for 26 per cent of world production. Impressive as this figure is, it constitutes a considerable understatement of the coverage of "trade" rules. Minimum standards in the Agreement on Trade-Related Intellectual Property Rights (TRIPS) are enforced by the WTO even if nothing crosses the border. Three of the four modes of delivery dealt with by the General Agreement on Trade in Services (GATS) do not involve the cross-border movement of services, and none enters normal merchandise trade statistics. Many of the "behind the border" agreements and requirements are important as well. The Subsidies Agreement is one example, as are disciplines relating to standards and technical regulations or the notification obligations that are requirements in many WTO Agreements.

A further obvious consideration is that the sectoral coverage of trade rules has expanded. Textiles and clothing trade were outside the normal multilateral rules, as was agricultural trade. Not only have textiles, clothing and agriculture now been brought under WTO rules, but new – and critical – sectors have been added in the form of the vast areas of trade in services and trade-related intellectual property rights. An important outcome of the Uruguay Round was that all WTO members were obliged to sign on to all Uruguay Agreements; the optional membership of the Codes that emerged from the Tokyo Round was no longer a possibility. The importance of these Agreements increased accordingly. In a similar vein, the number of countries whose trade is subjected to WTO rules has increased dramatically. The original 23 members of the GATT have grown to around 150 in the WTO, with another 25 countries in the process of accession. Even since the creation of the WTO in 1995, the number of members has grown from 132 to close to 150.

However, it is not just that the reach of the rules has become wider; the rules themselves have become far more exigent. Domestic regulations relating to patents, financial services, subsidies and support measures for agriculture are among those now subject to WTO disciplines. These rules extend well beyond border measures and reach deep into the domestic regulatory structures of WTO member countries. As a result, WTO Agreements raise key issues of public concern that far transcend those associated with the conventional political economy of trade policy. For example, the TRIPS Agreement raises ethical questions about the patenting of life forms, as does the Agreement on Sanitary and Phytosanitary Measures (SPS) about the role of precaution in the absence of scientific evidence in matters relating to public health. Agricultural negotiations embrace sensitive questions relating to the multifunctionality of agriculture, and the TRIPS Agreement addresses matters of geographical indications. In addition, the issues dealt with in the normal course of business have been expanded through the process of continuing negotiations. Limitations on subsidies that lead to the depletion of fish stocks and negotiations on the relationship between the WTO rules and multilateral environment agreements (MEAs) emerged naturally out of the ongoing work of the Committee on Trade and Environment (CTE).

Another development that has raised the profile and extended the reach of the WTO is its greatly strengthened dispute settlement mechanism. Unlike the GATT, the WTO process moves forward automatically: Panel and Appellate Body reports are adopted unless there is a consensus against them. The rule of negative consensus, backed up by a mechanism providing for compensation and sanctions in the case of non-compliance, has greatly increased public awareness of the WTO's existence. As a consequence, public interest has heightened, particularly in the light of recent high-profile disputes that extend into sensitive areas such as the role of science in risk management, the conservation of endangered species, and restrictions on the cross-border movement of genetically modified organisms (GMOs). These features, coupled with the fact that the dispute proceedings are closed to the public, have exacerbated the sense of exclusion and resentment among those outside the process.

Although the creation of a WTO Appellate Body may have added balance to the automaticity of the decision-taking in the dispute settlement system, it has left some with the view that it has extended the WTO's authority beyond that granted to it by member governments at the time of its creation.[3] The Dispute Settlement Understanding limited its jurisdiction to issues of law covered in Panel reports and to legal interpretations developed by Panels. It was prohibited from adding to or diminishing the rights and obligations provided in WTO Agreements. It has been argued that some Appellate Body reports seem to indicate a new concept of evolutionary policy formulation through litigation, which is very different from the normal interpretation of decision by consensus. Appellate Body rulings – such as the acceptability of *amicus* briefs submitted by non-governmental organizations (NGOs) – have led to considerable controversy among members while raising expectations among those hoping to achieve greater access to the process. Such controversies have also raised the profile of the WTO.

That two-thirds of WTO members are now developing countries has also raised its profile. Developing countries, having undertaken new and demanding obligations, rightfully look to assured market access through liberalized trade in merchandise and commitments in the services sectors to support their export-led growth strategies. Their legitimate expectation is that the WTO will provide a forum in which their views can be effectively expressed and their concerns adequately dealt with. An important feature of developing country participation in the WTO is not only their increased numbers but also that their participation is far better informed than in earlier years. Along with the increased complexity and breadth of coverage of the WTO Agreements, there has been a serious demand by developing countries for improved and extended technical assistance. Adequate technical assistance to ensure they are well informed is now a precondition for their participation in negotiations. Governments will not sign agreements if they do not feel their interests have been adequately covered and that they are fully aware of all the implications. If the WTO is to remain a consensus-based organization, all participants must be well informed.

As a result, developing countries are far more active in the WTO than in earlier times, have higher expectations about what the institution can and should do for them, and consequently have formed groups in which their specific interests can be better negotiated. Compared with earlier decades when the Group of 77 was held together on the basis of a common characteristic – poverty coupled with a sense of third world solidarity – today developing countries form coalitions around policy issues, not poverty, and have increased their negotiating clout accordingly. Their increased numbers, coupled with a better knowledge of their rights and obligations through technical assistance and use of their own resources, have led to their more demanding presence in the WTO.[4] The Group of Twenty developing countries formed at the time of the Cancún Ministerial Meeting in 2003 stands as testimony to this. At the same time, others – in particular least developed countries – feel they have not been integrated into the trading system at all and look to new initiatives to achieve this. The injustices that face the impoverished cotton-exporting countries of Africa, or the difficulties of gaining access to essential medicines for AIDS-stricken countries, have heightened the attention to least developed countries by development organizations, other public interest groups, researchers and some governments.[5]

Although many of these developments have been the result of conscious initiatives on the part of governments, others were not. In some instances, the importance of the WTO has increased almost on a de facto basis through events over which it has no control. One example is recent developments in genetic engineering that permit genetic information to be transferred from one organism to another that is too distantly related to permit natural cross-breeding. WTO rules are the centre of concern for both those who see potential conflict between WTO Agreements and recent MEAs, and those who see limitations on the cross-border movement of GMOs as trade restrictions. It is hard to imagine that all developments relating to biotechnology and their WTO implications were foreseen at the time of negotiation of the Agreements concerned. Another example is the proliferation of multilateral environment agreements, which are also outside the realm of influence of the WTO.

In addition, the heightened interest in the WTO has come against the backdrop of an incredible revolution in the speed with which information can be communicated and its cost. Non-governmental organizations are now linked through broad networks and coalitions that render them more effective and sophisticated than their earlier counterparts. The public image of the WTO – as well as public interest in it – has been greatly influenced by the information conveyed through these electronic means.[6]

Although many of these groups are not against trade per se, others are unabatedly protectionist, putting them on a collision course with supporters of an open and liberal trading system. The events in Seattle, fuelled by coalitions of NGOs built on the World Wide Web, placed the public for the first time at the centre of a vital public policy discussion that was traditionally dominated by governmental representatives in closed meetings.

What is the WTO?

In tandem with its growth in importance, the WTO has come under increasing attack from numerous quarters. These two developments are inextricably linked, because many of the areas of heightened importance are among the most controversial from a public policy perspective. As a result, the WTO – unlike the GATT – has become an object of attack for anti-globalization groups, environmental groups, human rights activists, organized labour, consumer groups, and development organizations, to mention a few. For the sake of convenience, such critics invariably target "the WTO" as an autonomous body with a life and personality of its own (*the WTO is undemocratic ... the WTO is not accountable to the public ... the WTO harms the environment ... the WTO is not transparent ...*). This may be a convenient approach, but in reality such an institution does not exist. The WTO is multifaceted in terms of its functions and institutional arrangements, and most criticisms are really addressing just one of its many faces. In dealing with the criticisms, it is important to decipher which face is involved. There are at least four choices in this respect.

- The WTO is a set of Agreements that create legally binding **rights and obligations** for all members, as do the schedules for tariffs and other restrictions on imports of goods and services attached to the respective Agreements. These schedules bind the degree of openness of the domestic markets and have been negotiated multilaterally and agreed to and ratified by all WTO members. Unlike other international agreements, the rights and obligations contained in the WTO Agreements are enforced through a dispute settlement mechanism that provides for both compensation and retaliation in cases of non-compliance. This process has also been agreed to and ratified by all WTO members.
- The WTO is a **trade forum** where delegations meet to discuss and negotiate a number of trade-related matters. In the Trade Policy Review Body, for example, governments periodically review the trade policies of other members. They discuss recent developments in the multilateral trading system in the General Council and elsewhere. WTO members also use the forum to negotiate both rules and the liberalization of

trade, normally in the context of formal multilateral rounds of negotiations. To date there have been eight such rounds; the most recently completed one, the Uruguay Round, lasted from September 1986 to December 1993. The current round is the Doha Development Agenda. The results of the Uruguay Round are embodied in the 30 legal Agreements and numerous supplementary Decisions all signed by ministers from over 100 countries in April 1994 in Marrakesh. The WTO and its Agreements entered into force in January 1995.

- The WTO is a relatively **small secretariat** with neither enforcement powers nor any role in the interpretation of the legal rights and obligations of WTO members. It has a total staff of around 600 and an annual budget of US$160 million. It is one of the smaller international organizations – dwarfed by the World Bank, the United Nations, the International Monetary Fund, the Organisation for Economic Cooperation and Development (OECD) and numerous other organizations, and smaller in terms of budget than either the United Nations Conference on Trade and Development or the United Nations Environment Programme.

- The WTO is an **intergovernmental organization** in which close to 150 governments have agreed not to discriminate against the trade in products and services between national and foreign suppliers of the same goods and services or between sources of supply. As an intergovernmental organization, WTO members are presumed to be acting on behalf of the collective interests of their diverse constituents. Although governments liberalize trade and agree to rules to secure benefits for the economy as a whole, they are aware that some interest groups may be adversely affected in this process; it is assumed that governments take into account the concerns of all domestic interest groups when they take decisions.

The bottom line is that the WTO is a collection of almost 150 governments that trade according to legally enforceable disciplines that have been adopted on a consensus basis. WTO members are sovereign states – the vast majority being democracies – and, although not all public interest groups approve all the decisions of the WTO, WTO members take decisions that they consider to be in their national interests. If they are not, it can be argued that the problem is a domestic one, where elected governments are not correctly representing the constituencies that elected them. If this is the case, the solution is to be found at the national level.

In short, on many occasions the WTO is a target of criticism when the target lies elsewhere. It is not the WTO that is slow in taking decisions on the limitation of fisheries subsidies that deplete fish stocks; it is the governments that oppose the initiatives. It is not the TRIPS Agreement that precludes access to essential medicines for impoverished people; it is the governments that are obstructive when it comes to interpreting flexibility. It is not the WTO that is non-transparent; it is the governments that have decided not to open meetings to public scrutiny.

A number of the common criticisms levelled at the WTO are discussed below. The spirit in which these criticisms are addressed is not in terms of defending the WTO at all costs, although there is certainly a defence of the WTO in what follows. The spirit is rather that, although there are good reasons to look for improvement in the WTO, it is important to shoot at the right target and to bear in mind the function of the WTO that is being commented on and who has assigned that role to the WTO.

The criticisms

The WTO is fiercely criticized by those who argue that, among other things, it is non-accountable to the public and non-transparent. Moreover, its rules and procedures constitute an unwanted intrusion into the domestic affairs of sovereign states and impede the proper workings of democratically elected governments.

Democracy

Those who argue that the WTO is a democratic institution point to the fact that decisions are made on the basis of a consensus, taking into account all members' views.[7] Agreements are negotiated by national officials, agreed to by trade ministers and signed off on by domestic parliaments before entering into force at the national level. Others argue that, if democracy means the active participation of all WTO members in the decision-making process, then the WTO is democratic only in principle. By way of example, they draw attention to developing countries. There have been numerous charges that developing countries are consistently excluded from critical meetings, and therefore from the decision-making process. Many of these charges come from developing countries themselves when voicing their long-standing dissatisfaction with their lack of involvement in the decision-making processes. This dissatisfaction has been particularly hostile at Ministerial Meetings such as those in Seattle and Cancún. In addressing this concern, there are a number of important considerations to take into account before drawing general conclusions.

It is important, for example, to draw a distinction between *lack of participation* in meetings and *systematic exclusion*. Informal groups meet frequently in the WTO, particularly when drafting texts. Limited participation is in many instances the most efficient – and sometimes the only –

way to proceed; agreement in a smaller group of the most concerned countries can later be extended to other less directly concerned countries. In such instances, absence is as common for industrial countries as it is for developing countries.[8] Few would take issue with this process. The problem arises, however, when not all interests are represented in such meetings and the results are not widely and rapidly communicated. In many instances, this has been a problem as much for transition economies and small developed countries as for developing ones. Representation in meetings and the communication of their outcomes have been far from perfect in the past and this process needs to be improved.

In principle, however, in any informal consultations where the chairperson is present, there is always representation from all groups that have an interest in the matter under discussion. A competent chairperson will ensure that any country with a particular interest that does not attend an informal consultation will be represented by a country with a similar interest. It is very much in the interests of the chairperson to act in this manner. Without broad representation in smaller groups, consensus could be blocked at a later stage by countries annoyed at not being part of the informal process or not seeing their interests reflected. It is, in fact, the responsibility of the member representing the interests of others – or of the chairperson – to keep other members informed of the outcome of smaller meetings.

Notwithstanding the existence of a process in which interests should be broadly represented, developing countries are indeed systematically *absent* from not only informal but also formal meetings. This absence, however, is the symptom of a problem, not the source of it. In the increasingly frequent, complex and resource-intensive negotiations at the WTO, most small delegations do not have the appropriate resources or expertise either in Geneva or in their own capitals to service the negotiating process and thereby participate meaningfully. The negotiation of special and differential treatment – which is of crucial importance to developing countries – was described in chapter 9 to exemplify the resource-intensive nature of the negotiations. Many small nations do not have a representative in Geneva, something that renders even ad hoc participation in the WTO process almost impossible.

Any increased participation of many developing countries can come only with a strengthening of their human and institutional capacity to service the WTO process. This, in turn, is possible only if resources are made available for technical assistance and training. In this respect, the regular WTO budget has been far from adequate. In more recent years, however, many developing countries – along with the WTO and other institutions – have invested a great deal in building a national capacity to service the WTO negotiations. Their well-informed representatives now expect to be present in all key meetings. It was most certainly the lack of opportunity to participate on the part of officials from some of these countries that created the strongest reactions in Seattle and Cancún.

Notwithstanding the lack of participation by a number of developing countries for whatever reason, it would be wrong to draw the overall conclusion that developing countries have had little influence in GATT and WTO negotiations. Latin American countries were major contributors both to the stalemate at the Montreal Ministerial Meeting (because of what they considered to be the unsatisfactory treatment of agriculture) and to the re-launching of the Uruguay Round some months later. Brazil, India, Argentina, Egypt, Colombia and other developing countries were all major players in their own way in the negotiation of the General Agreement on Trade in Services. The influence of developing countries in framing the GATS was taken up in some detail in chapter 8, the argument being that, contrary to popular belief (at least among some non-governmental organizations), developing countries directed the pace, substance and therefore the speed and orientation of these negotiations. In fact, the Group of Negotiations on Services had a developing country chairperson for the duration of the Uruguay Round.

Yet, if democracy means that each WTO member has the same power in the negotiating process, then the WTO is far from democratic. Very clearly, the more economically powerful countries are listened to more carefully. And, because agreement is by consensus, frequently achieved by trade-offs, powerful countries have far more bargaining chips to use in terms of trade-offs to offer and eventually leveraging less powerful countries into "agreeing" on the preferred "consensus" decision. An important reality is that the inequality in the power of nations is not entirely removed by the existence of rules – even if adopted on the basis of consensus. This situation has led to the creation of various developing and developed country groups to negotiate collectively to meet certain objectives.

With their new weight of numbers in the WTO, developing countries do have the opportunity to press for Agreements that are more sensitive to their development concerns. The diversity of their circumstances and commercial interests will not necessarily permit common negotiating positions to be adopted, and, indeed, a coalition with developed countries may be the most effective grouping for certain initiatives. The Cairns Group is a classic case in point. However, developing countries do have it in their power to make common cause for their collective good by ensuring that development considerations are taken fully into account in WTO Agreements.[9] The creation of the Group of Twenty in Cancún and the coordination of African cotton exporters stand as testimony to this fact.

Given the increased and diverse membership of the WTO, the question is frequently posed as to whether the practice of decision-taking by consensus can continue. The WTO maintains the practice adopted by the GATT-1947 that decisions were taken only after an issue had been discussed to the point where all countries were prepared to agree, or at least not to oppose, the outcome. Voting, when it took place, was normally a formality, and usually concerned the approval of the pre-negotiated terms on which a country either acceded to the GATT or was permitted to waive its normal obligations. It is not clear that this tradition can be continued.

The total membership of the WTO is already approaching 150. A requirement that three-quarters of the membership approve a proposed waiver could therefore necessitate the affirmative votes of more than 100 countries. From a procedural perspective, this condition could be difficult to fulfil, since the failure of a relatively small number of countries to vote (and many countries do not have permanent representation in Geneva) could be sufficient to block action. Also, from a substantive point of view, agreement among 100 countries with very different levels of economic development and interests in the vast area of economic activity dealt with by the WTO is a major, and sometimes impossible, task.

Transparency

For more than 50 years, access to information on GATT trade negotiations was difficult for all those outside the process. To be fair, however, interest in GATT proceedings was not of the same magnitude as with the WTO. The WTO inherited GATT traditions and, despite considerable efforts by the Secretariat to increase public awareness of the WTO, it is still paying the price in the form of a misunderstanding of its functions and criticisms of its lack of transparency. If it is hard to find out what the WTO is doing, the critics say, the organization must have something to hide.

Paradoxically, transparency has been fundamental to the workings of the GATT and now the WTO. The WTO Agreements assign the highest priority to the need for transparency in the conduct of international trade through the notification of domestic regulations and other means. Both the GATT-1994 and the GATS require members to publish all measures that affect the operation of the Agreements. The GATS also requires the establishment of inquiry points to ensure access to information on domestic regulations for foreign traders. The Sanitary and Phytosanitary

Agreement and the Technical Barriers to Trade Agreement require members to notify each other if new local standards affecting trade deviate from international standards. Members review the trade policies of other countries carefully. The clear preference in the WTO is for *ad valorem* tariffs because of their transparency.

Nevertheless, the WTO is bitterly criticized for a lack of transparency in its own procedural operations. Improving transparency has been discussed in the WTO under three broad headings: raising the general level of awareness about the WTO; establishing formal avenues of cooperation with public interest groups, intergovernmental organizations, academics and others; and accelerating the process of "derestricting" documents so that they become quickly available to all interested parties.

With respect to raising general awareness, much has been done to improve the situation – with no apparent adverse consequences. The creation of the WTO website was an important initiative, and one apparently much appreciated. Individual users rose to just under 1 million in 2004, a 50 per cent increase over the previous two years.[10] The section consulted most often is the one that provides access to WTO documents. In addition, the WTO Secretariat has organized joint symposia involving WTO members and representatives of intergovernmental organizations and development and environmental NGOs to discuss a variety of controversial issues. Representatives of well over 100 NGOs have been joined at recent meetings by delegations from the majority of WTO members. A symposium in March 2004 involved ministers, heads of international organizations and senior officials or heads of NGOs. Further, as part of raising the awareness of government officials, particularly in developing countries, the WTO Secretariat has regularly organized regional seminars in developing countries and transition economies. These have involved officials from national trade ministries as well as environment, finance and other ministries. The intention has been to improve national coordination in an area where WTO members themselves have pointed to this need.[11]

As far as the derestriction of documents is concerned, considerable progress was made some years ago when WTO members agreed in principle that all documents should be circulated as unrestricted.[12] Although this is subject to some exceptions, any document containing public information must be circulated as unrestricted; moreover, any WTO member is free to have any of its submissions circulated at any time it wishes.[13]

It is in the interests of the WTO to become far more transparent in its activities than the GATT was in the past. The organization has little to hide: all the rules and procedures are in the public domain, and there is no reason to delay publication through an artificial date for derestriction of documents that will eventually enter the public domain. The restricted nature of some WTO documents makes it harder for WTO members to explain clearly to domestic constituencies the rationale for national activities regarding the WTO. Yet, very few WTO documents contain genuinely confidential information that would justify restriction. As a general principle, procedures for delayed derestriction should apply only to WTO activities in which there is a strong case for maintaining a period of confidentiality while an issue is subject to consideration by WTO bodies; derestriction should come only when the information is no longer confidential. Such documents might contain tariff offers in liberalization negotiations, confidential information on the status of balance of payments in times of difficulty, and some requirements sought in terms of changes in regulations in countries in the process of accession.[14]

On this basis, Secretariat background notes, minutes and agendas of meetings should be derestricted when they are circulated to governments. Some members maintain that minutes and any formal summaries of meetings should be derestricted only after three months, to allow time to ensure that delegations have been correctly quoted. Misquotations are rare, however, and a correction can always be issued. In addition, these small inconveniences are far outweighed by the benefits of a well-informed public.

As regards the dispute settlement process and the availability of Panel reports, it has been argued that the reports are published too long after the Panel has completed its work. In fact, the Panel reports are circulated to governments and the public at the same time; nevertheless, this can indeed be some time after the Panel has completed its work. The reasons rest largely with practical considerations relating to the processing of documentation. The length of the Panel reports is such that their reproduction and distribution take time. The *Shrimp-Turtle* Panel report, which was one to which environmentalists wished to have rapid access, comprises 431 pages of tightly written single-spaced text. Its length is in turn a function of the fact that WTO members insist on the publication of their own argumentation coinciding with the publication of the Panel findings to provide evidence that the case has been comprehensively argued. Although this in itself ensures a certain delay before distribution, the time period is further prolonged because governments will permit the reports to be circulated only when they are available in all three working languages of the WTO. The reports can then be read by officials in each of the national capitals at the same time and reacted to accordingly.

To make Panel reports available more rapidly, three solutions would appear to present themselves. The first is to make reports available immediately in the working language of the Panel – in most cases in English. The second is to distribute only the findings of the Panel and not the summaries of the argumentation. In the *Shrimp-Turtle* case, the Panel findings consist of just 20 pages and the Panel conclusions of 2 pages. The third is to provide the Secretariat with the resources to enable it to produce the full reports more quickly. The same procedures could apply to Appellate Body reports.

Involvement: Intergovernmental organizations

Observer status for the secretariats of relevant multilateral institutions can help to create a clearer appreciation of the mutually supportive role of trade and other international policies.[15] Chapter 12 addresses the relationships between the WTO and the Bretton Woods institutions. Here I shall concentrate on multilateral environment agreements.

It is widely accepted that it is useful for MEA representatives to brief the Committee on Trade and Environment on the use of trade measures applied pursuant to the MEAs. This gives the CTE a chance to express its view to MEA authorities on such measures. At the June 2004 meeting of the CTE, seven MEAs were invited to send representatives for this information-sharing exercise.[16]

It should be possible to enhance transparency, dialogue and cooperation between MEAs, relevant international organizations and the WTO from the initial stage of negotiation of an MEA to its implementation. This cooperation might include the exchange of information, mutual participation in meetings, access to documents and databases, and briefing sessions, as necessary. It has been proposed in the CTE that a guide containing WTO principles could be compiled by the WTO Secretariat that, after being agreed by the CTE, could be used by MEA negotiators in their consideration of proposed trade measures.

Cooperation agreements between the WTO and MEA institutions could provide for the WTO Secretariat to respond to requests for technical information about relevant WTO provisions and for MEAs to inform the WTO of all envisaged trade provisions. These provisions could be examined by the CTE and a report sent to the MEA authorities. While acknowledging the importance of contacts between the WTO and MEA secretariats, some commentators maintain that – as with NGOs – policy dialogue must take place in national capitals, that the WTO and MEAs must respect their specific areas of competence, and that the WTO Secretariat already has the authority to provide factual information about the multilateral trading system.

Involvement: Non-governmental organizations

Unlike developing country governments, NGOs are precluded from attending negotiations by agreement among governments. In fact, the push for a presence by NGOs raises fundamental questions related to representation, advocacy and the legitimacy of a state to act on behalf of its citizens. Unlike a number of other international organizations, the WTO permits only representatives of governments and selected inter-governmental organizations to participate in, or observe, the processes of the regular WTO activities. This has led to claims that the WTO is not accountable, and therefore not responsive, to public concerns. The counter-argument is that it is the role of national governments to keep all parts of society fully informed of developments of relevance to them and to take their concerns into account as appropriate.

The General Council has established Guidelines for WTO relations with NGOs.[17] These Guidelines recognize the role that NGOs can play in increasing public awareness of the WTO and the need to increase the transparency of WTO operations. They mention specifically the need to make documents available more readily than in the past. The Guidelines mandate the Secretariat to play a more active role in its direct contacts with NGOs, and recommend the development of a number of ways to interact with NGOs, including symposia on specific WTO-related issues. They also envision the possibility of the chairpersons of WTO councils and committees participating in discussions or meetings with NGOs, al-though only in their personal capacity. The Guidelines do state that there is currently a "broadly held view that it would not be possible for NGOs to be directly involved in the work of the WTO or its meetings". They note that the WTO is a legally binding treaty of rights and obligations among its members and a forum for negotiations, and that the primary responsibility for taking into account the different elements of public in-terest lies at the national level. Based on these Guidelines, a number of steps have been taken by the WTO Secretariat to increase its interaction with NGOs.

In the view of most WTO members, however, closer consultation and cooperation with NGOs should be undertaken through appropriate pro-cedures at the national level, where the main efforts should be made to take into account the different elements of public interest in trade policy. It is apparent, however, that many governments have been far from ef-fective in creating such mechanisms. Against this backdrop, an important question is whether initiatives at the multilateral level could support im-proved national processes.

Less frequently, it is proposed that NGOs should participate in some manner in WTO meetings in order to improve their appreciation of the process. The fact that they are not permitted to attend WTO meetings has led to a number of proposals buttressed by a variety of arguments about how their direct involvement would enrich the functioning of the WTO.[18] The thrust of these proposals is not that NGOs should have a role in the process of intergovernmental negotiation; rather that it is in the interests of the WTO itself to be more receptive to NGO views and involvement, and better connected to the non-governmental organizations that represent the diverse strands of global civil society.[19] In this context, it is important to note that the composition of a national delegation is in the final analysis a prerogative of the government itself. If a government wants to have an NGO representative present at a particular meeting, that option is already available. In the past, most governments have resisted such requests – a pressure with which they are quite familiar. For example, business lobbyists frequently try to exercise their influence directly by being appointed to a national delegation.

Opening the door to the participation of NGOs raises very practical considerations. Which groups of civil society should be represented at different meetings, and who would decide on the criteria? Is the size of the NGO or whether it represents a large part of society an important consideration? Would non-profit groups representing business and labour interests be present? At negotiations on agricultural subsidies that lead to environmental degradation, should farmers' unions be present or should it be environmental NGOs? At negotiations discussing trade liberalization leading to lower consumer prices, should consumer groups be present or the sectoral interests that would be adversely affected by the removal of protection?

Rule change

A further criticism is the unwillingness of WTO members to consider changes in rules proposed by those outside of government. A case in point is spelled out in some detail in chapter 2 in the context of the "failure" of the CTE to make recommendations to modify the WTO to accommodate the concerns of environmentalists. Although changes in rules have been rare in both the GATT and the WTO,[20] the rules have proven to be very flexible instruments – "changes" have been possible through techniques ranging from simple non-enforcement of certain rules to a variety of relatively informal actions agreeing to allow some deviations from rules. It has been argued, for example, that the inexact status of the final actions taken by WTO members represents a practical answer to policy issues on which it is not possible to reach total agreement. Consequently, a well-known approach in WTO negotiations is to agree on texts that contain what has become known as *constructive ambiguity*. Rather than block negotiations because of a failure to agree on exact wording, and therefore the meaning and interpretation of the substance of the text, words are sought that allow negotiators to find an interpretation of the text that covers their own particular national position.

Constructive ambiguity is a fig leaf behind which disagreement can be hidden while searching for an acceptable conclusion to a negotiation without blocking it. Viewed from another perspective, it is betting on the ambiguous text never having to be interpreted as a result of a formal complaint. Bob Hudec reasons that trade ministries have a certain degree of mutual trust allowing them to leave long-term answers open while short-term pragmatic solutions are found. They are confident that there is enough common interest among members to make it likely that something will be worked out in the long run.[21]

The WTO affinity for ambiguous solutions to legal issues is not a solution for many NGOs. In reality, the means to address the problems seen by public interest groups (such as environmental NGOs) have been couched in terms of two rather rigid alternatives: formal decisions involving amendments or waivers; or changes to the interpretation of rules through the dispute settlement procedures. Environmentalists resist the WTO's pragmatic solutions to the interpretation of rules, believing that trade ministries do not have the same ultimate values as they do. They are therefore not prepared to trust the WTO to achieve a solution for them over the long run.[22]

Reform

A decade of experience with the WTO and the heightened public interest it has generated have already led to many calls for reform. Reform will not come easily, however, if it means unravelling existing trade agreements or introducing new restrictions on international trade. From a systemic perspective, the pursuit of free trade has been a powerful driving force behind many policy decisions, ranging from the removal of the Corn Laws in England in the early part of the nineteenth century to the adoption of outward-oriented development strategies in developing countries over the past few decades. Those who constructed the WTO are proud of what they have created. Martin Wolf has remarked that the "multilateral trading system at the beginning of the twenty-first century is the most remarkable achievement in institutionalized global economic cooperation that there has ever been".[23] The current trade rules permit world trade in goods and services to be conducted at the pace of close to US$1 billion per hour every hour of the day. This system will not be given up lightly. Thus, the central question that needs to be addressed is what wise policy makers ought to do to preserve the strengths of rules-based trading while responding to the pressures now falling on it.

The important point here is not to sing the praises of the multilateral trading system but rather to point to the degree of resistance that can be expected to be mustered to any change in the role of the WTO. This resistance has to be factored into proposals for major reform of the functioning of the WTO, particularly because it is an institution where change comes only through consensus decision-making.

In addition, less weight is given by seasoned trade negotiators to public anti-WTO demonstrations and the failure to conclude a Ministerial Meeting satisfactorily than is given by demonstrators, the press and others. Failed meetings are certainly not a new phenomenon at the GATT and the WTO, even at the ministerial level. The Mid Term Ministerial Review of the Uruguay Round in 1988 in Montreal ended in a stalemate, and the 1990 Ministerial Meeting in Brussels, which was to conclude the Uruguay Round, collapsed amidst large-scale violent protests, largely led by European farmers. Yet, the Uruguay Round was successfully completed, with all participating countries ratifying the results. Nor are violence and public demonstration new features of GATT/WTO meetings. The Seattle demonstrations pale into insignificance when compared with the violence and the size of the demonstration at the Brussels Ministerial in 1992. Similarly, the press coverage of the demonstrations in Brussels far exceeded that of Seattle. It is interesting that the Seattle meeting is seen by some to be such a landmark, when both Seattle and Cancún were just repeats of past performances.

Conclusion

Against the backdrop of the diverse criticisms levelled at the WTO, it is important to ask why sovereign states would spend years negotiating agreements that have the sorts of negative effects on their citizens that is claimed. If the answer is that nation-states unwittingly erred in joining or creating the WTO, then why do they not leave? All this requires is six months' notice; yet no country has ever expressed an interest in leaving either the GATT or the WTO. And if WTO Agreements mean a loss of national sovereignty, why would 25 sovereign nations be so intent on acceding to the WTO and forgoing this sovereignty?

A principal reason for the support for the WTO by both large and small governments is that they see adherence to multilateral rules – rather than political or commercial power – to be in their national interests. Rules bring predictability and stability to the world trading system and, although rule-governed trade may not guarantee peace, it does remove a potent cause of conflict. It offers an alternative to reliance on unbridled force in the trading relations among states. Although sovereignty is forgone by being a member of the WTO (as with any significant international agreement), what is gained is the possibility to participate in the global economy through cooperation.

Notes

1. WTO, *Doha Declarations: The Doha Development Agenda*, Geneva: WTO Secretariat, 2001, para. 10.
2. The GATT had an original membership of 23 countries. The volume of world trade has increased 19-fold since 1950 and 36-fold for manufactured goods.
3. For a comprehensive analysis of this view, see Claude E. Barfield, *Free Trade, Sovereignty, Democracy: The Future of the World Trade Organisation*, Washington DC: American Enterprise Institute Press, 2001.
4. See Clare Short, "Making the Development Round a Reality", in Gary P. Sampson (ed.), *The Role of the WTO in Global Governance*, Tokyo: United Nations University Press, 2001, pp. 59–80.
5. Among the original 23 signatories of the GATT-1947, 11 were developing countries. Currently, more than 100 out of nearly 150 members of the WTO are developing countries; 29 of these are least developed countries. Of the 25 countries in various stages of accession to the WTO, all are developing or transition economies. Not surprisingly, the participation of developing countries in WTO negotiations has increased greatly in recent times; for example, 25 developing countries took part in the Kennedy Round of negotiations in 1964–1967, 68 in the Tokyo Round in 1973–1979, and 76 in the Uruguay Round in 1986–1994.
6. See Frank Loy, "Public Participation in the WTO", in Gary P. Sampson (ed.), *The Role of the WTO in Global Governance*, Tokyo: United Nations University Press, 2001, pp. 113–137.
7. For an explanation of how decisions are taken in the WTO, see John Jackson, *The World Trade Organization: Constitution and Jurisprudence*, Chatham House Papers, London: Royal Institute of International Affairs, 1998, section 3.4. See also John H. Jackson, "Global Economics and International Economic Law", *Journal of International Economic Law*, March 1998.
8. Of course, as in any negotiations, groups of countries may meet privately of their own volition to discuss common interests, and choose whom they wish to have present. This is a normal procedure and no one can deny them this right.
9. On this point, see Short, "Making the Development Round a Reality".
10. The WTO home page is at ⟨http://www.wto.org/⟩.
11. See WTO, *Report of the Committee on Trade and Environment*, Geneva: WTO, WT/CTE/1, 12 November 1996, para. 168.
12. The General Council adopted WTO, *Procedures for the Circulation and De-restriction of WTO Documents*, Geneva: WTO Secretariat, July 1996.
13. These documents include draft agendas, draft decisions and proposals, working papers, confidential documents relating to negotiating positions, minutes of meetings, documents relating to the accession of future WTO members, reports on balance of payments consultations, and Panel reports that are derestricted 10 days after their circulation to members.
14. These would include documents relating to Working Parties on Accession (documents submitted by the acceding country could be subject to earlier derestriction if the acceding country so indicates to the Secretariat); documents relating to balance of payments consultations; and documents relating to the Budget Committee.
15. In July 1996, the General Council also adopted WTO, *Observer Status for International Intergovernmental Organisations in the WTO*, Annex 3 of *Rules of Procedure for Sessions of the Ministerial Conference and Meetings of the General Council*, Geneva: WTO Secretariat, WT/L/161, 25 July 1996. The CTE agreed to extend observer status on a permanent basis to the intergovernmental organizations that previously participated as

observers on an ad hoc basis, and it has subsequently further added to this list. Currently 23 intergovernmental organizations sit in as observers at the CTE.

16. Representatives attended from the Convention on International Trade in Endangered Species of Wild Fauna and Flora, the Montreal Protocol to the Vienna Convention for the Protection of the Ozone Layer, the Framework Convention on Climate Change, the Intergovernmental Forum on Forests and the International Tropical Timber Organization. The Convention on Biological Diversity and the Convention on the Conservation of Antarctic Marine Living Resources did not send representatives but did make written submissions.

17. WTO, *Guidelines for Arrangements on Relations with Non-Governmental Organizations: Decision Adopted by the General Council on 18 July 1996*, Geneva: WTO, WT/L/162, 23 July 1996. According to the Agreement Establishing the WTO (Article V.2), the "General Council may make appropriate arrangements for consultation and co-operation with non governmental organizations with matters related to those of the WTO". WTO, *Results of the Uruguay Round of Multilateral Trade Negotiations: The Legal Texts*, Geneva: WTO Secretariat, 1995.

18. See, for example, Daniel C. Esty, "Environmental Governance at the WTO: Outreach to Civil Society", in Gary P. Sampson and W. Bradnee Chambers (eds), *Trade, Environment, and the Millennium*, 2nd edn, Tokyo: United Nations University Press, 2002, pp. 119–144.

19. Ibid.

20. See Jackson, *The World Trade Organization*.

21. This thinking is developed in an excellent article on this and related topics by Robert E. Hudec, "The GATT/WTO Dispute Settlement Process: Can It Reconcile Trade Rules and Environment Needs?", in Rudiger Wolfrum (ed.), *Enforcing Environmental Standards: Economic Mechanisms as Viable Means*, Berlin: Springer-Verlag, 1996.

22. The reasoning in this paragraph draws on Hudec, "The GATT/WTO Dispute Settlement Process".

23. See Martin Wolf, "What the World Needs from the Multilateral Trading System", in Gary P. Sampson (ed.), *The Role of the WTO in Global Governance*, p. 155.

11

World trade and environment organizations

Introduction

Prior to the 1972 Stockholm Conference on the Human Environment there was very limited international activity in the field of the environment, but the past three decades have seen a great deal of useful international action. The negotiation of many global and regional conventions represents a considerable achievement in a relatively short period of time. However, it seems widely accepted that this has resulted in a proliferation of structures, agreements and conferences and that greater coherence among the various instrumentalities is now required, at both the inter-agency and intergovernmental levels. According to the Executive Secretary of the United Nations Environment Programme (UNEP), the environment instruments and institutions have "often been created without due consideration of how they might interact with the overall system, and questions have increasingly arisen concerning the coordination of this multifaceted institutional architecture. A new model of international environmental governance must be predicated on the need for sustainable development that meets the interrelated social, economic and environmental requirements."[1]

In 1997, the UN General Assembly undertook a five-year review of the outcome of the 1992 Earth Summit in Rio and adopted the Programme for the Further Implementation of Agenda 21. The Programme underscored that, given the increasing number of decision-making bodies concerned with various aspects of sustainable development, including international conventions, there was an ever greater need for better policy coordination at the intergovernmental level, as well as for continued and more concerted efforts to enhance collaboration among the secretariats of those bodies.

With the increasing number of treaties, conventions and institutional arrangements, the UN Secretary-General, Kofi Annan, officially placed the question of international environmental governance reform on the international political agenda. Within his 1998 programme for reform entitled "Renewing the United Nations", he appointed a Task Force on Environment and Human Settlements that was to examine, *inter alia*, the structures and actors involved in efforts to manage and protect the global environment.[2] A product of this Task Force was the Global Ministerial Environment Forum. At its first meeting, ministers called on the forthcoming World Summit on Sustainable Development (WSSD) in Johannesburg in 2001 to review the requirements for a greatly strengthened institutional structure for international environmental governance based on an assessment of future needs.[3]

On quite a separate track, and at about the same time, the Director-General of the World Trade Organization (WTO) opened a high-level trade and environment symposium at the WTO by informing the audience that the WTO was poised to create something truly revolutionary – a universal trading system bringing together developed, developing and least developed countries under one set of international rules. He went on to propose a similar multilateral rules-based system for the environment – a World Environment Organization (WEO) – to be the institutional and legal counterpart to the World Trade Organization. In the presence of the Executive Director of UNEP, the Secretary General of the United Nations Conference on Trade and Development and others, he said this should be a main message from the meeting.[4] He did not give the slightest hint of why this would be useful from the point of view of the WTO or what the WEO would look like.

The statement by the Director-General sent something less than a ripple through the trade community. An unsolicited personal proposal from the head of the bureaucracy – in the absence of consultation with governments – counts for little with trade negotiators in their everyday hectic business. This, however, was not the case for the environment community. Providing an added impetus and urgency to the call from Lionel Jospin, Helmut Kohl and others for a WEO, it added a new twist: the WTO, for some reason, needed a WEO. In fact, well-respected figures in the environment community even consider the international debate on the creation of a WEO to have "its origins in the frustration of those responsible for trade policy about being confronted by an ever growing list of environmental concerns relating more or less directly to trade. A situation has been reached where these environmental concerns threaten to block any further action on the trade agenda. For trade officials – and for trade analysts – the multitude of international environment regimes, ranging from small to infinitesimal, are a source of dismay."[5]

Key questions that follow from the literature around the WEO include: what would it look like; would the prevailing system of environmental governance be dissolved; would a new institution be created with a physical presence in a town such as Geneva, or would there be a consolidation of the existing components of global governance with a strengthening and rationalization of the status quo? In addressing these questions, the WTO sometimes emerges as a model – both good and bad. I think it is important to look at the various characteristics that could be relevant for a World *Environment* Organization when we have the experience of a World *Trade* Organization to draw on. Taking the logic further, just as we have a World Trade Organization to deal with the many multilateral *trade* agreements, do we need a World Environment Organization to deal with the many multilateral *environment* agreements? What features of the WTO could provide useful insights in addressing these questions? How does the WTO system differ from the environmental governance system? Indeed, what in fact is the environmental governance system and what is the system that governs international trade? Are there lessons to be learned by comparing the architectures of the two systems?

The objective of this chapter is to address these questions and to suggest relevant policy considerations. At the same time, I want to make some observations about the very different proposals for reform of the structure of international environmental governance when viewed through the prism of the WTO. In the following, I first describe some of the institutional characteristics of the multilateral trade agreements (MTAs) and the multilateral environment agreements (MEAs). My aim is to enquire into some of the relevant characteristics of the multilateral trade agreements in order to establish a yardstick against which to compare the governance structure for the multilateral environment agreements. I do not advocate one system in preference to another, but rather point to similarities and differences between the systems with a view to drawing useful conclusions from a policy perspective. The approach I adopt is selective. Certainly I do not address all of the characteristics of the trade agreements or of the environment agreements. However, I give sufficient examples to allow useful observations.

MTAs and MEAs

Multilateral trade agreements

The Uruguay Round of multilateral trade negotiations (1986–1994) was the most comprehensive of nine such rounds since the Second World War, extending far beyond the scope of the original GATT. The negotiations were conducted as a single undertaking, in which it was understood that the discussions on all issues had to progress broadly in parallel. All WTO members were obligated to accept all the multilateral trade agreements that emerged from the Uruguay Round. During the process of negotiations, governments frequently made concessions to other participants in one area in order to achieve their goals in another.

It became clear at the end of the negotiations that an organization was necessary to oversee and coordinate the functioning of the trading system. The World Trade Organization is the product of the Uruguay Round negotiations, coming into being on 1 January 1995. At the time of writing, it has close to 150 members, China and Taiwan being among the most recent additions, and Russia is expecting to accede shortly. All members of the WTO have ratified all the multilateral trade agreements according to their domestic parliamentary procedures and changed their domestic laws and regulations where necessary, and are therefore legally committed to each of the multilateral trade agreements.

The multilateral trade agreements are to be found in four Annexes attached to the Agreement Establishing the WTO (signed in Marrakesh on 15 April 1994). Many earlier GATT provisions and understandings have also been carried over into the WTO system. The first of the Annexes contains all the multilateral trade agreements administered by the WTO; that is, the updated GATT of 1947 (i.e. GATT-1994) plus 12 other Agreements. The second Annex contains the Understanding on Rules and Procedures Governing the Settlement of Disputes. The third Annex contains the procedures relating to the Trade Policy Review Mechanism. The agreements contained in the three Annexes constitute a total undertaking and there can be no choosing between individual agreements. The fourth Annex relates to the less important Plurilateral Trade Agreements (plurilateral, because they do not have the full multilateral membership of the WTO).

The World Trade Organization is the legal and institutional basis of the multilateral trading system. It embodies the main contractual obligations that determine how governments must formulate and apply their laws and regulations relating to trade. It is also the framework for the conduct of trade relations among its members, through a collective process of discussions, negotiations and decisions.

It is perhaps important to note at this stage that there are well over 200 regional or preferential trade agreements that are plurilateral in nature and function alongside the WTO. Although plurilateral trading arrangements based on preferences would appear to be the antithesis of a multilateral system based on non-discrimination, the general view is that they complement rather than undermine the multilateral system of the WTO. In terms of the formal relationship between the regional agreements and the WTO, each of the agreements is to be notified to the WTO if a member country is a party. Certain requirements are to be met to conform to WTO obligations.

The Preamble to the Agreement Establishing the WTO sets out, in the broadest terms, the objectives of the whole body of multilateral trade agreements. Much of the language of the Preamble is taken over from the GATT, with some minor modifications. As noted in earlier chapters, the most important modification for present purposes is that the Agreement adds the objective of sustainable development, seeking both to protect and to preserve the environment. The declared means of achieving these objectives is reciprocal and mutually advantageous arrangements directed to the substantial reduction of tariffs and other barriers to trade and the elimination of discriminatory treatment in international trade relations.

The Agreement Establishing the WTO specifies five functions for the WTO. The first is to facilitate the implementation, administration and operation of the multilateral trade agreements, and to further their objectives. The second is to be a negotiating forum for the multilateral agreements dealt with in the Annexes referred to above, as well as further negotiations concerning multilateral trade relations, as may be decided by the WTO's Ministerial Conference. The third function is to administer the multilateral trade arrangements in the Annexes and to settle disputes between members. The fourth is to review the trade policies of WTO member countries. Finally, the WTO is to cooperate with the International Monetary Fund and the World Bank with a view to achieving greater coherence in global economic policy-making. The United Nations and its various bodies are not specifically mentioned in this context. However, the General Council is to make appropriate arrangements for effective cooperation with other intergovernmental organizations that have responsibilities related to those of the WTO. This includes the specialized agencies of the United Nations.

The structure of the WTO is as follows. It is headed by a Ministerial Conference composed of all members of the WTO, which meets at least once every two years. There have been five such meetings: in Singapore, Geneva, Seattle, Doha and Cancún. The Ministerial Conference has full powers under the Agreement, and it is to carry out the functions of the

WTO. It has the authority to take decisions on all matters relating to any of the multilateral trade agreements. Between sessions of the Ministerial Conference, its functions are exercised by the General Council, also made up of the full membership of the WTO. The General Council is responsible for the continuing management of the WTO and supervises all aspects of its activities. The General Council also meets as the Dispute Settlement Body and the Trade Policy Review Body.

There are separate sets of subsidiary bodies reporting to the General Council. The most important group, responsible for the main operational aspects of the WTO, consists of the three councils that supervise work arising from the obligations all member countries have assumed under the Agreements on trade in goods, trade in services and trade-related aspects of intellectual property matters. Another group reporting to the General Council consists of the Committee on Trade and Development, the Committee on Balance of Payments Restrictions, and the Committee on Budget Finance and Administration. Many, or even most, of their tasks are specifically laid down elsewhere in the WTO Agreement or in its Annexes.

The WTO is located in Geneva, Switzerland. The organization has a permanent staff consisting of a Secretariat headed by a Director-General. The Director-General is appointed by the Ministerial Conference; s/he in turn appoints the staff and sets their duties and conditions of service in accordance with regulations adopted by the Conference. Because the WTO is a "member-driven" intergovernmental organization, unlike some other organizations (e.g. the Bretton Woods institutions), the Director-General has very limited powers. S/he cannot, for example, formulate policy for the organization, nor is s/he expected to comment on the policies of the member governments.

The funding of the WTO is relatively straightforward, stable and predictable. The scale of contributions is proportionate to the share of each country's exports and imports in the total trade among members. A minimum 0.03 per cent contribution is applicable to countries with a share of less than that amount in trade among WTO members. The WTO's resources are limited in comparison with a number of other multilateral institutions. Its budget was US$160 million for the year 2004 and it has a Secretariat of 600 staff members.

Multilateral environment agreements

It is well acknowledged that, unlike the multilateral trading system, international environmental governance is constituted by a complex and fragmented web of institutions and arrangements. This may well be a rational response to the very different nature of environmental problems, because the agreements address the regional nature of some of the problems. Within the United Nations system there are many bodies that have important roles in dealing with the environment. These include the General Assembly, the Economic and Social Council (ECOSOC), the United Nations Environment Programme (UNEP), many UN specialized agencies, the United Nations Commission on Sustainable Development (CSD), the Regional Commissions and, importantly, a plethora of multilateral environment agreements that are, to varying degrees, a part of the United Nations system. Outside the UN system are numerous other intergovernmental organizations and arrangements. There are also linkages between national and international institutional arrangements, regional treaties, diverse understandings, and networks and major interest groups centred in non-governmental organizations (NGOs).[6]

In what follows, I focus on UNEP and the MEAs, although I refer to other institutions and arrangements where necessary. As noted in chapter 2, UNEP was established by the General Assembly of the United Nations following the Stockholm Conference in December 1972. The Governing Council of UNEP reports to the General Assembly of the United Nations through ECOSOC, which transmits to the General Assembly any comments it may consider necessary. These comments relate primarily to the coordination of environmental policies and programmes within the UN system with overall economic and social policies and priorities. The 58 members of the UNEP Council are elected on a regional basis for four-year terms by the General Assembly.

UNEP is not a specialized agency of the United Nations. It is a Programme to promote international cooperation in the field of the environment and to recommend policies to this end; to provide general policy guidance for environmental programmes within the UN system; to review periodic reports on the implementation of environmental programmes within the UN system; to review the world environmental situation; to promote the exchange of environmental information; to review the impact of environmental policies on developing countries; and to approve the utilization of the resources of the Environment Fund.

The Committee of Permanent Representatives is a subsidiary organ of the Governing Council. It is composed of permanent representatives of UNEP members at the headquarters of UNEP in Nairobi. It consists of representatives of all UN member states and members of its specialized agencies. The Committee meets four times a year. It may establish subsidiary bodies, subcommittees and working groups on specific subjects that meet between the sessions of the Council. The mandate of the Committee is to review, monitor and assess the implementation of Council decisions on administrative, budgetary and programme matters; to review the draft programme of work and budget during their preparation by the Secretariat; to review reports requested of the Secretariat by the Governing Council; and, finally, to prepare draft decisions for consideration by the Governing Council.

As discussed in chapter 2, the United Nations Conference on Environment and Development (UNCED) focused on the relationship and balance between environmental protection and economic development. The stronger focus on economic and development issues was seen by some as a weakening of the environmental side of the balance sheet and a shift in favour of development. It is important in this respect that both UNEP and the Commission on Sustainable Development report to ECOSOC (sometimes on overlapping issues). In the case of UNEP, however, it reports to the UN General Assembly through ECOSOC. Because the mandate of the CSD overlapped somewhat with that of UNEP, there was confusion about the exact role of UNEP in the UN system. Thus, in 1997, the Governing Council adopted the Nairobi Declaration on the Role and Mandate of the United Nations Environment Programme, which acknowledged UNEP to be the leading global environmental authority that sets the global environmental agenda, promotes the coherent implementation of the environmental dimension of sustainable development within the UN system, and serves as an authoritative advocate for the global environment. The Declaration had as its objective a revitalization of UNEP, and went on to elaborate a mandate for UNEP, based partly on a more focused Programme for the Further Implementation of Agenda 21.

The UN Task Force on Environment and Human Settlements made a number of recommendations for improving the effectiveness of UNEP, one of which was the establishment of the Global Ministerial Environment Forum (GMEF). The GMEF is an annual ministerial-level forum. It meets as the UNEP Governing Council in regular session in one year, and in alternate years as a Special Session of the Governing Council. It has a purely advisory role. It reviews policy issues in the field of the environment and gives due consideration to ensuring the effective functioning of the governmental mechanisms of UNEP. It is to maintain the role of the CSD as the principal forum for high-level policy debate on sustainable development. Membership of the GMEF is not universal, being limited to members of the UNEP Council. Another recommendation was the establishment of an Environmental Management Group (EMG) as an instrument to enhance inter-agency coordination and cooperation in the field of the environment.

In 2001, the UNEP Governing Council created an open-ended Intergovernmental Group of Ministers to undertake a comprehensive policy-oriented assessment of existing institutional environmental governance. In February 2002, this group completed its deliberations and reported to the GMEF, which eventually accepted the proposals. The proposals included establishing a clear policy-making role for the GMEF/UNEP Council, with both having universal membership; a strengthening and regularizing of the financial situation of UNEP; enhanced synergies and linkages between the MEAs; and improved capacity-building and technology transfer. The group also proposed considerably strengthening the EMG. These proposals were adopted at the WSSD.[7] Notwithstanding its ambitious mandate from the point of view of environmental governance, its proposals fell far short of recommending the establishment of a World Environment Organization.

UNEP is headquartered in Nairobi, Kenya, and has a number of regional offices.[8] The budget for UNEP in 2004 was approximately US$140 million. In the same year, the staff numbered approximately 1,000, with about 55 per cent being professional posts. As far as the sources of funding are concerned, when the General Assembly originally established UNEP it was agreed that the budget for servicing the Governing Council and the Secretariat should come from the regular budget of the United Nations. While the total budget of UNEP is similar to that of the WTO, it differs in that it draws on several sources and can vary considerably over time.

Other funding comes from the Environment Fund, which was established by the UN General Assembly in 1972 to provide financing for environmental programmes. Altogether 126 countries pledged contributions to the Environment Fund in 2004, and total contributions were approximately US$56 million. There are also Trust Funds earmarked by donors for specific purposes. The general purpose Trust Funds provide financial resources for activities supporting the programme of work of UNEP as well as of Conventions and regional seas programmes and the activities of their secretariats. Contributions to Trust Funds in 2003 were approximately US$40 million. Finally, counterpart contributions are made in cash or kind by United Nations agencies, other organizations, non-state actors and individuals, and are earmarked for specific activities, services and facilities for individual projects. They have grown significantly in terms of the percentage of funding. In 2004, total support received through earmarked contributions was around US$20 million.

An important role for UNEP is in administering the secretariats for the environment Conventions.[9] Of the 41 core environmental Conventions, Protocols and related international agreements, UNEP provides the secretariat for 22 and has working relationships with all the others.[10] Most MEAs are legally binding instruments. Some are Framework Conventions that can develop Protocols, others are self-contained and work through Annexes or Appendices. Protocols, Annexes and Appendices can either be revised or adjusted by decisions of the parties, or be formally amended by means of a ratification procedure. The non-legally binding agreements are underpinned by plans of action adopted or approved intergovernmentally.

Multilateral environment agreements adopted since 1972 generally have the following institutional elements: a secretariat, a bureau, advisory bodies, a clearing house mechanism and a financial mechanism. Conferences and Meetings of the Parties are the ultimate decision-making bodies regarding implementation and the evolution of each agreement, including the work programme, the budget and the adoption of Protocols and Annexes. Non-binding agreements do not have such bodies. Decisions on their work and budget are made by the intergovernmental bodies that they report to or, for agreements for which UNEP provides the secretariat, by the Governing Council.

Some agreements have established standing committees or hold intersessional meetings to review and advise their secretariats on implementation. Subsidiary bodies, which are generally advisory in nature, reporting to Conferences or Meetings of the Parties on scientific, technical or financial matters or on progress in implementation, may be internal or external, and may be standing bodies or ad hoc bodies with limited mandates. Clearing house mechanisms may be operated by secretariats to facilitate the exchange of information. A few Conventions have established regional centres for training and technology transfer or to assist in implementation.

Although the scope and mandate of secretariats can vary, from a functional point of view they can be divided into two categories: first, secretariats that prepare for, and service, the meetings of the Conferences of the Parties and their subsidiary bodies and coordinate with other international organizations; second, secretariats that carry out the functions of the first category but are also involved in implementing programmes or projects at regional and country levels. An important function of most secretariats is the monitoring and evaluation of implementation, proposing formats for national reports, receiving and analysing reports submitted, and providing the Conference or Meeting of the Parties with syntheses of the information contained in national reports.

In most Conventions, NGOs, private industry, civic groups, local communities and indigenous groups are invited and allowed to participate in the deliberations of the parties. In some cases, however, this does not necessarily apply to meetings that are not open-ended, such as those of technical expert groups and liaison groups. Some secretariats maintain regular contacts with civil society organizations for exchange of information and views, receipt of documentation and preparation of background papers. Some also work with civil society groups and private industry in the implementation of activities.[11] Conventions recognize the involvement of all relevant stakeholders as fundamental.

In general, Trust Funds provide the funding for the individual agreements and are administered by the international organizations that provide the secretariats. Thus, in the case of UNEP-administered Conventions and related agreements, UNEP serves as the trustee. Most agreements have financial rules adopted by the parties that are applied to Trust Funds. Trustees are able to provide guidelines for the transactions and accounts of the Conventions and agreements, including systems and facilities that allow them to undertake their programme activities effectively. The accounts and finances of the agreements and their secretariats are audited and reported. Budgets are proposed by the secretariats, both for the operations of each secretariat itself and for the programme of work, and in most cases are negotiated and agreed to by the Conferences of the Parties. Conferences and Meetings of Parties are financed either through secretariats' core budgets or through separate budgets earmarked for this purpose.

The funding of MEAs is mainly through Trust Funds, one or more of which may be established under an agreement, with some for specialized purposes. Other sources of funding are the multilateral financing mechanisms addressing specific subject areas. In 1992, the UNCED recognized the Global Environment Facility as providing funding to developing countries and countries with economies in transition for project activities targeting global benefits in one or more of four focal areas: biodiversity, climate change, international waters and ozone layer protection. Land degradation, particularly deforestation and desertification activities as they relate to the four focal areas, is also eligible for funding. The World Bank, regional development banks, bilateral arrangements with donor countries, foundations such as the United Nations Foundation, private sector donors and non-governmental organizations also provide funding. In addition, traditional Trust Funds are financed by mandatory or voluntary contributions from parties, or both.

Institutions: Similarities and differences?

Lessons can be learned from comparing the governance of global trade with that of the environment. Reference to the WTO as an institution responsible for the global governance of trade has – not surprisingly – figured in one form or another in many of the proposals for the reform of the institutional structure that deals with global governance of the environment. The various references find themselves on a vast spectrum:

there are those that see merit in a virtual cloning of the WTO, whereas others see a number of features of the WTO to be avoided at all costs. Irrespective of a proposal's location on the spectrum, it is instructive to compare some of the features of the two global systems in order to identify similarities and differences that might permit some useful conclusions to be drawn. I make some observations below to demonstrate the very different nature of the two systems – viewed from a trade perspective – and to assist in advancing well-informed proposals for reform. One overriding consideration is that the WTO is a very centralized system of governance, and as such its relevant features in terms of institutional responsibilities are not difficult to identify. This is not the case for the environment institutions.

Fundamentals

Environment officials and trade officials have fundamentally different approaches to policy-making: one relates to comparative advantage and the need to remove trade restrictions and distortions, and the other to the grounds for discrimination and the need to introduce them.

The role of the principle of comparative advantage in the manner in which international trade should or should not be regulated has a long history in both theory and practice. Two hundred years ago, David Ricardo demonstrated that it is in the interests of two countries to trade, even if one country could produce all goods more cheaply than the other – even, in other words, if it has an absolute advantage in the production of all goods. With a simple numerical example, Ricardo showed that even the country without any absolute advantage still has a comparative advantage in some goods, and that these can be profitably traded.[12] Goods with a potential comparative advantage are those in which the opportunity costs of production (the resources forgone in their production) are relatively less than for the trading partner.[13] The simple logic of comparative advantage has been a driving force behind many powerful policy decisions, ranging from Ricardo convincingly arguing for the removal of the Corn Laws in England in the early part of the nineteenth century to the adoption of outward-oriented development strategies in developing countries over the past few decades.

Within the context of the negotiation of multilateral trade agreements, however, it would be wrong to argue that comparative advantage has been the driving force behind multilateral trade negotiations. If it had been, trade officials would accept the merits of unilateral trade liberalization and not spend years in multilateral negotiations attempting to obtain concessions from others. Nevertheless, the broad understanding that there is merit in removing trade barriers has contributed significantly to the belief that trade liberalization is beneficial for the economy even if some groups are adversely affected.

Even though the principle of comparative advantage is widely accepted in some sectors, it is viewed by many with considerable mistrust. Their scepticism stems from the important condition that resources will naturally flow to areas where they have a comparative advantage as long as distortions are not introduced by governments. The concern is that the unfettered functioning of comparative advantage can mean that, with prices determining the production and consumption patterns in a free market, the welfare of society is undermined. Market prices may well fail to capture the effects of environmentally damaging activities and send misleading signals regarding the appropriate use of environmental resources. Resource misallocation owing to inappropriate relative price structures can undermine effective environmental management. There may be a failure by the producer to shoulder the costs of environmental degradation borne by society, or inappropriate natural resource depletion because of pricing that fails to reflect scarcity value. Since these are conditions under which international trade can promote environmentally destructive production, there are calls for limits to trade. A clear case can be made for governments to intervene to make the necessary adjustments to the patterns of production or consumption to reflect their costs and value to society.

These simple facts go a long way to explain much of the difference in approach to policy formulation in the trade and environment arenas. Many policies designed to protect the environment are based on government intervention through the regulation of production activities – for example, through taxes, quantitative restrictions and subsidies. The GATT and the WTO, in contrast, have a long tradition of negotiating away government measures that affect trade: subsidies affecting exports, export bans, restrictions on imports.[14] Thus, many in the trade community would argue that the environmental degradation associated with trade liberalization is not a result of bad trade policy but rather a manifestation of the inadequacy of the environmental management policies in place at the time of the trade liberalization. Hence the call for sustainability impact assessment studies to precede or at least accompany trade liberalization (see chapter 3).

One common feature of the multilateral trade and multilateral environment agreements is the diversity of the subject matter they deal with. Protecting endangered species is very different from protecting the ozone layer, maintaining a stable climate, preserving wetlands or inhibiting the encroachment of deserts. These issues are all dealt with by multilateral environment agreements. So it is with trade agreements: quarantine measures, patents, financial services, dumping and agricultural price supports are all very different. Nevertheless, they too are all covered by multilateral trade agreements. As trade and environment agreements each deal with their own subject matter, they each have their own objective.

In broad measure, the objective of multilateral environment agreements is to safeguard environmental quality. However, because the environment itself cannot be controlled, the agreements' aim is to modify human behaviour in ways that will result in more satisfactory environmental conditions. This requires the use of carrots and sticks, and the success in modifying human behaviour is not always quantifiable. Further, these objectives do not translate into common legal obligations that can be enforced in the same manner as trade agreements.

Broadly speaking, the objective of the multilateral trade agreements is to increase trade in goods and services and to construct and enforce rules to ensure stability and predictability. The pace of liberalization can be controlled and agreed to, as can the nature of the rules. Thus, the extent to which the objective of trade liberalization has been met is identifiable in terms of reductions in tariffs, which are legally bound in tariff schedules. The removal of quantitative restrictions is also easily identified and recorded. In terms of rules, the core discipline of non-discrimination pervades most of the agreements in the form of national treatment and most favoured nation treatment. Breaches of these and other obligations can be identified and acted upon via authorized trade retaliation and compensation if necessary.

Another fundamental difference would appear to lie in the transparency with which trade and environment policies are formulated. The environment community appears to favour openness and transparency in policy formulation and the involvement of all stakeholders. This has not been the GATT practice in the past. The closed nature of GATT negotiations can arguably be traced to the realities of the political economy of protection. The vast literature on this topic makes clear that distributional coalitions form to resist policy change that is not in the specific interests of their members. WTO members – and GATT members before them – are familiar with taking decisions that are not in the interests of all groups in society but are nevertheless thought to be in the interests of the constituencies that the governments represent when elected democratically. This has very practical implications for governments that spill over to transparency considerations. If, for example, saving an efficient domestic motor vehicle manufacturing industry requires removing tariff protection for a highly protected and inefficient local steel industry, it is most unlikely that the government concerned would invite steel and car manufacturers to the multilateral negotiating table – at least not when it comes to bargaining with other countries on tariff reductions – though they are indeed stakeholders. After reviewing the evidence before it, the government would be expected to take decisions at the multilateral level that are in the interests of the community at large.

Thus, many GATT documents have traditionally been kept far from the eyes of the public. National proposals for tariff reductions, for example, continue to be among the most highly restricted documents during rounds of trade negotiations. Countries acceding to the WTO engage in negotiations to change their trade regime, with significant implications for business, and they would have great difficulty in proceeding if all information were in the public domain. For countries experiencing balance of payments difficulties, revealing the nature of their problems could lead to serious implications for capital flight, exchange rates and other key economic variables. As a result, GATT contracting parties in the past have built up a tradition of jealously guarding the intergovernmental character of GATT without the active participation of interested (industry) groups; and the WTO in some measure continues the tradition.

A further fundamental difference in the formulation of trade and environment policy is the grounds on which there can be legitimate discrimination between products during production and marketing. As noted on several occasions in chapter 3, the WTO does not inhibit governments from protecting (as they wish) against damage to the environment resulting from the manufacture and consumption of goods produced and used within national boundaries. Final products can be taxed and other charges levied for any purpose thought to be appropriate. However, the understanding behind a number of WTO Agreements is that the flexibility extends to regulation only of domestic products and processes and not of the processes used to produce imported products. For example, mandatory standards may be applied domestically that limit the use of energy in production processes, but an imported product cannot be discriminated against only because the production process is considered to be emitting excessive greenhouse gases (see chapter 5).

The underlying thesis is that should any country wish to influence the manner in which goods are produced in other countries – regardless of how appropriate it may seem to interest groups in the importing country – this should not translate into discriminatory trade measures. In general, WTO rules treat products that have the same physical form as "like" products, even if they have been produced in very different ways. From the perspective of the environment, environmentally unfriendly goods and services – and the processes that produce them – are categorically different from environmentally friendly ones. Thus, whereas the rationale for environmental regulation is to make discrimination between goods and services mandatory (based, for example, on life-cycle analysis), the rationale for WTO rules is to avoid discrimination as far as imports are concerned.

Balance of interests

The multilateral trade agreements are legally binding instruments in which the rights and obligations are carefully balanced after years of negotiations. They are a single undertaking in both the legal and negotiating sense of the term. This is not the case with the multilateral environment agreements. Moreover, the trade agreements have a common membership, and all rules and agreements are adopted on a consensus basis by all WTO members. The membership of some environment agreements, in contrast, varies greatly.

The common membership of all multilateral trade agreements means that there is not only a balance of rights and obligations across the totality of the agreements, but also a perceived balance of interests. The practical result is that, much to the annoyance of some, any individual agreement – such as the Agreement on Trade-Related Intellectual Property Rights (TRIPS) – is most unlikely to be changed without a change in others. Even if all members thought a particular change appropriate, it is doubtful that – in general terms – it would come about without some compensating change elsewhere. If one government is a *demandeur* for the change, another will take advantage of that fact and seek a change for which it is the proponent. Not surprisingly, rule change is rare, not only for this reason – that is, the search for consensus – but also because of the sometimes unknown implications of changes in rules that are legally enforceable.

Central body

As noted above, although the WTO is headed by a Ministerial Conference, the General Council is responsible for the day-to-day management of all the trade agreements. The centralization of the decision and management process means that the organization of the WTO's work differs significantly from that of the multilateral environment agreements. There is no such central body dealing with the totality of multilateral environment agreements, nor do all UN members belong to all MEAs, or indeed to the UNEP Governing Council itself.

It is clear that any reform of global environmental governance would involve the strengthening of the authority and mandate of UNEP to enable it to play the role of a global environmental authority effectively. As it stands, UNEP does not have a general assembly that can draft treaties negotiated by subcommittees under its auspices. Creating hard international law in the same manner as can be done in the WTO General Council would require a mechanism that goes far beyond the powers of the existing UNEP Governing Council, which can initiate intergovernmental negotiations but cannot adopt legal instruments on its own. An important question is whether it is possible to envisage governments agreeing to the creation of a general assembly of this nature to oversee the existing agreements and to create new ones.

The WTO is commonly referred to as one of the trio of institutions – along with the World Bank and the International Monetary Fund – popularly known as the Bretton Woods institutions. It is not. Nor is it a specialized agency of the United Nations. Both its budget and country membership differ from those of the United Nations, and the only formal relationship is through a stand-alone Agreement between the WTO and the United Nations. UNEP, on the other hand, is very much part of the United Nations system through the chain of communication discussed above – it reports to the General Assembly. This compares starkly with the centralization of the WTO in which control of members via the General Council and Ministerial Meetings is direct.

The budget of the WTO is regular and calculated objectively, with the standard yardstick being the share of a member in world trade. WTO members can increase the budget at any point if they agree to do so. As far as UNEP is concerned, it is frequently lamented that it is underfunded and only a Programme. However, it is not clear what the budget of the WTO should be compared with as regards institutions responsible for multilateral environment agreements. A number of MEAs operate under the auspices of UNEP, so perhaps this is the appropriate body. However, the comparison is far from clear and unambiguous because a large part of UNEP funding is for project and other activities outside the realm of MEAs.

One roof

An important difference between the trade and environment agreements is that the numerous trade agreements, with over 70 councils, committees, working parties and other processes, are all serviced in the same geographical location and even under the "same roof" in Geneva. Moreover, the WTO bodies are frequently serviced by the same people from capitals, national delegations based in Geneva as well as the WTO Secretariat. They too, of course, meet under the same roof. In this manner, a high degree of expertise is acquired all round, and there is a minimum of travel in servicing the various trade agreements for local delegations stationed in Geneva. Furthermore, an atmosphere has developed that reflects the continuing contacts of all the individuals involved, both between government officials and between the officials and Secretariat staff members.

This is not the case for environment agreements, which are dealt with by geographically dispersed secretariats located in Geneva, Montreal, Nairobi, Bonn and elsewhere. There are presently over 500 international treaties and other agreements related to the environment,[15] and national governments find themselves facing as many as 65 global and regional environmental Conventions and agreements.[16] This presumably has implications for the coherence of the diverse environment agreements and the effectiveness with which they can be managed. Each MEA normally has its own Conference of the Parties, secretariat, advisory bodies and subsidiary bodies (such as technical expert groups). It has been estimated that, if a minister of the environment had to participate in all the meetings of the Conferences of the Parties – as is sometimes expected – he or she would probably be on mission 600 days of the year.[17]

With the current arrangements with respect to multilateral environment agreements, there is no implementation mechanism through which environmental commitments and assets could be exchanged among themselves or exchanged for non-environmental assets such as finance. It has been argued that, if cash were offered in exchange for environmental commitments, flows of financial resources (not foreseen in the WTO framework) might be bargained for improved environmental quality.[18]

In terms of the possibility of bringing all MEAs into the one house, as is the case with the WTO, an important consideration is that the multilateral trade agreements were created at the same time as the WTO. Had individual agreements been in existence with their own secretariats, executive secretaries and the vested interests to which institutional structures give rise, it is not clear that it would have been possible to create a common institution such as exists today. One similarity, however, is that the secretariats that service the environment agreements are, with some exceptions, quite small (in many cases just five or six people). This is also the case in the WTO, where secretariats (i.e. the WTO Divisions servicing the individual trade agreements) rarely number more than half a dozen professionals and on some occasions fewer.

Dispute settlement

One important operational characteristic of the diverse multilateral trade agreements – the glue that holds them together – is the dispute settlement process. This lies at the heart of the WTO. In all the trade agreements, breaking the rules means being taken to court; if the offending measures applied by a country are found to be in error, and are not brought into conformity with WTO rules, then compensation and retaliation – with the approval of the General Council – are provided for. And, in this context, the interrelationship between the trade agreements is critical. Compensation can be sought in the form of improved market access in any of the areas covered by the multilateral trade agreements, and not necessarily with respect to the Agreement where the breach of obligations was committed. Similarly, retaliation can take place in any of the areas covered by the agreements, not necessarily with respect to the one where there was a breach of obligations. In MEAs, in contrast, many of the obligations are not subject to judicial application; they leave considerable discretion to parties on how they choose to implement their commitments.[19]

However, what many consider to be an effective WTO dispute settlement process is the culmination of 50 years of experience. It is important to be realistic about the WTO model being applied to the multilateral environment agreements if that were thought desirable.

WTO, WEO

Given the lack of institutional coherence in dealing with environmental policy globally, it is not surprising that the discussion about institutional reform has for some time focused on the creation of a World or Global Environment Organization (WEO/GEO).[20] Over the past decade or so, a number of proposals have been advanced in this respect. Nor is it surprising that some looked to the GATT – and later the WTO – as relevant in this respect.[21] This is perhaps all the more so because the origins of the argument for a WEO were not unrelated to the concerns in the 1990s among those who felt that the GATT/WTO system was ill equipped to respond when trade questions intersected with environmental issues. Even if the GATT system could be "greened", international environmental challenges require their own multilateral responses via the creation of a WEO.

There are numerous and very varied views as to what would constitute a World Environment Organization. As a point of reference, the models of reform that have been explored include: clustering of MEAs; strengthening UNEP; expanding the role of the Global Ministerial Environment Forum; reforming existing UN bodies; strengthening financing sources and mechanisms; building up the environmental competence of the WTO; reforming the UN Trusteeship Council; expanding the mandate of the UN Security Council; and establishing a World Environment Court.[22] Although these models are very different, a number of similar questions emerge: what functions would the WEO have; would it act as an umbrella for the various multilateral environment agreements; what financial resources and legal authority would it be endowed with?

These proposals have usefully been grouped into three different types: the cooperation, the centralization and the hierarchization models.[23]

In the cooperation model, UNEP would be upgraded to a UN specialized agency with new legal and political powers. It would approve certain regulations by a qualified majority vote and these would then become binding on all members. The WEO general assembly would be able to adopt draft treaties negotiated by subcommittees under its auspices. The centralization model would integrate various existing agencies, programmes and regimes into the WEO in the same manner that the WTO has various multilateral trade agreements integrated under its umbrella. Finally, the hierarchization model would be a quasi-supranational agency that would have decision-making, enforcement and sanctioning powers vis-à-vis a minority of non-consenting states if the global commons are at stake. All the models have a bit of the WTO in them.

Although the continuing debate on the virtues or otherwise of creating a World Environment Organization has been useful in identifying the shortcomings and possible improvements in the global governance structure, it seems increasingly clear that the improved framework being sought will not come via the creation of a separate WEO – at least in terms of the "big bang" that many of its advocates have envisaged.[24]

State of play

When addressing the need for improved global environmental governance, the Secretary-General of the United Nations noted: "There is no shortage of ideas on what should be done.... What we need is a better understanding of how to translate our values into practice, and how to make new instruments and institutions work more effectively."[25]

The debate on the need for a WEO has certainly not died. In a relatively recent article, Ford Runge, one of the original and most articulate promoters of the idea of a WEO, argues: "A Global Environmental Organisation (GEO) should be considered as one in a set of efforts to better coordinate international environmental policy, whilst protecting and insulating the World Trade Organization (WTO) from responsibilities for which it is both disinclined and unprepared."[26]

One question concerns how the existence of a WEO would make the life of the WTO easier. Runge argues that a GEO would offer the trading system the opportunity to disentangle trade from environmental matters, allowing the WTO to focus where it should: on expansion of market access and reductions in trade protectionism, and attending to environmental measures only in cases of obvious trade distortion. A GEO could clarify where environmental exceptions to the GATT Articles were justified (under Article XX) and provide guidelines for minimally trade-distorting MEAs. At the same time, a GEO could help fill the institutional gap in dispute resolution and coordination surrounding the many MEAs and institutions now responsible for global environmental issues.[27] Clearly this last point is important, because some of the proponents of a WEO have dispute settlement on their mind. However, it should be seen in perspective. Out of many hundreds of disputes brought to the GATT and the WTO, only nine could be considered to be environment related. Although they have been controversial and taken time to deal with, they have all been effectively resolved. Under the GATT, six Panel proceedings involving an examination of environmental measures or human health-related measures under Article XX were completed.[28] Of the six reports, three remained unadopted. Under the WTO, three disputes have so far led to the adoption of Panel and Appellate Body reports. No case has ever been brought to the dispute settlement system – and in my view never will be – where a WTO non-conforming measure was justified under an MEA (this is discussed in some detail in chapter 6). What is required are more effective MEAs that better define on a consensus basis the conditions under which WTO members are prepared to forgo their rights not to be discriminated against if certain predetermined standards in MEAs are not adhered to.

Conclusions

A shortcoming of many proposals relating to the creation of a WEO is that they lack specifics, particularly relating to why the creation of a new global organization would make any difference to the underlying problems of a lack of resources, a lack of political will and inadequate policy integration in matters relating to global environmental governance.

Some see the WEO as an intellectually attractive option for the longer term but argue that improved global environmental governance will come via an evolutionary, step-by-step approach rather than overnight structural reform of existing institutions through the creation of new ones. Thus, "the strengthening of international environmental governance should be based on existing structures, in particular UNEP, should aim gradually to adapt them to the new requirements and could ultimately lead to a World Environment Organization, respecting existing headquarters; it should try to respond to current challenges, particularly as regards the implementation of environmental agreements".[29] In the same vein, the emphasis in most intergovernmental Declarations has been on improved governance in the environmental sector through greater synergies and interlinkages between the multilateral environment agreements.[30]

Thus, a number of questions arise that could be usefully addressed based on the earlier sections of this chapter. First, does the WTO constitute a useful model that could be drawn on when seeking to improve the structure of global environmental governance? In my view, the answer to this question is "no", but that does not diminish the usefulness of examining another – albeit very different – model. Second, could the rules of the WTO be changed in order for it to play a more significant role in global environmental governance? My answer to that question is that, although rule change is not necessary, there are other tools that could usefully be considered, including Decisions (as in access to essential medicines and TRIPS), negotiations (as in fisheries subsidies) or sectoral agreements (liberalizing trade in environmental goods and services). The final question is whether the existing WTO rules and processes could be used in a more environmentally friendly manner. In my view, the answer to this question is in the affirmative, and changes on this front are evident in the dispute settlement process.

Notes

1. See UNEP, *International Environmental Governance; Report of the Executive Director, to the first meeting of the Open Ended Intergovernmental Group of Ministers in New York*, Nairobi: UNEP, UNEP/IGM/1/2, 4 April 2001.
2. See United Nations, *Report of the Secretary-General: United Nations Reform – Measures and Proposals – Environment and Human Settlements*, New York: United Nations, A/53/463, 6 October 1998.
3. *Malmö Ministerial Declaration*, Sweden, 31 May 2000; available at ⟨http://www.unep. org/malmo/malmo_ministerial.htm⟩.
4. Renato Ruggiero, *Opening Remarks to the High Level Symposium on Trade and the Environment*, WTO, 15 March 1999, available at ⟨http://www.wto.org/⟩.
5. See Konrad von Moltke, "The Organisation of the Impossible", *Global Environmental Politics*, Vol. 1, No. 1, 2001.
6. These components of international environmental governance are usefully described in UNEP, *International Environmental Governance; Report of the Executive Director*.
7. Philippe Roch, *International Environmental Governance: Striving for a Comprehensive, Coherent, Effective and Efficient International Environmental Regime*, Geneva: Graduate Institute of International Studies, Cahiers No. 8, 2003.
8. These regional offices are in Paris, Geneva, Osaka, The Hague, Washington, New York, Bangkok, Mexico City, Panama, Montreal and Bonn.
9. UNEP also hosts several environmental Convention secretariats, including the Ozone Secretariat and the Montreal Protocol's Multilateral Fund, the Convention on International Trade in Endangered Species of Wild Fauna and Flora, the Convention on Biological Diversity, the Convention on Migratory Species, and a growing family of chemicals-related agreements, including the Basel Convention on the Transboundary

Movement of Hazardous Wastes and the recently negotiated Stockholm Convention on Persistent Organic Pollutants.

10. See UNEP, *Multilateral Environmental Agreements: A Summary*, UNEP/IGM/1/INF/1, Nairobi: UNEP, 18 April 2001. The following paragraphs draw on this document and other relevant UNEP publications.

11. Examples of roles being played by the major groups of the civil society in the implementation of MEAs include: providing technical knowledge; awareness-raising; assisting the secretariat in communicating with non-parties; promoting implementation in the field; gathering and transmitting information about possible non-compliance; implementation of relevant national policies; pressuring governments to implement the MEAs; and participating in the decision-making process.

12. Writing in the early part of the nineteenth century, David Ricardo reasoned that "[a] country ... enabled to manufacture commodities with much less labour than her neighbours may, in return for such commodities, import a fraction of the corn required for its consumption, even if ... corn could be grown with much less labour than in the country from which it was imported." See R. M. Hartwell, *Introduction to D. Ricardo: The Principles of Political Economy and Taxation*, UK: H. Watson & Viney, 1971.

13. Teachers normally explain the principle of comparative advantage with an example along the lines of a neurosurgeon employing an administrative assistant to run her office even if the surgeon is more efficient in both surgery and office management. With the (less well paid) assistant releasing the (highly paid) resources of the surgeon to perform the professional tasks, it is profitable for the surgeon to employ the assistant, spending more time doing what the surgeon has a comparative advantage in doing, and profiting from the process.

14. The GATT and the WTO have certainly been less than pure in this respect. The Multifibre Arrangement is an example of the GATT providing legal cover for restrictions on international trade and of agriculture as a sector that has been left to one side during half a century of GATT-driven trade liberalization.

15. See UNEP, *International Environmental Governance; Report of the Executive Director*.

16. These statistics are drawn from UNEP, *International Environmental Governance: Multilateral Environmental Agreements*, Nairobi: UNEP, UNEP/IGM/2/INF/3, 10 July 2001.

17. See Roch, *International Environmental Governance*.

18. John Whalley and Ben Zissimos, "What Could a World Environmental Organization Do?", *Global Environmental Politics*, Vol. 1, No. 1, February 2001.

19. James Cameron comments that environmental regimes lack the power of the WTO dispute settlement mechanism, which has been "astoundingly popular" with states because it can "offer rewards for use", with political and economic benefits that can be cashed in – "There is no comparable mechanism in multilateral environment agreements". James Cameron, "Dispute Settlement and Conflicting Trade and Environment Regimes", in Agata Fijalkowski and James Cameron, *Trade and Environment: Bridging the Gap*, London: Cameron and May, 1998, p. 18.

20. Among the early advocates of a Global Environment Organization were Steve Charnovitz, "The Environment versus Trade Rules: Defogging the Debate", *Environmental Law*, Vol. 23, 1993, pp. 511–517; Daniel C. Esty, "GATTing the Greens", *Foreign Affairs*, Vol. 72, No. 5, 1993, pp. 132–136; and Ford C. Runge (with Francois Orlalo-Magne and Philip Van de Kamp), *Freer Trade, Protected Environment: Balancing Trade Liberalization and Environmental Interests*, New York: Council on Foreign Relations Press, 1994, pp. 100–107.

21. For example, when global environmental governance was discussed by EU environment ministers in July 2000, the "main issue" was whether to copy the WTO model in the

environmental field. European Commission, *An EU Contribution to Better Governance beyond Our Borders*, White Paper on Governance, Brussels: European Commission, Report of Working Group 5, May 2001.

22. Joy Hyvarinen and Duncan Brack, *Global Environmental Institutions: Analysis and Options for Change*, Report prepared for Department of the Environment, Transport and the Regions (UK), London: Royal Institute of International Affairs, September 2000.

23. See Frank Biermann, "The Emerging Debate on the Need for a World Environment Organisation: A Commentary", *Environmental Politics*, Vol. 1, No. 1, February 2001. The following description of each of the models is a summary drawn from the article by Biermann.

24. This has been convincingly argued by Hyvarinen and Brack, *Global Environmental Institutions: Analysis and Options for Change*.

25. Preface by the Secretary-General in UNEP, *Annual Report of UNEP*, Nairobi: UNEP, 2000, p. i.

26. Ford C. Runge, "A Global Environment Organisation and the World Trading System", *Journal of World Trade*, Vol. 35, No. 4, 2001, p. 399.

    Steve Charnovitz is of the view that, although many of the arguments for a WEO are not convincing, compelling arguments do exist. In a well-argued paper and in pragmatic vein, however, he reasons that a full centralization of environmental affairs is impossible. See Steve Charnovitz, "A World Environment Organisation", paper prepared for the UNU/IAS International Governance Reform Project, UNU/IAS, Tokyo, mimeo, 1 December 2001.

27. Runge, "A Global Environment Organisation and the World Trading System".

28. For a comprehensive study documenting all the Article XX environment cases in the GATT and the WTO, see WTO, *GATT/WTO Dispute Settlement Practice Relating to GATT Article XX paragraphs (b), (d) and (g): Note by the WTO Secretariat*, Geneva: WTO Secretariat, WT/CTE/W/203, 8 March 2002.

29. European Union, *Global Environmental Governance – Conclusions*, 2321st Council meeting, Brussels: European Commission, 18–19 December 2000.

30. The need for strengthening linkages between MEAs to facilitate synergies and promote coherence of policies was also stressed by the *Report of the United Nations Task Force on Environment and Human Settlement* (Töpfer Report), UN General Assembly, 53rd Session, A/53/463, 6 October 1998, Annex, para. 30, and supported by the General Assembly in its Resolution on International Institutional Arrangements Related to Environment and Development, A/RES/53/186, 2 February 1999.

12

Coherence and sustainable development

Introduction

There has long been a perception among the members of the General Agreement on Tariffs and Trade (GATT) – and now of the World Trade Organization (WTO) – that, owing to interlinkages at the international level, policies relating to trade and other areas of global policy formulation would be more coherent if there were a broadening and deepening of cooperation between other international institutions and the GATT/WTO. Although the desire to address these linkages institutionally has emerged at different times in GATT history, it received formal recognition as a result of the Uruguay Round of multilateral trade negotiations (1986–1994). A negotiating group was created, entitled the Functioning of the GATT System (FOGS) Group, which provided a forum for governments to identify the "contradictions" or "inconsistencies" that they believed to exist between the aims pursued by trade and by other policies. When adopting the results of the Uruguay Round in Marrakesh in April 1994, ministers stressed that "growing interactions between national economic policies meant that co-operation in each aspect of policy making was necessary for progress in other areas. In particular, if the origins of difficulties are outside the trade field, they cannot be redressed through trade measures alone".[1]

One outcome of the Uruguay Round is Article III of the Agreement Establishing the WTO, entitled "Functions of the WTO". It specifies the

289

five basic functions of the WTO, one of which is for the WTO to cooperate with the World Bank and the International Monetary Fund (IMF) to
achieve greater coherence in global economic policy-making.[2] Only the
Bretton Woods institutions are singled out in this respect. This mandate
is further elaborated in a Ministerial Declaration inviting the Director-
General to review with the heads of the World Bank and the IMF how
the institutions can cooperate to achieve this greater coherence. The
goal is for the institutions to ensure "consistent and mutually supportive
policies".[3] As far as other international institutions are concerned – and
none is specifically identified – Article V of the Agreement Establishing
the WTO, entitled "Relations with Other Organizations", instructs the
General Council to make "appropriate arrangements for effective cooperation with other intergovernmental organizations that have responsibilities related to those of the WTO" (para. 1). This falls far short of
mandating the WTO to work together with the specialized agencies of
the United Nations in order to bring greater coherence to global policy-
making.

   In the earlier chapters of this book I have focused on a number of
areas where there is a need for "consistent and mutually supportive policies" in the relationship between trade policy and sustainable development. Although there has been formal recognition of this need with respect to trade, money and finance, it could be argued that this is equally
the case for many of the issues addressed in this book. Ministers meeting
in Doha in Qatar in November 2001 strongly reaffirmed their "commitment to the objective of sustainable development", and, at the United
Nations World Summit on Sustainable Development in September 2002
in Johannesburg, ministers committed themselves to continue "to promote open, equitable, rules-based, predictable and non-discriminatory
multilateral trading and financial systems that benefit all countries in the
pursuit of sustainable development". The important question is how to
ensure "consistent and mutually supportive policies" between the many
institutions dealing with sustainable development.

   Political declarations are very much "top–down" in nature, frequently
stating the desirability of consistency and mutual supportiveness among
institutions pursuing common goals but with very little indication of
where and how this is to be achieved. On the basis of substance, it would
appear that there is considerable scope for improved cooperation between the WTO and the United Nations agencies and for greater coherence in the policies that governments pursue within them. It is, however,
important for there to be effective cooperation at the global level. As a
practical matter it is important to identify specific areas where complementary and mutually supportive policies could be pursued, not only
in the work of the WTO and the Bretton Woods institutions but in all

global intergovernmental institutions. Identifying these substantive areas would facilitate a "bottom–up" approach to the restructuring of collaboration, and could play an important role in complementing political declarations of good intent. In this exercise, we should not lose sight of the fact that the WTO as an institution with legally binding obligations and a powerful dispute settlement system is very different from the United Nations agencies and is viewed by governments as such. This difference was addressed in chapter 11.

The outline of the chapter is as follows. First, I look in some detail at how greater coherence in policy-making between the WTO and the Bretton Woods institutions has been achieved in practice. This serves as a useful model for the policy directions I suggest. Then I flag a number of areas where there is the potential for mutually supportive and consistent policies between the WTO and other international organizations – particularly the specialized agencies of the United Nations. I describe the experience in the Committee on Trade and Environment as a potential model for future cooperation of this sort. I close the chapter with four policy proposals as to how there could be a greater degree of coherence and complementarity between the WTO and other international institutions.

Coherence: The WTO and the Bretton Woods institutions

That coherence should be sought between the areas of responsibility of the WTO, the IMF and the World Bank should come as no surprise.[4] The three institutions share the same basic philosophy and have very similar objectives. According to the formal objectives of the institutions, they are all dedicated to, for example, expanding international trade, promoting high (or full) levels of employment, increasing standards of living and real incomes and developing the full use of productive resources. Apart from these general objectives, all three organizations have specific objectives with respect to international trade. The IMF, for example, is to "facilitate the expansion and balanced growth of international trade", recognizing "that the essential purpose of the international monetary system is to provide a framework that facilitates the exchange of goods, services and capital among countries". As far as the World Bank is concerned, it is to "promote the long range balanced growth of international trade ... by encouraging international investment".[5] The trade-related objective of the Bank is to promote trade, but its own role is limited to encouraging investment to contribute to this end.

The Punta del Este Declaration which launched the Uruguay Round included among the central objectives of the Round "to ... increase the responsiveness of the GATT system to the evolving international economic environment, through ... enhancing the relationship of the GATT with the relevant international organizations", to "foster concurrent cooperative action at the national and international levels to strengthen the inter-relationship between trade policies and other economic policies affecting growth and development, and to contribute towards continued, effective and determined efforts to improve the functioning of the international monetary system and the flow of financial and real investment resources to developing countries".[6] The Punta del Este Declaration called for action not only at the international level but also at the national level – better policy coordination at national level was identified as a precondition for effective international coordination.

To fulfil the mandate created by the Punta del Este Declaration, the Negotiating Group on the Functioning of the GATT System (FOGS) was created to, *inter alia*, "increase the contribution of the GATT to achieving greater coherence in global economic policy-making through strengthening its relationships with other international organizations responsible for monetary and financial matters".[7] One of the concerns of the negotiators was to remove perceived inconsistencies and contradictions in policy-making in the areas of trade, money and finance, and to render the institutions more consistent and mutually supportive in their approach.

The results of the negotiations in the FOGS Group can primarily be found in two outcomes. First, in the Agreement Establishing the WTO, the Article entitled "Functions of the WTO" (Article III:5) states that one of five functions of its members is to achieve greater coherence in global economic policy-making. In this respect, the WTO is to cooperate, as appropriate, with the IMF and the World Bank. Second, this mandate is further extended in an elaborate Ministerial Declaration on "The Contribution of the WTO to Achieving Greater Coherence in Global Economic Policy-Making", which invites the Director-General of the WTO to review with the heads of the Bretton Woods institutions how the institutions can cooperate to achieve greater coherence.[8]

Although the subject matter addressed in the Ministerial Declaration is far-reaching, there is a clear lack of specificity about the initiatives to be pursued. For example, the Declaration recognizes the ever-growing interactions between the economic policies pursued by individual countries (including trade and finance); that the task of achieving harmony between these policies falls primarily upon governments at the national level, but their coherence internationally is an important and valuable element in increasing the effectiveness of these policies; that greater exchange rate stability should contribute to the expansion of trade; that there is a need for further efforts to address debt problems; and that the

WTO, the IMF and the World Bank should follow consistent and mutually supportive policies. The Declaration also mandates the WTO to pursue and develop cooperation with the international organizations responsible for monetary and financial matters, while respecting their autonomy and avoiding the imposition on governments of cross-conditionality. Ministers also invited the Director-General of the WTO to review with the Managing Director of the IMF and the President of the World Bank how the institutions could cooperate to achieve greater coherence in global economic policy-making.

However, the term "coherence" was not clearly defined. It was generally perceived by governments in the Uruguay Round to relate to inter-linkages from a policy perspective between trade, money and finance, and to the role of institutional cooperation in improving the coherence of policy formulation in all areas. It had the potential to provide the basis for both broader and deeper relations than had existed in the past between the institutions in many areas. Advancing the practical implementation of the coherence mandate handed to the WTO by ministers in Marrakesh was more a matter of the institutions and/or their members deciding on the issues to address under the heading, rather than of attempting to define the term precisely. What was required was a bottom–up approach.

Since the entry into force of the WTO, formal Agreements have been concluded between the WTO and the World Bank and between the WTO and the IMF that provide the necessary specificity. Not surprisingly, the Agreements are very similar. Although the Agreement between the WTO and the IMF is more far-reaching than that with the Bank, this relates largely to the special relationship resulting from the balance of payments restrictions determinations.

The Agreements acknowledge the importance of cooperation between the WTO, the IMF and the World Bank in achieving greater coherence, and stipulate that attention is to be given to identifying possible means for cooperation in specific policies followed by each institution within their respective area of competence. One area in which a specific deepening of relationship is evident is the participation of the staff of each of the institutions in their respective meetings of members. The Agreements provide for WTO Secretariat attendance at Executive Board meetings of the World Bank and the IMF as well as the IMF Committee on Liaison with the WTO when matters of particular common interest or trade relevance are discussed. Participation in meetings of the Executive Board of the Bretton Woods institutions was not available to the GATT in the past, nor is it available to other organizations at present. For their part, Bank and IMF staff are offered observership in the vast majority of WTO bodies, including the Dispute Settlement Body provided certain conditions prevail (e.g. for the IMF when matters of jurisdictional relevance are considered). Among other things, the Agreements provide for the exchange of information between the organizations for their confidential use (e.g. in WTO trade policy reviews of members), and staff consultations to ensure consistency between members' obligations under WTO Agreements or the Articles of Agreement of the IMF.

Thus, the Agreements provide a framework within which the institutions can explore the precise mechanisms for intensifying institutional cooperation. In identifying these mechanisms, proposals in the FOGS Group are once again instructive. They included the sharing of research efforts; that the three organizations produce a biennial joint report on coherence between trade, monetary and finance policies; that they jointly analyse specific problems of interdependence among these policies, with each organization analysing the topic under discussion from its point of view; cooperation in the preparation of trade projections and joint research projects on subjects of common interest; a regular programme of staff exchanges; and staff meetings at head and deputy level on a regular basis.

Coherence: The WTO and the UN agencies

Given the ambitious objectives of the WTO and the extension of the subject matter covered by the WTO Agreements, it is not surprising that there is considerable overlap between the very specific subject matter dealt with by the WTO and that dealt with by the United Nations agencies. There are many examples.

The Agreement on Trade-Related Intellectual Property Rights (TRIPS) and its relationship to the United Nations Convention on Biological Diversity (CBD) is regularly singled out. The linkage comes from the fact that the CBD recognizes the sovereign rights of states over their natural resources and their authority to determine access to their genetic resources. The objective of the Convention is "the conservation of biological diversity, the sustainable use of its components, and the fair and equitable sharing of the benefits arising out of the utilization of their genetic resources".[9] Because the CBD recognizes that access, where granted, should be on mutually agreed terms and subject to prior informed consent of the provider party, intellectual property rights are clearly important. Yet the TRIPS Agreement makes no reference to the CBD, to access and benefits sharing, or to traditional knowledge. In this respect, the question is whether instruments contained in the TRIPS Agreement promote the equitable sharing of benefits between commercial users of genetic resources and indigenous communities. Some doubt that this is the case and ministers in Doha instructed the Council for

TRIPS to examine the relationship between the TRIPS Agreement and the CBD.[10]

Another example comes from the fact that recent dispute settlement cases at the WTO have dealt with the environment and public health. This is not appreciated by all: "Purists want environmental regulations left to specialised agencies, whereas many environmentalists want them enforced by the WTO. The argument for using the WTO is simple, for unlike most other international organisations, the WTO has a mechanism for enforcing its rulings: trade sanctions. The WTO convenes panels of experts to rule on trade disputes among member governments. If the losing government refuses to comply with the ruling, the panel authorises the winning government to impose trade sanctions."[11] The result is that the WTO dispute settlement process finds itself dealing with cases relating to non-traditional trade areas such as the environment and public health.

I argue in chapter 4 that the *Shrimp-Turtle* case should never have come to the WTO. It provides a good example of the potential for synergies between WTO rules and UN agreements. In this case, the Appellate Body was required to determine if a trade measure that had been invoked in relation to the conservation of an exhaustible natural resource qualified for provisional justification under the GATT-1994 Exceptions Article. At issue was whether a living creature should be considered to be an exhaustible natural resource. The Appellate Body ruled that, in the light of contemporary international law, living species, which are in principle renewable, "are in certain circumstances indeed susceptible of depletion, exhaustion and extinction, frequently because of human activities". In taking this decision, the existence of a UN multilateral environment agreement (MEA) was critical. Because "all of the seven recognised species of sea turtles are listed in Appendix 1 of the Convention on International Trade in Endangered Species of Wild Fauna and Flora (CITES)", the Appellate Body concluded that the five species of sea turtles involved in the dispute constitute "exhaustible natural resources" within the meaning of Article XX(g) of the GATT-1994.[12] CITES had an important complementary role to play, as did a number of other UN agreements.

There are other cases where complementarities are potentially very important. In the *EC-Asbestos* case discussed in chapter 4, the Appellate Body noted that the more "vital and important" the policy pursued by a national government, the easier it would be to prove that a nonconforming WTO measure was "necessary" to meet the objectives of the policy concerned. In this case, the public health objective being pursued was characterized as "vital and important in the highest degree".[13] This then begs the question of whose responsibility it is to decide whether the objective pursued is vital and important in the highest degree. The World Health Organization (WHO) of the United Nations is certainly one candidate for providing an input. The European Commission has also proposed a formal role for the WHO in settling questions surrounding compulsory licensing, access to essential medicines and the TRIPS Agreement.

Another useful example relates to fisheries subsidies. Concern about the effects of these subsidies is not new. Many international initiatives over the past decade have emphasized the adverse effects of subsidies on fish stocks. As spelled out in chapter 3, these have involved, among others, the United Nations Commission on Sustainable Development, the Committee on Fisheries of the Food and Agriculture Organization, the Asia-Pacific Economic Cooperation Conference, the United Nations Convention on the Law of the Sea, the Organisation for Economic Co-operation and Development and the United Nations Environment Programme (UNEP). In this instance, work in the WTO can progress only by involving the many intergovernmental organizations already active in the area. It also needs to address the concerns and integrate the information coming from various non-governmental groups. However, as with other areas of sustainable development, the WTO should not be drawn into the role of a fisheries management or conservation body, or infringe on the powers or autonomy of existing authorities.

Quite apart from specific WTO Agreements and the dispute settlement mechanism, it is the view of many that the everyday work of the WTO has an impact on matters dealt with by United Nations agencies. Human rights is one example. In reporting to the fifty-fifth session of the General Assembly, the UN Secretary-General stated:

[the] goals and principles of the WTO Agreements and those of human rights do share much in common. Goals of economic growth, increasing living standards, full employment and the optimal use of the world's resources are conducive to the promotion of human rights, in particular the right to development. Parallels can also be drawn between the principles of fair competition and non-discrimination under trade law and equality and non-discrimination under human rights law. Further, the special and differential treatment offered to developing countries under the WTO rules reflects notions of affirmative action under human rights law.[14]

From both an economic and a social perspective, it is argued that stable and rules-based societies constitute a necessary condition for sustainable development, a well-functioning world economy and an international trading system. There is thus a mutuality of interests between the international trading community and the implementation of international human rights law. "Yet the reality is that, whereas the rules that favour the expansion of the global economy have become stronger and more enforceable, equally important rules relating to human rights as well as environmental and labour standards have not kept pace in terms of their implementation. This has been at the heart of what the UN Secretary-General Kofi Annan has described as the 'backlash against globalization'."[15]

In this respect it is interesting that some international institutions, far from being mutually supportive, permit attacks on others. A much publicized report to the United Nations Sub-Commission on the Promotion and Protection of Human Rights declared that the WTO "has extended its purview to encompass additional areas beyond what could justifiably be described as within its mandate. Furthermore, even its purely trade and commerce activities have serious human rights implications. This is compounded by the fact that the founding instruments of WTO make scant (indeed only oblique) reference to the principles of human rights. The net result is that for certain sectors of humanity – particularly the developing countries of the South – the WTO is a veritable nightmare."[16] This was not a statement of government opinion, so not too much should be made of a report prepared by consultants that declares the WTO to be a veritable nightmare. Nevertheless, it had the potential to set two institutions on a collision course and should not have been published – at least not without the possibility for the WTO to comment on and correct many of the obvious errors. Here there is a clear lack of coherence.

Some areas dealt with by UN bodies have been proposed as candidates for collaboration with the WTO. An example is core labour standards, and the appropriate relationship between the WTO and the International Labour Organization (ILO) has been under review. In Singapore in December 1996, trade ministers renewed their commitment to the observance of internationally recognized core labour standards. They affirmed that the ILO is the competent body to set and deal with these standards, as well as their support for its work in promoting them. They stated their belief that economic growth and development fostered by increased trade and further trade liberalization contribute to the promotion of these standards and rejected the use of labour standards for protectionist purposes, agreeing that the comparative advantage of countries, particularly low-wage developing countries, must in no way be put into question. In this regard, they noted that the WTO and ILO secretariats would continue their existing collaboration.

As noted in the introduction to this chapter, the need for collaboration to increase the complementarities of the WTO and the United Nations and its specialized agencies is formally recognized by the WTO. Article V of the Agreement Establishing the WTO requires "the General Council [to] make appropriate arrangements for effective cooperation with other intergovernmental organizations that have responsibilities related to those of the WTO". But, if there is a need for greater collaboration between the WTO and UN bodies, the question remains what form this collaboration should take. The United Nations and its specialized agencies are charged, for example, with advancing the components of sustainable development: economic development, the environment, human rights and labour. However, it seems there is not the same willingness to forgo national sovereignty and accept strong compliance mechanisms in treaties negotiated under the auspices of the United Nations and its specialized agencies as in the WTO. As Peter Sutherland et al. have remarked, "The weakness of other multilateral institutions, and the inadequacy of existing decision-making fora, has increased the demands on the WTO to deal with issues not heretofore within its mandate. Labour and environmental issues are the two most notable cases.... These pressures have been brought to bear on the WTO not only because of the attraction of its unique enforcement power, but also because the institutions that might be expected to deal with labour and environment issues either do not exist or are weak."[17]

Trade and environment as a model

Against this backdrop, an important question is how to proceed in practice. One interesting case study is the relationship between the WTO and the trade provisions in the United Nations MEAs. The WTO's Committee on Trade and Environment (CTE) was created with broad terms of reference. Through intensive discussion in the ensuing years it has, in my view, been particularly effective in promoting a greater understanding on the part of trade and environment officials of their respective concerns and the policy tools available to deal with them. This has been achieved through practical initiatives such as the WTO organizing "trade and environment" symposia attended by national government officials, academics, representatives of the United Nations and specialized agencies; joint technical cooperation missions involving both WTO and UNEP staff; observer status for MEAs in the Committee on Trade and Environment; and regular presentations by representatives of MEAs to the CTE on the trade-related aspects of their agreements. These exchanges have certainly contributed to the fact that a dispute has never been brought to the WTO relating to a WTO-inconsistent measure provided for in an

MEA, and they have arguably led to a better understanding of the goals of trade and environment policy and the respective roles of the MEA treaties and secretariats as well as of UNEP.

At the Doha Ministerial Meeting in 2001, trade ministers welcomed "the WTO's continued cooperation with UNEP and other inter-governmental environmental organizations" and encouraged "efforts to promote cooperation between the WTO and relevant international environmental and developmental organizations, especially in the lead-up to the World Summit on Sustainable Development".[18] In concrete terms, pursuant to discussion in the CTE, ministers agreed at the Doha Ministerial to clarify and improve WTO disciplines on fisheries subsidies, taking into account the importance of this sector to developing countries.

There have also been unsuccessful proposals for changes in WTO rules and procedures to accommodate MEAs. One aspect of the debate has centred on the possibility of a conflict arising over trade-related measures contained in MEAs, and how potential inconsistency with WTO rules could be avoided or dealt with. Given the importance of the global trade and environment regimes, any clash over the application of rules agreed to among nations would have unfortunate ramifications for both regimes. Trade ministers in Doha therefore agreed to negotiations on the relationship between existing WTO rules and specific trade obligations set out in multilateral environment agreements.

It has been suggested that an "environmental window" be created by providing for exceptions for WTO-inconsistent measures being taken in light of the provisions of environment agreements. This has not met with the unanimous approval of WTO members. Nevertheless, it can be argued that it is very much in the WTO's interests to have effective multilateral environment agreements to ensure that trade-related disputes do not gravitate towards the WTO. To achieve this, any WTO-inconsistent measures should be clearly identified and agreed to by the parties to the MEA. The environment agreements would set the standards for environmental protection and enforce them. If WTO members forgo their WTO rights not to be discriminated against if certain environmental standards are not met, then they have the right to do so. This course of action however requires "effective" (from a WTO perspective) MEAs, characterized by clearly specified trade measures taken for environmental purposes, broad-based support in terms of country membership and a robust dispute settlement system. Unfortunately this is not the case today.

Although there has been clear evidence of collaboration to harness complementarities in trade and environment, it is difficult to envisage similar processes being established in the WTO for other areas in which the United Nations has responsibilities. It is hard to imagine the creation of a Committee on Trade and Human Rights or Labour Standards within the WTO. Developing countries are far too suspicious of hidden protectionist intentions behind any such initiatives, believing that these issues should be the responsibility of the United Nations and the specialized agencies with the mandate and expertise to deal with them.

Multilateral discussions on the trade and environment link are much further along than are discussions on trade and labour issues. Several WTO Agreements directly or indirectly address environmental matters, and the CTE, although criticized by many for failing to find solutions to key outstanding issues, has served as a useful focal point for discussion and analysis. On the labour standards issue, in contrast, there is nearly unanimous opposition to the creation of a working group on trade and labour standards inside the WTO.

Four proposals

In the foregoing chapters, I have addressed a number of issues that fall under the heading of trade and sustainable development, and I have argued that the WTO has evolved into a World Trade and Sustainable Development Organization. A number of conclusions can be drawn from this, not the least being that viewing the WTO through the prism of sustainable development clearly demonstrates the extent to which the study of the multilateral trading system is now an interdisciplinary task. The functioning of the WTO is not only based on traditional principles of economics, law and international relations; disciplines such as ethics, equity, the environment, public health and many others have a role to play. Recognition of this fact is important so that students of the WTO have the right toolbox to deal with the trade and sustainable development issues on the WTO agenda. I also believe there can be a far greater appreciation and public understanding of the role of the WTO – what it should and should not do – when studied in the context of sustainable development.

In the first chapter, I indicated that this book was about policy, and I have dealt with a number of policy considerations. It is not my intention to summarize what has gone before, but rather to make some proposals based on the contents of this chapter, and add others that derive from having already established an inventory of trade and sustainable development issues. In fact, I would like to add to earlier proposals by making four very different ones, all of which are potentially far-reaching but far from radical. They would also contribute in their own way to a better understanding of the role of the WTO in global governance.

A Functioning of the World Trade Organization System Group

In this chapter I have argued that, particularly in the area of trade and sustainable development, the specialized agencies of the United Nations and the WTO should pursue consistent and mutually supportive policies. I have not advocated any change in their mandates. It is clear that the WTO is in many ways unique, and governments will resist any move significantly to modify its role, particularly if it means becoming more "UN-like". Nevertheless, closer cooperation between the WTO and UN specialized agencies has the potential to bring many benefits, and this chapter has provided examples of how it could be achieved.

As noted above, the FOGS Group was created in the Uruguay Round to examine ways in which the WTO and the Bretton Woods institutions could bring greater coherence to global economic policy-making. The Group recognized that difficulties with origins outside the trade field could not be redressed through measures taken in the trade field alone. This was an important recognition of the complex interlinkages between trade and other global policies. The policy prescriptions of the FOGS Group look remarkably relevant for many of the issues confronting the global economy of today. From an institutional perspective, the Group declared that the interlinkages between different aspects of economic policy require the international institutions with responsibilities in each of these areas to follow consistent and mutually supportive policies. The outcome of the FOGS Declaration was the negotiation of formal agreements between the WTO and the Bretton Woods institutions to ensure consistent and mutually supportive policies in their own operations.

My first proposal then is top–down. A Functioning of the World Trade Organization System (FOWTOS) Group should be formed where governments could examine and make recommendations on how to bring greater coherence to policy-making at the global level – as the FOGS Group successfully did. The mandate of the FOWTOS Group should be to review and make proposals on collaboration between the WTO and other international bodies such as the UN agencies with a view to a possible restructuring of the relationship.

Useful as such an exercise could be, however, there is every likelihood that it would result in exhausting negotiations concluding merely in agreed language identifying the need for greater coherence. As in too many other instances, the ensuing declaration would be an end in itself rather than a means to an end. The experience of putting substance into the FOGS Declaration reveals that such declarations can be successfully pursued and implemented only if there is a solid understanding of where greater institutional coherence is required as well as the form it should take. In the earlier chapters of this book – and particularly in this chapter – I have pointed to the areas where this cooperation could be improved and indicated options as to how it could be achieved.

An inventory of issues

Thus, to be effective, political declarations should be complemented with an inventory of candidates for greater institutional coherence. Given the interdisciplinary and technical nature of the trade and sustainable development agenda, I believe that there is merit in conducting a serious and scholarly review of many of the issues that are found on the trade and sustainable development agenda. This review should, however, take place outside the negotiating context and be carried out by a group of eminent scholars and other well-informed individuals from various disciplines. The members of the group should be sufficiently familiar with the political realities of the WTO to be able to come forward with novel and ambitious proposals. Historically, many trade officials have been sceptical of those outside the negotiating processes, believing them to be so far removed from the realities of the workings of the GATT as to be naïve. This may have been the case in the past when the negotiating process was far more obscure than it is today, but it is no longer the case. Although the proposals emerging from the group would have no legal standing, they would be invaluable in terms of providing guidance on how the WTO might deal with the challenges it faces.

There is little doubt, however, that governments would not reach agreement on launching such a group, nor would they fund it from the regular WTO budget. Such was the case with the much-lauded Leutwiler Group. In any event, such a group should be independent of political processes, including in relation to the nomination of its members. The participants should be widely accepted as important scholars irrespective of their country of origin and affiliation. Nevertheless, such a group should have the blessing of the Director-General, who would have an input to the discussions, and its final output should be made available to all. Official status could also be acquired for the final report if any government thought it sufficiently useful to table it at the WTO for discussion.

The success or otherwise of such a proposal would depend on the terms of reference for the group, the suitability of the participants and the basic materials they would be working with. As far as the terms of reference are concerned, I would envisage an agenda that would complement the very useful report of the recent Group convened by the WTO Director-General and deal more with the detailed substance of the types of issue identified above.[19] As far as background material is concerned, there is now an abundance of scholarly contributions in numerous journals and other publications from economists, lawyers and experts in other disciplines that could be usefully drawn on.

Policy options

More is needed, however. A description of the issues should be accompanied by a menu of options for dealing with them. There are, indeed, many instruments available to governments that fall short of modifying agreed texts or entering into litigation, all useful in different situations and with different implications. We have seen an Understanding on financial services within the context of the General Agreement on Trade in Services, a Declaration to deal with access to essential medicines to accompany the TRIPS Agreement, a Decision on bringing greater coherence to global economic policy-making, and negotiations on how to deal with concerns over fisheries subsidies. There are many other examples of such instruments, and it should not be beyond the ingenuity of WTO members to create new ones.

Many important advantages flow from agreement between governments as a result of debate in the various WTO councils and committees rather than through a closed process of litigation. Because governments are identified in the various committee discussions, there is less of a tendency for the WTO *as an institution* to be held accountable for outcomes that are considered negative by public interest groups. This has been apparent, for example, in dealing with the Decision accompanying the TRIPS Agreement and access to essential medicines, just as it is proving to be with respect to negotiations on fisheries subsidies, as well as on the relationship between the WTO and MEAs. The advantage of this approach is that it makes clear that it is not the WTO that is blocking access to essential medicines or new disciplines on fisheries subsidies but certain governments. These governments can then become the target of criticism, praise or lobbying, depending on the interest group involved. As a result, a new dimension of clarity enters the debate about the role of "the WTO" in these contentious areas.

More specifically, I would like to propose that formal consideration be given to the situations where litigation could be avoided and various mechanisms (such as Understandings, Interpretations or Decisions) usefully drawn on to clarify a number of key aspects of the WTO Agreements. What is quite clear is that such an approach is not an option for all unclear texts – there are many contentious issues where governments would quite rightly want to "let sleeping dogs lie". Nevertheless, to improve the understanding of some concepts, particularly in the light of recent Appellate Body rulings, an open debate could have positive benefits for all. In this respect, it would be hard to argue that the six Understandings negotiated during the Uruguay Round to clarify a number of aspects of the GATT Articles did not serve a useful purpose.

Should there be threat of recourse to the dispute settlement process, the maximum effort should of course be made to find a solution that avoids formal litigation. I have proposed one approach in chapter 4 that is particularly suited to environment-related matters or sustainable development more generally. However, it is likely that more disputes relating to sustainable development will continue to find their way to the WTO in the coming years. Recent experience has shown that the rulings handed down, coupled with their automatic adoption, have led some to the view that the WTO legal system has extended its authority beyond that granted to it by member governments. In terms of the Appellate Body, for example, it has been argued that some of its reports indicate a new concept of evolutionary policy formulation through litigation, which is very different from consensus decision-taking after a debate by all members in the WTO General Council. The exploration of alternative courses of action as described above would respond to those who believe that interpretation of textual language where important policy considerations are involved is not the role of the Appellate Body, but rather the role of governments and consensus-based decision-making.

The Doha Development Agenda

In the Doha Development Agenda, ministers agreed that the "Committee on Trade and Development and the Committee on Trade and Environment shall, within their respective mandates, each act as a forum to identify and debate developmental and environmental aspects of the negotiations, in order to help achieve the objective of having sustainable development appropriately reflected".[20] To my mind, this agreement presents a golden opportunity to address many of the issues raised in this book.

However, as things stand, this potentially important mandate is dispensed with in a particularly low-profile manner. In fact, the WTO Secretariat briefs the Committee on Trade and Environment and the Committee on Trade and Development on how sustainable development is dealt with in the respective committees they service. It is significant that staff members carry no political weight, so the process is particularly low key. In addition, it seems an odd way to proceed, because governments are in any event expected to be fully aware of developments in all WTO Committees.[21]

A joint meeting of the Committees at senior official level – or, better, at political level – to address some of the issues arising from the interface of trade and environment policies holds the promise of great potential for more coherence in global policy-making. Once again, the success of such a meeting would depend heavily on the agenda for such a meeting and the material presented for discussion. A practical way of proceeding would be to link the existing mandate agreed at Doha to the above proposals in order to identify issues that could benefit from study as well as the mechanisms to deal with them.

Notes

1. See *Declaration on the Contribution of the World Trade Organisation to Achieving Greater Coherence in Global Economic Policy Making*, in WTO, *The Results of the Uruguay Round of Multilateral Trade Negotiations: The Legal Texts*, Geneva: WTO Secretariat, 1994, p. 386.
2. See WTO, *The Results of the Uruguay Round of Multilateral Trade Negotiations: The Legal Texts*.
3. Ibid., pp. 442–443.
4. The origins and outcome of the discussion on coherence in the Uruguay Round and the period preceding it can be found in Gary P. Sampson, "Greater Coherence in Global Economic Policy Making: A WTO Perspective", in A. Krueger, *The World Trade Organization: Its Effectiveness as an Institution*, Chicago: University of Chicago Press, 1997.
5. Ibid., p. 259
6. GATT, *Ministerial Declaration on the Uruguay Round*, Geneva: GATT, MIN.DEC, September 1986, p. 2.
7. Ibid., p. 6.
8. Relations between the institutions are also implied in the Decision on Measures Concerning the Negative Effects of the Reform Programme on Least-Developed and Net Food-Importing Developing Countries, which identified the need for countries that face difficulties as a result of agricultural liberalization to have access to the resources of the international financial institutions. Finally, the entry into force of the General Agreement on Trade in Services required an extension of the relations of the WTO with the IMF with respect to balance of payments restrictions beyond the traditional merchandise trade to include restrictions on trade in services.
9. CBD, *Convention on Biological Diversity: The Text*, Montreal: CBD Secretariat, 5 June 1992, Article 1.
10. See WTO, *Ministerial Declaration: Ministerial Conference, Fourth Session, Doha, 9–14 November*, Geneva: WTO, WT/MIN(01)/DEC/W/1, December 2001, para. 19.
11. Michael M. Weinstein and Steve Charnovitz, "The Greening of the WTO", *Foreign Affairs*, November–December 2001, p. 149.
12. See WTO, *United States – Import Prohibition of Certain Shrimp and Shrimp Products*, Appellate Body Report, WT/DS58/AB/R, 12 October 1998, para. 128.
13. WTO, *European Communities – Measures Affecting Asbestos and Asbestos-Containing Products*, Appellate Body Report and Panel Report, 5WT/DS135, April 2001.
14. United Nations, *Globalization and Its Impact on the Full Enjoyment of all Human Rights, Preliminary Report of the Secretary-General*, Fifty-fifth session of the General Assembly, UN Doc. A/55/342, 31 August 2000, p. 4.
15. Mary Robinson, "Making the Global Economy Work for Human Rights", in Gary P. Sampson, (ed.), *The Role of the WTO in Global Governance*, Tokyo: United Nations

University Press, 2001, p. 211; see also Kofi Annan, "Foundations for a Fair and Free World Trade System", in Sampson, (ed.), *The Role of the WTO in Global Governance*.

16. ECOSOC, *The Realisation of Economic, Social and Cultural Rights: Globalization and Its Impact on the Full Enjoyment of Human Rights*, Sub-Commission on the Promotion and Protection of Human Rights, E/CN.4/Sub.2/2000/13, 15 June 2000, p. 8.

17. Peter Sutherland, John Sewell and David Weiner, "Addressing Global Governance in the WTO", in Sampson (ed.), *The Role of the WTO in Global Governance*, p. 104.

18. WTO, *Ministerial Declaration: Ministerial Conference, Fourth Session, Doha, 9–14 November*, para. 6.

19. In June 2003, the Director-General of the WTO requested eight experts in GATT and WTO matters to reflect on the future of the WTO. The experts came from business, government, academia and policy-making positions. According to the Director-General, this group was to "examine the functioning of the institution – the WTO – and to consider how well equipped it is to carry the weight of future responsibilities and demands". See WTO, *The Future of the WTO – Addressing Institutional Challenges in the New Millennium*, Report by the Consultative Board to the Director General of the WTO, by Peter Sutherland et al., Geneva: WTO, 2004.

20. WTO, *Doha Declarations: The Doha Development Agenda*, Geneva: WTO Secretariat, 2001, para. 51.

21. For example, when the Committee on Trade and Development dealt with the services negotiations and sustainable development, there was little if any reference to sustainable development. See WTO, *Note on the Meeting of 27 and 28 November 2003*, Geneva: WTO, WT/COMTD/M/47, 14 January 2004.

Index